Begin to Code with C#

Rob Miles

PUBLISHED BY
Microsoft Press
A Division of Microsoft Corporation
One Microsoft Way
Redmond, Washington 98052-6399

Library of Congress Control Number: 2015942036
ISBN: 978-1-5093-0115-7

Printed and bound in the United States of America.

1 16

Microsoft Press books are available through booksellers and distributors worldwide.
If you need support related to this book, email Microsoft Press Support at mspinput@micro-
soft.com. Please tell us what you think of this book at http://aka.ms/tellpress.

Acquisitions and Developmental Editor: Devon Musgrave
Project Editor: John Pierce
Editorial Production: Rob Nance and John Pierce
Technical Reviewer: Lance McCarthy; Technical Review services provided by Content
            Master, a member of CM Group, Ltd.
Copyeditor: John Pierce
Indexer: Christina Palaia, Emerald Editorial Services
Cover: Twist Creative • Seattle

To Mary

Contents at a glance

Part 1: Programming fundamentals

Part 2: Advanced programming

Part 3: Making games

Contents

Part 1: Programming fundamentals

Give us feedback

Tell us what you think of this book and help Microsoft improve our products for you. Thank you!

http://aka.ms/tellpress

6 Repeating actions with loops 134

Part 2: Advanced programming

11 Making solutions with objects 336

Part 3: Making games

Introduction

I think that programming is the most creative thing you can learn how to do. If you learn to paint, you can make pictures. If you learn the violin, you can make music. But if you learn to program, you can create experiences that are entirely new (and you can make pictures and music too if you want to). Once you have started on the programming path, there's no limit to where you can go. There are always new devices, technologies, and marketplaces where you can use your programming skills.

You can think of this book as your first step on a journey to programming enlightenment. The best journeys are undertaken with a destination in mind, and this one is no different. I'd like to describe the destination as "usefulness." By the end of this book you won't be the best programmer in the world (unless I retire, of course), but you will have enough skills and knowledge to write properly useful programs. And maybe you can have at least one of your programs available worldwide for download from the Microsoft Store.

However, before we start off, I'd like to issue a small word of warning. In the same way that a guide would want to tell you about the lions, tigers, and crocodiles that you might encounter if you went on a safari adventure, I feel that I must let you know that our journey might not be all smooth sailing. Programmers have to learn to think slightly differently about problem solving because a computer just doesn't work the same way that we do. Humans can do complex things rather slowly. Computers can do simple things really quickly. It is the job of the programmer to harness the simple abilities of the machine to solve complicated problems. This is what we are going to learn how to do.

The key to success as a programmer is pretty much the same as for lots of other endeavors. If you want to become a world-renowned violin player, you will have to practice a lot. The same is true for programming. You will have to spend quite a bit of time working on your programs to get code-writing skills. But the good news is that, just as a violin player really enjoys making the instrument sing, making a computer do exactly what you want turns out to be a really satisfying experience. And it gets even more enjoyable when you see other people using programs that you have written and finding them useful and fun to use.

How this book fits together

I've organized this book in four parts. Each part builds on the previous one with the aim of turning you into a successful programmer. We start off considering the low-level programing instructions that programs use to tell the computer what to do, and we finish by looking at professional software practices.

Part 1: Coding fundamentals

The first part gets you started. It points you to where you will install and use the programming tools that you will need, and it introduces you to the fundamental elements of the C# programming language that are used by all programs.

Part 2: Advanced programming

Part 2 describes the features of the C# programming language that are used to create more complex applications. It shows you how to break large programs into smaller elements and how you can create custom data types that reflect the specific problem being solved. You'll also find out how programs can maintain data in storage when they are not running.

Part 3: Making games

Making games is great fun. And it turns out that it is also a great way to learn how to use object-oriented programming techniques. In this part, you'll build some playable games and at the same time learn the fundamentals of how to extend programming objects through inheritance and component-based software design.

Part 4: Creating applications

Part 4 is where you find out how to create fully fledged applications. You'll discover how to design graphical user interfaces and how to connect program code to the elements on the display. You'll also learn how modern applications are structured. Part 4 doesn't appear in this printed book but is available as an ebook, free to download from this book's webpage at https://aka.ms/BeginCodeCSharp/downloads.

How you will learn

In each chapter, I will tell you a bit more about programming. I'll show you how to do something, and then I'll invite you make something of your own by using what you've learned. You'll never be more than a page or so away from doing something or making something unique and personal. In each chapter we will use *Snaps*, prebuilt bits of functionality that I'll show you how to use. After that, it's up to you to make something amazing!

You can read the book straight through if you like, but you'll learn much more if you slow down and work with the practical parts along the way. This book can't really teach you how to program, any more than a book about bicycles can teach you how to ride a bike. You have to put in the time and practice to learn how to do it. But this book will give you the knowledge and confidence to try your hand at programming, and it will also be around to help you if your programming doesn't turn out as you expected. Here are the elements in the book that will help you really learn, by doing!

MAKE SOMETHING HAPPEN

Yes, the best way to learn things is by doing, so you'll find "Make Something Happen" elements throughout the text. These elements offer ways for you to practice your programming skills. Each of them starts with an example and then introduces some steps you can try on your own. Everything you create will run on a Windows PC, tablet, or phone. You can even publish your creations to the whole wide world via the Windows Store.

CODE ANALYSIS

A great way to learn how to program is by looking at code written by other people and working out what it does (and sometimes why it doesn't do what it should). In this book's "Code Analysis" challenges, you'll use your deductive skills to figure out the behavior of a program, fix bugs, and suggest improvements.

If you don't already know that programs can fail, you will learn this hard lesson very soon after you start writing your first program. To help you deal with this in advance, I've included "What Could Go Wrong?" elements, which anticipate problems you might have and provide solutions to those problems. For example, when I introduce something new, I'll sometimes spend some time considering how it can fail and what you need to worry about when you use the new feature.

PROGRAMMER'S POINTS

I've spent a lot of my time teaching programming. But I've also written many programs and sold a few to paying customers. I've learned some things the hard way that I really wish I'd known right at the start. The aim of "Programmer's Points" is to give you this information up front so that you can start taking a professional view of software development as you learn how to do it.

"Programmer's Points" cover a wide range of issues, from programming to people to philosophy. I'd strongly advise you to read and absorb these points carefully—they can save you a lot of time in the future!

Programs and Snaps

Nobody builds programs from scratch any more. All software is built using pieces of software that have already been built. If one program wants to display text, make a sound, or play some video, it simply asks another program to do it. Every popular computer language is underpinned by a huge library of existing code, and one of the things that a programmer needs to understand is how to use these libraries and software written by other people.

I've created the Snaps library specially for this book. It provides a set of functional behaviors that are easy to use and fit together. You will use the Snaps library in your first programs. Later in the book you'll discover other libraries of functionality that you can use to build programs.

Programs that use Snaps run inside the Snaps engine, which is a self-contained environment in which programs can speak messages, get input from a user, draw images, make sounds, and even find out what the weather is like.

I'll provide examples of how the Snaps work and then leave it up to you to see what you can come up with. The principle we'll follow is this: "If you can't use programming to impress your friends and family, what's the point of it?" I really hope you'll come up with some impressive programs of your own and maybe even publish them for other people to enjoy.

PROGRAMMER'S POINT

Everything is built on someone else's code

It seems fitting that the first Programmer's Point is about how "creatively lazy" a good programmer can be. They'll never write a program if they can find a way to use one that has already been written. (Why reinvent the wheel?) The Snaps that I've provided are an example of this. You'll take a look inside some of them later in the book and discover that they themselves make use of other libraries.

Software and hardware

You'll need a computer and some software to work with the programs in the book. I'm afraid I can't provide you with a computer, but in the first chapter you will find out where you can get Visual Studio 2015 Community Edition, the free software that you'll use to create your programs. You'll also learn where to download the Snaps library and the demonstration code we'll examine and use.

The computer you use must run the 64-bit version of the Windows 10 operating system. Here are the other requirements:

- A 1 Ghz or faster processor, preferably an Intel i5 or better.

- At least 4 gigabytes (GB) of memory (RAM), but preferably 8 GB or more.

- The full Visual Studio 2015 Community installation takes about 8 GB of hard disk space.

There are no special requirements for the graphics display, although a higher resolution screen will enable you to see more when you are writing your programs. The Snaps library works with touchscreens, a mouse, pen input devices, and the Xbox One and Xbox 360 controllers for the games you'll develop in Part 3.

Visual Studio 2015 Community Edition is a freely available application that can be used to create C# programs on a Windows 10 PC. If you have an earlier version of Visual Studio on your computer already (Visual Studio 2013, for example), I'm afraid that you can't use it with this book. However, the 2015 version of Visual Studio will work quite happily alongside existing installations. In Chapter 1, I provide a link to detailed instructions for how to install Visual Studio and get it going. To make use of Visual Studio, it's best to have a Microsoft account so that a development license can be assigned to you.

Downloads

In every chapter in this book, I'll demonstrate and explain programs that teach you how to begin to program—and that you can then use to create programs of your own. You can download the Snaps library, this book's sample code, installation and setup instructions for Visual Studio, and the ebook for Part 4, "Creating applications," from the following page:

https://aka.ms/BeginCodeCSharp/downloads

Follow the instructions you'll find in Chapter 1 and in the setup document to install the sample programs and code.

Acknowledgments

I really like to write books. Huge thanks to Devon Musgrave and the folks at Microsoft Press for giving me the chance to write another one, to Rob Nance for the wonderful artwork, and to John Pierce and Lance McCarthy for doing such fantastic work on the text. It turns out that the acknowledgment is the olny part of the buk that they don't see, and I must give them both greatful thanks for making sure that all my text reads rightly.

Errata, updates, & book support

We've made every effort to ensure the accuracy of this book and its companion content. You can access updates to this book—in the form of a list of submitted errata and their related corrections—at:

https://aka.ms/BeginCodeCSharp/errata

If you discover an error that is not already listed, please submit it to us at the same page.

If you need additional support, email Microsoft Press Book Support at *mspinput@microsoft.com*.

Please note that product support for Microsoft software and hardware is not offered through the previous addresses. For help with Microsoft software or hardware, go to *http://support.microsoft.com*.

You'll also find "author's notes" about this book, including other projects and information about the Snaps library at:

http://www.robmiles.com/begintocode

Free ebooks from Microsoft Press

From technical overviews to in-depth information on special topics, the free ebooks from Microsoft Press cover a wide range of topics. These ebooks are available in PDF, EPUB, and Mobi for Kindle formats, ready for you to download at:

http://aka.ms/mspressfree

Check back often to see what is new!

We want to hear from you

At Microsoft Press, your satisfaction is our top priority, and your feedback our most valuable asset. Please tell us what you think of this book at:

http://aka.ms/tellpress

We know you're busy, so we've kept it short with just a few questions. Your answers go directly to the editors at Microsoft Press. (No personal information will be requested.) Thanks in advance for your input!

Stay in touch

Let's keep the conversation going! We're on Twitter: *http://twitter.com/MicrosoftPress*.

Part 1

Programming fundamentals

Let's begin traveling toward programming enlightenment. You'll start by installing the programming tools you need. Next you'll discover what a computer actually does and what a programming language is. You'll also take your first small steps in using the C# language to tell a computer to do things for you, and you'll find out how to work with Snaps, small helpers I've created for you to use in your first programs.

The aim of Part 1 is to introduce you to fundamental elements of the C# programming language that are used by all programs. Then, in Part 2, you'll look at how a modern programming language like C# builds on these programming fundamentals to make it easier to create applications.

1

1
Starting out

What you will learn

Programmers have a set of tools and techniques they use when they create programs. In this chapter, you're going to learn what kind of computer you need to write programs and how to find and install the tools you'll use in this book to build your code. You'll also take your first actual coding steps using the Begin to Code with C# sample apps.

Building a place to work

If you were a truck driver who spends many hours in the cab hauling goods across the country, you'd want a truck with a comfortable seat, a good view of the road, and controls that were light to use. It would also help if your truck had enough power to climb hills at a reasonable speed and was easy to handle on twisty mountainside roads.

In the same way, if you expect to spend any amount of time at a keyboard writing programs, you should have a decent place to work. If you can, find somewhere to set up a computer, a keyboard, and a screen and then pull up a chair that you don't mind spending quite a few hours sitting in.

You don't need a particularly fancy computer to write programs, but your machine will need a reasonable amount of memory and processor performance to handle the tools we're going to use. I suggest that you find a Windows 10 device with at least an Intel i5 or equivalent processor, 4 gigabytes of memory, and 256 gigabytes of hard-disk space. You can use smaller computers than this, but they can make the development process somewhat frustrating because they will take a while to update your program after you make any changes to it.

One thing that is very important is that *you must have a computer that is running the 64-bit version of Windows 10.* Very small devices run a 32-bit version of Windows 10. This works fine for most applications, but it cannot be used to build Windows 10 applications with Visual Studio, the tool we'll be using.

Getting the tools and demos

All the tools we're going to use are free to download and install. I find it astonishing and wonderful that such powerful software is available for free for anyone to use. The Visual Studio program makes it very easy to create applications and games. It even helps you make your programs available for sale in the Windows Store.

I strongly advise anyone starting to program that they should take at least one of their programs to market. It's lovely to think that software you have made is available in the Store to everyone.

However, before you can start sharing or selling your programming wares, you have to download and install the tools that will make this possible. Installation will take a little while, depending on how fast your network connection is. There will be a few occasions when you'll just have to sit and wait while things are fetched from the Internet and installed. While Visual Studio is downloading and installing, you'll probably have enough time to tidy things up and do a little housekeeping. One note, though:

it's important to perform the actions in the order I give you. The good news is that you have to do this installation only once for each computer that you want to use.

The steps you follow to install Visual Studio change from time to time, and they might vary depending on whether you have a Microsoft account or other factors. Instead of including the detailed steps here, I've provided that information online (so that I can update it whenever necessary).

If you haven't already downloaded the sample code and the other online content described in the "Downloads" section in this book's introduction, go to the following website and download the files now:

https://aka.ms/BeginCodeCSharp/downloads

Open the file named GettingStarted.pdf, and follow the instructions it provides to install Visual Studio Community 2015 and extract and set up the sample code and applications.

Once you've finished the installation, just to make sure you're ready to start, use File Explorer to open the folder with the demo code. You should see the files and folders shown in **Figure 1-1**. You're now ready to open Visual Studio and begin to code with C#, which we'll do in the next section!

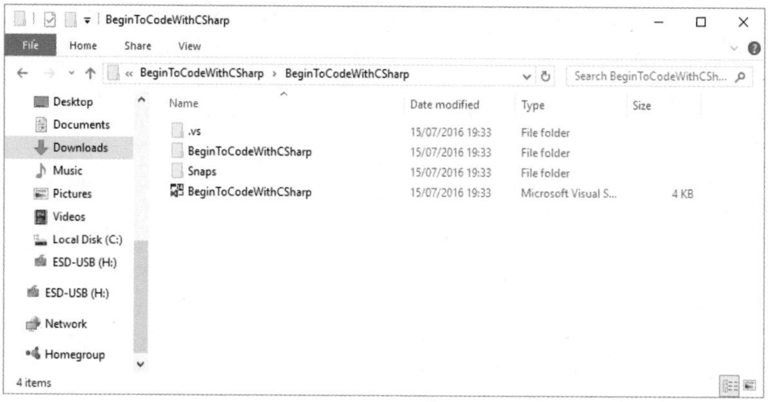

Figure 1-1 The contents of the BeginToCodeWithCSharp folder. You'll start from here in just a moment.

Using the tools

You've reached a significant point in the process of learning how to program. You're about to open Visual Studio and start working with this book's demo code. This is a bit like opening the front door of a new apartment or house or getting in a shiny new car you've bought.

Visual Studio projects and solutions

As you'll learn, Visual Studio organizes your programming work as *projects* and *solutions*. When you use Visual Studio to develop an app, an application, a website, a Web App, a script, a plug-in, or something else, you create a new project. A project is a set of resources (code files, images, and so on) that are used in the program you're developing. When you create the project, Visual Studio also creates a solution and includes the project in that solution. A solution can contain a single project, but you can add additional projects to a solution when your program needs the resources another project contains. All the projects in a solution are combined by Visual Studio to make the solution work.

Visual Studio is automatically associated with solution files (.sln files) in the same way that a word processor is associated with a document file. This means that when you open the **BeginToCodeWithCSharp** solution, shown selected in **Figure 1-2**, the Visual Studio environment and the solution are opened automatically. Go ahead and open that solution file (by double-clicking it, for example) now.

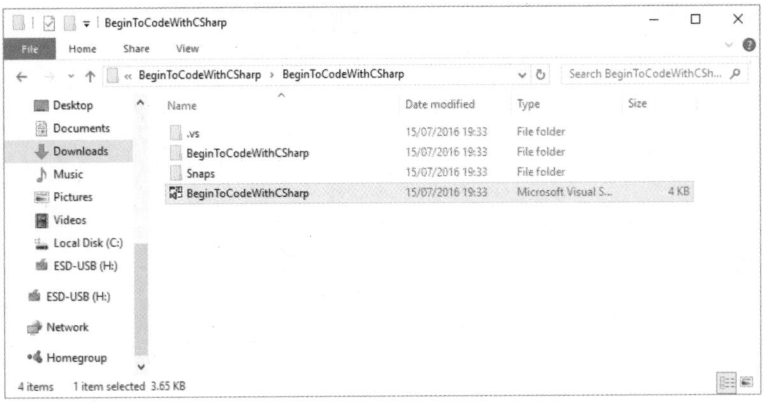

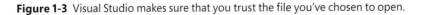

Figure 1-2 Open the solution by double-clicking the solution file.

Visual Studio is a protective sort of program that doesn't automatically trust projects that have been downloaded from the Internet, so it asks you to confirm that the projects in the solution are okay, as you can see in **Figure 1-3**. In this case the projects are fine (after all, I wrote them), so select OK.

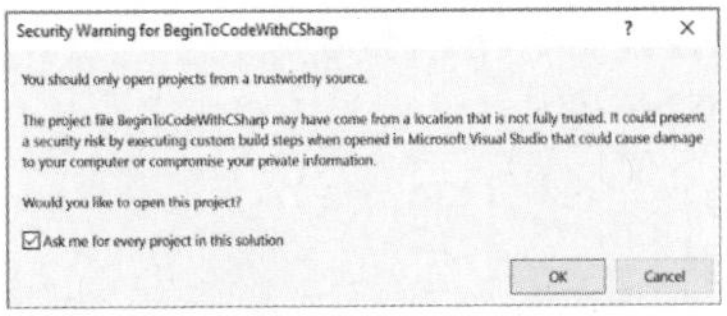

Figure 1-3 Visual Studio makes sure that you trust the file you've chosen to open.

Visual Studio provides *Solution Explorer*, a tool that you can use to browse the projects in a solution and to look at each of the files in the solution and its projects. Solution Explorer provides an organized view of your solutions and projects, so let's start using it. **Figure 1-4** shows what you should see when Visual Studio opens the **BeginToCodeWithCSharp** solution. (Your display might look slightly different depending on what options you have installed.)

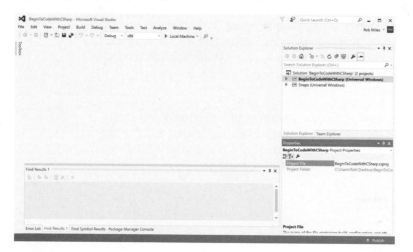

Figure 1-4 The main page in Visual Studio. Solution Explorer is at the top right of the page.

The solution contains two projects. One is the **BeginToCodeWithCSharp** project, and the other is the **Snaps** project, which contains a set of tools that are used by the sample applications. (The **Snaps** project provides facilities that can be used by any program, including ones that you will create later. You'll learn a lot more about Snaps later in this book.)

Running a program with Visual Studio

Visual Studio is called an *integrated development environment* (or IDE). It's a place where programmers can not only write their program code but also see their programs running. Let's begin to get to know Visual Studio by running some of the sample applications created by the demo code you downloaded for this book.

When you want to give control to a program, you tell Visual Studio to run it by using the run button, which is the button with the green arrowhead I've pointed to in **Figure 1-5** on the next page.

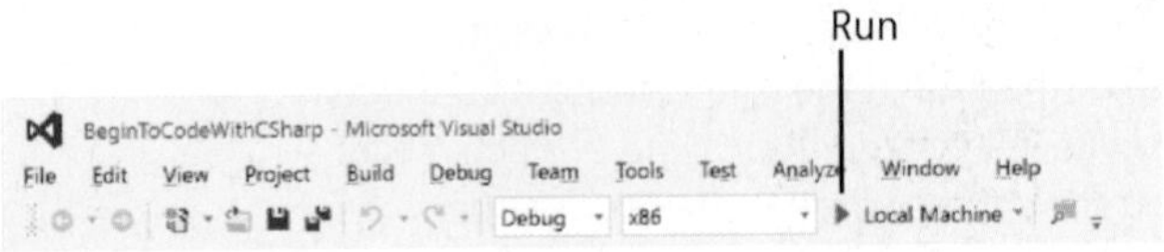

Figure 1-5 Visual Studio's run button starts the program you are working on.

When you use the run button to start an application, Visual Studio actually does two things. First it creates the application from the components that are managed within the solution. This process is called *building the application*. After the application has been built, Visual Studio then hands over control and lets it run. For our solution, the build process requires an Internet connection in order to work.

Go ahead and press the run button now to make the application run. Visual Studio displays the "Begin to Code with C#" window that's shown in **Figure 1-6**. If you like, you can move this window around the screen, minimize it, and display it full screen by using the **Maximize** button (the square) in the top-right corner.

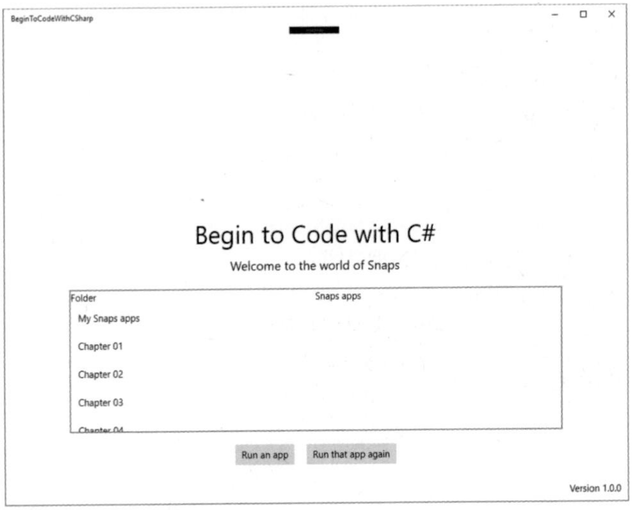

Figure 1-6 The BeginToCodeWithCSharp application is now running.

The **BeginToCodeWithCSharp** solution is an application I've created for you that lets you navigate the book's sample applications. Each of the book's demonstration programs, in other words, is included in the solution as a separate application, and by running the solution you can then choose a particular sample application to run. Some of the apps are fully fledged applications that you could use (or even sell in the Windows Store), and others are simple demonstrations of specific programming points that we will look at together.

The buttons at the bottom of the window are the controls for running these sample apps. To run an app, first select it by using the navigation panels above the buttons. In the left panel, labeled **Folder**, you select a particular app folder, most of which are named after the book's chapters. In the right panel, you select an app from that folder. When you select **Run an app**, the app you selected runs.

🚀 **MAKE SOMETHING HAPPEN**

Select and run an application

This is our first "Make Something Happen" sidebar—welcome! Sometimes in these sidebars I'll ask you to make something, and at other times I'll ask you to simply try something out. In all cases you'll be doing what developers do. This time I want you to just select and run some of the apps in **BeginToCodeWithCSharp**. (Yes, this is the simplest "Make Something Happen" in the book.)

Make sure that you have the solution running. Select a folder from the left panel and a sample app in the right panel. There are lots of apps to choose from. You can start by looking in the **Chapter 03** folder for the **Ch_03_03_Speaking** app, which will make your computer introduce itself to you via sound.

Select **Run an app**, and the app you selected runs. When the app finishes, the navigation panels are displayed again. Have a go at selecting and running some more apps. If you fancy playing a game, take a look at **Ch_13_08_KeepUpGame** in the **Chapter 13** folder.

Stopping a program running in Visual Studio

After you finish trying out some of the apps, you need to stop the **BeginToCode-WithCSharp** application. You need to do this because Visual Studio will not let you change the contents of a program while it is still running. (Doing so would be like performing maintenance on a plane while it's still in the air.) And yes, you're about to do some coding to change a program!

When you want to stop the program, you can simply close the window by using the Close button (the X) in the top-right corner, just like you would for any other application. However, Visual Studio also provides a button (pointed to in **Figure 1-7**) that you can use to stop a running program. You can use this in the unlikely event that your program gets "stuck" in some way.

Figure 1-7 Use this button to stop a running program in Visual Studio.

Repeating an app

You can use the **Run that app again** button to rerun the last app you ran. The name of that last app is remembered even if you shut down your computer and return to the **BeginToCodeWithCSharp** solution at a later date.

WHAT COULD GO WRONG

Getting "stuck" in an app

Welcome to our first "What Could Go Wrong" sidebar. Here we look out for any pitfalls that you might encounter as you work with the code. In this sidebar, we are going to consider how you can move between the sample applications.

Some of the apps are simple demonstrations that run and then complete, allowing you to select and run another app from the main application's navigation panels. Other apps are designed to run continuously, just like a "real" application. For example, you might have discovered earlier that there is no way to stop the Keep Up! game; the program was designed to run continuously.

If you find yourself "stuck" in an app and want to run another one, simply stop the **Begin-ToCodeWithCSharp** solution within Visual Studio (as shown earlier) or select the X in the top-right corner of the running application to stop it. Although I showed you how to stop a program a moment ago, I wanted to include a "What Could Go Wrong" sidebar here to show you that I'll be looking out for you as you learn.

The MyProgram application

As you've seen, when you first run the **BeginToCodeWithCSharp** solution, the application displays a welcome message: "Welcome to the world of Snaps." This message is displayed by a program that is, of course, built into the solution. Let's take a look at the C# code that does this.

Visual Studio lets you manage a program you are writing in the same way that the Windows operating system lets you manage files. When you create a program, you often bring together lots of different parts, as you can see in **Figure 1-8**. For example, modern applications contain sounds and images, and all these items need to be kept together so that they can be used to build the finished program.

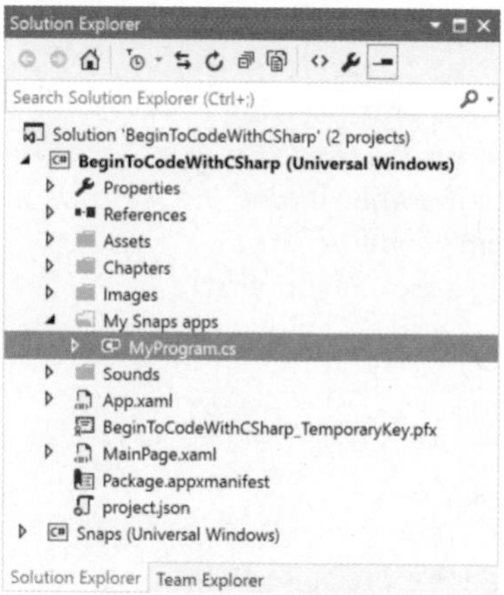

Figure 1-8 The MyProgram.cs source file and other program resources in Solution Explorer.

In Visual Studio, Solution Explorer helps a programmer manage the different elements that make up the completed program. You can think of Solution Explorer as a special file browser. It provides a view of the folder that contains all the files that are used when the application is built and run in Visual Studio. The **BeginToCodeWithCSharp** project contains a number of folders that hold different files. You can navigate the elements and folders in the solution by clicking the arrowhead near the item. Later in the book, we'll take a look inside more of the folders, but for now let me draw your attention to the **MyProgram.cs** source file, which is stored inside the **My Snaps apps** folder and which is shown selected in **Figure 1-8**. This file contains the program code that runs when the **BeginToCodeWithCSharp** solution starts.

Double-clicking this file in Solution Explorer makes its code appear in Visual Studio's editor window, shown in **Figure 1-9**.

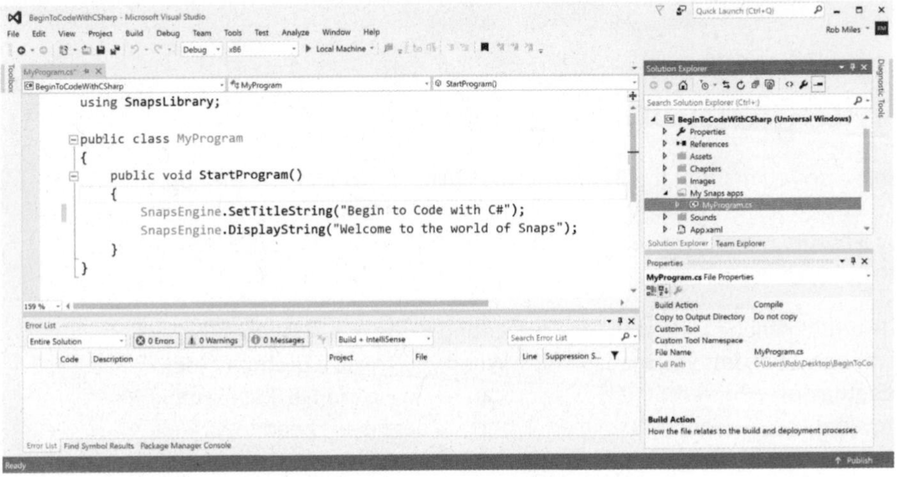

Figure 1-9 Visual Studio shows the contents of the MyProgram.cs file in the editor window.

What you have done is something like opening a document in a word processor, but instead of revealing a string of words that make up a story (or a poem or a report), you're looking at a sequence of instructions that the computer follows when it runs the program—or, put another way, you are examining the program's code. What you see in **Figure 1-9** is actual C#, so—congratulations!—you're taking a look at your first piece of C#.

PROGRAMMER'S POINT

Programming languages are not that special

If you were thinking that a programming language must be something complicated and hard to understand, you're mistaken. I think that many people (who can read English) would be able to grasp that the program shown in **Figure 1-9** displays the messages "Begin to Code with C#" and "Welcome to the world of Snaps".

Part of the clarity of the program comes from the C# language, which was designed to be easy to follow, but the rest comes from carefully choosing names that describe the components in the program. I could have used "xyzzy" instead of SetTitleString to name the behavior that displays the title message in the window. The computer really doesn't care what I call things as long as I'm consistent and it can tell them apart. However, I wasn't just writing this program for the computer. I was also writing it for beginners like you, who will learn to code by working out what the program does and then begin to write your own programs.

Modify the messages

Click the arrows in Solution Explorer to open the **BeginToCodeWithCSharp** project and the **My Snaps apps** folder. Double-click the **MyProgram.cs** file to open it for editing (if it isn't already open). You can create your very first program by changing this program so that it works slightly differently. You can start by just changing the messages that the program displays. The program code that we are running (which you can also see in **Figure 1-9**) looks like this:

```
public class MyProgram
{
    public void StartProgram()
    {
        SnapsEngine.SetTitleString("Begin to Code With C#");
        SnapsEngine.DisplayString("Welcome to the world of Snaps");
    }
}
```

Visual Studio has been specially written to display different parts of the code in different colors. One convention is that text that will be displayed on the screen when a program runs—this text is referred to as a *string*—appears as red text in the program's code. You don't have to make the string text red; this happens automatically when the string is framed correctly in the code. (More on this in a moment.) Make some changes to the strings, as I have below, without changing any of the other code. Then run the program again by using the run button in Visual Studio. The messages on the screen will change to reflect the changes you made to the code. The screenshot on the next page, for example, shows the results of my changes.

```
public class MyProgram
{
    public void StartProgram()
    {
        SnapsEngine.SetTitleString("Rob Miles will one day rule the world");
        SnapsEngine.DisplayString("...oh yes he will");
    }
}
```

Rob Miles will one day rule the world

...oh yes he will

Be careful when you change the text that you don't remove the double quotation mark characters (") that mark the start and end of the strings in the program. If you remove those, you'll find that the text no longer makes sense within a C# program, and you will get errors when you try to run the program. If this happens, don't worry: the Visual Studio editor has a powerful undo feature that you can use to undo the changes that you made to the file. Just hold down the **Ctrl** key and press **Z** to undo successive changes to a file. If you press **Ctrl+Z** several times when you are in the editor (the window where the code appears), you will eventually return to the original state of the program.

You've just written (or at least edited) your first program. Now, if you get asked to make something that can display a message on a screen, you have a partial idea of how to do it. I will, of course, explain the various other aspects of the code you just tweaked to help you complete your understanding!

PROGRAMMER'S POINT

There's no such thing as a "professional" program

What you are running here—after your edits to the **MyProgram.cs** file—is a "proper" program. If you wanted, you could use tools built into Visual Studio to submit this program to the Windows Store for anyone in the world to download and use (although, to be honest, I'm not sure anyone would find it useful yet). People learning to program sometimes wonder when they will reach the point where they are as good at programming as a "professional" developer. The answer is that as soon as someone pays you for writing a program, you are a professional developer.

Of course, being given money to do something doesn't automatically make you better at it, but in this case it should provide a useful focus for your efforts. If you want people to give you money for your programs, you need to make sure that your programs are worth paying for. Throughout this book, we'll be looking at examples of good programming practice so that when someone says, "I'd pay money for that" when they see one of your programs, you'll give them something of good quality and value.

What you have learned

In this first chapter you've built yourself a place to work, installed the Visual Studio tools that you're going to use to write your programs, and taken a look at some of the sample applications provided with the book.

You've discovered that Visual Studio is essentially a "word processor for programmers," where programmers can create and test their software. You've also seen that Visual Studio uses solutions and projects to organize the resources and program code that are put together to make a modern application. And you have created your very first application by changing the messages a program displays.

To reinforce your understanding of this chapter, you might want to consider the following questions about computers, programs, and programming.

What is the difference between a program and an application?

When people talk about software, you will find the words *program* and *application* (or *app*) used interchangeably. When I talk about a program, I am describing some code that tells the computer what to do. I regard an application as something larger and more developed. An application brings together program code and assets such as images and sounds to make a complete experience for a user. A program can be as simple as a few lines of C#.

What is the difference between a project and a solution in Visual Studio?

A *solution* is the outermost container. A solution can contain projects and is frequently used to create a complete application or product. A *project* can contain C# source files and is frequently a complete subcomponent of a solution. For example, all the C# program files that make up the Snaps framework are packaged as a project—the **Snaps** project in the **BeginToCodeWithCSharp** solution—that can be used in any solution that needs to make use of Snaps resources. You'll be using the resources in the **Snaps** project a lot as you begin to code your own applications in this book.

Why do we need a special language like C# to program a computer?

My favorite answer to this question is the pair of sentences "Time flies like an arrow. Fruit flies like a banana." A human being can work out that the first one refers to something flying, whereas the second sentence is all about insects and what they like to have for lunch. A computer would have a horrible time getting the correct meaning from these two statements. The way that humans use language is packed with ambiguity and confusion. Fortunately, we have really powerful computers between our ears that are hard-wired for languages, and we spend all our early years programming them. By contrast, the poor computer has a very simple thinking machine that works best only when given hard and fast rules. A programming language contains a set of specific constructions that we can make the computer understand so that it can follow our instructions correctly.

Is Visual Studio the only way to write programs?

No. There are a great many tools that you can use to create software. Some are tied to one particular programming language, and others are more general purpose. Visual Studio is one of the best, however.

What do I do if I break the program?

Some people worry that things they do with a program on the computer might "break" it in some way. I used to worry about this too, but I've conquered this fear by making sure that whenever I do something I always have a way back. You are currently in that happy position. You know exactly how to put Visual Studio on a computer, and you are using a copy of the demo code that you extracted from the .zip folder you downloaded. Even if something goes horribly wrong and you end up breaking a program so that it won't work, you simply have to extract a clean copy of the demo code from the .zip folder and start again.

2
What is programming?

What you will learn

In this chapter, you'll work with more C# programs. But before you do, we're going to take on some detective work and discover what makes a programmer and what a computer really does.

What makes a programmer?

If you have not programmed before, don't worry. Programming is not rocket science—it is, well, programming. The hard part about learning to program is that you get hit at the start with a lot of ideas and concepts, and this can be confusing.

However, if you think that learning to program sounds like hard work and that you might not be able to do it, I'd strongly suggest that you put those thoughts aside. Programming is as easy as organizing a birthday party for a friend.

Programming and party planning

If you were organizing a party, you'd have to decide who to invite. You'd have to remember who wanted vegetarian pizza and which kids can't sit next to each other without causing trouble. You'd have to work out what presents the kids would take home and what everyone would do when they were at the party. And you'd have to organize the timing so that the magician or the band doesn't arrive just as the food is being served. To help, you'd organize the party using lists like those shown in **Figure 2-1**. Programming is just like this. It is all about organization.

Guest List	Menu	Schedule	Guest Presents
Jim	Crisps	3:00 pm Arrival	Hat
Simon	Pizza	3:30 Xbox Party Games	Whistle (maybe)
Anita	Lemonade	4:30 Food	Sweets
Josh	Cola	5:15 Magician	Puzzle
Mo	Orange juice		Book
Kevin			
Sunil			
Albert			

Figure 2-1 Party planning is a lot like programming—you have to stay organized.

If you can organize a party, you can write a program. What happens in a program is a little different, but the basic principles are the same. And because a program contains elements that you create and manage (unlike unruly kids), you have complete control over exactly what happens. What's more, once you've done some programming, you might start to approach all tasks in a systematic way, so a bit of programming experience can turn you into a better organizer overall.

Programming is defined by most people as "earning huge sums of money doing something that nobody can understand." I define programming as "determining a solution to a given problem and expressing it in a form that a computer system can understand and execute." One or two things fall out of this definition:

- You need to be able to solve the problem yourself before you can write a program to do it.

- The computer has to be made to understand what you are trying to tell it to do.

You can think of a program as a bit like a recipe. If you don't know how to bake a cake, you can't tell someone else how to do it. And if the person you are talking to doesn't understand instructions such as "Fold the flour and sugar into the mix," you still can't tell him how to bake the cake.

To create a program, you have to take a solution that you have worked out and then write it down in simple steps that the computer can perform.

Programming and problems

I also like to think of a programmer as a bit like a plumber. A plumber arrives at a job with a big bag of tools and spare parts. Having looked at the plumbing problem for a while, he opens his bag, takes out various tools and parts, fits the parts together, and solves your problem. Programming is like that. You are given a problem to solve, and you have at your disposal a big bag of tools, in this case a programming language. You look at the problem for a while, work out how to solve it, and then fit the bits of the language together to solve the problem. The art of programming is knowing which bits you need to take out of your bag of tools to solve each part of the problem.

The art of taking a problem and breaking it down into a set of instructions you can give to a computer is the interesting part of programming. However, learning to program is not simply a matter of learning a programming language. Nor is programming simply a matter of coming up with a program that solves a problem. You must consider many things when writing a program, and not all of them are directly related to the problem at hand.

To start, let's assume that you're writing your programs for a customer. He or she has a problem and would like you to write a program to solve it. We'll also assume that the customer knows even less about computers than we do. Initially, you're not even going to talk about the programming language, the type of computer, or anything like that; you are simply going to make sure that you know what the customer wants. Because programmers pride themselves on their ability to come up with solutions, as soon as they are given a problem, they immediately start to think of ways to solve it—this is almost a reflex action. Unfortunately, many software projects have failed because the problem that they solved was the wrong one. Coming up with a perfect solution to a problem the customer doesn't have is something that happens surprisingly often in the real world. The developers of the software quite simply did not find out what was required or desired. Instead, they created what they thought was required. The customers assumed that because the developers stopped asking questions, the right solution was being built. Only at the final handoff was the awful truth revealed. It is very important that a programmer should hold off making something until she knows exactly what is required.

The worst thing you can say to a customer right away is "I can do that." Instead, you should first think, "Is that what the customer wants? Do I really understand what the problem is?" Asking these questions is a kind of self-discipline. Before you solve a problem, you should be sure that you have a watertight definition of what the problem is, which both you and the customer agree on.

In the real world such a definition is sometimes called a *functional design specification,* or FDS. An FDS tells you exactly what the customer wants. Both you and the customer sign it, and the bottom line is that if you provide a system that behaves according to the design specification, the customer must pay you. Once you have your design specification, you can think about ways of solving the problem.

You might think that having a specification isn't necessary if you are writing a program for yourself, but this is not true. Writing some form of specification forces you to think about your problem at a very detailed level. It also forces you to think about what your system is not going to do. You need this clarity when building something for yourself as much as when you are working with a customer. The specification sets expectations right at the start.

PROGRAMMER'S POINT

The specification must always be there

I have written many programs for money. I would never write a program without getting a solid specification first. This is true even (or perhaps especially) when I do a job for a friend.

Modern development techniques put the customer at the heart of development and involve them in the design process in an ongoing way. These techniques reflect the assumption that it is very hard to get a definitive specification at the start of a project. As a developer, you don't really know much about the customer's business, and the customer doesn't know the limitations and possibilities of the technologies that can be used to solve the problem. With this in mind, it's a good idea to make a series of versions of the solution and discuss each version with the customer before moving on to the next one. This is called *prototyping.*

Programmers and people

Finding out what the customer wants is one of the most important aspects of any programming task. However, communication with other people is important in lots of other situations, too. Perhaps you want to convince a wealthy backer that you have the idea for the next big thing or persuade a customer that you have the best solution to his problems.

Not all programmers are great communicators at the start. But the important thing to remember is that communication skills can be learned, just like a new programming language. This might mean going outside your comfort zone—nobody likes standing in front of an audience for the first time—but with practice you can master communication skills and vastly increase your chances of going a long way in this business.

Effective communication also extends to writing. Being able to create text that other folks can read is a very useful skill, and again, the best way to do this is with practice. My advice is to start writing a blog or a diary. It doesn't matter that only your mom reads your blog at first; the important thing is that you write regularly. If you write about something you are interested in (I write about programing—surprise, surprise—at www.robmiles.com), you will quickly become much better at it.

PROGRAMMER'S POINT

Programmers who can communicate well get the most money and the interesting work

It's possible to make a good living from programming even if you can communicate only in single words and grunts—as long as you can write code quickly that meets the given requirements. But the really interesting tasks go to developers who can communicate well. They are the ones who can sell their ideas and are best at talking to customers to find out what the customer wants.

Computers as data processors

Now that you know what programmers do, we can start to consider what a computer is and what makes it so special.

Machines and computers and us

The human race is a race of toolmakers. We invent things to make our lives easier, and we've been doing it for thousands of years. We started with mechanical devices, like the plough, which made farming more efficient, but in the last century we've moved into electronic devices. **Figure 2-2** offers a quick summary.

Inputs		Outputs
Human Effort Steering	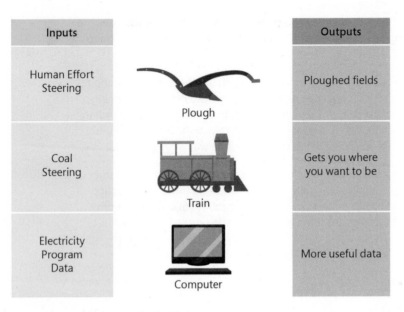 Plough	Ploughed fields
Coal Steering	Train	Gets you where you want to be
Electricity Program Data	Computer	More useful data

Figure 2-2 Machines that do things for us.

Machines usually involve something going into them, or inputs, and they produce things or events that we want as outputs. A plough, with human effort and steering as inputs, provides a field that will grow more crops. Given coal and a track to follow, a train takes us where we want to go. A computer is given power, a program to tell it what to do, and some data to work on. It then outputs data that is useful.

As computers became smaller and cheaper, they found their way into things around us, and many devices—the mobile phone, for example—are possible only because we can put a computer inside to make them work. But we need to remember what the computer actually does; it automates operations that used to need brain power. There's nothing particularly clever about a computer; it simply follows the instructions that it's given. In this respect, a computer has a lot in common with a plough—it's not conscious in any way. It is simply something that we can use to make our lives easier.

A computer works on data in the same way that a sausage machine works on meat: something is put in one end, some processing is performed, and something comes out the other end. You can think of a computer program as similar to the instructions that a coach gives to a football or soccer team before a play. The coach will say something like, "If they attack on the left, I want Jerry and Chris to run back, but if they kick the ball down the field, I want Jerry to chase the ball." Then, when the game unfolds, the team will respond to events in a way that should let them outplay their opponents.

However, there is one important distinction between a computer program and the way a team might behave in a football game. A football player would know that some instructions make no sense. If the coach says, "If they attack on the left, I want Jerry to sing the first verse of the national anthem and then run as fast as he can toward the exit," the player would raise an objection.

Unfortunately, a program is unaware of the sensibility of the data it is processing, in the same way that a sausage machine is unaware of what meat is. Put a bicycle into a sausage machine, and the machine will try to make sausage out of it. Put meaningless data into a computer, and it will do meaningless things with it. As far as computers are concerned, data is just a pattern of signals coming in that has to be manipulated in some way to produce another pattern of signals. A computer program is the sequence of instructions that tell a computer what to do with the data coming in and what form the data sent out will have.

Examples of typical data-processing applications include the following (and are shown in **Figure 2-3**):

- **Mobile phone** A microcomputer in your phone takes signals from a radio and converts them into sound. At the same time, it takes signals from a microphone and makes them into patterns of bits that will be sent out from the radio.

- **Car** A microcomputer in the engine takes information from sensors telling it the current engine speed, road speed, oxygen content of the air, setting of the accelerator, and so on and produces voltages that control the setting of the carburetor, the timing of the spark plugs, and other things to optimize the performance of the engine.

- **Game console** A computer takes instructions from the controllers and uses them to manage the artificial world that it is creating for the person playing the game.

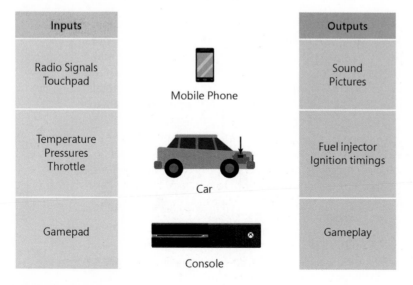

Figure 2-3 Many different devices use computers.

Most reasonably complex devices created today contain data-processing components to optimize their performance, and some exist only because we can build in such capabilities. It is into this world that you, as a beginning programmer, are moving. It is important to think of data processing as much more than working out the company payroll—calculating numbers and printing out results (the traditional uses of computers). As a software engineer, you will inevitably spend a great deal of your time fitting data-processing components into other devices to drive them. These embedded systems mean many people will be using computers even if they're not even aware of it!

Making programs work

Inside every computer is hardware—physical machinery, that is—that actually does the data processing I've been describing. This hardware is called the *central processing unit,* or CPU. The programs that directly control the CPU, telling it what to do, are called *machine code.* Different kinds of CPUs have different designs of machine code, in the same way that humans communicate by using many different languages.

Machine code contains the individual steps that tell the CPU what to do. Simple operations—for example, adding one number to another—are performed by a sequence of machine-code instructions. To write machine code, you have to know exactly how the hardware works and the particular instructions that it understands. To understand what this means, take a look at **Figure 2-4,** which shows part of a program that totals up what a customer buys at a supermarket. This program adds the price of an item to the customer's total bill.

High Level Program	Low Level Program
1. Add the price of a can of beans to the bill.	1. Fetch the bill value.
	2. Fetch the price of a can of beans
	3. Add the two values together.
	4. Put the value back.

Figure 2-4 A single step in a high-level program is broken down by a low-level program.

The instructions on the right are the lower-level instructions that the computer is actually able to perform. These describe the individual steps that the computer has to go through to perform the action, adding the price of an item to a bill. Writing low-level programs is rather tedious because an action, as you can see, needs to be broken down into a number of smaller ones.

The good news, however, is that programmers over the years have thought about this and invented new languages that can be used to tell a CPU what to do. These languages are "higher level" than machine code. A program written in a high-level language doesn't provide the individual machine-code steps required to perform a particular action. It just contains an instruction such as, "Add this number to another." A special program called a *compiler* takes this high-level program and generates the machine code required for the computer to be able to perform the task. After you have written your high-level program (in C#, for example), it will be compiled to produce the machine code that runs inside the computer.

A useful side effect of using a high-level language is that by changing the compiler you can generate machine-code programs for different hardware platforms. The C# programs you are going to write over the course of this book can be made to work on Windows, Android, and Apple devices because compilers are available that will convert the high-level statements into machine code for those devices. If anyone asks you which type of computer you are learning to program, you can correctly reply "All of them."

Programs as data processors

Figure 2-5 shows what every computer does. Data goes into the computer, which does something with it, and then data comes out of the computer. What form the data takes and what the output means is entirely up to us, as is what the program does.

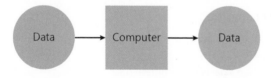

Figure 2-5 A computer as a data processor.

As I quickly mentioned earlier, another way to think of a program is as a recipe, which is illustrated in **Figure 2-6.**

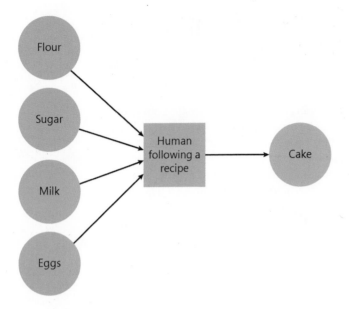

Figure 2-6 Recipes and programs.

In this example, the cook plays the role of the computer and the recipe is the program that controls what the cook does with the ingredients. A recipe can work with lots of different ingredients, and a program can work with lots of different inputs, too. For example, a program might take your age and the name of the movie you want to see and provide an output that determines whether you can go see that particular movie.

CODE ANALYSIS

Mystery program investigations

Welcome to our first "Code Analysis" section. In these sections, you'll take a look at some program code and consider questions posed by it. In this first case, you're going to take the idea of what a computer is and consider what happens when a particular program runs— you're going to try to work out what the program does with the input to produce the output. This is a bit like detective work, where a great detective arrives at the scene of a crime and then uses the available evidence to deduce what happened. The following screenshot shows the window that you saw when you ran the first program in Chapter 1. The program displays a welcome message and a list of folders and Snaps applications, as you see here.

Question: What are the inputs and the outputs from this program?

> **Answer:** Identifying the output is very easy. It's the display the user sees on the screen. The inputs to the program are slightly trickier to identify, but it turns out that they were put into the program when it was written. In the previous chapter, you saw how to use Visual Studio to look at the contents of a program. Here is the program code that you found when you opened the file MyProgram.cs.

```
public class MyProgram
{
    public void StartProgram()
    {
        SnapsEngine.SetTitleString("Begin to Code with C#");
        SnapsEngine.DisplayString("Welcome to the world of Snaps!");
    }
}
```

Built-in title string

Built-in display string

I've called out the two strings in the program that provide the input to the program. In this case, the inputs are built into the program code in the form of the text strings that are displayed when the program runs. You can tell that these are the inputs because if you changed these strings, the program would do something different when it runs. In fact, we actually did this at the end of Chapter 1, when I made some alterations that reflect my urge for world domination.

Some programs are entirely self-contained like this, with all their information built into their code. But it is much more likely that a program will receive data from the outside and work on that. So now let's look at a program that receives data from the program's user.

This program is one of the Snaps apps that are supplied with the sample code. Each chapter presents a number of sample programs, and you can run any of these by selecting the chapter folder in the list on the left, selecting the program in the list on the right, and then selecting the **Run an app** button. The first sample application we're going to run is called Ch02_01_MysteryProgram1, which you see selected in this screenshot.

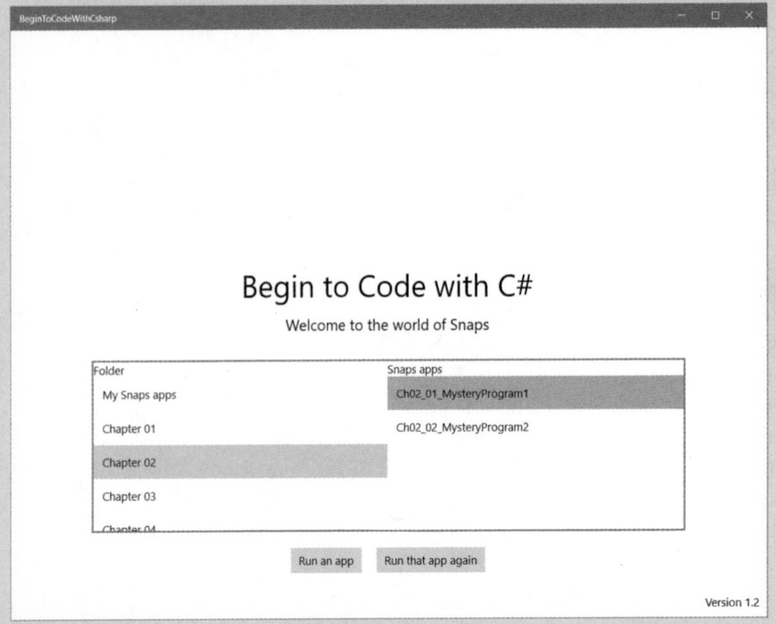

If you do this for our mystery program, you are presented with a request to enter a number, as shown here:

The data going into the program is a number; here I've entered the value 1. When you select **Enter,** the program takes the number, does something with it, and then returns a result:

It turns out that when you enter **1**, the output from the Mystery Program is 2. You might have a theory about what happens to the input to produce this output. Here are a couple of theories that fit what we see:

- The program might always output 2.

- The program might add 1 to the input.

You can use the **Run that app again** button to run the Mystery Program again and try different numbers. I've tried it with a few more numbers and received the following results:

- 1 produces 2.

- 2 produces 4.

- 3 produces 6.

- 0 produces 0.

From these results I think that we can deduce that the behavior of the program is to take the number coming in and double it.

Programmers call this form of program examination *black-box testing*. The program is being treated as a black box that we can't look inside of. Input values are fed into the black box, and the outputs are checked to see whether they match what we think the program should do.

The idea behind black-box testing is to build confidence that the program actually does what we want. If someone offered to pay us large sums of money to produce a program that would double the value of the number that was entered, from the tests we have performed it looks like we have something here that would do the job.

The tests we've done seem fairly convincing, but there is no way that we can be sure that the program always produces an output that is double the input unless we try every possible number. This illustrates a problem with this form of testing: it can prove that there is a fault in the program, but it can't prove the absence of faults.

As an illustration of the limits of black-box testing, try entering **40** to see what the program does when it is given that value:

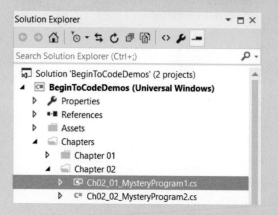

It turns out that for every input value apart from 40, the program produces double the input. But for the input value 40, the Pirate King message is displayed. It is as if the program is specifically looking for the value 40 and behaving in a different way if it is given that value. This turns out to be exactly what is happening. If you want to find out how this code works, open the sample program in Visual Studio and take a look. Use Solution Explorer to find the source file, as shown here, in the same way that you opened the MyProgram.cs file in Chapter 1.

When you do this, you find the following program code:

```
public class Ch02_01_MysteryProgram1
{
    public void StartProgram()
    {
        SnapsEngine.SetTitleString("Mystery Program 1");
        double inputNumber = SnapsEngine.ReadFloat("Enter a number please");
        if (inputNumber == 40)                                         Test for
            SnapsEngine.DisplayString(@"'Arr. That be my age.' said the   the value
            Pirate King");                                                 40.
        else
        {
            inputNumber = inputNumber + inputNumber;        Double the input.
            SnapsEngine.DisplayString("Output: " + inputNumber);
        }
    }
}
```

For now, don't worry too much about the curly brackets and the different colored words in the program text; just consider the elements that have been called out. You can see that the code has some form of test (performed by an `if` construction, which you'll learn more about in Chapter 5) and a statement that appears to double a value by adding it to itself.

If you want to guard against faults in your programs, you have to take a look at the actual program code. Programmers call this form of program evaluation *white-box testing* or *code review*. Instead of looking at the outputs produced by the program in response to particular inputs, you look at the actions that are called for by the code and make sure that these match the behaviors that you want. You do this by pretending to be a computer and working through the program statements to see what happens.

PROGRAMMER'S POINT

Testing is really hard to do—but you must try

One of the dangerous things about black-box testing is that all it can do is prove that a program has faults. If we feed a bunch of inputs into the program and all the outputs are correct, this does not mean that the program is fault free; it just means that we haven't found a test that the program fails. The only way to really be sure that the program will work is to take a look at the actual code itself.

Please don't confuse testing with "that thing I've done to see whether the program looks like it works." In the case of the number-doubling machine in Mystery Program 1, we could put a few numbers in and see whether it generated results that look okay, but that's not testing. That's just seeing whether the program looks like it works.

If I was serious about testing a program like this, I'd create a set of specific tests. I'd make sure the tests included very large and very small numbers, as well as negative values and the value 0, and I'd formalize the tests so that when they've been performed successfully the program is "signed off" as tested. If I was really clever, I'd create a program that did the testing for me. This program could feed in many millions of values and check that each matching output is correct. Of course, if my tests never fed in the "pirate value" of 40, then the program would be passed as tested but still have the potential to fail when it's used. But as I said, tests prove only the existence of faults, not that there aren't any.

The good news is that a combination of black-box and white-box testing can produce programs that are reliable enough. But please remember that proper tests are planned, managed, and documented and not just "this thing I did to see whether it works."

MAKE SOMETHING HAPPEN

Get rid of the pirate

This exercise is not really programming as such, but you should be able to make a version of the doubling program that works correctly for every value that is input. You can do this by removing the code that checks for the value 40 and the code that runs if the value 40 is found. You can do this by editing the chapter example itself (in which case, you can be said to have "personalized" your copy of the sample code).

Data and information

Now that you understand computers as machines that process data and that programs tell computers what to do with the data, let's delve a little bit deeper into the nature of data and information. People use the words *data* and *information* interchangeably, but I think it's important to make a distinction between the two because the way that computers and humans consider data is completely different. Take a look at **Figure 2-7.**

What the computer sees   What we see

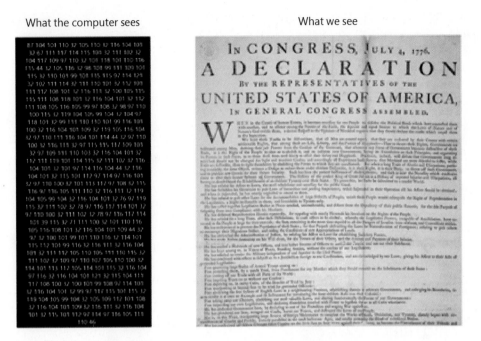

Figure 2-7 Data on the left; information on the right.

The two items in the figure contain exactly the same data, except that the image on the left is closer to how the document would be stored in a computer. The computer uses a numeric value to represent each letter and space in the text. If you work through the values, you can figure out what each of them are, starting with the value 87, which represents an uppercase W.

Because of the way that computers hold data, another layer sits underneath the mapping of numbers to letters. Each number is held by the computer as a unique pattern of on and off signals, or 1s and 0s. In the realm of computing, each 1 or 0 is known as a *bit*. (For a wonderful explanation of how computers operate at this level and of how these workings form the basis for all coding, see Charles Petzold's *Code: The Hidden Language of Computer Hardware and Software*.) The value 87, which we know means "uppercase W," is held as the following bit pattern:

1010111

I don't really have the space to go into precisely how this works (and Charles Petzold already did this!), but you can think of this bit pattern as meaning "87 is made up of a 1 plus a 2 plus a 4 plus a 16 plus a 64."

Each of the bits in the pattern tells the computer hardware whether a particular power of two is present. Don't worry too much if you don't fully understand this, but do remember that as far as the computer is concerned, data is a collection of 1s and 0s that computers store and manipulate. That's data.

Information, on the other hand, is the interpretation of data by people to mean something. Strictly speaking, computers process data and humans work on information. As an example, the computer could hold the following bit pattern somewhere in memory:

11111111 11111111 11111111 00000000

You could regard this as meaning "You are $256 overdrawn at the bank" or "You are 256 feet below the surface of the ground" or "Eight of the thirty-two light switches are off." The transition from data to information is usually made when a human reads the output.

So why am I being so pedantic? Because it is vital to remember that a computer does not "know" what the data it is processing actually means. As far as the computer is concerned, data is just patterns of bits; it is the user who gives meaning to these patterns. Remember this when you get a bank statement that says that you have $8,388,608 in your account!

CODE ANALYSIS

Mystery program investigations

You are now going to run another mystery program to take a look at how data is stored in a computer. This program has the rather unoriginal name of Ch02_02_MysteryProgram2. You can select and run it by using the same steps as before. (You can also use Visual Studio to look at the code right at the start if you like, but I'd call that cheating.)

When you run the program, you're asked to enter something. Type the word **hello,** select the Enter key, and the program displays what you see here:

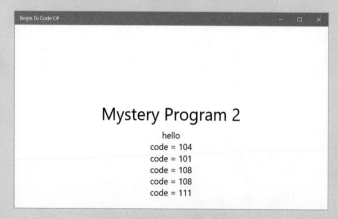

The program displays the word you just typed in, followed by a list of mysterious codes. If you look carefully, you can start to work out what the codes mean. The program displays five code values, which is the same number of letters contained in the word "hello." What's more, the third and fourth codes are the same number, just like in "hello," in which the third and fourth letters are the same.

It turns out that these "codes" are actually the numbers that are used by your computer to represent those letters of text. Modern digital devices use a standard called Unicode that provides a mapping of character codes to particular numeric values. This mystery program just takes each character in the word you type in, converts it to a number, and then displays the number. Let's take a look at exactly how it works by analyzing the code.

```csharp
public class Ch02_02_MysteryProgram2
{
    public void StartProgram()
    {
        SnapsEngine.SetTitleString("Mystery Program 2");

        // Read a string from the user
        string inputText = SnapsEngine.ReadString("Enter something please");

        // Only display the first 10 characters from the string
        if (inputText.Length > 10)
            inputText = inputText.Substring(0, 10);

        SnapsEngine.AddLineToDisplay(inputText);

        // Get each character in the string
        foreach (char ch in inputText)
        {
            // Get the number that represents this character and
            // display it
            int chVal = (int)ch;
            SnapsEngine.AddLineToDisplay("code = " + chVal);
        }
    }
}
```

This is a more complex program than the first mystery program. It contains a loop—a kind of programming device that lets a program repeat an instruction—that is applied to each character in the word you type, converting the character to an integer and then displaying it. There are some quite advanced C# constructions used in this code, which we will get to later in the book, but you should be able to pull out some elements that make sense. And for the moment, that's enough.

Over the years I've looked at a great many programs. Some were programs that I wrote, and some were written by other people. Some programs were written by using a programming language that I know, while others were written in a language I'd never seen before.

I've learned not to be distracted by the bits of the program I don't understand yet and to focus on the parts that make sense to me. You might not know what the `public class` bit of the program listing means, but the line `string inputText = SnapsEngine .ReadString("Enter something please");` should kind of make sense and leave you thinking this might be where the program gets a string of text.

Americans use the term "spelunking" to describe the hobby of exploring underground caves. The term is also used to describe the "hobby" of exploring unfamiliar program code. You should try to get good at spelunking the programs in this book. You can start by looking for landmarks that you know are there and then work from those, refining your understanding of the program's behaviors. For example, you know that somewhere in the program it performs an action *for each* character in the string. Knowing that, you should be able to work out where in the code this action happens.

What you have learned

In this chapter you've learned a bit about how computers actually work and what programming is about. You have discovered that a computer views the entire universe as patterns of ons and offs (1s and 0s), which represent the data the computer is working with. The computer performs data processing by transforming one pattern of bits—the input—into another pattern of bits—the output.

When human beings take a look at the data output and act on it, the data becomes *information*. Computers are unaware of the meaning that we place on the patterns of bits that they process, which means that a computer will do things with data that make no sense.

A program tells the computer what to do with the pattern of bits. The computer itself understands only very simple instructions, but programs called *compilers* can take in a higher-level description of the actions that are required and produce the simple instructions for the computer to perform.

The job of the programmer is to create a program as a sequence of instructions that describes the tasks to be performed. To solve a problem successfully, the programmer must not only write a good program but also make sure that the program actually does what the user wants. This means that before a programmer can write any code, she will have to make sure that she has a good understanding of exactly what is required. Talking to people and finding out what they want is a very valuable skill and worth acquiring if you want to be a successful programmer.

To reinforce your understanding of the content, you might want to consider the following questions about computers, programs, and programming.

Would a computer "know" that it is nonsensical for someone to have an age −20?

No. As far as the computer is concerned, the age value is just a pattern of bits that represents a number. If we want a computer to reject ages that are negative, we have to actually build that understanding into the program ourselves.

If the output from a program is the settings for the fuel-injection system on a car, is the output data or information?

As soon as something starts acting on data, I think it becomes information. A human being is not doing anything with these values, but they will cause the speed of the engine to change, which might well affect humans, so I reckon this makes this information rather than data.

Is the computer unintelligent because it can't understand English?

It is very hard to write something in English that is completely unambiguous. Large parts of the legal profession are built on precise interpretation of the meaning of texts and how they are applied in particular situations. Since we humans can't agree on how to understand something, I don't think it is fair to call a computer stupid because it can't do this either.

If I don't know how to work out the answer, can I write a program to do it?

No. You can put some statements together and see what happens when they run, but this is very unlikely to make what you want. It is rather like throwing a bunch of wheels, gears, and an engine against a wall and expecting them to land and form a working car. In fact, the best way to write a program is frequently to get away from the keyboard for a while and just think about what the program is supposed to do.

Is it sensible to assume that the customer measures everything in inches?

It is never sensible to assume anything about a project. A successful programmer needs to make sure that everything he is doing is built on a solid understanding. Every assumption that you make increases the potential for disaster.

If the program does the wrong thing, is it my fault or the customer's fault?

It depends:

- Specification right, program wrong: programmer's fault

- Specification wrong, program right: customer's fault

- Specification wrong, program wrong: everyone's fault

3
Writing programs

What you will learn

Now that you know a bit about computers, programs, and programmers, you can start to think about writing program code.

In this chapter, you'll closely examine some C# programs to find out how they run. I call these programs "Snaps applications" because they use the Snaps library, a simple collection of programming resources that help you get things done "in a snap." By analyzing how these programs use various Snaps—discrete pieces of programming functionality or behaviors provided by the library—you'll learn some fundamentals of C# programming. Along the way you'll learn more about using Visual Studio to create and manage the code elements in the **BeginToCodeWithCSharp** solution and what to do when the compiler complains that your program doesn't make sense as far as it is concerned.

At the end of this chapter, you will be creating programs that provide simple solutions to some realistic problems.

C# program structure

Let's take a very detailed look at some Snaps applications to understand their elements and the organization of those elements. The welcome that you witness when you first run the **BeginToCodeWithCSharp** solution isn't complicated, but it's a good place for us to start. We quickly examined the code that creates that experience when we analyzed **MyProgram.cs** in Chapter 2. Take a look now at the file named **Ch03_01_WelcomeProgram.cs**. (In case you've forgotten: use Solution Explorer to navigate through the solution's chapter folders to find the file, and then select the file to show its code in the editor window.)

Notice that the code is almost exactly the same as the code as in **MyProgram.cs**, so this program should give us the same experience, right? Let's check that. Go ahead and run the solution again, select **Chapter 03** in the **Folder** list and **Ch03_01_WelcomeProgram** is the **Snaps apps** list, and then run the app. Yep, same experience, which makes perfect sense. Now let's really break down this program to figure out how it's working. Its code is shown next, and I've indicated each part of the program with a callout. We'll examine these parts line by line in the following sections.

```
using SnapsLibrary;                                          Identify resources.

public class Ch03_01_WelcomeProgram                          Start a class definition.
{
    public void StartProgram()                               Declare the
    {                                                        StartProgram method.
        SnapsEngine.SetTitleString("Begin to Code with C#");
        SnapsEngine.DisplayString("Welcome to the world of Snaps");   Set the title
    }                                                                 and display
}                                                                     a message.
```

Identify resources

```
using SnapsLibrary;
```

I described the C# *compiler* in Chapter 2. This is a program that converts a high-level C# program (like the one we're analyzing) into machine code that can run inside your computer. When you run your C# code, the compiler built into Visual Studio converts the program into machine code so that it can be run. A C# program can contain lines called *directives* that give the compiler instructions. This first line of the program is a using directive.

As a programmer, you will frequently want to use prebuilt pieces of software, in the same way that a cook will sometimes use readymade pastry. Readymade C# programs are packaged as libraries of components that can be added to a Visual Studio solution. As I've mentioned, the Snaps library is an example of such a library that I've provided to help you get started. The using directive here identifies the library as a resource that has been added to our solution and, as you'll see in a moment, this program is going to use something from it, specifically the SnapsEngine. This using directive says to the compiler, "If I mention something you haven't seen before, go and look in SnapsLibrary to see if you can find it there." This is a bit like saying to our cook, "If you need to use some pastry, take a look in the fridge." The first programs that we're going to write in this book use only items in SnapsLibrary. Later on we will create programs that use other libraries.

CODE ANALYSIS

Using the using directive

In some "Code Analysis" sections, like this one, you don't need to look at any code to consider some code-related questions.

Question: Does the using directive actually fetch the library that a program wants to use?

Answer: No. This might sound confusing, but the using directive just tells the compiler where to look for the items that are available for use in a program. The resources available to a program are set up in the Visual Studio project. We can change the using directive to direct the compiler to use code from different places. This would be like telling the cook, "If you need to use some pastry, check by the sink" so that he would use a resource from a different location.

Question: If I add lots of using directives, will this make my program bigger?

Answer: No. The directive just tells the compiler where to look for things. It doesn't add anything to the size of the program.

Start a class definition

```
public class Ch03_01_WelcomeProgram
```

C# can be called an *object-oriented* programming language. This is because, in the universe of C#, everything is an *object*. Objects in a C# program can be as simple as a single number or as complex as an entire video game. An object can contain other objects. Anything that is contained within another object is called a *member* of that object.

We can express an object design in the form of a C# *class* definition. A C# class definition can describe data members (values that the object can hold) and behavior members (things you can ask the object to do for you). When you design an object, you write C# that specifies these two things. This line of the program tells the compiler that we are expressing the design of a `class` named `Ch03_01_WelcomeProgram`.

You'll find out much more about classes and objects later in the book.

CODE ANALYSIS

Classes and objects

Question: Is a class definition the only way to define an object?

Answer: No. There are other kinds of C# objects, which you will see later.

Question: Does defining a class actually create an object?

Answer: No. Think of the class as the blueprint or design of an object, just like you might have plans for a treehouse. In the same way as having the plans for a treehouse doesn't actually give you a treehouse, having a class definition doesn't actually give you an object.

Question: Do all classes have to contain both data and behaviors?

Answer: No. Some classes contain just data members, and others contain only behavior members. For example, the Math library, which we haven't seen yet, contains classes that can perform mathematical functions.

Question: When does the program actually make an object based on the class `Ch03_01_WelcomeProgram`?

Answer: This happens automatically. The sequence goes like this: The user is running the **BeginToCodeWithCSharp** application and then selects **Ch03_01_WelcomeProgram** and runs it. The **BeginToCodeWithCsharp** application creates an object based on the `Ch03_01_WelomeProgram` class and then runs the `StartProgram` behavior inside this object.

Declare the StartProgram method

```
public void StartProgram()
```

Behaviors in an object are expressed in the form of *methods*. A method is a piece of C# code that is given a name. A program can run the code in a method simply by giving the name of the method—this is known as *calling the method*. You are going to start by calling methods that have already been written (by me), but later you will create methods of your own.

This program's single class—Ch03_01_WelcomeProgram—has just a single behavior, a method called StartProgram. The declaration public void StartProgram() marks the beginning of the StartProgram method. (The *method modifier* public and the *return type* void tell us about the nature of this method, but these are details we don't need to get into at the moment.) The StartProgram method is special. It is the entry point for a Snaps application. In other words, to start running a Snaps application, the StartProgram method is called.

This program's class does not contain any data members but later we will design some objects that do contain data.

CODE ANALYSIS

Declaring methods in classes

Question: What is the difference between a behavior and a method?

> **Answer:** A behavior is an action that an object can perform. The method is the actual C# code that delivers that behavior.

Question: Can a class contain more than one method?

> **Answer:** Yes. A programmer decides how many behaviors a class should provide, and she writes a method for each one. The demo program we've been looking at has only one behavior: to start the demo. Later on we'll create classes with many methods in them.

Question: How does the StartProgram method get used?

> **Answer:** StartProgram is a special method, in that it defines the starting point for any Snaps application. While we're working in the Snaps environment provided by the Snaps library, we will always call the StartProgram method to start a program running.

Set the title and display a message

```
SnapsEngine.SetTitleString("Begin to Code with C#");
SnapsEngine.DisplayString("Welcome to the world of Snaps");
```

The first of these two lines of code is the first C# *statement* in the `StartProgram` method. Statements are the parts of a program that get things done. A statement might call a method, make a decision, or manipulate some data. Statements are held inside methods and are performed when the method is used. The `StartProgram` method contains only two statements; larger programs will contain many more. The two statements within the `StartProgram` method do indeed call other methods.

Each statement in a method is performed in sequence, starting with the first one and then moving on to the next. There are several types of statements that you can use, and you'll find out about these as you learn the C# language. The semicolon (;) character marks the end of each statement.

This first statement sets the title of our program to "Begin to Code with C#". It uses the `SnapsEngine` class to do this. The `SnapsEngine` class is part of the Snaps library—the resource we identified in the first line of this program—and the class provides lots of behaviors that we can use in our programs. You can think of `SnapsEngine` as a kind of "program butler" that can do things for programs that you write.

Each `SnapsEngine` behavior is provided as a C# method that our programs can call. In this example, you can see how to use the `SetTitleString` method in the `SnapsEngine`. Then, in the same way that a "Get me a drink" command to a butler needs to be accompanied by the type of drink you want, the `SetTitleString` method needs to be given the string of text to be used as the title of the program. A C# string is given in parentheses after the name of the method that we're calling. Information added to a call of a method is called an *argument* to the method.

Regarding the string itself, the double quotation mark characters (") in the statement mark the start and end of the string—the string starts immediately after the first double quotation mark and ends immediately before the second one. It's a convention in C# that whenever you want to specify a string of text, you enclose it in double quotation marks like this. If we added spaces in the string text—for example, " `Welcome to Snaps` "—those spaces would also be displayed in the program's title (although a user might not notice them).

The second statement works in the same way as the previous one. It calls a method in the `SnapsEngine` class that displays a string as a message on the screen of the Snaps application (rather than setting a string as a title on the screen). When you saw the `DisplayString` method name, did you expect to see quotation marks and string text within the method's parentheses? Good!

Calling methods in classes

Question: Where is the SetTitleString method declared?

> **Answer:** The SetTitleString method is declared in the SnapsEngine class in exactly the same way as the StartProgram method is declared in the Ch03_01_WelcomePro-gram class. Later you will discover how to create your own methods in classes.

Question: What happens if I don't give SetTitleString a string to work on?

> **Answer:** The design of SetTitleString specifies that a string will be supplied when it is called. The compiler will complain that a program is invalid if the program doesn't provide a string argument to the method call.

Question: Why do we have to put parentheses around the string that we're providing to SetTitleString? Surely the compiler can figure out that the string to be displayed will start with a double quotation mark character.

> **Answer:** The reason why we need to include the parentheses is to tell the compiler the start and end of the list of arguments being fed into the method. SetTitleString has only one item being fed into it, but other methods might have lots of items. If you look at the text of the program, you'll find that the StartProgram method has been specified to accept an "empty" list of arguments, which means that it doesn't work on any items. The designers of the C# language have used different characters to define the limits of (or *delimit*) different elements of the program. As we've seen, strings are *delimited* by double quotation mark characters. Lists of arguments are delimited by open and close parentheses: (and). The contents of a class and the body of a method are delimited by curly brackets: { and }. As you might expect, the compiler is very careful to make sure that the use of these delimiters "makes sense," and it will reject any program that has mismatched delimiters.

You can think of the two statements we just analyzed—which set the screen's title and display a message—as the "payload" of the sample program. The rest of the code around those statements provides the structure around those actions. To write larger programs, you just have to replicate this structure and add more statements. Now that you know how a simple program fits together, you can start to make your own, using the Snaps applications as a starting point. For example, you could make a program that displays two message strings rather than a title and a message, like I've done with **Ch03_02_MoreStatements.cs:**

```
using SnapsLibrary;
```

```
public class Ch03_02_MoreStatements
{
    public void StartProgram()
    {
        SnapsEngine.DisplayString("Hello world");          First statement
        SnapsEngine.DisplayString("Goodbye chickens");     Second statement
    }
}
```

In this program, `SetTitleString` isn't called and two statements call the `Display-String` method so that the program displays one message followed by a second message. You can put a very large number of statements in a program. You could write a program that displays the Gettysburg Address (or any other long text) one string at a time simply by adding more statements. It's important to remember that each statement is obeyed in order when the program runs. The preceding program will always display "Hello world" before it displays "Goodbye chickens". (Let me point out just one more time that the program doesn't display the double quotation marks you see in the previous sentence because no quotation marks appear in the string's text itself between the double quotation marks that delimit it. The double quotation marks I use in this paragraph are there only for clarity's sake, as I describe the text the program displays.)

So when you display a string via the `DisplayString` method, it replaces the string that was displayed by a previous call of `DisplayString`, if any. In our example, this is why "Hello world" is replaced by "Goodbye chickens". Later you'll discover how to build up multiple lines of text on the screen. Also, you can use `DisplayString` to display very long messages if you want to; the text is automatically wrapped if it extends over the edge of the screen. If you display a message that is extremely long, you'll find that it extends off the bottom of the screen and the user won't be able to read all of it.

Extra Snaps

Every now and then I will introduce other Snaps—behaviors enabled by the Snaps library—that you can play with. You can use these in your programs just like the programs we've been analyzing use `DisplayString`.

SpeakString

You can make programs that speak text instead of displaying it. Here's an example:

```
using SnapsLibrary;

class Ch03_03_Speaking
{
    public void StartProgram()
    {
        SnapsEngine.SpeakString("Hi there. I'm your friendly computer.");
    }
}
```

The SpeakString method is used in the same way as the DisplayString method, but it causes the computer to speak the text provided instead of displaying it on the screen. This is a useful method because it makes it easy to create programs that can talk.

CODE ANALYSIS

Speak and display

Let's take a look at some code and try to work out why it doesn't do what it should. Let's say that your younger brother wrote this program. He wanted something that displays "Computer Running" and then says "Computer Running," but he complains that the visual message doesn't appear until after the computer has finished speaking.

```
using SnapsLibrary;
class Ch03_04_DoubleOutput
{
    public void StartProgram()
    {
        SnapsEngine.SpeakString("Computer Running");
        SnapsEngine.DisplayString("Computer Running");
    }
}
```

Question: Why does the message appear on the screen after the computer finishes speaking?

> **Answer:** When you are trying to work out what a program does, it is often useful to "behave like the computer" and work through the statements one at a time in sequence. The computer speaks before the message is displayed because it strictly follows the sequence of the statements. The DisplayString method doesn't run until after the SpeakString method has completed. This problem is fixed by reversing the order of the statements. Take a look at **Ch03_05_DoubleOututFixed.cs** in Visual Studio to see that.

Creating new program files

Programming is very creative, and you'll create your own programs as we go through the book. What I'm really hoping is that you'll have your own ideas for programs and build those along with the ones that I suggest. Each new program that you create will be a new Snaps application that other learners can analyze or use.

You can create a new Snaps app by using the **MyProgram.cs** program file as a starting point. Begin (like we always do) by opening the **BeginToCodeWithSharp** solution file, and then in Solution Explorer find the file in the **My Snaps apps** folder in the **BeginToCodeWithCSharp** project. Right-click the file in Solution Explorer to open the context menu, and then select **Copy**, as shown in **Figure 3-1**.

Figure 3-1 Copying a program.

Now paste this copy into the **My Snaps apps** folder by right-clicking the folder and selecting **Paste**, as shown in **Figure 3-2**.

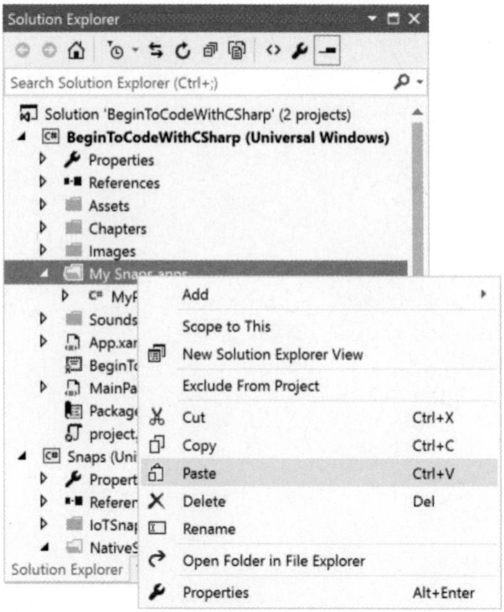

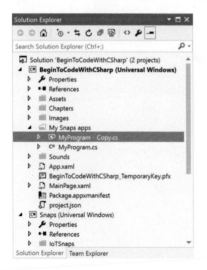

Figure 3-2 Pasting the program.

Figure 3-3 shows the copy, called **MyProgram - Copy.cs**, in the folder.

Figure 3-3 The copied program appears in the folder.

Let's rename this new file to reflect the new Snaps app you're going to build. Right-click the file (the one that includes "Copy" in its name) in Solution Explorer to open the context menu again, and select **Rename**. (I won't show this step because I'm sure you know what to do!) Now you can enter the new name for your application, as shown in **Figure 3-4**.

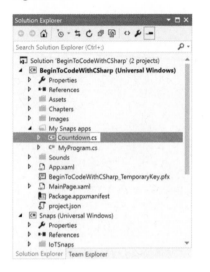

Figure 3-4 Entering the new name.

Change the name of the program to "Countdown". Be very careful not to remove ".cs" at the end of the name. If you remove this part of the file name, Visual Studio will not know the file is a C# program and will not work correctly when you try to run the program. When you have finished entering the name, press Enter. You now have a copy of the original program in a file called **Countdown.cs**. The reason I chose this name will become apparent soon.

The next thing we need to do is rename the class that holds our program. Click the **Countdown.cs** file in Solution Explorer so that its code appears in the editor window, as shown in **Figure 3-5**.

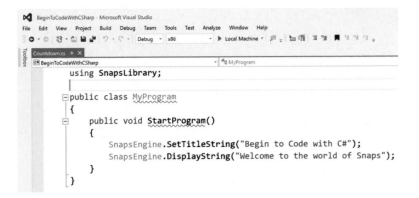

Figure 3-5 The Countdown.cs file open in the Visual Studio editor.

Looking at **Figure 3-5**, you can see that Visual Studio is trying to tell us something. The wavy red lines indicate that Visual Studio thinks some elements of the program's code are wrong. Visual Studio is unhappy in this case because our **BeginToCode-WithCSharp** solution contains two versions of the `MyProgram` class—the original in **MyProgram.cs** and now another in **Countdown.cs**. We can fix this problem by giving the class a new name.

In **Figure 3-6**, I've changed the name of the class to `Countdown` and also changed what the program does by altering one statement (the one that calls `SetTitleString`) and by deleting the other statement (the one that was calling `DisplayString`). The program now just sets its title to "Countdown". You can put whatever you want in the string, of course, but be sure that it has a double quotation mark at each end; otherwise, your program won't compile.

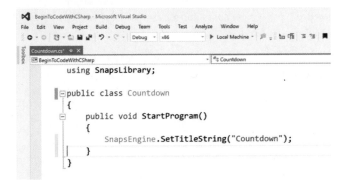

Figure 3-6 Defining a `Countdown` class.

Visual Studio is happy now because we removed the duplicate of the `MyProgram` class. You should now be able to run the program by using the run button (the green arrow).

Class names and file names

A C# solution can be spread over a large number of separate program files. It is worth giving some thought to how this works.

Question: Why do we have to change the name of the class when we have already changed the name of the file?

> **Answer:** To answer this question, you have to understand the difference between *logical* and *physical* names in a program. You can think of the names of the files that hold our programs as physical names because a file name is connected to an actual file that is stored on the computer. However, the names of the elements in a program are not tied to the physical file that holds the program's text. They exist in a "logical" namespace that is defined by the programmer.
>
> When the C# compiler is compiling a program, it reads all the source files and builds up a list of all the different items that are defined in the program. This is the logical namespace of the program. Each of the items in this logical namespace must have a unique name. If we create two items with the same name, the compiler will complain, and that is what happened earlier when we copied the **MyProgram.cs** file. After the copy, there were two classes with the name `MyProgram`. We fixed the problem by changing the name of one of the items to a new, unique name.

Question: Does the name of a program's source file (the physical name) and the name of a class (the logical name) in that source file have to match?

> **Answer:** No. It is often convenient to make the two names match because it can make it easier to find particular items, but the C# compiler does not enforce this.

Question: What would have happened if the program already contained a class named `Countdown` and we added another one?

> **Answer:** You can probably guess what would happen. The compiler would complain because it doesn't like having two items with the same name.

By the way, perhaps you were expecting the **Countdown** app to run immediately when you clicked the run button? Whenever the **BeginToCodeWithCSharp** application is first run, the Snaps environment looks for a class named `MyProgram` and then calls the `StartProgram` method in that class. This means that whenever you start the **BeginToCodeWithCSharp** application, it will first run the original program: **MyProgram.cs**. Then you use the **Folder** and **Snaps apps** lists to select other apps you want to run.

You can follow this copy, paste, and revise process each time you want to make a new application and add it to our Snaps environment. Or, now that you know that **MyProgram** is the app that runs automatically when the Snaps environment starts up, here's a tip that can make things easier: start by editing the content of the **MyProgram.cs** file. This way, the code you've created will run without you having to find and select the new app in the environment (like we just had to do to run the **Countdown** app).

Remember: as long as the class in **MyProgram.cs** is called `MyProgram`, this program will run first in the environment. When you finish building your new app in the **MyProgram.cs** file, you can copy and paste the program code into a new source file (a new **.cs** file), give that new source file a unique name, and rename the new program's class so that Visual Studio won't wave red lines at you and prevent your program from compiling. And, at this point, if you really want the **MyProgram** app to function as it has in these first three chapters—setting the same title and displaying the same message we've seen in these chapters—you know how to get it back to that state.

Is it obvious now why I've called this source file **MyProgram.cs**? It's ready for you to use to build lots of programs!

Build a Countdown announcer

This "Make Something Happen" is quite momentous. It represents a very important milestone on your journey toward programming enlightenment. Up until now you've been modifying or fixing existing programs, which is a great way to get started, but at some point you're going to have to create your own program from scratch. That time is now. If you think about it, even Bill Gates had to start somewhere. But I'm fairly sure that his first program wasn't able to speak to its users. Making computers speak was very difficult at the time Bill Gates was learning to write code, but he would have felt the same sense of excitement as you are about to.

After you build this application, you'll have written your first program. You can make the program more personal by using whatever messages you want to, and in the next section you'll discover some more Snaps that you can use to make the program even more interesting.

You should already have an "empty" app named **Countdown**. At the moment it does almost nothing—it only sets a title string in the state we last saw it—but now you're going to write your own statements to give it life. You can use the `SpeakString`, `DisplayString`, and `SetTitleString` methods provided by the `SnapsEngine` class to create your program.

All you have to do is make a program that counts down from 10 to 0. A clue: your program will contain at least 10 statements. Improve the program so that it displays the numbers on the screen as well as speaks them. This should double the number of statements in your program.

Compilation errors

Before a program can run, it must be checked by the compiler. You can think of this process as a bit like the preflight checks performed on aircraft. Before a flight, the captain must walk around the plane, count the wings, ensure that all the tires have air in them, and be sure that the craft is safe to fly. In the same way, the compiler performs preflight checks on a program before it can run. If the program doesn't adhere to the rules of C#, the compiler will generate errors that you, the programmer, need to fix.

Unfortunately, the compiler is much pickier about errors than humans are. I can walk up to someone and ask "What you doing?" I'll get an answer, even though the question I asked is not properly formed English. However, if I try to compile the following program, I will get errors:

```
using SnapsLibrary;

public class BadBrackets
{
    public void StartProgram()
    (
        SnapsEngine.SpeakString("Hello world");
        SnapsEngine.SpeakString("Goodbye chickens");
    )
}
```

This code looks very similar to a program that we know works, but there are two tiny mistakes in the text. The bad news is that they generate 11 highly confusing errors, as shown in this screenshot.

The hard part about this state of affairs is that none of these messages actually tell you what you did wrong (and some of them look really scary). The compiler is a very clever program, but it's not smart enough to say, "You've used parentheses where you should have used curly brackets." Update this code so that the statements are preceded by an open curly bracket ({) and followed by a closed curly bracket (}), and the program will run. When you mark the start and end of parts of a program, you must always use curly brackets. Parentheses are used for something else.

The best way to deal with mistakes like this is, of course, not to make them in the first place. But because we are human, this is impossible. Here are my tips for dealing with compilation errors:

1. Start from a program that *compiles*, or runs successfully. (Remember: compilers take our high-level code and generate the machine code that enables a computer to perform the actions we want it to perform. This is why we say that a program that runs successfully without errors compiles.) Visual Studio provides software wizards that can be used to make a program that doesn't do much but that does compile.

2. Compile often (in Visual Studio with the run button). If the number of changes you have made since the last successful compilation is small, you can isolate the error to just a few places.

3. Look for the three classic compilation mistakes:

   a. Missing something—for example, not putting a semicolon at the end of a statement.

   b. Using the wrong character—for example, using [rather than }.

   c. Spelling something incorrectly—for example, writing "startProgram" rather than "StartProgram". In the world of C#, it matters whether you use capital letters or lowercase letters.

4. Don't expect the error to be where the compiler has detected it. Some mistakes—for example, a missing curly bracket—may be detected many lines further down the program.

5. Use the color highlighting to help you. Words that are part of C# are shown in blue. Strings of text are red. If a word is not the color you think it should be, you might have typed it incorrectly.

6. Fix all the errors that you can see, and then compile again. Sometimes the compiler becomes confused and reports errors on lines that are sensible. Once you have fixed all the errors you can see, compile again and see if that works.

7. Use Undo and Redo. Visual Studio contains a very powerful editor with an Undo button (or Ctrl+Z) and a Redo button (Ctrl+Y), which you can use to step backward and forward through the changes you have made to your code. You can use these commands and the wavy red lines Visual Studio uses to highlight errors to find out where the mistakes are.

CODE ANALYSIS

Find the compilation errors

This program produces 20 errors when it is compiled. See if you can find all the mistakes.

```
using SnapsLibrary;

public Class MyProgram
{
    public void StartProgram()
    {
        SnapsEngine.SetTitleString("Begin to Code with C#");
        SnapsEngine.DisplayString(Welcome to the world of Snaps");
    }
}
```

Here are the errors:

```
using SnapsLibrary;

public Class MyProgram                          ─── Class should use a
{                                                    lowercase c
    public void StartProgram()
    {
        SnapsEngine.SetTitleString("Begin to Code with C#");

        SnapsEngine.DisplayString(Welcome to the world of Snaps");  ─── Missing
    }                                                                    the double
}                                                                        quotation
                                                                         mark
                                                                         before
                                                                         Welcome
```

If you fix these two mistakes, we have a program that compiles just fine.

Extra Snaps

At the end of some chapters, I will introduce extra Snaps that you can play with. You can use these in your programs just like you used the `SpeakString` Snap earlier.

Delay

You might want to make your program delay for a while with the `Delay` Snap:

```
using SnapsLibrary;

class Ch03_06_TenSecondTimer
{
    public void StartProgram()
    {
        SnapsEngine.DisplayString("Start");
        SnapsEngine.Delay(10);                          Delays 10 seconds
        SnapsEngine.DisplayString("End");
    }
}
```

This program displays "Start", pauses for 10 seconds, and then displays "End". The `Delay` method is different from `DisplayString` in the type of data you provide to it. You give the `DisplayString` method the string that you want the program to display. You give the `Delay` method the number of seconds you want the program to pause. This number can be a fraction if you want the program to pause for less than a second:

```
SnapsEngine.SpeakString("Tick");
SnapsEngine.Delay(0.5);                          Delays the program
SnapsEngine.SpeakString("Tock");                 for half a second
```

You can use `Delay` to make a program look like it is thinking about something or to give the user time to read some information on the screen.

SetTextColor

This Snap lets you set the color of the text in the message on the screen:

```
using SnapsLibrary;

class Ch03_07_BlueText
{
    public void StartProgram()
    {
        SnapsEngine.SetTextColor(SnapsColor.Blue);
        SnapsEngine.DisplayString("Blue Monday");
    }
}
```

Built-in Snaps color that represents the color blue

You can also call this method to change the color of the text already on the screen.

```
using SnapsLibrary;

class Ch03_08_DelayedBlueText
{
    public void StartProgram()
    {
        SnapsEngine.DisplayString("Blue Monday");
        SnapsEngine.Delay(2);
        SnapsEngine.SetTextColor(SnapsColor.Blue);
    }
}
```

This program displays "Blue Monday" in the default color to start with. After two seconds, it changes the text's color to blue.

SetTitleColor

This Snap lets you set the color of the text in the title message on the screen:

```
using SnapsLibrary;

class Ch03_09_GreenSystemStarting
{
    public void StartProgram()
    {
        SnapsEngine.SetTitleColor(SnapsColor.Green);
```

```
            SnapsEngine.SetTitleString("System Starting");
    }
}
```

This program sets the title text to green and then displays "System Starting" as the title of the page. Generally, it's best to set the color of titles and messages before they are displayed; otherwise, they will "flick" into the requested color once they come into view. Reverse the order of the statements in **Ch03_09_GreenSystemStarting.cs** to see what I mean. This effect was minimized in **Ch03_08_DelayedBlueText.cs** because of the delay.

SetBackgroundColor

This Snap lets you set the background color of the screen. You can use this to indicate alarms or other conditions.

```
using SnapsLibrary;

class Ch03_10_RedScreen
{
    public void StartProgram()
    {
        SnapsEngine.SetBackgroundColor(SnapsColor.Red);
    }
}
```

Creating your own colors

The Snaps library includes a number of built-in colors that you can use in your programs. You can see these SnapsColor values in the examples we've been looking at: SnapsColor.Blue, SnapsColor.Green, and SnapsColor.Red. However, you might want to use colors that are not in the library. For example, I like the color lilac. When you describe a color to a computer, you have to use numbers because, as we know, computers only really work with numeric values. To describe a particular color, we can use three values: the amount of red, the amount of green, and the amount of blue in that color. In the case of Snaps (and lots of other computer platforms, including Windows), each of the numbers that describes a color level is in the range 0 to 255.

You can go online and look up the amount of red, green, and blue in particular colors. It turns out that lilac is made up of 200 red, 162 green, and 200 blue. Here's how you use these kinds of values in the Snaps that deal with colors:

```
using SnapsLibrary;

class Ch03_11_LilacScreen
{
    public void StartProgram()
    {
        SnapsEngine.SetBackgroundColor(red:200,green:162,blue:200);
    }
}
```

Amount of red, green, and blue to make the color lilac.

The SetBackbroundColor method can be given one or three items to work on. It can be given one SnapsColor value, or it can be given values for red, green, and blue. Each of the color intensity values are identified by name, which makes it easier for the programmer to see which of the values is being used for which purpose.

When a method is designed, the programmer has to decide how much information the method needs to do its work and what form the information should take. In the case of SetBackgroundColor, this version of the method needs to be told the amount of red, green, and blue to be used. The items supplied to the method are given as a list in which each item is separated from the next by a comma. If you omit an item or list too many, the compiler will complain when it tries to create the program.

```
SnapsEngine.SetBackgroundColor(red:255,green:255);
```

```
Error 1    No overload for method 'SetBackgroundColor' takes 2 arguments
```

The compiler doesn't like this statement because SetBackgroundColor in the Snaps library hasn't been created (by me) to accept only two items.

WHAT COULD GO WRONG

Bad color schemes

You will not get any errors if you write a program that displays red text on a red background, but what will your program's users say? I personally like using default colors (that is, the ones that you get when you start the program running). If you want to show your creative side, you can pick other colors, but make sure you test your color scheme on many different devices because some machines can display colors much better than others. You should also make sure to check your proposed color scheme with your customer, if you have one, because colors are one thing that customers have very strong opinions about. Also, different people see different colors with varying degrees of success. Don't assume that others see colors the way you do!

Build an egg timer

You can now use your programming skills to make a program that will time how long to cook an egg. By using the `Delay` method from the Snaps library, you can make the program pause while the egg is cooking and then announce when the egg is ready. My tests indicate that to get a perfect egg, you should cook it for five minutes (or 300 seconds). This code serves as a good starting point—copy this code rather than copying or editing **MyProgram.cs** when you make your egg timer:

```
using SnapsLibrary;

class Ch03_12_EggTimerStart
{
    public void StartProgram()
    {
        SnapsEngine.SetTitleString("Egg Timer");
        SnapsEngine.DisplayString("There are five minutes left");
        SnapsEngine.Delay(60);
        SnapsEngine.DisplayString("There are four minutes left");
    }
}
```

I think this is another important milestone for you as a developer. Unlike the countdown timer you created before, this program has all the makings of a proper product. Your mom would find this program useful. The Windows Store has quite a few products that work as timers, and there's no reason why a timer that you've made could not be one of them.

You could add extra features to your timer to do things like change the screen color when the egg is nearly ready and even provide a 30-second warning before the timer expires—and maybe a "ten, nine, eight" style countdown right at the end. You could also make the timer speak how much time is left as well as display it.

You can also use this design to make timers that could be useful in lots of other situations. Here are four that I can think of:

- Your best friend has discovered a passion for developing her own photographs and wants a timer she can use in the dark. The timer should just announce how many seconds have gone by every five seconds.

- You and your coworkers have started a quiz club and want to control how long each team has to answer a question. Each team gets 10 seconds.

- Your brother has a game where each player has to use a toothpick to eat as many baked beans as they can in thirty seconds (I didn't say it was a sensible game), and he needs a timer for that.

- Your mom is into exercise and needs something to time each stage of her workout and tell her what the next activity is. There are five activities: jogging in place, push-ups, jumping jacks, stand and sit, and squat thrusts. Each activity should be performed for 30 seconds, followed by a 10-second rest period.

Try your hand at making these timers and any other ones that you might think of. In the next chapter, you'll discover how a program can get input from a user so that you can make even better timers that allow the user to set the length of time the timer should run.

What you have learned

In this chapter, you've become more familiar with the Visual Studio environment in which you're creating your programs. You've seen that a C# program is expressed as a sequence of statements that are performed in order when the program runs. You've also seen the high-level C# that you and I have written converted into lower-level computer instructions by a program called the compiler. Sometimes the code has compiled, so the program runs successfully, and sometime the code hasn't compiled because of errors.

You've seen that the compiler ensures that the program conforms to the rules of the C# language. The compiler will reject programs that don't have statements that are completely correct. Whereas a human reader will tolerate missing or incorrect punctuation, the compiler will reject anything that does not obey the rules of the programming language.

The programs that we have written so far make use of a set of Snaps provided by the Snaps library that let us do things such as speak messages, display colors, and delay the execution of the program for a while. These components are provided as methods that are passed data to tell them what to do. For example, the `SpeakString` method is given the text of the string that is to be spoken.

Here are some questions you might like to ponder about programs, statements, and compilers.

Does the user of the program need to have a copy of Visual Studio to run the program?

No. Visual Studio can produce a program file that users can run without Visual Studio.

Do I have to know how every Visual Studio command works?

No. You can get along by working with just a few of the buttons to start with. You will discover more features as you go through the book.

Is the compiler incompetent because it is confused by invalid program code?

You might think that the compiler is a bit silly, because sometimes it does things like complain when it has seen the wrong character. You would be forgiven for wondering why the compiler doesn't just substitute the right character and keep going. However, it turns out there is a very good reason for the compiler not to do this. If the compiler inserts things that it thinks are missing, it is making an assumption about what you, the programmer, were actually trying to do. We have already seen that assumptions are dangerous. It is much safer for the compiler to insist that you express exactly and correctly what you want the program to do.

Can any C# method accept any number of things to tell it what to do?

No. Each method is custom-made to accept a specific set of information. The `Delay` method needs to be told how many seconds to delay for. The `SpeakString` method needs a string of text to speak. The compiler knows what a method was built to accept, and it will feed only that kind of data into it. If you attempt to feed a string to `Delay`, the program will not compile.

Are the statements in a program always performed in the order they are written in the program?

Yes. You can think of a program as a story or recipe or a sequence of instructions. It would be meaningless for the steps to be performed in any order other than the one that has been set out.

Are the Snaps part of the C# language?

No. The Snaps library and these methods have been provided to help you learn how to program and to create simple applications. They are not part of C#, but they were created with C#. You will learn about other library classes and methods supplied with C# a little later in the book.

4

Working with data in a program

What you will learn

In the previous chapter, you learned how a program is a sequence of instructions that the computer follows. You saw this in the programs we created that use some of the Snaps. In this chapter, you are going to find out how a computer program manipulates data. You will discover the different forms that data can take—the difference between text data and numeric data, for example, and the two kinds of numeric data, whole numbers and real numbers. You'll also learn how to create your own data storage in a C# program and how to work with this data by using expressions.

Starting with variables

The programs we've worked with up until now used data that was built in. For example, the following statement takes data (the text "Hello world") and then does something with it—in this case, converting it to words the computer speaks.

```
SnapsEngine.SpeakString("Hello world");
```

Lots of programs have data built in in this way—a video game, for example, includes images and sounds alongside the program code. This data comes from values that are "hard wired" into the program's code. These values are known as *literal* values.

Literal values are fine for the fixed data in a program, but you need to do something else if you want your code to be flexible. To change a literal value in a program, you have to change the actual code (change "Hello world" to the new message you want, for example) and then recompile the program. To make your code more flexible, you use *variables*. Variables accept input from the user, and the program can then work with this input.

CODE ANALYSIS

Literal values

Question: What is the literal value in the statement SnapsEngine.SpeakString("Hello world");?

   Answer: The literal value is the string "Hello world".

Question: Is the method named SpeakString a literal value?

   Answer: No. To understand why, consider the difference between the code in a program that provides instructions (things that do the work) and the data in a program (things that the work is done on). SpeakString is the identifier of a method that enables the computer to speak a text string. "Hello world" is the literal string of text that we want the program to speak.

Question: Are strings the only kind of literal values?

   Answer: No. Later in this chapter, you will learn about numeric literal values.

Variables and computer storage

For a program to be fully useful, it must be able to accept and work with data from an external source. Every time you press a key, tap the screen of your mobile phone, or move your mouse, you provide input to a program that is stored in a variable of some kind. But where is that variable stored?

When a computer owner says proudly, "My computer has 16 gigabytes of RAM," what she is really saying is that the *random access memory* (RAM) in her computer contains a huge number (16 thousand million) of individual memory locations, each of which can hold a tiny piece of data called a *byte*. Each memory location is numbered, and the computer can access any location at any time (which is why this is called *random access memory*). These memory locations are used to store the instructions given to the computer (the program) and the data that the program works on. As an example, when you use a word processor, some of the RAM in your computer is holding the word-processor program, and some of the RAM is holding the text being worked on.

There is a difference between data that is held in RAM and data stored on devices such as disk drives or thumb drives. When you use a word processor, the program loads your document from the disk drive and copies it to RAM. When you save a document, it is copied from RAM back to the disk storage. Programs and data are held in RAM while you work with them because that lets the data be accessed extremely quickly. But RAM is also volatile. When you exit a program or the computer is switched off, the contents of RAM are destroyed. (Later in this book, you'll find out how to make a program store data on storage devices, but for now we are going to consider how programs can work with data held in RAM.)

You can think of a variable as a named location in memory that stores something that the program is "thinking about." While a program is running, it works on the variables to generate a result, which the program then outputs. Another way to think of a variable is as a "box with a name." In a program, the box is used to store stuff. The programmer provides a name for the variable and also specifies the kind of data (such as text or a number) that can be stored in it.

Declaring a variable

Let's say we want to create a program that's used to announce people who arrive at a posh party we are organizing. Using the program, each guest would enter his or her name. The person's name would be stored in a variable defined in the program, and the program would then announce the person's arrival by retrieving the variable from memory.

To make this program work, we need a variable that can be used to store the name that the guest enters. A name is a string of text, so we need a variable that can hold a string.

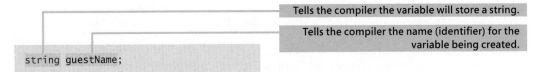

Tells the compiler the variable will store a string.

Tells the compiler the name (identifier) for the variable being created.

```
string guestName;
```

This code is a *declaration* that tells C# to reserve space in memory for a variable that can store a string of text. The C# compiler understands that the word *string* is the beginning of the declaration. The word *string* is followed by the name of the variable to be created, in this case guestName.

The name you use for a variable is called the *identifier* for that variable. The C# compiler makes sure that you don't declare two items that have the same identifier. It also enforces some rules for identifiers:

- An identifier can contain letters, digits, and the underscore (_) character.

- An identifier must start with a letter or an underscore.

- You can't use an identifier that matches any of the keywords that are built into C#. The word *string*, for example, is a keyword, so you can't use *string* as an identifier. Each keyword has a specific meaning in the context of the programming language.

CODE ANALYSIS

Identifiers

Question: Would my$name be a good identifier?

> **Answer:** No. It contains a dollar sign, which is not allowed in an identifier. It would be okay to use MyName or my_name.

Question: Would 2ndInningsScore be a valid identifier?

> **Answer:** No. It starts with a number, which is not allowed.

Question: Would x29zog be a good identifier?

> **Answer:** Yes, this is a legal identifier—C# would not object to it. But even though it is valid, it is not meaningful. The identifier for a variable should indicate what it is being used for, and this name doesn't do that.

Question: Would textstring be a good identifier?

Answer: This is a valid identifier. It contains the word *string*, which is a keyword, but the compiler doesn't mind in this situation because *string* is part of a larger word. However, I'm not keen on identifiers like this because they don't really tell me much about what is being stored. I'd much prefer something like nameString.

Simple assignment statements

After a variable is declared, a program can give the variable a value. Here's an example:

The name of the variable being assigned to . . .

. . . a literal string value.

```
guestName = "Rob";
```

This type of statement is called an *assignment*. The variable on the left is assigned the value on the right. The result of a program running this statement is that the variable guestName would be made to hold the string "Rob".

The equal sign between the variable and the value is not performing a comparison. Instead, it says that we want to make the variable on the left equal to the value on the right. I call this a *gozzinta* operation, in that the value "goes into" the destination on the left.

Assignment statements are a very important part of a program. Whenever a program is processing data, it does so by assigning values to variables. We will take a more detailed look at assignments later in the book.

WHAT COULD GO WRONG

Assignment issues

An assignment statement is how a program gives a value to a variable. However, things can go wrong, and here are a few ways in which assignments can fail:

```
newKidInTown = "Nowhere";
```

This is a perfectly legal statement, as long as the variable newKidInTown has been declared. If it has not been declared, the compiler will generate an error. In C#, you must declare a variable if you are going to assign a value to it.

```
string Name;
name = "Rob";
```

On the face of it, this code looks quite legal. But if you look carefully, you'll see that the variable declared has the identifier Name, whereas the one that's used has the identifier name. The C# language makes a distinction between uppercase and lowercase letters in identifiers. The fact that the case of *n* is different here means that the compiler will complain that the variable name has not been declared.

```
string age;
age = 21;
```

This code looks legal, but the compiler will complain because in C#, strings of text must be enclosed in double quotation marks—"21" is a string, but 21 (without the quotation marks) is a number.

Using a variable in a program

In your programs, you can use a string variable everywhere you can use an actual string. For example, when we used SpeakString in previous chapters, we gave the method the literal string value that we wanted the computer to speak. But you can also give SpeakString or DisplayString the value of a variable that contains a string, as here:

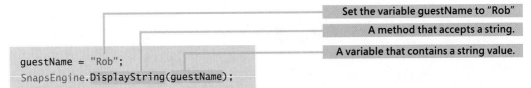

Set the variable guestName to "Rob"

A method that accepts a string.

A variable that contains a string value.

```
guestName = "Rob";
SnapsEngine.DisplayString(guestName);
```

Using a variable's identifier in a program (guestName in this example) makes the program use the value that's held (assigned to) that variable. By putting the lines of code we've been looking at together, you can see how this works. Here's a program that runs and displays "Rob":

```
using SnapsLibrary;
```

```
class Ch04_01_SimpleVariable
{
    public void StartProgram()
    {
        string guestName;                         Declare the variable.
        guestName = "Rob";                        Put a value in the variable.
        SnapsEngine.DisplayString(guestName);     Display whatever is in the variable.
    }
}
```

But what have we achieved by doing this? Why not just put the literal string "Rob" in the call to DisplayString as we've done in programs in earlier chapters? Well, things get much more exciting when you get the value of guestName from the user instead of setting it to a fixed value.

To see how this works in more detail, we'll use another Snap method, the ReadString method. It does what you might expect—it reads a string that is entered by the user.

```
                                                    Destination for the assignment.

                                                    Put a value in the variable.

                                                              Prompt displayed
                                                              by ReadString.

guestName = SnapsEngine.ReadString("What is your name?");
```

In this statement, the ReadString method is given a string that is used as a prompt for the user—"What is your name?" When this statement is obeyed, the program displays the prompt and a text box for user input. It then pauses and waits for the user to type in his or her name, as shown in **Figure 4-1**.

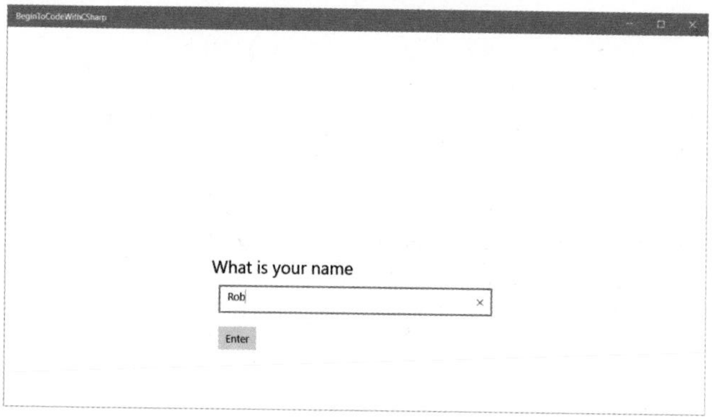

Figure 4-1 This program stores the name you enter in the text box as a string variable.

When the user presses the Enter button, the ReadString method returns whatever the user entered as a string, so the string assigned to guestName is read from the user's input rather than being fixed to the value "Rob" as it was in the previous example. You can use the ReadString method any time you want to get some information from the user. Here's a more complete example.

```
using SnapsLibrary;

class Ch04_02_ReadingAString
{
    public void StartProgram()
    {
        string guestName;                                        Declare the variable.
        guestName = SnapsEngine.ReadString("What is your name?");  Read the value
        SnapsEngine.DisplayString(guestName);                      from the user.
                                                     Display whatever is in the variable.
    }
}
```

Reading data from the user makes this program into a "proper" data processor that accepts information in one form (the text that the user types in) and produces output in another form (the screen display).

MAKE SOMETHING HAPPEN

Create an announcer

You can try out this program right now. Just run the Snaps app named **Ch04_02_Reading-AString**. The Snaps methods will take the name you enter and then display it. You can add a call to the SpeakString method to make the program also announce the user by name. If you want to display the name in large letters, you could use the SetTitleString method as well.

Assigning values in a declaration

C# lets you assign a value to a variable at the same time that you declare it. Here is a single statement that replaces the two you have just seen:

```
string guestName = Snaps.ReadString("What is your name?");
```

This statement gets a string from the user and stores it in a `string` variable with the identifier `guestName`. This kind of statement makes programs slightly shorter, and makes it less likely that a program will try to use a variable that has not been given a value.

Adding strings together

Earlier in this chapter, we set out to make a program that will announce people's names as they arrive at a party. Now we want to make the announcement a little fancier. In my case, I want the program to say "The honorable Mister Rob Miles." I could try doing this by using the following C# code:

```
string guestName;
guestName = SnapsEngine.ReadString("What is your name?");
SnapsEngine.SpeakString("The honorable Mister");
SnapsEngine.SpeakString(guestName);

Ch04_04_StiltedAnnouncer
```

Get the name to be announced.

Speak the introduction.
Speak the name.

This code snippet (which you can find in the Snaps app called **Ch04_04_StiltedAnnouncer**) runs correctly, but because the two parts of the message are produced by separate statements, the speech output process treats them as separate items and they sound a bit stilted. What we want is to assemble a single greeting for the program to speak. To do this, we need to combine the introduction and the name in a single string, like this:

```
string fullMessage = "The honorable Mister " + guestName;
```

This is the first *expression* that we have seen for a C# program. An expression is something that expresses an action to be performed. It is made up of *operands,* which are the items to work on, and *operators,* which denote the particular action to be performed. The elements of the expression in the announcer program are illustrated in **Figure 4-2**. This expression has two operands and one operator. One operand is the string "The honorable Mister," and the other is the variable `guestName`. The operator is the plus sign (+), and the result of this expression is placed in the variable called `fullMessage`.

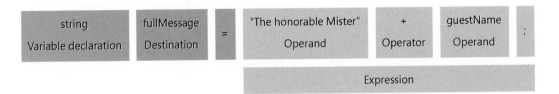

| string Variable declaration | fullMessage Destination | = | "The honorable Mister" Operand | + Operator | guestName Operand | ; |

| | | | Expression | | |

Figure 4-2 Anatomy of an expression.

Expressions are a fundamental part of the way that C# works with data. You will see more of them in future chapters.

WHAT COULD GO WRONG

Invalid operators

The C# language provides lots of operators. Programs can not only combine strings or add numbers with the plus sign, they can also subtract, multiply, and divide, among other things, and you will see examples of this soon. But for now, take a look at this statement:

```
string fullMessage = "The honorable Mister " - guestName;
```

This statement looks like it is trying to subtract guestName from the introductory string. This operation will not work because C# does not allow one string to be subtracted from another. It is only meaningful for a program to add strings to each other. The compiler always checks the context of an operator. While it is fine to subtract one number from another, it is not possible to subtract one string from another. When you write a program (and particularly when the compiler complains about an operation you are performing), be sure to consider the context of the actions you are performing.

MAKE SOMETHING HAPPEN

Speak the day: Using patterns

The announcer program gets a string from the user and then displays it. You can use the same pattern to make a program that tells you the day of the week—and then you can run this program and decide whether you need to get out of bed in the morning. To make this program, you can use a Snaps method named GetDayOfWeekName. When you call the method, it reads the clock in the computer and works out what day of the week it is. It returns this value as a string.

```
string day = SnapsEngine.GetDayOfWeekName();
```

The best way to construct this program is to base it on an existing one, and the approach for using this Snap method is identical to the announcer program. Here is what the announcer program does:

```
string guestName = Snaps.ReadString("What is your name?");   ── Set up guestName
Snaps.DisplayString(guestName);   ──────────────────── Display the contents of guestName
```

A program that speaks the day of the week would be very similar. The main difference is where the message comes from.

```
string dayName = SnapsEngine.GetDayOfWeekName();
SnapsEngine.SpeakString(dayName);
```

You can use the announcer program pattern everywhere you want to create a program that asks a method a question and gets a response. When you are faced with a new problem, it is a very good idea to consider whether you have already solved that problem with a particular pattern. The full version of a program that tells you which day it is would look like this.

```
using SnapsLibrary;

class Ch04_04_SpeakingDay
{
    public void StartProgram()
    {
                                                          Get the day of the
                                                          week as a string.
        string dayName = SnapsEngine.GetDayOfWeekName();
        SnapsEngine.SpeakString(dayName);   ──────────── Speak the day of the week.
    }
}
```

You can make the program display the day of the week as well as announce it. You could also add a title display so that the user knows what the program is doing for them. By adding strings together, you could even make the program greet you and say "Good day, Rob. And how are you doing this fine Thursday?"

Working with numbers

We have worked mainly with strings of text to this point in our programming. Now it's time to learn how a program can represent and manipulate numeric values.

Whole numbers and real numbers

As far as C# is concerned, there are two kinds of numbers, *whole numbers* and *real numbers*. Whole numbers have no fractional part. A computer stores the value of a whole number exactly. Real numbers, on the other hand, have a fractional element. As a programmer, you need to choose which kind of number you want to use to store a particular value.

CODE ANALYSIS

Whole numbers vs. real numbers

You can learn about the difference between whole numbers and real numbers by looking at a few situations when they might be used.

Question: I'm building a device that can count the number of hairs on your head. Should I store this value as a whole number or a real number?

   Answer: This should be a whole number, since there is no such thing as half a hair.

Question: I want to use my hair-counting machine on 100 people and work out the average number of hairs on all their heads. Should I store this value as a whole number or a real number?

   Answer: When you work out the result, you'll find that the average has a fractional part, which means that you should use a real number to store it.

Question: I want to keep track of the price of a product in my program. How should I do it?

   Answer: This is actually very tricky. You might think that the price should be stored as a real number—for example, $1.50 (one and a half dollars). However, you could also store the price as the whole number, 150 cents. The type of number you use in a situation like this depends on what you are using the number for. If you are just keeping track of the total amount of money you take in selling your product, you can use a whole number to hold the price and the total. However, if you are also lending money to people to buy your product and you want to calculate the interest to charge them, you would need a fractional component to hold the number more precisely.

The way you store a variable depends on what you want to do with it

It seems obvious that you would use a whole number to count the number of hairs on your head. However, one could argue that we could also use a whole number to represent the average number of hairs on 100 people's heads. This is because the calculated average would be in the thousands, and fractions of a hair would not add much useful information. When you consider how you are going to represent data in a program, you have to take into account how it will be used.

C# whole number types

As I mentioned, whole numbers have no fractional part. They are frequently used in programs for counting things. Also, the value of a whole number is stored exactly by a computer program. In other words, every whole number value is mapped into the computer's memory in a way that perfectly preserves the value.

When I use a whole number in a program, I tend to use the `int` type, which has a range up to 2,147,483,647. If the number I want to store is larger than this, I can use the `long` type, which has a range as large as 9,223,372,036,854,775,807. And if I want to count only as far as 32,767, I can use a type called `short`. All of these types have an equivalent negative range.

Each type takes up a different amount of space in RAM. The `long` type takes up eight memory locations, whereas the `short` type takes up only two. In most of my C# programs I tend to use the `int` type because I am confident that I will never exceed its range.

Be careful that you don't exceed the range of whole number types

You might think that the computer would detect that the range of a particular type is exceeded. In other words, you might expect a program to stop if it tries to put the value 32,768 into variable that is of type `short` (which can store values only up to 32,767). However, this is not guaranteed to happen. Instead, you might find that the value in the variable becomes completely incorrect and the program continues on its way. This can lead to the most awful problems. The main reason I use the `int` type instead of the `short` type is that I can think of situations where I might want to store values that are more than 32,000, but it is very unlikely that I will exceed a value of 2,000,000,000.

When you are picking a type for a variable, it is important to consider the range of the type you are using. If you're in doubt, pick a type with plenty of room. In a world where computers routinely have enormous amounts of RAM, it is unlikely that you need to save storage space by taking a risk with the size of the variable types you are using.

C# real number types

Real number types have a fractional part, which is the part of the number after the decimal point. Real numbers are not always stored exactly. A particular real number is mapped to computer memory in a way that stores a value that is as close as possible to the original. You can increase the accuracy of the storage process by using larger amounts of computer memory, but you are never able to hold all real values precisely.

This is actually not a problem. We are used to the fact that values such as pi can never be held exactly because they "go on forever." (I've got a book that contains the value of pi to 1 million decimal places, but I still can't say that this is the exact value of pi. All I can say is that the value in the book is many more times as accurate as anyone will ever need.)

When you create a variable to hold a whole number, you should start by considering what the variable will be used for. Do the same thing when considering how to store real numbers in a program. Start by thinking about the *range* and *precision* that your application needs from the variable.

Precision sets out how precisely the number is stored. As an example, C# provides a real number type called `float` that holds a number with seven digits of precision. A `float` variable could store the value 1234567.0 or 0.1234567, but it could not store 1234567.1234567 because it does not have enough precision to hold 14 digits. The range of a real-number type tells you the largest and smallest values that it can store. In the case of the `float` type, it can hold a number with 38 digits (that's a 1 followed by 38 zeroes).

If I want to store a value very precisely, I use the `double` type. (The name is short for *double precision*.) This type gives me 15 or so digits of precision and is able to store numbers with over 300 digits. There is also a type called `decimal`, which has a lower range than `double` (it can handle 28 digit values), but it provides 28 digits of precision.

Most of the time, I use the `float` data type, which is accurate enough for my needs. I would use the `double` precision type if my program was using a particular variable in calculations that were repeated many millions of times a second. In such a program, the `float` type would be unsuitable because calculation errors might accumulate over time and become noticeable. I would use the `decimal` type if I was performing interest calculations on amounts of money. The high precision of the decimal type would be able to hold even very tiny amounts of interest very accurately.

Variables are not perfect, but they are good enough

You might think that your all-powerful computer should be able to hold all values precisely. It comes as a bit of a shock to discover that this is not true, and that a simple 10-digit pocket calculator can outperform your powerful PC.

However, this lack of accuracy is not really a problem in programming because we don't usually have incoming data that is particularly precise anyway. For example, if I refine my hair-counting device to measure hair length, it would be very difficult for me to measure hair length with more than a tenth of an inch (2.4 millimeters) of accuracy. This means that there is no point in storing hair length in a variable of type double because the data is simply not there in the first place.

The important thing to remember is that with whole numbers, as well as real numbers, you should pick the type that you are going to use by considering what it will be used for.

Performing calculations

You have seen how a program can manipulate strings by creating expressions that join them together. You can also create statements that contain expressions involving numbers. The expressions can be evaluated to produce a result, and you can then use the result as you need to in your program. Expressions can be as simple as a single value or as complex as a large calculation. Here are a few examples of numeric expressions:

    2 + 3 * 4

    -1 + 3

    (2 + 3) * 4

These expressions are worked out (evaluated) by the computer working from left to right, just as you would read them yourself. Again, just as in traditional math, multiplication and division are performed first in an expression, followed by addition and subtraction.

C# achieves this order by giving each operator a priority. When C# works out an expression, it finds all the operators with the highest priority and applies them first. It then looks for the operators next in priority and so on, until the final result is obtained. The order of evaluation means that the expression 2 + 3 * 4 will calculate to 14, not 20.

If you want to force the order in which an expression is worked out, you can put parentheses around the elements of the expression you want to evaluate first, as in the final example above. You can also put parentheses inside parentheses if you want—provided you make sure that you have as many opening parentheses as closing ones. Being a simple soul, I tend to make things very clear by putting parentheses around everything.

It is probably not worth getting too worked up about *expression evaluation* (as people in the know call it). Generally speaking, things tend to be worked out how you would expect them.

Here is a list of some other operators, what they do, and their precedence (priority). The operators are listed with the highest priority first

OPERATOR	HOW IT'S USED
–	Unary minus, the minus that C# finds in negative numbers, e.g. –1. Unary means applying to only one item.
*	Multiplication; note the use of the asterisk (*) rather than the more mathematically correct but confusing x.
/	Division; because of the difficulty of drawing one number above another during editing, we use this character instead.
+	Addition.
–	Subtraction. Note that we use exactly the same character as for unary minus.

This is not a complete list of the operators available, but it will do for now. Because these operators work on numbers, they are often called *numeric operators*. However, one of them, the + operator, can be applied between strings, as you've already seen.

CODE ANALYSIS

Work out the results

Question: See if you can work out the values of a, b, and c when the following statements have been evaluated:

```
int a = 1;
int b = 2;
int c = a + b;
```

```
c = c * (a + b);
b = a + b + c;
```

Answer: a=1, b=12, c=9. The best way to work this out is to behave like a computer would and work through each statement in turn. When I do this, I write down the variable values on a piece of paper and then update each as I go along. This is actually a useful thing to do. It means that you can predict what a program will do without having to actually run it.

WHAT COULD GO WRONG

Dumb calculations

One of the operators that can be used in an expression is the division operator. This means that you can write silly code such as this:

```
int factor = 0;
int kaboom = 1 / factor;
```

This code tries to divide 1 by 0, giving a result that is not sensible. You might think that this would cause the computer itself to crash. In the old days, this might have happened. I have fond memories of a calculator I used to own. If I tried to divide 1 by 0, it would just keep counting up, trying to reach a result of infinity. In the case of a C# program, what will happen is that the C# run-time system will simply stop your program from going any further.

Working with different types of data

You've already discovered that in the C# language, every variable has a characteristic type, such as `string` or `int`. Now we are going to explore matters of type in a bit more detail. You can think of a type as something like a garage that will fit only one particular kind of car. The C# compiler enforces type checking to make sure that a program doesn't try to combine types in a way that is not meaningful. Just as you can't put a stretch limo into a garage made for a compact car, you can't directly put variables of one type into another. However, programs often have to move values between types—for example, to display numeric values in text form—so how do you do this?

Converting numbers into text

C# lets you write programs that can manipulate text and numbers so that you can represent numbers as text or convert text into numeric values. We'll explore how to do this by making a digital clock. Earlier, we used a Snap that gets the day of the week. There's also one that obtains the date and time. The Snap method `GetHourValue` returns the hour value of the current time as an integer. The following statement declares a variable of type `int` with the identifier `hourValue`. It then sets this variable to the result of the `GetHourValue` method.

```
int hourValue = SnapsEngine.GetHourValue();
```

Now that you have the hour value, you can make the program output it. You might make part of the digital clock by using the `DisplayString` method to display the hour value, like this:

```
SnapsEngine.DisplayString(hourValue);
```

But unfortunately, this doesn't work. Visual Studio generates an error when you try to run the program.

```
Error CS1503 Argument 1: cannot convert from 'int' to 'string'
```

Here, it looks like the compiler wants to have an argument with us, but this is not actually what the message means. An *argument* is what C# calls the bit of data you provide to a method to tell it what you want it to do. In the case of the `DisplayString` method, the argument is the string that you want the program to display. This error occurs because we are not giving `DisplayString` an argument of the `string` type. We are giving it an `int`, which contains a numeric value. The error message tells you that `DisplayString` has been given the wrong type of input and that the C# compiler doesn't automatically convert an `int` to a `string`. To make this program work, we need to convert the number in `hourValue` into a string that the program can feed to `DisplayString`. (You would see the same problem if you tried to use `SpeakString` because that method also expects to be given a string of text to speak.)

A program can obtain a string version of any type of variable by asking the variable to provide a string version of itself. Every type in C# provides a method named `ToString`, which returns a string that describes the contents of that type.

```
string hourString = hourValue.ToString();
```

This statement creates a new `string` variable called `hourString` that holds the hour value as a string of text. Now the program can provide the time. Here's the complete program that displays the hour when we run it.

```
using SnapsLibrary;

class Ch04_05_DisplayHour
{
    public void StartProgram()
    {
        int hourValue = SnapsEngine.GetHourValue();
        string hourString = hourValue.ToString();
        SnapsEngine.DisplayString(hourString);
    }
}
```

Get the hour as a number.

Ask the hour to give us its string version.

Display the hour as a string.

CODE ANALYSIS

Display the full time

The time-telling program we started earlier would be improved if it displayed the minute value along with the hour. For this, we have the Snaps method `GetMinuteValue`. By adding this method to the program, you can create a complete time message by joining the hour and minute strings together, which turns out to be very easy:

```
int hourValue = SnapsEngine.GetHourValue();
int minuteValue = SnapsEngine.GetMinuteValue();
SnapsEngine.DisplayString(hourValue + ":" + minuteValue);

Ch04_06_TimeDisplay
```

The above statements fetch the hour and minute values and then display them with a colon in between, as shown here:

Current Time
19:27

But if you look at the code that displays hours and minutes, you should notice something strange about it. Previously we had to convert the numbers into strings when we wanted to display them.

Question: Why does `DisplayString` now work with the values of `hourValue` and `minuteValue` with no problems?

> **Answer:** The reason this code works has to do with a quirk in the way that the + operator handles strings in a program. If one of the operands being applied to the + operator is not a string, the operand is automatically converted to a string by the C# compiler. I really do not like this behavior. I can see that it has been added to make it slightly easier to write programs, but when you are learning to write code, you can find this behavior very hard to understand. It implies that a program can use number values (in this case, hours and minutes) everywhere that it can use a string. But we know that this is not the case.

MAKE SOMETHING HAPPEN

Speak the time, and grow it

One simple enhancement you can make to the clock is to have it speak the time as well as display it on the screen. But it might also be fun to make a clock that gives an indication of the time by enlarging the size of the letters on the screen. The Snaps method `SetDisplay-StringSize` can be used to set the size of the text that is displayed. It is given a single number to work on, and it uses the value supplied to set the size of the text on the screen.

```
SnapsEngine.SetDisplayStringSize(20);
```

This statement sets the size of the text in the display string to 20, which is the text's size when the program starts. If you want larger text, you can put a larger value in. You can experiment with your system to see which values work best for you. (You will learn exactly how the size of objects is expressed in a program a bit later in the book.) I got good results by multiplying the hour value by 20 and setting the text size to the result, but you might like to try some other values. If you multiply by a number that is too large, you might find that the program display "pushes" the Snaps control panel off the bottom of the application window, and you will have to stop the program in order to select another Snaps application to run.

Whole numbers and real numbers in programs

C# also enforces type checking when real numbers and whole numbers are used in a program. We can look at what happens by working with a simple program that converts a temperature expressed in Fahrenheit to the corresponding value in centigrade.

Variable types and expressions

To convert a temperature from Fahrenheit to centigrade, you subtract 32 from the Fahrenheit value and then divide the result by the value 1.8. You could write a C# expression to work out this result:

```
int tempInFahrenheit = 54;
int tempInCentigrade = (tempInFahrenheit - 32) / 1.8;
```

I quite like this code. It calculates the centigrade temperature for 54 degrees Fahrenheit. It makes good use of parentheses to make sure that the program subtracts 32 from the Fahrenheit value before the division is performed. Unfortunately, the program produces an error when it is compiled:

```
Error 1    Cannot implicitly convert type 'double' to 'int'. An explicit
           conversion exists (are you missing a cast?)
```

This error occurs because the result of the calculation is a number with a fractional part, and we are trying to store this result in a variable that was declared as an integer, a type used with whole numbers. The C# compiler won't allow this.

Losing data

It is not obvious which statement in the temperature-conversion code is causing the problem. This raises some questions:

Question: Where is the "double" value coming from?

> **Answer:** The double-precision element in this program is the literal value 1.8. When the compiler sees a whole number literal value, it regards it as an integer. When the compiler sees a literal value that contains a decimal point, it regards it as a double-precision real number. When C# evaluates an expression, the result has the type of the "largest" type used in the expression. This means that an expression with a double-precision value will return a double-precision result.

Question: Why is the compiler complaining?

> **Answer:** Converting a value from double precision to an integer isn't a problem for the computer. It's a simple operation for a program. However, the compiler is concerned that the programmer (that's you) might lose valuable data in the conversion because the fractional part of the real number will be discarded. It is essentially saying, "I won't just do this conversion; you have to explicitly tell me you want the program to do it."

Question: What is this "cast" the error message refers to?

> **Answer:** If you cast a play, you have the job of deciding which actor will play which role. Once you decide, you can tell Kevin that he is playing the role of Macbeth—and the best of luck to him. In programming terms, casting is rather similar. It is like saying, "I know that this value is a double-precision value, but for this statement I'd like it to play the role of an integer." The compiler is happy that you are aware that a conversion is taking place and allows the operation to go forward. You'll see how to perform casting later in this section.

We can fix the error by using `double` to change the type of the variable that holds the temperature in centigrade:

```
int tempInFahrenheit = 54;
double tempInCentigrade = (tempInFahrenheit - 32) / 1.8;

Ch04_07_CentigradeAndFahrenheit
```

Precision and accuracy

When I run the temperature-conversion statements we've been studying, I get the following results:

   tempInFahrenheit = 54

   tempInCentigrade = 12.222222222222221

At first sight, it looks like the temperature in centigrade is being stored much more accurately than the temperature in Fahrenheit. But this is not really the case; this is just how the numbers worked out. When the program does the calculation, it generates a result that is stored with this high level of precision, but this doesn't mean that there is more detail in the data.

For most of my programs I don't use the double-precision type because I don't need its level of precision. Instead, I use the `float` type, which is short for *floating-point number*. As I mentioned earlier, this type holds numbers less accurately than `double`, but the values take up half as much space in memory, and they are much faster to calculate. These considerations can be important if you are thinking of running your programs on small devices such as mobile phones.

PROGRAMMER'S POINT

Don't confuse precision with accuracy

It is very important to remember that numbers don't become more accurate just because they are stored with more precision. Scientists in a laboratory measuring the length of ant legs will not be able to do this to more than a few digits of accuracy (unless they have some amazing technology), so there is no point in them using much higher precision to store and process their results. Using higher precision has the effect of slowing down the program and also means that the variables take up more space in memory.

I could change the temperature-conversion program so that the variable `tempInCentigrade` is held in a floating-point variable instead of the double-precision one, like this:

```
int tempInFahrenheit = 54;
float tempInCentigrade = (tempInFahrenheit - 32) / 1.8;
```

But, unfortunately, these statements will not compile:

```
Error 1    Cannot implicitly convert type 'double' to 'float'. An explicit
           conversion exists (are you missing a cast?)
```

This is the same problem we had when we tried to put a double-precision value into an integer. If you think about it, the error makes perfect sense. Moving a double-precision result into a floating point variable may result in a loss of data because floating point values aren't held as precisely as double-precision ones.

PROGRAMMER'S POINT

The compiler is on our side, really

As you write more programs, you'll get used to the compiler being fussy like this. The annoying thing is that in the case of our program, it doesn't really make any difference whether we use `float` or `double`. However, one day you might find yourself writing programs that do rocket-guidance calculations, where a tiny error in the results could result in a disaster. The compiler must make sure that all programs are as safe as possible, and so the best thing you can do is just get better at dealing with these errors and try not to introduce them in the first place.

Converting types by casting

We can solve the problem of mismatched number types by *casting*. You use a cast to explicitly inform the compiler that you are aware an action might lose data, but you know that it won't affect the behavior of the program. Look at this line of code:

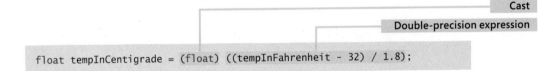

```
float tempInCentigrade = (float) ((tempInFahrenheit - 32) / 1.8);
```

Here, I've wrapped the entire expression in parentheses and then used a cast to tell the compiler, "I don't care what the type of this value is. I want you to regard it as a floating-point value." The statement instructs the compiler to perform an explicit conversion and, if necessary, to discard some of the detail in the result.

Casting is strong magic. You can also use casting to convert from real numbers to integers:

```
int tempInCentigrade = (int) ((tempInFahrenheit - 32) / 1.8);
```

This cast is actually quite a dangerous one. It tells the compiler to convert a real number to an integer by discarding the fractional part. In other words, the value 0.999 would be converted to 0, losing a lot of data in the process. Here is a better way to perform this conversion:

```
int tempInCentigrade = (int) (((tempInFahrenheit - 32) / 1.8) + 0.5);
```

Adding 0.5 to the value before we cast it ensures that 0.999 is rounded up to 1.

Using casting on operands in an expression

Another way to fix the type problem is to give the compiler more information about the values it is working with. If we tell it that the value 1.8 is actually a floating-point value, it will generate a floating-point version of the expression. You can do this by a bit of cunning casting:

```
float tempInCentigrade = (tempInFahrenheit - 32) / (float) 1.8;

Ch04_08_FloatCentigrade
```

Now the value 1.8 has been cast to a floating-point value, leading to a floating-point result for the calculation.

CODE ANALYSIS

Casting and program performance

The type of a variable in an expression can have an effect on performance. This is worth exploring.

Question: Casting the value of 1.8 to a floating-point value makes the program more efficient. Why do you think this might be?

> **Answer:** If we cast the double-precision result of the calculation to a floating-point value, we are effectively performing a high-precision calculation and then doing work to discard some detail. It is much more efficient to just perform the calculation by using floating-point values and then not have to convert the value at all. In an ordinary program this might not make much difference, but it is the kind of issue that programmers concerned with performance (for example, games developers) worry about a lot.

It turns out that the designers of C# have provided a quick way of saying that an operand is a floating-point value—you just have to put an *f* after the value in the program code:

```
float tempInCentigrade = (tempInFahrenheit - 32) / 1.8f;
```

Putting *f* at the end of a literal value casts that value to the float type.

The value 1.8f is a literal value in the program; it is not a variable. There are actually two literals in this statement—the values 1.8 and 32. Unless we give the compiler more information, it will assume that literals with no decimal point are integers and ones with a decimal point are double precision. However, if we put an *f* after a value, this tells the compiler it is really a floating point.

Types and errors

Errors that occur when you convert one type to another are some of the hardest ones for a programmer to deal with. The intent of the program may be correct—there is, in fact, nothing wrong with what you are telling the computer to do—but the realization of the program (the statements that implement this intent) may result in data loss. The compiler will notice this and refuse to compile the program unless you explicitly take responsibility for the conversion.

CODE ANALYSIS

Type checking

Sometimes, finding problems in programs involves a bit of detective work. You have to work with the clues to work out just what is happening.

Say a friend of yours has decided to write a program that will work out the average of three temperatures, held in variables called t1, t2, and t3. The program compiles and runs just fine. It contains the following statement:

```
int average = (t1 + t2 + t3) / 3;
```

Question: What does this tell you about the variables t1, t2, and t3?

Answer: They must be integers. If they were float or double, the compiler would not allow the result of the calculation to be stored in an integer variable.

Question: Your friend would like to get fractional parts in the results. He's tried the following statement, but it doesn't seem to add any more detail, although it compiles and runs fine. What's the problem?

```
float average = (t1 + t2 + t3) / 3;
```

Answer: The calculation is producing an integer result because all the operands in the expression are integers, and the compiler always works with the highest precisions of the operands.

Question: You've told your friend that he needs to make sure that the expression that works out the average produces a floating-point result. He changed the code to the following statement, but it doesn't compile, and now he's angry. How do you fix this?

```
float average = (t1 + t2 + t3) / 3.0;
```

Answer: The problem is that the compiler regards the literal value 3.0 as a double-precision value. The calculation generates a double-precision value, which then can't be placed in a floating-point variable. The best way to fix the problem is to tell the compiler that 3.0 is a floating-point value by putting an *f* after the value (3.0f)

Extra Snaps

Before you go on to the next chapter, you might want to exercise your programming skills by using some more Snaps. Here are a few you can try:

Weather snaps

Converting from Fahrenheit to centigrade is even more useful if you actually have some weather data to work from. The Snaps method named GetTodayTemperatureInFahrenheit returns the temperature of a location in the United States. (The information is provided by the US National Weather Service, www.weather.gov). You must supply the method with the latitude and longitude of the location for which you want the temperature. Here's an example that gets the temperature for Seattle, Washington.

```
int temperature = SnapsEngine.GetTodayTemperatureInFahrenheit (latitude: 47.61,
    longitude: -122.33);

Ch04_09_TemperatureDisplay
```

You can find the latitude of a town or city in the United States by using the Bing search engine. Just search for *"MyLocation* Latitude," and you will get the values you need to use. The `latitude` and `longitude` items in the call to the method are *named arguments*. You first saw examples of these in Chapter 3, in the description of how to create color values. Here we are giving two arguments that describe a location.

If you want a brief description of the weather conditions at a location, you can use the `GetWeatherConditionsDescription` method, which returns a short string describing the conditions.

```
string conditions =
    SnapsEngine.GetWeatherConditionsDescription(latitude: 47.61,
                                                longitude: -122.33);

Ch04_10_WeatherConditionsDisplay
```

I've just run the method, and it returned the message "Partly cloudy" for Seattle.

Keep in mind that these methods provide weather information only for locations in the United States. If you try to use latitude and longitude values for other countries or regions, you will get a rather silly temperature (1000 degrees) or a message that indicates the weather information is not available.

ThrowDice

So far, our programs have worked in a totally consistent way. When we run the program with the same inputs, we get the same outputs. But sometimes it's useful for a program to obtain some random data to work with. You can use randomness to make games more interesting. The Snaps library provides a method named `ThrowDice` that simulates a single throw of the dice. There is no need to feed any information into the method; a program can just use the result that is provided. The next three statements show how the method is used:

```
int spotCount = SnapsEngine.ThrowDice();
SnapsEngine.SetTitleString(spotCount.ToString());
SnapsEngine.SpeakString("You have rolled a " + spotCount.ToString());

Ch04_11_Dice
```

The first statement sets the integer variable spotCount to the result of a throw of the dice. The second statement sets the title string of the page to the dice throw (converting the integer to a string), and the third statement speaks the result.

You could create a program that you could use in place of the dice in a game. You could also use it to create a random delay. The random dice throw could be the basis of a "nerves of steel" game. The program picks a random time by getting a random dice throw and then multiplying it by another random dice throw. This produces a number between 1 and 36. The program then pauses for that number of seconds before saying "Nerves of steel." Everybody stands, and the program runs. The last person who sits down before the program speaks the message is the winner.

What you have learned

In this chapter you have learned that programs use random access memory (RAM) to hold program data and code. RAM is a series of numbered locations, each of which stores one byte. You don't need to worry where in memory your data is stored because C# allows you to create named variables that are managed automatically.

Each variable is created with an identifier that is chosen by the programmer. The identifier should reflect the purpose of the variable. Variables can have values assigned to them, and a variable can be used within expressions in a program. An expression is made up of operands (variables and literal values) and operators (like the plus and minus signs). Expressions can contain multiple operators and operands, and the order in which operators are applied is defined in C# so that results tend to work out the way you would expect them to. If a calculation is performed that will generate an invalid result—for example, dividing 1 by 0—a program will fail at that point.

A given variable is defined as being able to hold a particular type of data, like an integer or a string. C# forces the programmer to be explicit when moving variables from one type to another so that data is never lost unintentionally by the conversion process.

Here are some questions you might like to ponder about types, variables, and expressions.

Are values held in the computer to unlimited accuracy?

No. Each numeric type has a particular range (the highest and lowest values available) and precision (the number of significant digits). You can increase the accuracy of stored data by selecting a type that uses more bytes of memory to hold each value. For example, a `double` variable is held in 8 bytes, whereas a `float` variable is held in only 4.

Can I can get more accuracy by using double-precision values?

This really depends on the accuracy of the numbers coming in. If you are measuring the length of your desk with a ruler and using that value in your program, it is unlikely that you could improve anything by using double precision, as the precision of the input value is not that great.

Does adding parentheses to an expression make the program go faster?

No. It might help the compiler make sense of your program, but it does not affect the speed at which the program actually runs.

Does the type of a variable really matter?

Yes. If you try to store text in a location that has been created to store a number, this will obviously not work. But you can get even worse problems if you use a numeric type that has an insufficient range for the value you want to put in it. For example, you might declare a variable of type `byte` (in an attempt to save memory) and then store the value 10,000 in that variable. This will not fit (the biggest value you can put in a byte is 255), and your program will do very strange things as a result.

5

Making decisions in a program

What you will learn

I've described a computer as a sausage machine, which accepts an input, does something with it, and then produces an output. This is a great way to start thinking about computers, but a computer actually does a lot more than that. Unlike a real-life sausage machine, which simply tries to create sausage from anything you put in it, a computer is able to respond to different inputs in different ways. In this chapter, you'll discover how to make your programs respond to different inputs. You'll also learn about the responsibility that comes with making the computer work in this way—you have to be sure that the decisions your programs make are sensible ones.

With this information in hand, we'll build an application that behaves according to the user's selection. As we build this application, you'll learn more about the logical expressions you can use to control a program. Then, at the end of the chapter, we'll expand on your newfound programming skills by exploring how to incorporate images and sounds in your programs.

Understanding the Boolean type

You've seen that C# provides different types, such as `string` and `float`, that you can use to represent data in a program. I like to think that you will forever associate the number of hairs on your head with whole numbers (integers) and the average length of your hair with real numbers (floating-point and double). Now it's time to meet another type, the *Boolean* type. Unlike the numeric types, which provide a range of values, the Boolean type has only two possible values: true or false.

Declaring a Boolean variable

A program can declare and assign a Boolean variable in the same way as for any other type of variable. The following statement declares a Boolean variable called `ItIsTimeToGetUp` and sets its value to `true`. (In my world, it seems that it is always time to get up.) Note that the designers of C# decided to shorten the program text slightly by giving the Boolean type the name `bool`.

```
bool ItIsTimeToGetUp = true;
```

In the highly unlikely event of me ever being allowed to stay in bed, we could change the assignment to set the value to `false`:

```
bool ItIsTimeToGetUp = false;
```

CODE ANALYSIS

Boolean values

Question: What happens if I try to set a Boolean variable to a number rather than to `true` or `false`?

Answer: I think we both know the answer to this one. The compiler enforces type rules on Boolean values as it does for all other types. The keyword `true` in a C# program is actually a literal Boolean value that means *true*, just like the value 12 is a literal integer value that means the value 12.

Question: Why do we need Boolean variables?

Answer: If you think about it, we don't really need Boolean variables. We could simply use an integer and adopt a convention that 0 means false and any other value means true. However, we'd have to rely on all programmers understanding the convention and using it correctly. If we were ever interested in storing only `true` or `false` (for example, I am either handsome or I am not handsome), then it makes sense to use a type that can represent just those two states. Another good reason to have Boolean types is to perform logic in a program, which you will be doing later in this chapter.

Question: What are `true` and `false`?

Answer: The words *true* and *false* are literal values in the program that mean *true* or *false*. You've seen literal values before. A program can contain the literal integer 1 or the literal string "Rob". If we use `false` in a program, the C# compiler regards it as a Boolean value that is false. The C# compiler will make sure that we assign these literal values only to Boolean variables.

Boolean expressions

A Boolean variable can be assigned to any expression that returns a value that is true or false. As an example, each day I need to get up at 7 a.m. We can use a Boolean expression involving the hour value of the current time to see whether I need to get up:

```
int hourValue = SnapsEngine.GetHourValue();
bool ItIsTimeToGetUp = hourValue > 6;
```

Get the hour value from the clock.

Set ItIsTimeToGetUp to true if the hour is greater than 6.

The first statement creates an integer variable called `hourValue` and sets it to the current hour of the time by using the Snaps method `GetHourValue`. The second statement sets the value of `ItIsTimeToGetUp` to the result of a Boolean expression that evaluates to `true` if the value in `hourValue` is greater than 6.

You can invert the value of any Boolean expression (converting `true` to `false` and vice versa) by using the ! (not) operator. This statement creates a Boolean variable called `ICanStayInBed` that holds the inverse of `ItIsTimeToGetUp`.

```
bool ICanStayInBed = !ItIsTimeToGetUp;
```

Boolean expressions

Question: What does the > character mean?

Answer: If you've done any math in school, you'll be familiar with the > character. It means greater than. In the same way that the + operator adds two operands together and returns their sum, the > operator compares two values and returns true if the value on the left of the operator is greater than the value on the right.

Question: Why is the test "greater than 6" rather than "greater than 7"?

Answer: We use this test because I need to get up at 7. Therefore, the expression must evaluate to true when hourValue is 7. If we used the test "greater than 7," the expression would not become true until the hour value reached 8 (because 7 is not greater than 7).

I think the best way to test your Boolean expressions is to say them out loud, replacing the variable with the actual value. If you say that the result of the expression would be true if "7 is greater than 7," you can tell that it is wrong because it sounds wrong. Of course, it turns out that I'm all in favor of software bugs that let me have an extra hour in bed.

Question: Can a program compare real numbers as well as whole ones?

Answer: Yes. For example, the greater-than (>) operator will work between two float values.

Question: How would I make a test to determine whether I can stay in bed?

Answer: C# provides a logical operator called "less than" (<) that can be used to perform this test.

```
bool ICanStayInBed = hourValue < 7;
```

Using **if** constructions and operators

Let's say I want to make a program that displays a message to tell me whether I need to get out of bed just yet. We can use a Boolean variable to control the execution of this program by using the if construction provided by C#. In a C# if construction, the if keyword is followed by a Boolean value enclosed in parentheses. This is often called the *condition*. The condition controls what the program does. If the condition is true, the statement after the condition is obeyed. If the condition is false, this statement is ignored when the program runs.

Here is a program that uses an `if` construction to display the message "Time to get up" only if you run it at 7 o'clock or later.

```
using SnapsLibrary;

class Ch05_01_GetUpAlarm
{
    public void StartProgram()
    {
        int hourValue = SnapsEngine.GetHourValue();
        bool ItIsTimeToGetUp = hourValue > 6;
        if (ItIsTimeToGetUp)
            SnapsEngine.DisplayString("Time to get up");
    }
}
```

Get the hour value.

Set ItIsTimeToGetUp to true if it is time to get up.

Start of the if condition.

Statement that is obeyed when the if condition is true.

We can simplify the program by including the logical expression inside the `if` construction, like this:

```
if (SnapsEngine.GetHourValue() > 6)
    SnapsEngine.DisplayString("Time to get up");

Ch05_02_SimplifiedGetUpAlarm
```

Get the hour value and test it using a Boolean expression.

Adding an `else` part to an `if` construction

Many programs want to perform one action if a condition is true and another action if the condition is false. An `if` construction can include an `else` element that identifies a statement to be performed if the condition is false.

The message the following program displays depends on the time of day the user runs it. In the morning, before 7:00 a.m., it displays "Go back to sleep." After 7:00 a.m., it displays "Time to get up."

```
if (SnapsEngine.GetHourValue() > 6 )
    SnapsEngine.DisplayString("Time to get up");
else
```

Condition that controls this if construction.

Statement performed if the condition is true.

```
SnapsEngine.DisplayString("Go back to sleep");
```

Statement performed if the condition is false.

Ch05_03_GetUpDeciderWithElse

CODE ANALYSIS

If constructions

Question: Does an `if` construction have to have an `else` part?

Answer: No. Including an `else` part is very useful sometimes, but it depends on the problem that the program is trying to solve.

Question: Does the condition in an `if` construction control what the compiler does?

Answer: No. Remember that the compiler is the tool that converts your C# program text into machine code that can run on the computer. When the C# compiler compiles an `if` construction, it creates the machine code that makes the decision and then runs the selected statement. The decision is made when the program runs, not when it is compiled.

Question: What happens if a condition is never true?

Answer: If a condition is never true, the statement controlled by the condition never gets to run. The compiler will give you the warning "Unreachable code detected" if it detects this situation.

Question: Why is the statement underneath the `if` condition indented a few spaces?

Answer: This statement doesn't need to be indented. The C# compiler would be able to understand what we want the program to do even if we put everything on one line. The indentation is there to make the program easier to understand. It shows that the statement underneath the `if` construction is being controlled by the condition above it. Indenting code like this is such a common practice that the behavior is baked into the Visual Studio editor. In other words, when you type an `if` construction and then press the Enter key at the end of the condition part, Visual Studio automatically indents the next line.

Relational operators

The less-than operator (<) is called a *relational operator* because it measures the relationship between two values. There are other relational operators you can use. The operator you choose depends on what you want the program to do.

RELATIONAL OPERATOR	NAME	BEHAVIOR
<	Less than	Evaluates to true if the value to the left of the operator is less than the value to the right.
>	Greater than	Evaluates to true if the value to the left of the operator is greater than the value to the right.
<=	Less than or equal to	Evaluates to true if the value to the left of the operator is less than or equal to the value on the right.
>=	Greater than or equal to	Evaluates to true if the value to the left of the operator is greater than or equal to the value on the right.

CODE ANALYSIS

Relational operators

Question: Two of the operators, the ones with *or equal to*, are expressed as two characters. How does this work?

Answer: When the C# compiler goes through your program, it looks for character combinations and converts them to symbols that represent the elements in the program. These elements are then used to build your program. Some of the symbols are keywords, such as `if` and `int`. Other symbols are elements such as strings of text (which are enclosed in double quotation marks) and literal values. The character sequence <= is recognized and converted into the less-than-or-equal-to symbol.

Question: How do I remember which symbol is which?

Answer: When I was learning to program, I used the way that *less than* looks a bit like an *L* to remember which is which.

Equality operators

In addition to the relational operators, C# also provides a couple of *equality* operators that a program can use to test equality.

OPERATOR	NAME	BEHAVIOR
==	Equal to	Evaluates to true if the value to the left of the operator is equal to the value on the right.
!=	Not equal to	Evaluates to true if the value to the left of the operator is not equal to the value on the right.

Here is an example of using the equal-to operator to display a message if the hour value of the time is 9.

```
if (SnapsEngine.GetHourValue() == 9)
    SnapsEngine.DisplayString("Nine hours, and all is well");


Ch05_04_IsItNineOclock
```

Compare the hours with the value 9.

Display the message if the hours value is 9.

The == operator can be a bit confusing. You saw that you use the = operator when you want to assign a value to a variable. C# uses the == symbol to indicate a test for equality so that programmers don't get confused between these two actions. The equality operator is used to generate true or false answers, while the assignment operator moves data around. The behaviors of the operators are quite different, so it makes sense to identify them with different symbols.

WHAT COULD GO WRONG

Comparing real numbers

In Chapter 4, we started working with real numbers, which have a fractional part as well as a whole part. For example, the value 1.1 has a whole part (1) and a fractional part (.1, or one-tenth). C# programs can hold real values in the float, double, and decimal types. You discovered that the value of a real number is not always held precisely by the computer; instead, it holds a number that is close enough to the actual value. This can lead to problems if you try to compare two numbers.

```
using SnapsLibrary;

class Ch05_05_NumberCompare
{
    public void StartProgram()
    {
        double calculatedPoint3 = (0.1 + 0.2);
        if (calculatedPoint3 == 0.3)
            SnapsEngine.DisplayString("Calculation works");
    }
}
```

Calculate the value 0.3 by adding 0.1 and 0.2.

Compare the calculated value with the literal value 0.3.

This statement is not performed because the calculation is inaccurate.

We know that 0.1 + 0.2 should be 0.3, so the message should be displayed. But because the computer does not hold values completely accurately, the value of 0.1 + 0.2 works out to be 0.30000000000000004. This is an extremely small difference, but as far as the equality test is concerned, the two numbers are not the same, so the message is not displayed.

Note that this does not reflect a problem with the computer or the programming language; it is just a consequence of the way that numbers are stored using digital systems. Some numbers—for example, one-third—can't be accurately represented as a decimal number. The same is true for some numbers stored by computers, and your programs must allow for this. If you want to compare floating-point values, your program should subtract one from the other and see whether the difference is very small.

Comparing strings

A program can use the equality operators to compare two strings. This program gets the name of the day of the week and then displays the message if it's Saturday.

```
if (SnapsEngine.GetDayOfWeekName() == "Saturday")
    SnapsEngine.DisplayString("Yay! It's Saturday");

Ch05_06_IsItSaturday
```

Compare the name of the day of the week with the string "Saturday".

Display the message if it is Saturday..

You can use similar code to make a program that recognizes people by name:

```
using SnapsLibrary;

class Ch05_07_HelloGreatOne
{
    public void StartProgram()
    {
        string name;
        name = SnapsEngine.ReadString("What is your name?");
        if (name == "Rob")
            SnapsEngine.DisplayString("Hello, Oh great one");
    }
}
```

Variable that holds the name of the user.

Read the name entered by the user.

Test to see if the name matches "Rob".

Display the message if the name matches.

Big and little characters

If you tried to show off by using the Great One program, you might have a problem, depending on how you type your name. The equality test regards uppercase and lowercase characters as different; in other words, if you enter the string "ROB", you will not get special treatment.

As a way around this, you can ask any string to provide the uppercase version of itself. A string value provides a ToUpper method that returns a version of a string that has all the lowercase letters replaced by uppercase characters. You can use the ToUpper method like this:

```
using SnapsLibrary;

class Ch05_08_GreatOneUpperCase
{
    public void StartProgram()
    {
        string name;                                        Variable that holds the name of the user.
                                                            Read the name entered by the user.
        name = SnapsEngine.ReadString("What is your name");
                                                            Obtain an uppercase
        string upperCaseName = name.ToUpper();              version of the name and
                                                            assign it to the variable.

        if (upperCaseName == "ROB")                         Compare the name with an all uppercase version.
            SnapsEngine.DisplayString("Hello, Oh great one");  Display the message if
    }                                                       the names match.
}
```

This version of the program will work whether the user enters "rob", "Rob", or "ROB". Whenever you write a program that accepts string input, you need to decide how the program should behave if the user enters text that is case sensitive. There is also a method called ToLower that you can use to convert uppercase letters in a string to lowercase ones.

Creating blocks of statements

The if condition controls the execution of a C# statement. Sometimes, however, you want to perform multiple statements if a condition is true. For example, you could write an announcer program that asks for the user's name and then offers a personalized greeting in that person's favorite color. To do this, a program needs to control multiple statements from a single condition.

You write code for a task like this by creating a *block* of statements. A block of statements is a sequence of C# statements enclosed in a pair of curly braces—the { and } characters. You have already seen blocks of statements in the programs we've examined and written; in those programs, the statements in the `StartProgram` method are enclosed in a block. You can create a block anywhere in a program, and it is equivalent to a single statement.

```
using SnapsLibrary;

class Ch05_09_ColorfulGreeter
{
    public void StartProgram()
    {
        string name;
        name = SnapsEngine.ReadString("What is your name?");
        string upperCaseName = name.ToUpper();
        if (upperCaseName == "ROB")
        {                                    Marks the start of a block of statements.
            string dayOfWeek = SnapsEngine.GetDayOfWeekName();
            string fullMessage = "Hello Rob. Hope you are having a great " +
                                 dayOfWeek;
            SnapsEngine.SetTextColor(SnapsColor.Blue);
            SnapsEngine.DisplayString(fullMessage);
        }                                    Marks the end of a block of statements.
    }
}
```

This program would recognize me by name and then display an uplifting message in my favorite color. All the statements in the block are controlled by the single condition defined in the `if` construction.

Local variables in blocks of code

If you take a look at the ColorfulGreeter program, you'll notice that the variables `dayOfWeek` and `fullMessage` are declared inside the block of code controlled by the `if` condition. C# programmers say that these variables are *local* to this block of code, which means that these variables exist only inside this block. Once the last statement in the block has completed and the program has moved out of the block of statements controlled by the `if` condition, these two variables are discarded automatically. If the program reenters the block at a later time, the variables will be created again. The part of a program within which it's valid to use a particular variable is called the *scope* of that variable.

The C# compiler will not allow you to use a variable outside the block—the scope—in which it is declared because as far as the compiler is concerned, the variable does not exist at that point in the program. This is a very sensible way to organize the use of variables. It makes programs clearer in that a programmer can declare variables much closer to the point in a program where they are being used. Also, if two programmers are working on the same program and each of them want to use a variable named count, they can do that, as long as they declare it inside separate blocks of code. (Discarding variables when they are not being used also saves memory, although you usually have plenty of memory to spare when you write programs these days.)

CODE ANALYSIS

Considering variable scope

Take a look at the following statements:

```
{
    int i=99 ;
}
{
    int i = 100;
}
```

Question: How many variables are being used in the above snippet of code?

Answer: There are two variables. Both are named i, and both are local variables in the blocks where they appear. In the first block, the value of i is set to 99; in the second block, the value of a different variable i (one local to the second block) is set to 100.

```
{
    int i=99 ;
}
{
    string i = "I am i";
}
```

Question: Is this code legal?

Answer: Yes. The integer variable i has been discarded (it is out of scope) before the string variable i is declared.

```
{
    int count=99 ;
}
count = 100;
```

Question: Is this code legal?

Answer: No. The scope of the variable count is restricted to the block of code in which it's declared, which means that an attempt to set count to 100 outside the block will not work. The compiler will complain if you try to use a variable outside the block in which it is declared. Programmers say that the variable is "out of scope."

```
{
    int i;
    {
        int i;
        i = 99;
    }
}
```

Question: Is this code legal?

Answer: No. The C# compiler does not let you create nested blocks that contain a variable with the same name as a variable in an enclosing block. Doing so might lead to confusing code. In this example, it is not necessarily clear whether the statement i = 99 refers to the version of i declared in the inner block or the outer one.

Creating complex conditions using logical operators

A program sometimes needs to make a more complicated decision than just a simple relational test. C# provides *logical* operators that you can use to do this. For example, on Saturday I'm allowed to stay in bed until 9:00 rather than 7:00, so if the day of the week is Saturday, I need to perform a different test to see whether I need to get up. This program must test whether the day of the week is Saturday *and* the time is 9 o'clock. The critical word in this requirement is "and"—which means both conditions need to be true.

C# provides a *logical* operator, a single ampersand (&), that works with two logical operands. The & operator evaluates to `true` if the operand on its left and the operand on its right are both true. Here's a program that displays the message if the day is Saturday and the hour value is larger than 8.

```
if (SnapsEngine.GetDayOfWeekName() == "Saturday" & SnapsEngine.GetHourValue() > 8)
    SnapsEngine.DisplayString("It is time to get up");


Ch05_10_WeekendAlarm
```

There are several logical operators that you can use to combine logical values.

LOGICAL OPERATOR	NAME	BEHAVIOR
&	AND	Evaluates to true if the value to the left of the operator and the value on its right are true.
&&	"short circuit" AND	Evaluates to true if the value to the left of the operator and the value on its right are true. This operator does not evaluate the value on the right if the value on the left is false.
|	OR	Evaluates to true if the value to the left of the operator or the value on its right is true.
||	"short circuit" OR	Evaluates to true if the value to the left of the operator or the value on its right is true. This operator does not evaluate the value on the right if the value on the left is true.
^	Exclusive OR	Evaluates to true if the value to the left of the operator or the value on its right is true, but it evaluates to false if they are both true or both false.

CODE ANALYSIS

Logical operators

Making decisions using logic is a huge part of being an effective programmer. We can explore this by looking at some more code. Take a look at this code, to which I have added an `else` part.

```
if (SnapsEngine.GetDayOfWeekName() == "Saturday" & SnapsEngine.GetHourValue() > 8)
    SnapsEngine.DisplayString("It is time to get up");
else
    SnapsEngine.DisplayString("When is this message printed?");
```

Question: When is the `else` part of the `if` construction actually performed?

Answer: To work out the answer, you have to think logically. The "It is time to get up" message is produced when the day is Saturday and the hour value is greater than 8. So the `else` part must be performed whenever this is not the case. This means that the `else` statement is performed on every other day of the week and on Saturday up to 8 o'clock.

Question: Would this code display "When is this message printed?" at 6:00 a.m. on Friday?

Answer: Yes. 6:00 is before my get-up time, but because the day is not Saturday, the first condition is false. The AND operator (&) needs both operands to be true, so it will not trigger the message "It's time to get up."

Question: What would happen if I replaced the & operator in the above statement with the "short circuit" version, &&?

Answer: The behavior of the program would be exactly the same, except that it would run slightly faster in some situations. If the weekday was not Saturday, the && operator would not bother testing the hour value because for an & operation to be true, both operands have to be true, and if the first operand is false, there is no point testing the second.

Question: Your friend has tried to make an alarm program that will tell you to get up at 9:00 a.m. on Saturday and 7:00 a.m. on all the other days of the week. However it doesn't work. This is his code:

```
if (SnapsEngine.GetDayOfWeekName() == "Saturday")
    if (SnapsEngine.GetHourValue() > 8)
        SnapsEngine.DisplayString("It is time to get up");
else
    if (SnapsEngine.GetHourValue() > 6)
        SnapsEngine.DisplayString("It is time to get up");
```

Answer: The logic of the code is correct. If the day of the week is Saturday, the program tests for an hour greater than 8. For any other day of the week, the program tests for an hour greater than 6. However, your friend has made a mistake in his coding. The `else` statement is associated with the second `if` condition (an `else` always associates itself with the nearest `if`). You can see the effect of this by changing the layout to reflect the way the code actually behaves:

```
if (SnapsEngine.GetDayOfWeekName() == "Saturday")
    if (SnapsEngine.GetHourValue() > 8)
        SnapsEngine.DisplayString("It is time to get up");
    else
        if (SnapsEngine.GetHourValue() > 6)
            SnapsEngine.DisplayString("It is time to get up");
```

This shows that the test for an hour greater than 6 is actually performed if the hour is not greater than 8. The layout of the above code shows which part of the program is controlled by which condition. We can fix the problem by putting the statements into blocks.

```
if (SnapsEngine.GetDayOfWeekName() == "Saturday")
{
    if (SnapsEngine.GetHourValue() > 8)
        SnapsEngine.DisplayString("It is time to get up");
}
else
{
    if (SnapsEngine.GetHourValue() > 6)
        SnapsEngine.DisplayString("It is time to get up");
}
```

Working with logic

Writing code that makes logical decisions like this is one of the hardest parts of learning to program. It is like solving a logic puzzle, because that is just what you're doing. The best advice I can give you is to write down what you want the program to do and then work through it, converting that description to a logical expression. For example: "I want to pay overtime when the hours worked are more than 40 or the day of the week is Saturday." Even after many years of programming, I still resort to this technique sometimes. And once I've written some code that I think will work, I test it by trying some values and observing what the decision would do.

Make the "time to get up program" work with minutes

You now know quite a bit about making programs that tell you when you need to get up. However, the programs we've made up to now have a serious limitation in that they work only with the hour value. See if you can make a version that will tell me to get up after 7:15 rather than after 7:00.

Hint: You can tie yourself in knots trying to combine conditions that test the hour and the minute values and decide when to trigger the alarm. My strong advice is to make the clock work with the minute value only. You can calculate the minute of the day by multiplying the hour value by 60 and then adding the time—for example, 7:15 is (7*60) + 15 = minute 435 of the day. Using the "minute of the day" means that your tests become a lot simpler.

Adding comments to make a program clearer

It is very important that you write programs in a way that makes it easy for people reading your code to understand what's going on. You've seen that in choosing names for variables, you need to be sure that the name describes what the variable is being used for. You can also make programs clearer by adding explanatory comments, and as soon as you start directing your program to make decisions, you should add comments that explain what your program is doing. You don't write comments for the computer; you write comments for someone reading your program. You can also use comments to indicate the particular version of the program, when it was last modified and why, and the name of the programmer who wrote it—even if it was you.

A single-line comment starts at the character sequence // and finishes at the end of that line, like this:

```
string name;
name = SnapsEngine.ReadString("What is your name?");
string upperCaseName = name.ToUpper(); // Convert name to uppercase
```

Single-line comment

You can add single-line comments to the end of a statement or on a line by themselves. In Visual Studio, comments are displayed in green to make them stand out.

You can write a comment that spreads over several lines by enclosing your comment with /* and */, like this:

```
string name;
name = SnapsEngine.ReadString("What is your name?");
string upperCaseName = name.ToUpper();
/* Check the name to provide the personalized greeting;
   change "ROB" to the name of the person you want to greet */        Comment
if (upperCaseName == "ROB")
{
    // Personal greeting code goes here
}
```

The comment in this program makes it very clear what the code does and how to work with it. When the compiler sees the character sequence /* in a program, it ignores the text that follows up to the point where it sees */, which ends the comment's text. You can put comments anywhere in your program. The compiler will completely ignore them.

Some people say that writing a program is a bit like writing a story. I'm not completely convinced that this is true, but I think that although a program is not a story as such, a good program does have some of the characteristics of good literature:

- It should be easy to read. At no point should a hapless reader be forced to backtrack or brush up on knowledge that the writer assumes is there. All the names in the text should impart meaning and be distinct from one another.

- It should have good punctuation and grammar. The various components should be organized in a clear and consistent way.

- It should look good on the page. A good program is well laid out. The different blocks of code should be indented, and statements should be spread over the page in a well-formed manner.

- It should be clear who wrote a program and when it was last changed. If you write something good, you should put your name on it. If you change what you wrote, you should add information about the changes that you made and why.

Comments that the programmer adds are a big part of a well-written program. A program without comments is a bit like an airplane that has an autopilot but no windows: there is a chance that it might take you to the right place, but it will be very hard to tell where it is going from the inside.

Comments help make your program much easier to understand. You will be very surprised to find how quickly you can forget how you got your program to work. Be generous with your comments, but you should not add too much detail. Remember that the person who is reading your program can be expected to know the C# language and doesn't need everything explained to them:

```
goatCount = goatCount + 1; // add one to goatCount
```

This comment is simply insulting to the reader, I reckon. If you choose sensible names, you should find that quite a lot of your program will express what it does directly from the code itself. From now on, the sample code that you see will have what I consider an appropriate level of comments.

Funfair rides and programs

Now that you know how to make decisions in your programs, you can start to make more useful software. Let's say that your next-door neighbor is the owner of a theme park and he has a job for you. Some rides at the theme park are restricted to people by age, and he wants to install computers around his funfair so that people can find out which rides they are allowed to go on. He needs some software for the computers, and he's offering a season pass to the park if you can come up with the goods, which is a very tempting proposition. He tells you the following information about the rides:

RIDE NAME	MINIMUM AGE INFORMATION
Scenic River Cruise	None
Carnival Carousel	At least 3 years old
Jungle Adventure Water Splash	At least 6 years old
Downhill Mountain Run	At least 12 years old
The Regurgitator (a super roller coaster)	Must be at least 12 years old and less than 70

You discuss with him the design of the program. What he'd like is for users to select the ride they want from a menu. The program will then ask for the user's age and display a message indicating whether they can go on the ride.

To create this program, we'll use a Snaps function that displays just the kind of menu required. It's a method named SelectFrom5Buttons.

```
using SnapsLibrary;

class Ch05_12_SelectFunfairRide
{
    public void StartProgram()
    {
        SnapsEngine.SetTitleString("Super Funfair Rides");
        string ride;
        ride = SnapsEngine.SelectFrom5Buttons(          Selects from five buttons.
            "Scenic River Cruise",
            "Carnival Carousel",
            "Jungle Adventure Water Splash",
            "Downhill Mountain Run",
            "The Regurgitator");

        SnapsEngine.SetTitleString(ride);               Displays the selected ride.
    }
}
```

The SelectFrom5Buttons method displays five buttons on the screen and then waits for the user to select one of them. When the user selects a button, the method returns with the name of the button selected. The program then sets the page's title to the name of the ride that was selected. **Figure 5-1** shows the display when the program runs.

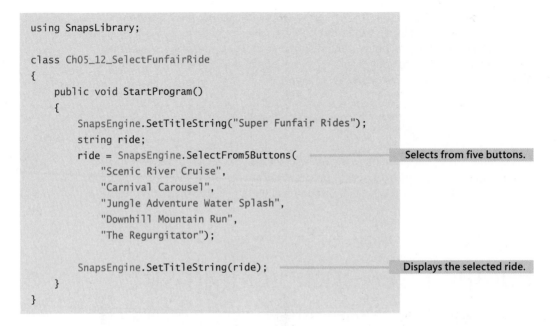

Figure 5-1 The menu used to select a funfair ride.

Here, the user is about to select **The Regurgitator** item. You can use the `Select-FromButtons` method anywhere you want a user to select something from a range of options. The Snaps framework includes versions of the method for two and up to six buttons.

Now let's add an `if` construction to the program to make it behave differently depending on which ride is selected:

```
using SnapsLibrary;

class Ch05_13_HandleRiverCruise
{
    public void StartProgram()
    {
        SnapsEngine.SetTitleString("Super Funfair Rides");
        string ride;
        ride = SnapsEngine.SelectFrom5Buttons(
            "Scenic River Cruise",
            "Carnival Carousel",
            "Jungle Adventure Water Splash",
            "Downhill Mountain Run",
            "The Regurgitator");

        SnapsEngine.SetTitleString(ride);

        if (ride == "Scenic River Cruise")
        {
            SnapsEngine.DisplayString("There are no age restrictions on this
                                       ride. Enjoy.");
        }
    }
}
```

This code handles the case when a user selects the Scenic River Cruise ride, displaying the message shown in **Figure 5-2**.

Scenic River Cruise

There are no age restrictions on this ride.
Enjoy.

Figure 5-2 The message confirming that the river cruise has no age restrictions.

With the information you received from the theme park's owner, you know that if the user selects any ride other than the Scenic River Cruise, the program must obtain the age of the user. You can add an `else` statement to the code to meet this need. Remember that the `if` construction will perform the `else` part of the code if the ride selected is one other than Scenic River Cruise, which is exactly what we want. Here I've put a comment in the code at the point where the program needs to read the age value.

```
if (ride == "Scenic River Cruise")
{
    SnapsEngine.DisplayString("There are no age restrictions on this ride.
                              Enjoy.");
}
else
{
    // We need to get the age of the user
}
```

Reading in numbers

The selection of the Scenic River Cruise is easy to handle because anyone can go on this ride. For the other rides, the program has to get the age of the person wanting to go on it. Fortunately, there is a Snaps method, named `ReadInteger`, that we can use to do this. The `ReadInteger` method reads a number entered by the user. It's similar to the `ReadString` method you have seen before:

```
using SnapsLibrary;

class Ch05_14_ReadAge
{
    public void StartProgram()
    {
        SnapsEngine.SetTitleString("Super Funfair Rides");
        string ride;
        ride = SnapsEngine.SelectFrom5Buttons(
            "Scenic River Cruise",
            "Carnival Carousel",
            "Jungle Adventure Water Splash",
            "Downhill Mountain Run",
            "The Regurgitator");
```

```
        SnapsEngine.SetTitleString(ride);

        if (ride == "Scenic River Cruise")
        {
            SnapsEngine.DisplayString("There are no age restrictions on this
                                ride. Enjoy.");
        }
        else
        {
            // These rides have age restrictions - read the age
            int ageInt = SnapsEngine.ReadInteger("What is your age?");  ——— Read in
                                                                            the age of
                                                                            the user.
            SnapsEngine.DisplayString("You are " + ageInt + " years old");
        }
    }
}
```

The ReadInteger method displays a prompt asking for the user's age and then returns the integer value that the user types in. **Figure 5-3** shows how the age value is read in when the user selects the Carnival Carousel ride. If the user doesn't type in a valid integer value (perhaps the user types in the string "twenty-five"), the ReadInteger method will display an error message and then ask the user to try again.

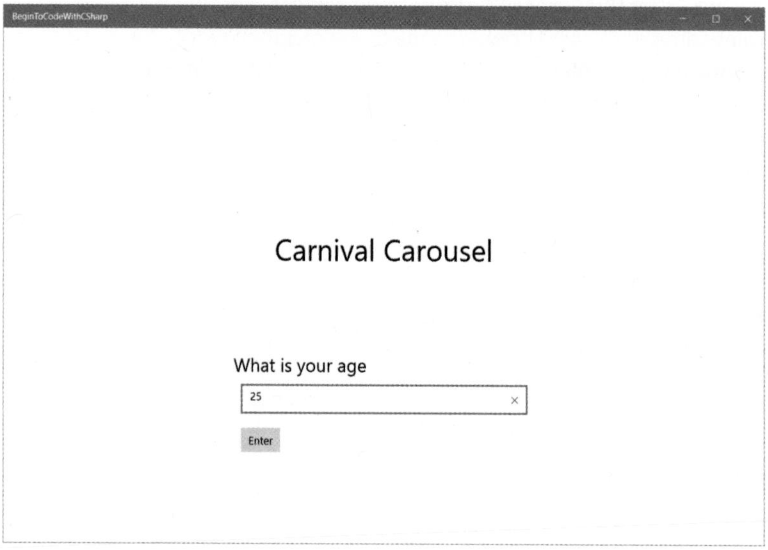

Figure 5-3 Getting the age of a user.

Building logic using `if` conditions

Once our funfair program knows the age of the user, it can decide whether the user can go on the ride. The program has two items of data to work with.

- The selected ride, held in a string variable named `ride`.

- The age of the user, held in an integer variable named `ageInt`.

The program can use a sequence of `if...else` constructions to make its decision:

```
if (ride == "Carnival Carousel")
{
    if (ageInt >= 3)
        SnapsEngine.DisplayString("You can go on the ride.");
    else
        SnapsEngine.DisplayString("I'm sorry. You are too young.");
}
```

These conditions work for the Carnival Carousel. The first (outer) `if` statement is used to determine the ride selected. The inner `if` statement makes the appropriate decision based on the age of the user.

Now that you have code that works for the Carnival Carousel, you can use it as the basis for the code that handles some of the other rides. To make the program work correctly for the Jungle Adventure Water Splash, you need to check for a different ride name and confirm or reject the user based on a different age value. Remember that for this ride, a visitor needs to be at least six years old. You could check whether the visitor is older than five (`ageInt > 5`) or use the greater-than-or-equal-to operator when you test for the value of `ageInt`.

```
if (ride == "Jungle Adventure Water Splash")
{
    if (ageInt >= 6)
        SnapsEngine.DisplayString("You can go on the ride.");
    else
        SnapsEngine.DisplayString("I'm sorry. You are too young.");
}
```

Completing the program

You can implement the Downhill Mountain Run very easily by using the same pattern as for the previous two rides. But the final ride, the Regurgitator, is more difficult. The ride is so extreme that the owner of the funfair is concerned for the health of older people who use it and has added a maximum age restriction as well as a minimum age. The program must test for users who have an age greater than 70 as well as for those with an age less than 12. We have to design a sequence of conditions to deal with this situation.

The code that deals with the Regurgitator is the most complex piece of the program that we have to write. To make sense of how it needs to work, you need to know more about the way that `if` constructions are used in programs. Consider the following code:

```
if (ride == "The Regurgitator")
{
    // If we get here we are dealing with the Regurgitator
}
```

The comment makes it clear that all the statements we add inside this block will run only if the selected ride is the Regurgitator. In other words, there is no need for any statement in that block to ask the question, "Is the selected ride the Regurgitator?" because the block is run only if this is the case. The decisions leading up to a statement in a program determine the context in which that statement will run. I like to add comments to make it clear what the context is, like this:

```
if (ride == "The Regurgitator")
{
    // If we get here we are dealing with the Regurgitator
    if (ageInt >= 12)
    {
        // If we get here the age is not too low
        if (ageInt > 70)
        {
            // If we get here the age is too high
            SnapsEngine.DisplayString("I'm sorry. You are too old.");
        }
        else
        {
            // If we get here the age is in the correct range
            SnapsEngine.DisplayString("You can go on the ride");
```

```
        }
    }
    else
    {
        // If we get here the age is too low
        SnapsEngine.DisplayString("I'm sorry. You are too young.");
    }
}
```

These comments make the program slightly longer, but they also make it a lot clearer. This code is the complete construction that deals with the Regurgitator. The best way to work out what it does is to work through each statement in turn with a particular value for the user's age. I've used the layout to make it clear where the blocks are and which else and if parts are matched. You can run the entire program from the sample **Ch05_15_CompleteFunfairProgram**.

MAKE SOMETHING HAPPEN

Fortune teller

The ThrowDice method from the Snaps framework, which I introduced in Chapter 4, can be used in if constructions to make programs that perform in a way that appears random.

```
if (SnapsEngine.ThrowDice() < 4)
    SnapsEngine.SpeakString("You are going to meet a tall, attractive stranger");
else
    SnapsEngine.SpeakString("You are not going to meet anyone at all");
```

The if construction tests the value produced by a call to the ThrowDice method. If the value returned by the method is less than 4 (in other words, 1, 2, or 3), the program tells the user that she is going to meet a tall, handsome stranger. Otherwise, it tells the user that she is not going to meet anyone interesting at all. You could use a sequence of such conditions to make a fun fortune-teller program.

Working with program assets

There is more to an application than just program code. Programs also often contain images and sounds. When the application is built, the images and sounds are incorporated into the program and can be used by it. We can refer to images, sounds, and things like them as *assets*. Some applications will contain additional kinds of assets. For example, a game might contain maps of the game area.

Asset management in Visual Studio

You can manage the assets in your programs by using Solution Explorer, the component in Visual Studio that we've been using to manage the C# source code we've written. Assets are added to a project in the same way as program code. You can also create folders that you use to organize your program's assets.

Figure 5-4 shows some of the assets that have been added to the BeginToCode-WithCSharp project. The storage structure you see in Solution Explorer is mirrored in the folders and files on your computer that are used to store the project. You may have noticed that there is already a folder named Assets in the solution. You could put asset files in that folder, but it is reserved for specific program assets managed by Visual Studio, so it is better to create your own folders to store your own assets.

Figure 5-4 Assets in a Visual Studio solution.

Each of the sound effects (beep.wav, ding.wav, and so on) are files that are identified in the Visual Studio solution and stored in the SoundEffects folder on your computer. When Visual Studio builds the application, it finds each of these files and incorporates them into the application. You can then use methods in the Snaps library to use these assets in your programs. Let's start by playing some sounds.

Playing sound assets

Computer programs are greatly improved by sound effects. Some simple ones are included in the BeginToCodeWithCSharp solution. With the PlaySoundEffect method, you provide a string that identifies the sound to be played. The following statement causes the ding sound to be played:

```
SnapsEngine.PlaySoundEffect("ding");
```

You can also use the strings "beep", "gameOver", and "lose". If you use any other name to specify a sound effect, the program will not make any sound. But you can add sound-effects files of your own if you want to. The PlaySoundEffect method works with .wav and .mp3 sound files and looks in the SoundEffects folder for sounds to play. Just drag a sound file from the folder where it's stored on your computer to the SoundEffects folder in the BeginToCodeWithCSharp Visual Studio solution. You can then use the sound in your program by using the name of the asset file. Here's a small program that lets a user select from the four built-in sound effects by pressing a button. You could easily modify this to make a sound-effects application of your own.

```csharp
using SnapsLibrary;

class Ch05_16_SoundEffects
{
    public void StartProgram()
    {
        string effectName = SnapsEngine.SelectFrom4Buttons("beep", "ding",
                                                "gameOver", "lose");
        SnapsEngine.PlaySoundEffect(effectName);
    }
}
```

Make some noise

You might go back at this point and add sound effects to the programs that you have already written. The egg-timer program would benefit from an alarm sound, for example. If you can find some suitably eerie background sounds, you could add these to the fortune-teller program.

Displaying image content

You can also display images in your programs. You can display images from the Internet and by using files that are built into the application. The Snaps library provides a method that will fetch and display images from either location. Here is the form of the method that displays an image that is stored with an application:

```
using SnapsLibrary;

class Ch05_17_CityImage
{
    public void StartProgram()
    {
        string url = "ms-appx:///Images/City.jpg";
        SnapsEngine.DisplayImageFromUrl(imageURL: url);
    }
}

Ch05_17_CityImage
```

Create a URL that identifies where the asset can be found.

Display the image

I've called the string variable that holds the name of the image url (short for *uniform resource locator*). You may have heard the term URL in the context of webpages. For example, my world famous (in my world) blog has the URL http://www.robmiles.com. The first part of a URL (the part before the // character sequence) is called the *scheme* and describes how to access the data. The scheme "ms-appx" means "look in the content for this asset." The second part of the URL is the actual address of the resource, which in this case is "/Images/City.jpg". If you use Solution Explorer to look in the Images folder, you will find that the folder does contain a file named City.jpg. If you want to add your own images to your applications, you can store them in this folder and then display them by using the DisplayImageFromUrl method.

The schemes *http* and *https* mean "look on the Internet and use World Wide Web protocols to find the asset."

```
string url = "https://farm9.staticflickr.com/8713/16988005732_7fefe368cc_d.jpg";
SnapsEngine.DisplayImageFromUrl(url);


Ch05_18_BridgeImage
```

Here you can see how to display an image held in my Flickr account. You can use a statement like this to incorporate pictures from the Internet in your programs (but remember that you must observe any copyright restrictions).

The `DisplayImage` method can use most of the popular image file types, including the JPEG, PNG, GIF and TIFF formats. Keep in mind that if you add a large number of images to your program, it will become larger, because the image files are stored as part of the application. One way to reduce the size of the application is to resize the images. Don't use images directly from your digital camera. Resize these so that they are no more than 1,500 or so pixels wide. This should provide you with enough detail in almost all cases. The best program that I have found for resizing images (and doing lots more besides) is the free image-processing program called Paint.Net, which you can download from http://www.getpaint.net/index.html.

WHAT COULD GO WRONG

Missing files

The `DisplayImageFromUrl` method is prone to failure. It might not be able to load an image because the device the program is running on doesn't have a network connection. Alternatively, the programmer might have mistyped the address of the image in the program. In these situations, the method will not be able to display a picture, which is a problem.

However, the method has been written so that it will not stop the program; instead, it displays a placeholder image to the user that indicates that something went wrong in fetching the image, as you can see here:

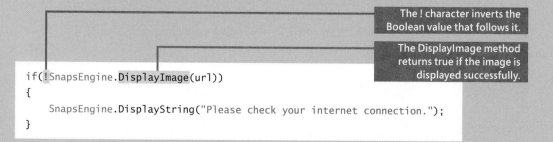

You can change this to a message image of your own by replacing the file named ImageNot-Found.png in the Images folder in the BeginToCodeWithCSharp solution.

The DisplayImage method returns a bool value that indicates whether it was able to display the image that was requested. Here is the code.

```
bool displayedOK = SnapsEngine.DisplayImage(url);
if(displayedOK == false)
{
    SnapsEngine.DisplayString ("Please check your internet connection.");
}
```

If the image is not displayed correctly, the program displays a message prompting the user to check his or her Internet connection. This illustrates an important point about methods when you use them in C# programs: a program does not have to use the result that a method returns. The DisplayImage method always returns whether it worked or not, but the first times we used it we ignored this result.

We can simplify the code a bit by using the result from DisplayImage directly:

The ! character inverts the Boolean value that follows it.

The DisplayImage method returns true if the image is displayed successfully.

```
if(!SnapsEngine.DisplayImage(url))
{
    SnapsEngine.DisplayString("Please check your internet connection.");
}
```

If you think about it, we want the program to display a message if the image is not displayed—in other words, if `DisplayImage` returns false. We therefore take the result that `DisplayImage` returns and then use the ! operator (not) to invert this.

Display some pictures

You can now make programs that display pictures. You can use the `Delay` method to provide a pause between each picture. You could even add some sound effects and use buttons to let the user select the pictures that they want to see. If you display text on the screen, you will find that it is drawn on top of the picture, so you can use this to add captions to the pictures as they are displayed.

What you have learned

In this chapter, you've learned that the C# `if` construction lets you change a program's behavior depending on the data that it is given to work with. This allows a programmer to make software that might be considered "sensible" in that it can respond to input in a useful way.

You also learned that the decision process in C# is based on the Boolean type, which allows programs to work with values that can only be true or false. C# conditions are controlled by the value of Boolean expressions, and the language provides a set of logical operators that can be used in programs to manipulate Boolean values. You can make things happen if two Boolean values are true by using the logical AND operator (&). You can also make things happen if one or the other of two values is true by using the logical OR operator (|).

You discovered how to write useful programs that work with logical conditions to create code that makes decisions. The best way to implement complex logic is to transcribe a plain description of the decision into C# conditional statements. For example, "If it is Saturday or Sunday and it is after 9:00 a.m., I must get out of bed" could be converted to a single logical expression that makes that decision.

Finally, you have seen how to add and use assets in a program, making use of Visual Studio to manage the asset files and Snaps methods that let you use the images and sound files. You have also seen how a unified resource locator string allows a program to load assets from the Internet.

Here are some questions that you might like to ponder about the process of making decisions in programs:

Does the use of Boolean values mean that a program will always do the same thing given the same data inputs?

It is very important that, given the same inputs, the computer does exactly the same thing each time. If the computer starts to behave in an inconsistent way, this makes it much less useful. When we want random behavior from a computer (for example, when we are playing a game against a computer opponent), we have to obtain values that are explicitly random and make decisions based on those. Nobody wants a "moody" computer that changes its mind (although, of course, it might be fun to try and program one by using random numbers).

Will the computer always do the right thing when we write programs that make decisions?

It would be great if we could guarantee that the computer will always do the right thing. However, the computer is only ever as good as the program that it is running. If something happens that the program was not expecting, this can cause it to do the wrong thing in response. For example, if a program was working out the cooking time for a bowl of soup and the user entered 10 servings rather than 1, the program would set the cooking time to be far too long (and probably burn down the kitchen in the process). In that situation, you can blame the user (because he put in the wrong data), but there should probably also be a test in the program that checks to see whether the value entered was sensible. If the cooker can't actually hold more than three servings, it would seem sensible to perform a test that limits the input to three. When you write a program, you need to anticipate what the user might do and create decisions that make your program behave sensibly in each situation.

6

Repeating actions with loops

What you will learn

In this chapter, you'll learn another step in how to control what a program does. Until now, we've written programs that run once and then stop when they're complete. But you often need to make a program repeat a sequence of actions. For example, if a user enters an invalid value, you want the program to reject that value and repeat the sequence to ask for another value. To repeat a series of actions, programs use what's known as a *loop*. In a video game, for example, the "game loop" continuously reads the positions of the game controllers, updates the variables that reflect the status of the players and the game world, and then draws the game world on the screen. In this chapter, you'll discover the C# constructions that you can use to create loops.

Using a loop to make a pizza picker

The Pizza Picker will be the first program we make that we can actually think about selling to the public. You can use it when a group you're with wants to order some pizzas. With this program, a user presses a button to select a piece of pizza with a particular topping. The program keeps count of how often each button is pressed and displays the totals on request. This program will also work on a Windows Mobile device, so you could pass your device around and get each person to tap the button that identifies the topping he or she wants. **Figure 6-1** shows what the program's main menu will look like.

Select Pizza

Cheese and Tomato
Pepperoni
Chicken
Vegetarian
Show Totals

Figure 6-1 The Pizza Picker app.

Each time a user presses a button, the count for that type of topping is increased. Then, the user can press the **Show Totals** button to see how many portions for each topping have been ordered. We'll build the Pizza Picker program in two stages. We'll start by writing the code that counts one pizza-topping selection. After that, we'll add a loop so that the program can accept multiple selections. As we build the program, you'll get a chance to use some of the C# constructions you've learned about in earlier chapters.

Counting selections

If you think about it, the Pizza Picker's menu shown in **Figure 6-1** tells us the first thing we need to do in this program. We need a variable for each pizza topping that counts the number of requests for that topping. The following statements create four `int` variables, with sensibly named identifiers, and set each of the variables to the value 0.

```
int cheeseAndTomatoCount = 0;
int pepperoniCount = 0;
```

```
int chickenCount = 0;
int vegetarianCount = 0;
```

Each time a topping is selected, the count for that particular topping must increase by one. The following statement increases the value in the counter for pepperoni pizza:

```
pepperoniCount = pepperoniCount + 1;
```

If this code looks a bit confusing, remember that when the program obeys this statement, it works out the value on the right side of the equal sign and assigns this result to the variable on the left side. Adding 1 to the value of a variable, which is what this statement does, is a behavior that's called an *increment* operation.

At this point, we have code that stores pizza selections and increments them when someone makes a choice. Next we need a way to display the buttons and determine which topping a user has selected. This part of the program is easy to create thanks to the Snaps button-selection methods that you used in Chapter 5 for the funfair ride application. Here's the statement that creates the pizza-picker menu by using the `SelectFrom5Buttons` method:

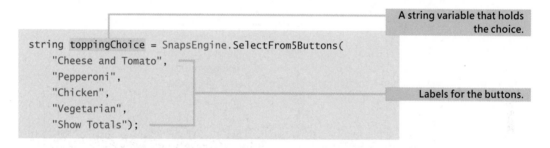

```
string toppingChoice = SnapsEngine.SelectFrom5Buttons(
    "Cheese and Tomato",
    "Pepperoni",
    "Chicken",
    "Vegetarian",
    "Show Totals");
```

A string variable that holds the choice.

Labels for the buttons.

Remember that the `SelectFrom5Buttons` method displays five buttons and waits for the user to select one of them. When the user selects a button, the method returns the string that refers to that button as the result. We can use an `if` construction to test the result and then increment the selected topping choice. The following statement increments the counter for pepperoni when the user chooses that button:

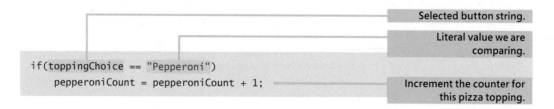

```
if(toppingChoice == "Pepperoni")
    pepperoniCount = pepperoniCount + 1;
```

Selected button string.

Literal value we are comparing.

Increment the counter for this pizza topping.

Bug swatting

The Pizza Picker program needs an `if` statement to test for each topping type. If I asked you to write this program, you might write the first statement, like the preceding one, and then copy that block of code to set up the other condition tests. However, copying blocks of code like this can be dangerous. Take a look at this code:

```
if (toppingChoice == "Cheese and Tomato")
    cheeseAndTomatoCount = cheeseAndTomatoCount + 1;

if (toppingChoice == "Pepperoni")
    pepperoniCount = pepperoniCount + 1;

if (toppingChoice == "Chicken")
    chickenCount = chickenCount + 1;

if (toppingChoice == "Vegetarian")
    vegetarianCount = chickenCount + 1;
```

The programmer who wrote this code is very proud of how quickly he managed to write the program, but it has a serious problem—it contains a *bug*, which means that users will hate it. A bug is something in a program that makes it do the wrong thing. (One story is that the first time the term "bug" was used, an insect had flown into the circuitry of an early computer and caused it to fail. The programmer dutifully wrote in her laboratory log book that she'd found a bug in the program, and the name stuck.)

Question: Can you find the bug?

> **Answer:** The bug is in the very last statement. Rather than incrementing the vegetarian counter, the program sets this variable to the number of chicken pizzas plus 1. Depending on who you are with, this could mean that you get a lot more or a lot fewer vegetarian pizzas than you expected.

Question: How would you find the bug?

> **Answer:** The only way to spot this bug is to methodically work through the options and check the counter values each time you add to one of them. If you never add a vegetarian pizza during testing, you'll never know that the program contains a bug. This is another cause of many bugs: the programmer knows exactly what the code is supposed to do, but he made a typing mistake when he entered the code. But since he knows exactly what the code is supposed to do, he assumes that the code is perfect and doesn't bother testing all the possibilities.

Displaying the totals

We've got the Pizza Picker program to the point that it can update the counter values for each pizza topping. Now we need a way to display the totals. The user will request this action by selecting the **Show Totals** button rather than a pizza topping.

When the user selects **Show Totals**, we want the program to display the current count for each of the pizza toppings. To do this, we'll use a couple of other Snaps methods that allow you to build up a display line by line. We'll use the Snaps method named ClearTextDisplay to clear the text display area and the AddLineToTextDisplay method to add another line to the display. Here's the code:

```
if (toppingChoice == "Show Totals")                        If the Show Totals option is selected.
{
    SnapsEngine.ClearTextDisplay();                        Clear the text display.

    SnapsEngine.AddLineToTextDisplay("Order Totals");      Add a heading.
    SnapsEngine.AddLineToTextDisplay(cheeseAndTomatoCount.ToString() +
        " Cheese and Tomato");                             Add the cheese and tomato count.
    SnapsEngine.AddLineToTextDisplay(pepperoniCount.ToString() + " Pepperoni");
    SnapsEngine.AddLineToTextDisplay(chickenCount.ToString() + " Chicken");
    SnapsEngine.AddLineToTextDisplay(vegetarianCount.ToString() + " Vegetarian");
}
```

Getting user options

There are two things that a user can do after she has read the current totals. She can continue to accept and count topping choices, or she can reset the counters to 0 for the next time she needs to run the program. We can create these options by displaying two buttons under the totals display, as you can see in **Figure 6-2**.

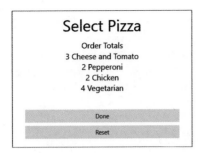

Select Pizza

Order Totals
3 Cheese and Tomato
2 Pepperoni
2 Chicken
4 Vegetarian

Done

Reset

Figure 6-2 The Done and Reset buttons provide options for the program's users.

The user can press the **Done** button when she has viewed the total counts and wants to return to entering topping choices. The **Reset** button is used to reset the count values to 0. You can use the following code to do this—and by now, most of it should be familiar:

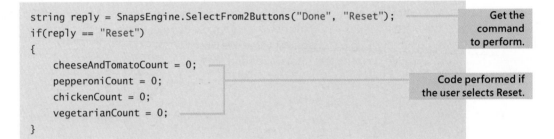

```
string reply = SnapsEngine.SelectFrom2Buttons("Done", "Reset");
if(reply == "Reset")
{
    cheeseAndTomatoCount = 0;
    pepperoniCount = 0;
    chickenCount = 0;
    vegetarianCount = 0;
}
```

Get the command to perform.

Code performed if the user selects Reset.

Remember that the Snaps library has button-selection methods for two to six buttons. This code uses the two-button version. With the Snaps library, these buttons are always displayed underneath any text, so the screen appears as you see it in **Figure 6-2**.

At this point, the user has viewed the total values and can use the **Reset** button to set the counters back to 0. Here's all the code that runs when the user selects the **Show Totals** option from the menu. As you read it, consider what the program needs to do when the user asks for the totals to be displayed:

- Display the totals

- Find out whether the user wants to clear the totals

- Reset the totals if requested

- Clear the display of the totals from the screen

```
if (toppingChoice == "Show Totals")
{
    SnapsEngine.ClearTextDisplay();

    SnapsEngine.AddLineToTextDisplay("Order Totals");
    SnapsEngine.AddLineToTextDisplay(cheeseAndTomatoCount.ToString() +
        " Cheese and Tomato");
    SnapsEngine.AddLineToTextDisplay(pepperoniCount.ToString() + " Pepperoni");
    SnapsEngine.AddLineToTextDisplay(chickenCount.ToString() + " Chicken");
    SnapsEngine.AddLineToTextDisplay(vegetarianCount.ToString() + " Vegetarian");

    string reply = SnapsEngine.SelectFrom2Buttons("Done", "Reset");

    if (reply == "Reset")
    {
        cheeseAndTomatoCount = 0;
        pepperoniCount = 0;
        chickenCount = 0;
        vegetarianCount = 0;
    }
    SnapsEngine.ClearTextDisplay();
}
```

Back at the start of this book, I said that programming was about organization more than anything else, and I compared writing a program to planning a party. What we have written with this code is very similar to party planning. If you were organizing a party, you would be sure that everything happened in the right sequence. You would not serve the food until everyone had arrived. And you'd hand out the thank-you gifts just as the guests were leaving.

In the same way, the sequence in our code clears the totals after the user has read them, and not before. And it clears the totals only if it is asked to. If you are not clear how to write a program to solve a problem, the best way to start is by writing down the actions that need to be performed, in the order they must happen. You can do this in your own language first and then "debug" the sequence by working through it to make sure it makes sense. Then you can take the description of your solution and create the C# statements that will tell the computer how to solve the problem.

Add some comments

You saw in Chapter 5 how to add comments to a program. Up until now in the Pizza Picker program, I've not added any comments to the code because the variable names are clear and the flow of the code is easy to follow. But we've arrived at a point where adding a comment would be a really good idea. Consider this statement:

```
SnapsEngine.ClearTextDisplay();
```

A programmer reading through the code might take a look at this statement and be a bit confused. What is the point of displaying nothing on the screen? Help other programmers understand the purpose of this statement by adding a comment. You might do something like this:

```
// Clear the total display from the screen, ready for the more choices
SnapsEngine.ClearTextDisplay ();
```

Now programmers can understand that you are clearing text from the screen to prepare for more choices.

Adding a `while` loop

The Pizza Picker program now has the behaviors it needs to process a single button press and select a pizza topping for one person. However, the statements we've written must be repeated for each person who wants to select a topping. We can achieve this by adding a loop construction to the program.

The C# language provides several ways of creating loops. The first one we are going to look at is the `while` loop, which is constructed as shown in **Figure 6-3**. In a `while` loop, a statement is repeated while the condition specified by a logical expression is true.

Figure 6-3 The structure of a `while` loop.

You could use a `while` loop to make a really annoying program. Here's a program that repeatedly says "Rob will rule the world" until the user gets bored with it and stops it. Remember that in this context, `true` means a logical value that is always true.

```
while (true)                                          Logical expression controlling the loop.
    SnapsEngine.SpeakString("Rob will rule the world");      Statement controlled
                                                                by the loop.
```

Or you could just as easily write the following:

```
while (1==1)
    SnapsEngine.SpeakString("Rob will rule the world");
```

This `while` loop will also run forever. The conditional expression that controls it is always true because 1 is equal to 1.

In a C# program, you can put a block of statements everywhere you can put a single statement. If you want the program to repeat more than one inspiring message, you can use the `while` construction to repeat a block of statements. Here, both statements in the block will be repeated by the `while` loop:

```
while (1==1)
{
    SnapsEngine.SpeakString("Rob will rule the world");
    SnapsEngine.SpeakString("Oh yes he will");
}
```

CODE ANALYSIS

Looking at loops

You can learn more about loops by considering what the following bits of program code would do:

```
while (false)
    SnapsEngine.SpeakString("Rob will not rule the world");
```

Question: Would this code speak the message? How many times would it speak it?

Answer: The loop is controlled by the Boolean expression given after the `while` keyword. (The statement controlled by the loop is obeyed *while* the condition is true.) Since this condition is false at the start, the statement in the loop is never performed, so the code will never speak the message.

```
bool flag = true;
while(flag)
{
    SnapsEngine.SpeakString("Hello again");
    flag = false;
}
```

Question: How about this code? Would it speak the message? If so, how many times would it speak it?

Answer: This code is completely legal and would compile just fine. The quick answer to this question is that the program would say the message only once. But work through the statements one by one to understand why. To make this easier, I've added line numbers to this listing. (I'll follow this practice from time to time to help you understand what each lines does as the program runs.)

```
1   bool flag = true;
2   while(flag)
3   {
4       SnapsEngine.SpeakString("Hello again");
5       flag = false;
6   }
```

- Line 1 creates a Boolean variable called `flag` and sets the value of `flag` to `true`.

- Line 2 starts the `while` loop. The keyword `while` is followed by the logical expression that will be tested before the loop is repeated. If this expression has the value `true`, the code in the body of the loop will be performed.

- Line 3 is the curly bracket that marks the start of the block that is controlled by the `while` loop. Because `flag` is true, the `while` loop performs the loop statement, so it moves to line 4.

- The statement at line 4 speaks the message "Hello again," and then the program moves to line 5.

- Line 5 is an assignment that sets the value of the `flag` variable to `false`.

- Line 6 is the curly bracket that marks the end of the block controlled by the `while` loop. At the end of this block, the program loops back to line 2, which is the `while` construction controlling the loop.

- At line 2, the `while` loop tests the value of `flag`. Remember that the body of the loop is performed only if the test is true. Because the `flag` variable now has the value `false` (set at the statement at line 5), the loop is not performed any more.

Question: Here's some code that looks similar to the previous example, but it uses an integer rather than a Boolean variable. What does it do?

```
1   int count = 0;
2   while(count < 10)
3   {
4       SnapsEngine.SpeakString("tick");
5       count = count + 1;
6   }
```

Answer: I've numbered the lines again so that you can work it out for yourself. Remember that the less than (<) logical operator means that a logical expression is true if the value on the left (in this case, the variable `count`) is less than the value on the right (in this case 10). This means that the loop will repeat while the value in the `count` variable is less than 10.

A loop in the pizza picker

Let's add a `while` loop to the Pizza Picker to make the program repeatedly ask for toppings and display totals when requested. Here is the code for the complete Pizza Picker program. Note that I've used the simplest form of loop construction here because we simply want the program to repeatedly ask for pizza selections. The user will quit the program when she wants to do something different.

```
using SnapsLibrary;

class Ch06_01_PizzaPicker
{
    public void StartProgram()
    {
        SnapsEngine.SetTitleString("Select Pizza");

        int cheeseAndTomatoCount = 0;
```

```
int pepperoniCount = 0;
int chickenCount = 0;
int vegetarianCount = 0;

// repeatedly ask for pizza selections
while (true)
{
    string toppingChoice = SnapsEngine.SelectFrom5Buttons(
        "Cheese and Tomato",
        "Pepperoni",
        "Chicken",
        "Vegetarian",
        "Show Totals");

    if (toppingChoice == "Cheese and Tomato")
        cheeseAndTomatoCount = cheeseAndTomatoCount + 1;

    if (toppingChoice == "Pepperoni")
        pepperoniCount = pepperoniCount + 1;

    if (toppingChoice == "Chicken")
        chickenCount = chickenCount + 1;

    if (toppingChoice == "Vegetarian")
        vegetarianCount = vegetarianCount + 1;

    if (toppingChoice == "Show Totals")
    {
        SnapsEngine.ClearTextDisplay();

        SnapsEngine.AddLineToTextDisplay("Order Totals");
        SnapsEngine.AddLineToTextDisplay(cheeseAndTomatoCount.ToString() +
            " Cheese and Tomato");
        SnapsEngine.AddLineToTextDisplay(pepperoniCount.ToString() +
            " Pepperoni");
        SnapsEngine.AddLineToTextDisplay(chickenCount.ToString() +
            " Chicken");
        SnapsEngine.AddLineToTextDisplay(vegetarianCount.ToString() +
            " Vegetarian");

        string reply = SnapsEngine.SelectFrom2Buttons(item1: "Done",
            item2: "Reset");
```

```
            if (reply == "Reset")
            {
                cheeseAndTomatoCount = 0;
                pepperoniCount = 0;
                chickenCount = 0;
                vegetarianCount = 0;
            }
            // clear the total display from the screen ready for more choices
            SnapsEngine.ClearTextDisplay();
        }
    }
}
```

PROGRAMMER'S POINT

The same code can have lots of uses

You can use the basic logic of the Pizza Picker program in lots of different situations. You could count votes at a school council meeting, count the number of people who come to your party, or let the audience pick the winners at a talent show. All you have to do is change the text strings in the program, and you can use it for just about anything. When you get asked to write a program, try to remember whether you have ever written anything that does the same kind of thing.

MAKE SOMETHING HAPPEN

Doing more with Snaps and loops

The Pizza Picker works fine, but at the moment it's a bit boring, as it just has a plain display. You can make it much more interesting by adding an image of a pizza as a background for the display. See if you can use the DisplayBackground method in the Snaps library to liven up the program. You can take a picture of your favorite pizza with your phone, extract the image, and add it to your program. (Look back at the example in Chapter 5 to tell you how to do this).

One thing to remember though: you need to be sure that your program is both good looking and still useable, so be sure that the color scheme of your background doesn't interfere with the display. You can change the color of the text and the program title if you want to get really artistic.

You could also make the program calculate how many pizzas of each type to order. If you work on the basis of one pizza for every two people, it is a simple calculation to convert the number of orders into the number of pizzas that are to be ordered. However, remember that it is not possible to order less than one pizza, and your program must behave sensibly if only one person in the group orders a particular type.

You could also use speech output to make the program comment on choices people make. By putting conditions in (by using `if` statements), you could make the program say things like, "So, you all like vegetarian pizza" or "Chicken wins" as the program is being used.

Here are some other ideas to try out:

- The funfair ride age checker we created in Chapter 5 would benefit from a loop construction. At the moment, the user has to run the program each time he wants to use it. You could add a `while` loop so that the program repeatedly asks for ride selections and requests ages.

- A neighbor of yours wants to open a diner for truck drivers. He is doing research on the traffic in the area because he wants to know how many trucks pass his site each day. He wants a way of counting cars, vans, trucks, and bikes as they go past, and wants to simply press a button for each different kind of vehicle that he sees go by. Write a program that will do this for him. You can use the Pizza Picker as a starting point for the code.

- Your fame is spreading, and another friend of yours wants your help. She works at the local observation tower as a guide. She has to make sure that no more than 10 people at a time get into the elevator to the top of the tower. She wants a program that she can run to count people as they enter the elevator. The program should display the count for each person in turn, and when 8 people are in the elevator, the program should say "Room for two more"; when 10 people are in the elevator, the program should say "Elevator full, enjoy your trip up." Provide a Reset button your friend can use to clear the count, set it back to 0, and start with the next set of passengers. Here, too, you can use the Pizza Picker program as a starting point, but you will need to add some extra logic to speak the messages. Remember that you can use an `if` condition in the loop to determine when your program should speak a message.

WHAT COULD GO WRONG

Never-ending loops

The never-ending loop in the Pizza Picker program is perfectly correct. It would be a problem for the user if the loop stopped repeating because this would prevent the program from accepting input. However, consider the following loop:

```
while (true)
{
}
```

This is completely legal C# that is also highly dangerous. It does nothing, repeatedly. You might think that the computer would be clever enough to work out that the loop does nothing, and therefore ignore it, but this is unfortunately not the case. What would happen here is that the computer would try to run this code as fast as it can. If this code ran on a desktop PC, you would find that the processor usage would go up (and maybe the fans would start running after a few seconds). If this code ran on a mobile device, you would find that the case would warm up and the battery would start to drain very quickly. It is interesting to note that this kind of code has actually been used to create "hand-warmer" apps for some mobile phones. These programs don't actually do anything useful, but they do make the phone get nice and warm to the touch, at least for a short while, until the battery goes flat.

As you learn to program, you will probably make this kind of mistake a few times and create programs that never stop. Remember that in Visual Studio, you can use the stop button to end a program that gets stuck in this way.

Performing input validation with a **while** loop

Let's look again at the format of one of the loop constructions we examined earlier:

```
while (false)
    SnapsEngine.SpeakString("Rob will rule the world");
```

This statement performs the test for the loop's condition at the start of the loop. This code will not speak the message because the logical expression that controls the loop is explicitly set to the value false, and this value is tested before the code in the loop is obeyed.

Sometimes, however, you need a loop construction that performs the test at the end of the code in the loop rather than at the beginning. C# also provides a loop construction that will do this:

```
do {
    SnapsEngine.SpeakString("Rob will rule the world");
} while (false);
```

Block controlled by the loop.
Logical expression.

This is a slightly different arrangement of the while construction. Here, the test is performed after the code in the block has been obeyed. This code would speak the message "Rob will rule the world" even though the value of the expression controlling the loop is set to false. However, the loop would speak the message only once because the value false means that the loop would not be repeated again.

This form of a while loop can be used when a program needs to validate input. Validation is a big part of building a program. It is how you ensure that a program never does anything that's not smart. When you design a program, you need to think about the valid range that a value can have. For example, if you are asking for the age of a user, you might accept ages in the range 1 to 100 as valid.

This type of loop is useful when you need to get a value from the user before you can decide whether the value is valid or not. You can design the program so that it loops around if the value entered by the user is not valid—in other words, the program will repeatedly ask for a value until the user gives one that is valid. Here's an example that shows how this works. Remember that if the age entered is less than 1 or greater than 100, the input must be rejected and the program must ask for the age value again.

```
1  int age;
2  do
3  {
4      age = SnapsEngine.ReadInteger("Enter your age");
5  } while (age < 1 | age > 100);
```

The best way to work out what is going on here is to work through the statements as a computer would.

- At line 1, the program creates an integer variable called age. This variable will hold the value that the program gets from the user.

- Line 2 marks the start of the loop.

- Line 3 is the open curly bracket that marks the start of the block of code that is controlled by the loop. This loop contains only one statement, but I've added the brackets to show that you could run many statements in the loop's body.

- Line 4 contains the statement that reads in the age entered by the user.

- If the number is read successfully, the program moves to the end of the `while` construction, at line 5. The `while` keyword is followed by a logical expression that will evaluate to true or false depending on the value in the `age` variable. If `age` is less than 1 or greater than 100, the expression will be true, which will cause the loop to repeat. This turns out to be exactly what we want—we want the program to keep asking for age values until a valid one is entered.

It is worth reading through this description very carefully to be sure that you understand what is going on. Remember that here the code controlled by the loop is always performed at least once because the repeat condition appears at the end of the loop. This makes perfect sense because we need to have a value before we can test it. This also means that the condition in the loop must evaluate to `true` if the value is not valid so that the loop will go around again.

Using Visual Studio to follow the execution of your programs

You can check your programs by working through them on your own, one line at a time, as we've done a couple of times already. But you can also use Visual Studio to view the actions of a program as it runs. To do this, you use the Visual Studio *debugger*. As the name implies, the debugger is a tool that helps you find and remove bugs from your programs. You can use a debugger to track the path that your program is actually following, rather than the one that you think it is following.

Adding breakpoints

We'll start by adding a breakpoint to our program. A breakpoint doesn't cause the program to break; it causes the program to "take a break." When a program reaches a statement designated as a breakpoint, Visual Studio pauses the program and hands control back to the programmer, who can then check that each variable has the content that it should have.

A program can contain many breakpoints. The first breakpoint that the program reaches is the one that will pause the program. You can even set and remove breakpoints as the program itself is running. You can create a breakpoint in any of your code or in any of the samples that are part of the BeginToCodeWithCSharp solution.

We'll use a breakpoint to investigate the behavior of the loop that we just worked through. You can find the code we've been looking at in the file

Ch06_02_AgeReader. Locate that file by using Solution Explorer, and then open it in Visual Studio, as shown in **Figure 6-4**. You set a breakpoint by clicking in the margin at the left of the statement where you want the program to pause.

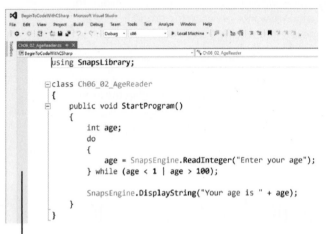

Click here to add a breakpoint

Figure 6-4 Add a breakpoint in the margin to the left of a statement.

Breakpoints are represented by a red circle on the left of the page, and the statement containing the breakpoint is highlighted in brown. You can't put a breakpoint on the declaration of the age variable or the do keyword that starts the loop. Here, I've put a breakpoint on the while part of the loop, as shown in **Figure 6-5**.

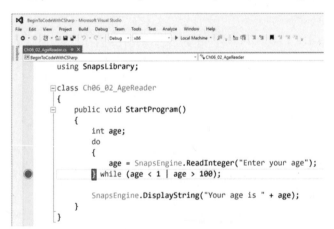

Figure 6-5 Setting a breakpoint.

Hitting a breakpoint

To start debugging, run the BeginToCodeWithCSharp solution as usual, select the **Ch06_02_AgeReader** demo application, and select **Run an app**. The program will ask for your age. Then, when the program reaches the breakpoint, Visual Studio will pause the program and wait for a command from you. **Figure 6-6** shows what you see when a breakpoint is reached. Note that the statement at the breakpoint has not been obeyed yet.

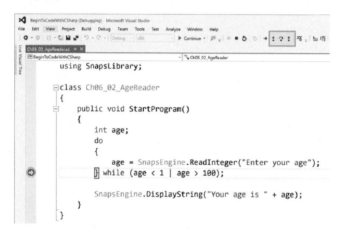

Figure 6-6 Hitting a breakpoint.

Viewing the contents of variables in the program

You can view the contents of a variable by resting the pointer over the variable's name. **Figure 6-7** shows the content of the age variable after I entered a rather optimistic value. The display is removed if you move your pointer away from the variable. If you want the age value to remain visible, click the pushpin to the right of the displayed value.

Figure 6-7 Viewing the age value.

Stepping through program statements

When a program is paused, you can tell Visual Studio to step through the program's statements by using a set of buttons that control this activity. These buttons appear on the Visual Studio toolbar only when the program is paused. I've identified them in **Figure 6-8**, along with the function key assigned to them. (You can press the function key instead of clicking the button.)

Step into method (F11)
Step over a method (F10)
Step out of a method (Shift+F11)

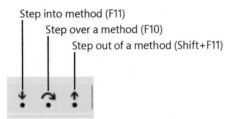

Figure 6-8 Use these buttons to step through a program in Visual Studio.

If you select **Step into a method** or press F11 when the program is paused at a statement that is about to call a method, Visual Studio will open the file that contains that method and navigate to the statements inside that method. Doing this is useful if you want to investigate the contents of methods that your program is using. We'll cover exactly what a method is in Chapter 8, but for now consider the ReadInteger method. It contains code that returns an integer. If we want to step through each statement in the ReadInteger method, we can press F11 to enter it. When you want to leave a method that you are stepping through and return to the one that called it, you can use the **Step out of a method** button (or hold Shift and Press F11).

The most useful button at the moment is **Step over a method** (F10). This command lets you step through the program and follow the path of execution. Each time you enter this command, Visual Studio performs one statement and then pauses the program again. In our program, what happens when you perform a step depends on the value of age. If you entered a valid age (one in the range 1 to 100), the loop will end and the program will move on to the call of DisplayString. If you entered an invalid age, the program will loop around again.

Continuing the program

When you want to stop stepping through a program and run it normally, press the **Continue** button (or F5) to resume. The program will stop at the next breakpoint it reaches (if it finds one). Visual Studio also has a breakpoint window that you can use to see the breakpoints you have created. You can display this window by going to the **Debug, Windows** menu in Visual Studio and selecting the **Breakpoints** option. You can do some very interesting things with breakpoints. For example, you can make them take effect only when certain conditions are true (so that you make the program break only when age is invalid). I'll let you find out more about how to do this on your own. For now, use breakpoints and single stepping to get a feel for how a program executes.

Design your code for debugging

Single stepping through code is a great way to find out what it is doing. When you write code, it's useful to design it so that you can easily step through it and find out what's going on. I am a great believer in spreading my code over a number of statements and even using extra temporary variables when it runs. This makes debugging easier and doesn't cost your program more memory since in the "smaller" version of the code above, the compiler will still have to create some internal temporary variables to perform the calculation. The only difference with the "more efficient" version above is that you can't take a look at them.

CODE ANALYSIS

When good loops go bad

You can learn a bit more about how loops work by taking a look at another one. At first glance, the following code might seem identical to the previous code. And if you actually run this program, it seems to work fine. If you give a valid age, the program says thank you.

```
1  public static void StartProgram()
2  {
3      SnapsEngine.SetTitleString("Age between 1 and 100");
4      int age;
5      do
6      {
7          string ageString = SnapsEngine.ReadString("Enter your age");
8          age = int.Parse(ageString);
9      } while (age < 1 & age > 100);
10     SnapsEngine.DisplayString("Thank you for entering your age of " + age);
11 }
```

Ch06_02_BadAgeReader

Question: What is the fault in the program?

Answer: The fault is in line 9. We have seen this problem before. The logical expression used here is slightly different from the one used earlier. This expression says, "while age is less than one *and* age is greater than 100." When you read it out loud, it sounds silly. How can a number be less than one and greater than 100? No such value exists. But it turns out that the compiler is quite happy to compile a program that contains a mistake like this.

Question: What will the fault cause the program to do?

Answer: Since there is no number that is both less than 1 and greater than 100, this means that the expression controlling the `while` loop can never be true, which means that the loop will *never* repeat. In other words, it will regard every age value as a correct one. This is very dangerous because if you don't test the program with invalid values, you will never notice this problem.

WHAT COULD GO WRONG

Always test failure behaviors along with successful ones

This is a really important point to consider when you write software. You need to test the code you write that is supposed to deal with errors. Software engineers talk about the "happy path" through a program, where the user enters the right values, the network connection works, there's enough space on the disk drive, and the printer doesn't jam. When programmers write software, they tend to focus on this happy path without giving too much thought to the depressingly large number of ways that a program can go wrong. However, this is a dangerous way to write code. A great programmer will proactively look for things that can go wrong, build in the code to deal with the error conditions, and then—crucially—take the trouble to test that this code works.

In the case of the age-reading program we've been looking at, I'd insist on testing it with the ages 0,1,50,100, and 101. These values should let me be sure that the invalid ages (0 and 101) are rejected and that all the other ages (including the values on the boundaries) are accepted. In fact, I would find a way that I could test the code automatically so that I can perform the tests at regular intervals.

Counting in a loop to make a times-table tutor

The loop in the Pizza Picker program was the simplest kind of loop. It repeats forever because the logical expression that controls it is the Boolean value true. However, you can also make loops that repeat a particular number of times. This is achieved by using a variable to count the number of times the loop has been performed. The program can set the counter variable to a starting value, and each time around the loop, the variable can be updated until it reaches the limit, which causes the loop to stop.

You could use this kind of loop to create a times-table tutor to help you (or someone else) with multiplication, which can be one of the tedious parts of learning arithmetic. You could use the loop to make the program say, "One times two is two, two times two is four," and so on. Here is the entire program. It uses a while loop that produces each successive output as it runs.

```
using SnapsLibrary;

class Ch06_04_TalkingTimesTables
{
    public void StartProgram()
    {
        SnapsEngine.SetTitleString("Talking Times Tables");

        int count = 1;                                          Create a counter.
        int timesValue = 2;                                     Set the times value.

        while (count < 13)                                      Stop the loop at 13
        {
            int result = count * timesValue;                    Calculate the
                                                                result.

            string message = count.ToString() +
                " times " + timesValue.ToString() +
                " is " + result.ToString();                     Assemble the
                                                                message.

            SnapsEngine.DisplayString(message);
            SnapsEngine.SpeakString(message);

            count = count + 1;                                  Update the count.
        }
    }
}
```

There are two parts of this program that you really must understand. The first is the loop and the expression that controls it:

```
while(count < 13)
```

The `while` loop is controlled by a logical expression that becomes false when the value of the `count` variable reaches the value 13 (this is because the value 13 is not less than 13, it is equal to 13).

The second important part of the program is the assignment statement that updates the counter:

```
count = count + 1;
```

This is the same pattern we used to update the pizza-topping counters in the Pizza Picker. Each time this statement runs, it calculates the value of `count` plus 1 and then stores this in the variable `count`.

CODE ANALYSIS

Counter intelligence

Here is the times-table code with line numbers. Let's take a closer look:

```
 1   using SnapsLibrary;
 2
 3   class Ch06_04_TalkingTimesTables
 4   {
 5       public void StartProgram()
 6       {
 7           SnapsEngine.SetTitleString("Talking Times Tables");
 8
 9           int count = 1;
10
11           int timesValue = 2;
12
13           while (count < 13)
14           {
15               int result = count * timesValue;
16
```

```
17              string message = count.ToString() +
18                   " times " + timesValue.ToString() +
19                   " is " + result.ToString();
20
21              SnapsEngine.DisplayString(message);
22              SnapsEngine.SpeakString(message);
23
24              count = count + 1;
25          }
26      }
27  }
```

Question: Which statement would you have to change if you wanted to generate the times table for 3 instead of 2?

Answer: You would change the assignment statement at line 11. If you set the variable timesValue to 3, this will cause the times table to display multiples of 3.

Question: What would happen to the program if I changed the statement at line 24 to the following statement?

```
count = count - 1;
```

Answer: This statement makes the variable count smaller each time the statement is obeyed. The code in the times-table loop would calculate and display negative multiples, and the loop would never stop because the count variable would always be less than 13.

Question: What would I have to do if I wanted the program to produce another times table?

Answer: The best way to do this would be to put the entire program inside another loop. It is perfectly okay to nest one loop inside another. If you did this, you would have to add some code that would allow the user to restart the program; otherwise it would just carry on forever, which users might not like.

```
using SnapsLibrary;

class Ch06_05_RepeatingTimesTables
{
    public void StartProgram()
    {
        SnapsEngine.SetTitleString("Talking Times Tables");

        while (true)                        Outer loop that
        {                                   continues forever.
```

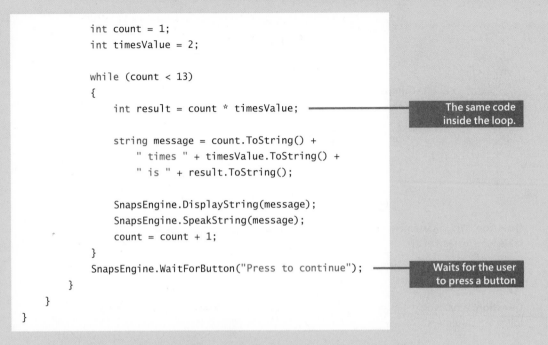

```
        int count = 1;
        int timesValue = 2;

        while (count < 13)
        {
            int result = count * timesValue;                    The same code
                                                                inside the loop.

            string message = count.ToString() +
                " times " + timesValue.ToString() +
                " is " + result.ToString();

            SnapsEngine.DisplayString(message);
            SnapsEngine.SpeakString(message);
            count = count + 1;
        }
        SnapsEngine.WaitForButton("Press to continue");         Waits for the user
    }                                                           to press a button
}
```

This version of the program uses an outer loop that never ends. The times-table loop is inside this loop. The code uses another Snaps method, `WaitForButton`, that waits for a button to be pressed. This allows the user to select when the times table is to be presented.

🚀 MAKE SOMETHING HAPPEN

Allow the user to select the times value

You can improve the times-table program to make one that asks the user what value to work with. You could allow the user to hear multiples of 25 if you like, or you could use validation so that the only times tables that can be produced are in the range 2 to 12.

Using a **for** loop construction

You have seen that you can manage perfectly well with `while` loop constructions. The times-table program works fine. However, the designers of C# decided to make it even easier to create loops that perform counting. To do this, they created a construction called the for loop. Its general structure is illustrated in **Figure 6-9**.

Figure 6-9 The structure of a for loop.

A for loop lets a programmer create the setup, test, and update elements of a repeating loop in a single statement. Each element of the loop is a C# statement.

- The setup element is performed once when the for loop is started

- The test element is performed before the execution of the loop. Just as in the while construction you saw earlier, the loop statement is performed only while the logical expression that is the test returns true.

- The update element is performed after each execution of the loop.

You could use this form of loop to make the times-table tutor program a lot simpler:

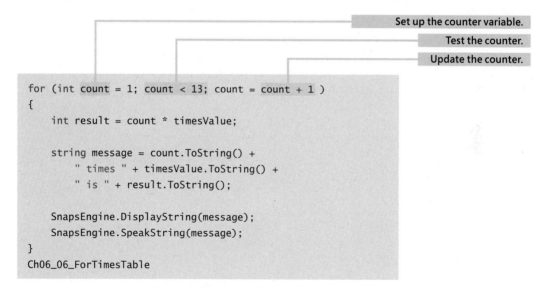

Set up the counter variable.
Test the counter.
Update the counter.

```
for (int count = 1; count < 13; count = count + 1 )
{
    int result = count * timesValue;

    string message = count.ToString() +
        " times " + timesValue.ToString() +
        " is " + result.ToString();

    SnapsEngine.DisplayString(message);
    SnapsEngine.SpeakString(message);
}
Ch06_06_ForTimesTable
```

The for loop at the top of this block does all the work that is spread over three statements in the previous version of the program. Any time that a program needs to repeat something a particular number of times, you should think about using a for loop.

For loops don't make anything new possible; they just make things easier

It turns out that we really need only one loop construction to write every program that has ever been written. The programs might be a bit longer and harder to understand, but they would work. The reason we have two different forms of the do loop and the for loop constructions is that they make writing programs easier. If you want to make a program count a particular number of times, a for loop is easier and quicker to write than a while loop. It is also more expressive, in that anyone seeing a for loop in your program will know exactly what you are trying to do. Later in the book, you will see other kinds of loops that you can use.

Unpacking loops

We can learn more about how for loops work by unpacking some loop designs.

Question: What does this program do?

```
for (int countdown = 10; countdown >= 0; countdown = countdown - 1 )
{
    SnapsEngine.SpeakString(countdown);
    SnapsEngine.Delay(1);
}
```

Answer: This program performs a 10-second countdown. It will speak the numbers 10, 9, 8, and so on over 10 seconds.

Question: Will this program speak the number zero?

Answer: Yes. The terminating condition (the condition that must be true for the for loop to continue) is countdown >= 0 (countdown greater than or equal to zero). When the counter has the value 0, the condition is still true, so the loop will continue working.

Question: How many times will the loop go around?

Answer: You might think that the answer is simple: 10. But you'd be wrong. The loop will go around 11 times. The first time around the loop, the value in countdown will be 10, and the last time around the loop, the value will be 0. If you write out the values, you can count them: 10,9,8,7,6,5,4,3,2,1,0. There are 11 values, so the loop must go around 11 times. You need to be very careful when designing loops that you make sure that you check that the terminating condition makes the loop stop at the right time. The first time I wrote this loop, I used the end condition `countdown > 0`, and I was confused as to why the program did not speak the value zero.

Breaking out of loops

Sometimes you'll need your program to escape from a loop while you are in the middle of it—in other words, your program might decide that there is no need or point to going on and want to leap out of the loop and continue the program from the statement after it.

You can do this with the `break` statement, which is a command to the program to leave the loop immediately. Your program will usually make some kind of decision before quitting in this way. I find the `break` statement useful when I need to provide a "get the heck out of here" option in the middle of something.

As an example, suppose we want to let a user stop the times-table tutor in the middle of its operation. It could be annoying for the user if there is no way to stop the program once it has started. To do this, we can use a Snaps method, named `ScreenHas-BeenTapped`, that lets a program detect when the user taps on a touchscreen or clicks on the screen with a mouse.

```
if (SnapsEngine.ScreenHasBeenTapped())
    // statement that we perform if the screen has been tapped
```

The ScreenHasBeenTapped method returns true if the screen has been tapped. The Snaps framework maintains a *flag* (a type of indicator) that is set when the framework detects that the screen has been tapped. If you want your program to detect a further screen-tap event, the program must call ClearScreenTappedFlag to clear the flag and be ready for the next tap.

```
SnapsEngine.ClearScreenTappedFlag();
```

The flag is cleared by a call of ClearScreenTappedFlag and will be set again when the screen is tapped again. You can use these Snaps methods along with the break keyword to allow the user of the times-table program to tap the screen to stop the program from producing output. Here is the code:

```
using SnapsLibrary;

class Ch06_07_TapScreenToStop
{
    public void StartProgram()
    {
        SnapsEngine.SetTitleString("Talking Times Tables");

        while (true)
        {
            int timesValue = 2;

            // Make sure that the screen tapped flag is clear
            SnapsEngine.ClearScreenTappedFlag();

            for (int count = 1; count < 13; count = count + 1)
            {

                int result = count * timesValue;

                string message = count.ToString() +
                    " times " + timesValue.ToString() +
                    " is " + result.ToString();

                SnapsEngine.DisplayString(message);
                SnapsEngine.SpeakString(message);
```

Clear the tapped flag and make it ready for use.

```
            // If the screen is tapped, break out of the for loop
            if (SnapsEngine.ScreenHasBeenTapped())
                break;
        }
        SnapsEngine.WaitForButton("Press to continue");
      }
    }
}
```

Test the flag, and exit the loop if the screen has been tapped.

This version of the times-table tutor displays and speaks the times table for 2 from 1 to 12. If the user taps the screen while the program is running, the program breaks out of the inner for loop and goes to the next statement after it—in this case, the statement that calls the WaitForButton method.

A program can break out of any of these loops. In every case, the program continues running at the statement after the last statement in the loop. If the loop is inside another loop (as with this example), the break takes the program out of only one loop. In other words, obeying the break statement inside the for loop that is speaking the times table does not cause the program to exit the outer while loop, just the inner for loop.

Going back to the top of a loop by using **continue**

Every now and then you will write a program that needs to go back to the top of a loop and run the loop again. You'll do this when you have gone through the statements as much as you need to for a particular pass around the loop. To perform this operation, C# provides the continue keyword, which says something along the lines of "Please do not go any further this time around the loop. Go back to the top of the loop, do all the updating and other work (if there is any), and then go around again if you are supposed to."

As an example, imagine that a user of the times-table program has a thing about the number 4. They don't know why, but they don't want to hear the program announce the times-table value for that number. We can use the continue keyword to control this behavior.

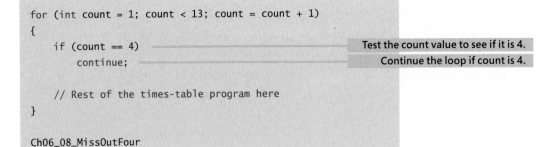

```
for (int count = 1; count < 13; count = count + 1)
{
    if (count == 4)                    ──── Test the count value to see if it is 4.
        continue;                      ──── Continue the loop if count is 4.


    // Rest of the times-table program here
}
```

Ch06_08_MissOutFour

The effect of the `continue` keyword is to send the program back to the top of the loop, increment the count value to make it 5, test the end condition (the loop will continue because `count` is less than 13), and then go around again. If you run the program, you will see that the times-table announcement for the value 4 is omitted.

PROGRAMMER'S POINT

You don't use `continue` as often as you use `break`

There are quite a few situations in programs where the `break` keyword is useful. However, the `continue` keyword is used much less frequently. Don't feel like you aren't a proper programmer if you don't find yourself using `continue` very often.

CODE ANALYSIS

Loops, break, and continue

You can improve your understanding of the way that `break` and `continue` are used by taking a look at a couple of simple programs.

```
1  for (int count = 1; count < 13; count = count + 1)
2  {
3      if (count == 5)
4          break;
5        SnapsEngine.SpeakString(count.ToString());
6  }
7  SnapsEngine.SpeakString("Done");
```

Question: What would this code actually say?

Answer: It would say "1,2,3,4" and then "Done." When the value of count reaches 5, the logical expression in the `if` condition at line 3 becomes `true` (because count is now equal to 5). The `break` statement would cause the program to exit the loop immediately and continue running the program at line 7. The program would not speak the value 5 because it breaks out before it reaches the `SpeakString` method that speaks that value.

```
1 | for (int count = 1; count < 13; count = count + 1)
2 | {
3 |     if (count == 5)
4 |         continue;
5 |     SnapsEngine.SpeakString(count.ToString());
6 | }
```

Question: What would this code say?

Answer: It would say "1,2,3,4,6,7,8,9,10,11,12". Note that it would not say "5" because when the value of count is 5, the conditional statement at line 3 will cause the program to continue back at the start of the loop, which means that the `SpeakString` method is not called for the value 5.

```
1 | while (true)
2 | {
3 |     break;
4 |     SnapsEngine.SpeakString("Looping");
5 | }
```

Question: Would this program run forever?

Answer: No. It is true that the logical expression controlling the loop is set to `true`, which means always repeat the loop, but the content of the loop body contains a `break` statement that would cause the loop to exit.

Question: Would this program say the message "Looping"?

Answer: No. This statement is never reached because the program breaks out of the loop first.

```
1 | while (true)
2 | {
3 |     continue;
4 |     SnapsEngine.SpeakString("Looping");
5 | }
```

Question: Would this program run forever?

> **Answer:** Yes. The `continue` keyword does not cause a loop to end. Instead, it causes the end condition to be tested, and the loop repeats if the condition is found to be true.

Question: Would this program say the message "Looping"?

> **Answer:** No. This statement is never reached because the program continues back to the top of the loop first.

Extra Snaps

Here are a couple of extra snaps that you might find useful as you write more programs of your own.

Voice input

The Snaps framework provides a set of methods that you can use to make your programs respond to voice input. They work in a similar way to the button-selection methods you have already seen. The only difference is an additional string that is provided as a prompt displayed to the user. In the following code, I've used voice input to get a pizza choice from the user. (Here I have used named arguments in the call of the `SelectFromFiveSpokenPhrases` method. You'll learn more about using named arguments in Chapter 8. In this code, the named arguments make it easy to tell the difference between the prompt and the phrases to be used.)

```
string toppingChoice = SnapsEngine.SelectFromFiveSpokenPhrases(
        prompt: "What pizza topping do you want",
        phrase1: "Cheese and Tomato",
        phrase2: "Pepperoni",
        phrase3: "Chicken",
        phrase4: "Vegetarian",
        phrase5: "Show Totals");

Ch06_09_VoicePizzaPicker
```

When this program runs, it displays the Windows 10 voice-input panel, shown in **Figure 6-10.**

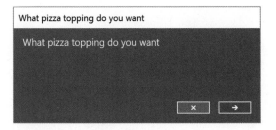

Figure 6-10 Voice-input panel.

The voice-input methods return the phrase that was detected, but if the user doesn't say anything recognizable or presses the Cancel button on the dialog box, the method returns an empty string.

The following code checks to see whether the pizza topping was recognized. If it was not, and the result returned was an empty string, the program tells the user that the choice was not recognized and then uses the `continue` keyword to continue looping and get a pizza choice.

```
if (toppingChoice == "")
{
    SnapsEngine.SpeakString("Sorry, choice not recognized");
    continue;
}
```

I've included versions of the voice-input method that you can use to select between two and six phrases. You can use these methods to make voice-controlled versions of many of the applications we have already built. You could make a voice-controlled egg timer in which the user speaks the delay required. You could also change the funfair ride programs to work with voice response, or you could make a completely new voice-controlled program.

Secret data entry

The Snaps `ReadString` method lets a program read a string, but anyone able to watch the program will be able to see what is being entered. The `ReadPassword` method is used in exactly the same way as `ReadString`, but the characters are replaced with dots as they are typed. This statement sets the string `password` to a secret password entered by the user.

```
string password = SnapsEngine.ReadPassword("Enter your secret password");
```

You can use the ReadPassword method to make password-protected versions of your apps.

What you have learned

In this chapter, you have learned how to create programs that contain statements that are repeated when the program runs. To learn this, you have worked with three different looping constructions that are provided by C#.

The first of these, the "while(condition) statement" construction, repeats the statement as long as the logical expression in the condition is true. If you simply put the Boolean value true as the condition, the loop will never end. In some cases this is a reasonable thing to do because many programs (games, for example) contain behaviors that must be repeated while they run.

The second loop configuration, "do statement while condition," is very similar to the first one, with the important difference that the statement is always performed at least once. In the "while(condition) statement" construction, the test that determines whether the loop repeats is performed at the start of the loop. This means that if the condition controlling the loop is false at the start, the loop code is never performed. In the second configuration, "do statement while condition," the test is performed *after* the code in the loop has been executed once. This second configuration is useful in situations where you are reading in a value and then testing its validity.

The third loop configuration is completely different from the other two. The "for (setup; test; update) statement" construction is designed for situations in which the programmer wants to manage a loop by setting up a counter of some kind, testing for when it reaches its limit, and using a third statement to update the counter. This configuration is especially useful in situations where a program must perform an action a particular number of times.

The C# language also provides a way for a program to break out of a loop by using the break keyword. This is useful if the program has reached a state where it is not meaningful for the loop to be repeated. And there is also the continue keyword, which causes a loop to continue from the start of the loop statements, once the end condition has been tested.

Here are some points to ponder about loops.

Do we really need loops?

No. In theory, we could write every program by using a sequence of statements and conditions. Loops could be "unrolled" into sections of repeated code. A loop that performs an action 10 times could be replaced by 10 copies of the code in the loop. Doing without loops would make programs much larger, but it would work.

Are loops dangerous?

In a way. An "unrolled" loop is guaranteed to run through to completion. There is no way it can get stuck or execute the wrong number of times. However, you have seen several times that if you get the end conditions wrong or update a counter incorrectly, you can have loops that get stuck looping forever or go around the wrong number of times. In other words, using loops in a program introduces the potential for new kinds of errors. It is interesting to note that in some absolutely critical programs, such as ones controlling aircraft or nuclear reactors, programmers sometimes avoid loops for just this reason.

7
Using arrays

What you will learn

You might find this surprising, but you've already learned most of what you need to know to tell a computer what to do. You can write a program that stores items of data, makes decisions based on data values, and repeats behaviors as long as particular conditions are true. These are the fundamentals of programming, and all programs are built on these core capabilities.

However, there is one more thing you need to know before you can write most any kind of program. You have to understand how to manage large amounts of data in your programs. In this chapter, you'll learn how to work with "collections" of data by using arrays and how to use loops to work through them.

Have an ice cream

Your fame as a programmer is beginning to spread far and wide. Now the owner of a group of ice-cream stands comes to you and asks that you write a program to help her track sales results. She has 10 ice-cream stands around the city, and each day they sell a different number of ice-cream treats. What she wants is quite simple—she wants to enter the sales value from each stand and then view the data in different ways: sorted from lowest to the highest, sorted from highest to the lowest, just the highest and the lowest numbers, the total number of sales, and the average sales value. She can use this information to help plan the location of her stands and reward the best sellers. If you get this right, you might be getting some free ice cream, so you agree to help.

> **PROGRAMMER'S POINT**
>
> ## Getting the specification right: Storyboarding
>
> It's important to agree on a specification with your customers. There are lots of ways that you can develop a specification. I find that the best way is to sit down with your user and a large pad of paper—as far away from the computer as you can get—and draw up a "storyboard." Storyboards are used in moviemaking to show everyone how the film will tell the story. Programs can have storyboards, too.
>
> Whereas a movie storyboard describes one sequence—the narrative of the film—the storyboard for a computer program has branches that show how the user follows different paths through the application. For example: When the ice-cream sales program starts, it asks for 10 sales values, one after the other. It then moves to the menu screen. The menu screen has options to view data (lowest to highest, highest to lowest, and so on) and an option to read in a new set of numbers. If the user selects **High to Low**, the program will show the sales numbers with the highest value first and provide a button the user can use to return to the menu screen. You would list and describe all the other operations in this way as well.
>
> In a storyboard, you can also draw up how the screens are supposed to look and agree with the customer what users must do to move from one screen to the next. You could even decide what color scheme to use. Remember that one of the worst things is for the user to say, "I'm really not that bothered about how it should work. I'll leave that to you. I'm sure it will be fine." No it won't. Designing a program must be done by working with the customer. That way, you can be sure you are delivering exactly what is required. What's more, doing the design like this means that when you start writing the program, you'll know exactly what you need to do, since the storyboard will tell you what happens first. And if there is anything the customer hasn't thought of, these will most likely be spotted as you build the storyboard. Building an understanding of how programs fit together can be a big help when you get to the point of creating them.

With the information you've gathered, all you have to do now is write the actual program itself. The program will use variables to hold the sales values entered by the user, and it can use a logical expression to compare two sales values and choose the bigger of the two (so that it can sort values and find the biggest sales). You also know from earlier chapters how to display results to the user.

Storing the data in single variables

When you write a program, a good place to start is to declare all the variables that the program will use. This program needs to store 10 sales figures, so start by declaring 10 variables, one for each of the values you want to store in the program. You can use integers (the `int` type) to hold the number of sales because you can't sell half an ice cream.

```
int sales1, sales2, sales3, sales4, sales5, sales6, sales7,
    sales8, sales9, sales10;
```

Now we need to get the sales figures from the user. We've used the `ReadInteger` method before to do this. (It is how the funfair rides program in Chapter 5 reads in the age of customers wanting to go on a ride.) In this program we are going to use the method to read in sales values. Using this approach, we could write 10 statements that read in the sales values for each ice-cream stand:

```
sales1 = SnapsEngine.ReadInteger("Enter the sales for stand 1");
sales2 = SnapsEngine.ReadInteger("Enter the sales for stand 2");
sales3 = SnapsEngine.ReadInteger("Enter the sales for stand 3");
sales4 = SnapsEngine.ReadInteger("Enter the sales for stand 4");
sales5 = SnapsEngine.ReadInteger("Enter the sales for stand 5");
sales6 = SnapsEngine.ReadInteger("Enter the sales for stand 6");
sales7 = SnapsEngine.ReadInteger("Enter the sales for stand 7");
sales8 = SnapsEngine.ReadInteger("Enter the sales for stand 8");
sales9 = SnapsEngine.ReadInteger("Enter the sales for stand 9");
sales10 = SnapsEngine.ReadInteger("Enter the sales for stand 10");
```

Now that we have the data in our program, we can start to work with it. First, we could create an `if` condition to decide whether the sales from stand 1 are the largest. Also, as you saw in Chapter 5, we can combine conditions to make complicated logical expressions. The output from the following condition is true only if `sales1` is larger than all the other sales values:

```
if(sales1>sales2 && sales1>sales3 && sales1>sales4 &&
   sales1>sales5 && sales1>sales6 && sales1> sales7 &&
   sales1>sales8 && sales1>sales9 && sales1>sales10)
{
    SnapsEngine.DisplayString("Stand 1 had the best sales");
}
Ch07_01_UnworkableSales
```

The problem (as you may have already spotted) is that this program would have to repeat this condition 10 times to display the correct message for all the ice-cream sellers. The problem would become worse if your customer added another 20 sales stands, because the program would become even more complex—it would require 20 more variables, 20 more read statements, and 20 more complex conditions. That's not the path we want to follow to manage this volume of data.

Making an array

Storing and working with large amounts of data is actually quite easy, but you need something better than single variables. You need to create a collection, and the simplest form of a collection is the C# array, so let's take a look at that.

Arrays have one or more dimensions. A one-dimensional array is something like a list. A two-dimensional array is more like a table or a grid (where each element is identified by what you might think of as a row and a column position).

An array will let us do what we really want to do to manage the data in our ice-cream application: create a single variable that can hold all 10 sales values at once. To declare an array variable for our program, you use the following statement, which creates an array called sales that can hold 10 sales values, each of which is of type int:

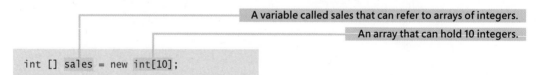

A variable called sales that can refer to arrays of integers.

An array that can hold 10 integers.

```
int [] sales = new int[10];
```

This statement looks a bit like an assignment—for example, int age = 21;—which is a type of statement you've seen before. It creates an integer variable called age and then puts the value 21 in it. The array declaration is the same kind of thing. It creates a variable (called sales) that can refer to arrays of integers and then makes the sales variable refer to a brand-new array that can hold 10 integer values. (This is the first *reference* variable that we have seen in our C# programs. You will learn a lot more about references later in the book.)

If you think of a single variable as a box that can hold one value, you can think of an array as a row of boxes, each of which can hold a value. In C# terminology, each of the boxes in an array is called an *element*—an array is made up of a number of elements. When an array of integers is created, each element is initially set to the value 0.

You can create arrays that hold values of any type. And you can use an array element everywhere you can use a variable of that particular type.

Using an index

A program addresses a particular element in an array by using an *index*, which is a number that identifies the element in the array. (Some programmers call indexes *subscripts*.) The index value is given in square brackets after the array reference (such as [5]). The following statement sets the element at the start of the array (which is at index 0) to hold the value 99. **Figure 7-1** shows the effect of this statement.

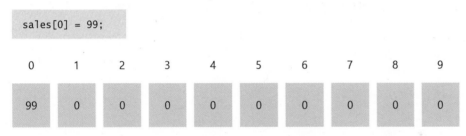

```
sales[0] = 99;
```

Figure 7-1 A set of array elements. The first element has the index 0 and the value 99.

It is very important to understand that array indexes start at 0. In other words, the *first* element has the index 0. This can be confusing for two reasons.

- It's not how humans number things. We never say, "I'll have the zeroth item on the menu" or "I live at house number zero at the top of the street." There is a natural human tendency to link "first" with the number one.

- It's not how some other programming languages work. Some other languages—for example, Basic—number their array elements starting at 1.

I find it best to think of the index as the distance down the array that you have to travel to get to the element that you want. The initial reference to the array takes you to the start of the array, so an index of 0 must be how you refer to that element.

Falling off the end of an array

When a program runs, it allocates exactly the right amount of memory needed for an array of a particular size. This can lead to problems. The next statement is trying to set the sales for the last ice-cream stand to 50.

```
sales[10] = 50;

Ch07_02_ArrayExceptions
```

At first glance this looks okay. The array contains 10 elements, and we are accessing the tenth one. How can this fail? It turns out that this statement fails because the first element of the array has the index 0, which means the tenth element has the index 9. (If you don't believe me, count the array elements in **Figure 7-1**, and you'll see that you have 10 of them, numbered 0 to 9). There is no element in the array with an index value of 10 for the program to use. So it does the only thing it can. It throws an exception.

Throwing an exception is the software equivalent of kicking over the table if you are losing in a game of chess. The current activity is abandoned. If you are using Visual Studio to develop the program, you might see a scary description of what just happened. **Figure 7-2** shows you the kind of information you see in Visual Studio if your program throws an exception.

Figure 7-2 Exception details displayed by Visual Studio for an IndexOutofRange exception.

If the program is running outside Visual Studio, the user won't see this message, but there is a very good chance that the program will just stop running when the exception is thrown.

You might think that this behavior is a bit extreme. All we did was get an index value wrong. Why such a fuss? The answer is very important. When a program goes wrong, it is crucial that the user knows this as soon as possible. There is only one thing worse than a broken program, and that is a broken program that the user doesn't know is broken. It is one thing for a word processor to give you an error when you try to save a file. It is quite another thing (and much worse) for a word processor to leave you thinking the file was saved when it wasn't.

In Chapter 11, you will find out how to capture and deal with exceptions that may arise when a program runs.

Working with arrays

At the moment you might not be very impressed. You've learned how to declare a large number of variables using a single statement, but how does this help us process the ice-cream sales figures? Well, consider the following code:

```
using SnapsLibrary;

class Ch07_03_ForLoopStorage
{
    public void StartProgram()
    {
        int[] sales = new int[10];
        for (int count = 0; count < 10; count = count + 1)
        {
            sales[count] = SnapsEngine.ReadInteger("Enter the sales value");
        }
    }
}
```

Arrays become very useful when you index their elements by using a variable rather than a fixed value. The preceding code uses a for loop to repeat a block of code. The for loop uses a counter called count. The first time around the loop, the count variable holds the value 0. Next time around the loop, the value of count is 1. The loop ends when count reaches the value 10, which is the end of the array.

Here is the statement in the loop that reads each sales value:

```
sales[count] = SnapsEngine.ReadInteger("Enter the sales value");
```

In this statement, the variable count is used to index the array and tell the program where to put the number it reads. The first time around the loop, the counter is 0, so the integer entered by the user goes into the element at the start. Then the value of `count` is increased to 1. This means the next value entered will be read into the element with the index of 1, and so on.

Investigating arrays

Here is an array that is being filled with data as the program runs, part way through the data entry.

0	1	2	3	4	5	6	7	8	9
50	54	29	33	22	0	0	0	0	0

Question: The program has just stored a value in an element in the array. What is the value of `count` at this instant? What is the value of the most recently entered sales?

Answer: You learned that an array element is filled with 0 when it is created. This means that the first element in the array that is not 0 must be the one whose value is most recently entered. If you look at the array, that element is the one at index 4. This element contains 22. So `count` is 4, and the most recently entered sales value is 22.

Question: How many ice creams did the third ice-cream stand sell?

Answer: It sold 29 ice creams. If you think the answer is 33, remember that array elements are indexed starting at 0. The first stand sold 50 (that element has the index 0), the second stand sold 54 (that element has the index 1), and the third sold 29.

Question: If I wanted to store the sales from 100 ice-cream stands, what would I have to change in the program?

Answer: This is where using arrays starts to really pay dividends. It turns out that all I would have to change is the size of the array so that it can hold 100 values and make the loop go around 100 times. C# has a feature that makes this easier. A program can determine the length of an array. The length value can be used to control the `for` loop so that it automatically works for an array of any size.

> Uses the array's length to count through the array.

```
int [] sales = new int[100];
for (int count = 0; count < sales.Length; count = count + 1 )
{
    sales[count] = SnapsEngine.ReadInteger("Enter the sales value");
}
```

This version of the program would work for 100 sales figures. You can make it work for any number of sales simply by changing 100 to a different value. You could even ask the user how many ice-cream stands she has:

```
int noOfStands = SnapsEngine.ReadInteger("How many ice cream stands?");
int [] sales = new int[noOfStands];
Ch07_04_VariableArraySizes
```

This code allows the user to decide just how much data he or she wants to process.

WHAT COULD GO WRONG

Flexibility can be dangerous

It is a great idea to allow a user to change the size of the storage that they want to use. But this might also be very dangerous. Take a look at this screenshot:

Data entry like this is going to end very badly. The program will try to make an array that will hold 100 million sales values. If that succeeds, it will then ask the user to enter each value in turn, which will take a very long time.

To stop this from happening, you must discuss the feature with the user and agree that she will never have less than 10 stands or more than 100. The program can then reject values outside the agreed range.

Index issues

Sometimes, trying to be helpful can give you new problems. The original version of the program asked the user for the details of each ice-cream stand in turn. The present version doesn't do this, and the user would very much like to know which particular value is being entered. The good news is that the program can use the count value in the prompt.

```
for (int count = 0; count < sales.Length; count = count + 1 )
{
    sales[count] = SnapsEngine.ReadInteger("Enter the sales for stand " + count);
}
Ch07_05_BadlyNumberedStand
```

Question: But the bad news is that this program doesn't actually work properly. Can you spot the problem and how to fix it?

Answer: The array is indexed starting at 0, which means that the first time around the loop, the program will display the prompt "Enter the sales for stand 0." This will confuse the user because she wants to count starting at 1. So you change the program as follows:

```
sales[count] = SnapsEngine.ReadInteger("Enter the sales for stand " + count + 1);
```

The idea here is that the program will add 1 to count so that it displays 1,2,3,4 instead of 0,1,2,3. However, when you run the "fixed" program, the output doesn't look right:

And after you have added the details of the first sales stand, things get even worse:

Enter the sales for stand 11

[   ]

Enter

What's happening here? It turns out that the problem is in the prompt statement:

```
sales[count] = SnapsEngine.ReadInteger("Enter the sales for stand " + count + 1);
```

The program is constructing the string to be displayed by adding items together using the + operator. When an expression contains the + operator between strings values, it *concatenates* the items (it strings them together). So, rather than adding 1 to the value of **count**, the code + 1 causes the value 1 to be concatenated to the end of the string that is displayed. To make the program work properly, you have to force it to work out the sum first and then display this result as an integer. You can use parentheses to tell the compiler that you want one part of the expression to be evaluated first, so you can do this:

```
sales[count] = SnapsEngine.ReadInteger("Enter the sales for stand " +
                                       (count + 1));
```

When the program builds the string now, it calculates **count + 1** before it does anything else, which means that the program displays the stand number correctly. But I would make one more change and write the code like this:

```
for (int count = 0; count < sales.Length;count = count + 1 )
{

    // User likes to count from 1, not zero
    int displayCount = count + 1;
    sales[count] = SnapsEngine.ReadInteger("Enter the sales for stand " +
                                           displayCount);

}
Ch07_06_ProperlyNumberedStand
```

This version explicitly creates a counter (displayCount) for use in the display message. The code also contains a comment that explains why it is doing this. I would consider this to be much more professional-quality code. Some programmers might say that this code is less efficient, in that I'm making a new variable each time around the loop, but this is probably not the case. Compilers today are very good at optimizing how they create the program. And anyway, I'm very happy to trade a tiny amount of computer power for a huge improvement in readability.

Displaying the contents of the array by using a for loop

We can create a loop that lets us display the contents of the array on the screen so that we can see the sales values.

```
using SnapsLibrary;

class Ch07_07_ReadAndDisplay
{
    public void StartProgram()
    {
        SnapsEngine.SetTitleString("Ice Cream Sales");

        // Find out how many sales values are being stored
        int noOfStands = SnapsEngine.ReadInteger("How many ice cream stands?");
        int[] sales = new int[noOfStands];

        // Loop round and read the sales values
        for (int count = 0; count < sales.Length; count = count + 1)
        {
            // User likes to count from 1, not zero
            int displayCount = count + 1;
            sales[count] = SnapsEngine.ReadInteger("Enter the sales for stand " +
                                                   displayCount);
        }

        // Got the sales figures, now display them

        SnapsEngine.ClearTextDisplay();
```

```
        // Add a line to the display for each sales figure
        for (int count = 0; count < sales.Length; count = count + 1)
        {
            SnapsEngine.AddLineToTextDisplay("Sales: " + sales[count]);
        }
    }
}
```

Ch07_07_ReadAndDisplay

The count variable is used to index elements in the array so that each element in turn is displayed. **Figure 7-3** shows the output when the program displays the sales values.

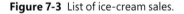

```
Ice Cream Sales

        Sales: 50
        Sales: 54
        Sales: 29
        Sales: 33
        Sales: 22
        Sales: 100
        Sales: 45
        Sales: 54
        Sales: 89
        Sales: 75
```

Figure 7-3 List of ice-cream sales.

You can use this pattern in other programs when you need to read some data in and then display it.

MAKE SOMETHING HAPPEN

Read the names of guests for a party

Arrays can hold any type of data that you need to store, including strings. You could change the ice-cream sales program to read and store the names of guests for a party or an event you are planning.

Make a modified version of the sales program that reads in some guest names and then displays them. Make your program handle between 5 and 15 guests.

Displaying a user menu

After the program has read in the sales data, it must determine what the user wants to do with it. The program can use the `SelectFromButtons` methods we've used in other chapters to get a command from the user. The following code should be familiar to you. Remember that this method displays a set of buttons (here we are displaying six) and then waits for the user to select one. **Figure 7-4** shows the menu the statement creates.

```
string command = SnapsEngine.SelectFrom6Buttons(
    "Low to High",
    "High to Low",
    "Highest and Lowest",
    "Total sales",
    "Average sales",
    "Enter figures");
```

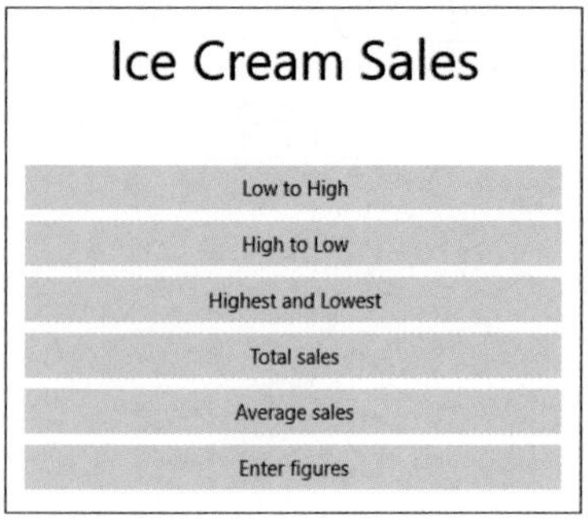

Figure 7-4 Ice-cream sales analysis menu.

The user can press the button that matches the data she wants, and then the program can test the result that comes back and decide which function to perform. In the following example, the code inside the block is obeyed if the command is **Low to High**. I've added a comment that tells someone reading the code what the code will do.

```
if (command == "Low to High")
{
    // Need to display the contents of the sales array
    // sorted lowest to highest
}
```

Sorting an array using the Bubble Sort

As the comment in the preceding code block tells you, the next thing we need to do is write code that does some sorting. Sorting is something that computer programs spend a lot of time doing, but as with other operations, you have to tell a computer exactly how to do it. A computer can't sort the whole array at once. It can work on only one item at a time. Examining how sorting programs work is a good idea because it helps you understand how a complex problem can be broken down to a series of smaller steps.

Computer scientists talk a lot about *algorithms*. An algorithm is a way of doing something. Programming is really about taking an algorithm and converting it to a sequence of instructions that tells the computer what to do. This brings into focus one of the most important points of programming: if you don't have the algorithm, you can't write the program. In other words, if you don't know the sequence of steps that solves the problem, you can't make a program to solve the problem.

When it comes to sorting collections of data, there are a number of different algorithms. Bubble Sort is one of them. Bubble Sort works in a way that progressively makes an array a little bit more sorted (one step at a time) by comparing adjacent elements and swapping elements that are in the wrong order. Next, we'll look in detail at how bubble sorting works and then convert the algorithm into C# programming. (Bubble sorting works well for small data sets, but it is not always the best way to sort large amounts of data. If you are interested in how computers do sorting, you can find lots of resources online to look at.)

Let's start with the sales data that we've been working with, which is shown in **Figure 7-5**.

0	1	2	3	4	5	6	7	8	9
50	54	29	33	22	100	45	54	89	75

Figure 7-5 The contents of the sales array, waiting to be sorted.

To sort the array, we can start by comparing the elements at the beginning of the array:

```
if(sales[0]>sales[1])
{
    // The elements are in the wrong order, need to swap them round
}
```

The `if` construction is controlled by a logical expression that compares `sales[0]` with `sales[1]`. If `sales[0]` is larger than `sales[1]`, it's in the wrong order (we want the largest at the bottom), and the two elements need to be swapped because we're sorting from lowest to highest.

CODE ANALYSIS

Swapping two numbers

As it happens, the first two elements in our sales array are in the right order, but we will need to swap values at some point further down the array, so take a look at this code:

```
if(sales[0]>sales[1])
{
    // The elements are in the wrong order, need to swap them around
    sales[0] = sales[1];
    sales[1] = sales[0];
}
```

Question: This code looks like it might work, but in fact it is broken. Any idea why?

Answer: What the code actually does is put a copy of `sales[1]` into `sales[0]`. Here's why:

- The first statement puts the value of `sales[1]` into `sales[0]`. Both array elements now contain `sales[1]` (in our case, 54).

- The second statement puts the value of `sales[0]` (which is 54, remember) back into `sales[1]`.

- So both elements end up with the same value in them, which is bad.

The way to fix this is to store the value of `sales[0]` temporarily so that we don't lose the value when we put `sales[1]` into it:

```
if(sales[0]>sales[1])
{
    // The elements are in the wrong order, need to swap them around
    int temp = sales[0];
    sales[0] = sales[1];
    sales[1] = temp;
}
```

The variable temp is created to hold this temporary value. It exists only within the block of code that is obeyed if the elements are in the wrong order.

By swapping two elements that are in the wrong order, we make the array a bit less out of order. Our program can now move on to the next pair of numbers and repeat the process to improve things still more.

```
if(sales[1]>sales[2])
{
    // The elements are in the wrong order, need to swap them around
    int temp = sales[1];
    sales[1] = sales[2];
    sales[2] = temp;
}
```

We could repeat this construction all the way to the end of the array, but it would be rather time-consuming to write the program. And when your customer with the ice-cream stands comes to you and says that she now has 50 sales outlets, you would be forgiven for bursting into tears.

However, if you take a careful look at the code used for swapping elements, you'll notice something interesting. The action the code performs is the same for each pair of numbers; it is just that we move one position down the array to perform the second test. This means we can use a loop to count through the array and work through it with just a single if construction:

```
for (int count = 0; count < sales.Length - 1; count = count + 1)
{
    if (sales[count] > sales[count + 1])
    {
        // The elements are in the wrong order, need to swap them around
        int temp = sales[count];
        sales[count] = sales[count + 1];
        sales[count + 1] = temp;
    }
}
```

The first time through the loop, the count variable will contain the value 0, so the test will compare sales[0] and sales[1]. Next time around the loop, count will contain the value 1, so the test will compare sales[1] and sales[2]. The loop will continue through the array until it reaches the end.

This loop has been written so that it can sort an array of any size. It also has one other bit of cleverness: it terminates when the counter reaches the value `length - 1`. I did this because we are always comparing an element with the one after it, and I don't want to go off the end of the array.

Run the Snaps app **Ch07_08_BubbleSortDemo** to see the first pass of the sorting. This demo contains the sales values that we've been working with in the text. Once the loop has been completed, the array is sorted as you can see in **Figure 7-6**.

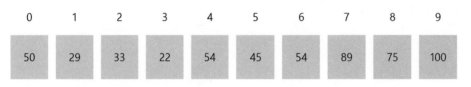

Figure 7-6 A slightly more sorted array

You can see in the figure that some values have not moved while others have moved quite a bit. The value 54 moved down the array until it met up with the value 100, which then went to the end of the array. This is how the Bubble Sort technique gets its name. While the array is sorted, the smaller values bubble up to the top as they are swapped with the larger values that move toward the bottom. After one pass through the array, we can be absolutely sure that the largest value is now at the end of the array, and we can now make another pass to push the next largest value into position. In a worst-case scenario, where the smallest value was at the "wrong" end of the array, it would take nine (or `length - 1`) passes to bubble this value to the top. The smallest value would be swapped with a value in the array each time a pass was made.

Here is the code that performs multiple passes by using a loop to repeat the sort. The outer loop causes the program to make multiple passes through the code. The variable `pass` is used to count the passes through the array. When the loops finish, the numbers will be sorted as you can see in **Figure 7-7**.

```
for (int pass = 0; pass < sales.Length - 1; pass = pass + 1)
{
    for (int i = 0; i < sales.Length - 1; i = i + 1)
    {
        if (sales[i] > sales[i + 1])
        {
            // The elements are in the wrong order, need to swap them around
            int temp = sales[i];
            sales[i] = sales[i + 1];
            sales[i + 1] = temp;
        }
```

```
    }
}
Ch07_09_BubbleSortWorking
```

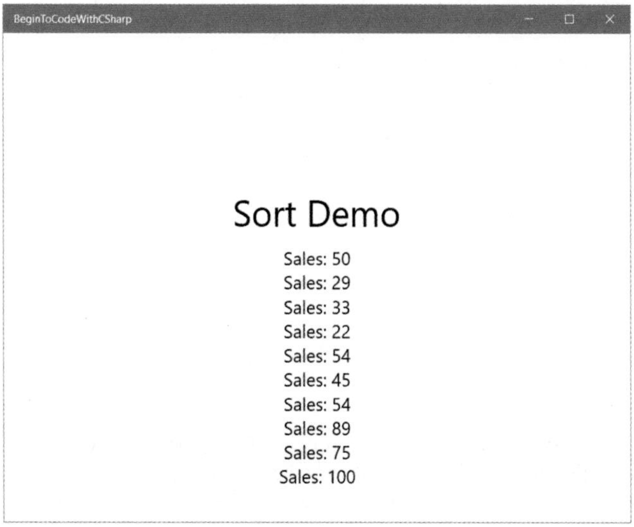
BeginToCodeWithCSharp
Sort Demo
Sales: 50
Sales: 29
Sales: 33
Sales: 22
Sales: 54
Sales: 45
Sales: 54
Sales: 89
Sales: 75
Sales: 100

Figure 7-7 The fully sorted array, lowest to highest

This is a good demonstration of how repeating a simple action (swapping two adjacent numbers) can solve a complex task (sorting a set of numbers).

CODE ANALYSIS

Improving performance

The sorting process works correctly, but it might be possible to improve the efficiency of the program.

Question: Is the program doing more comparisons than it needs to?

> **Answer:** Yes. If you think about it, once the program has made one pass through the array, the largest number is guaranteed to be at the bottom of the array. It's now a waste of time to check to see whether this value needs to swapped, as it never will be. We can use the pass counter to make the program go down the array only as far as it needs to with each pass:

```
for (int pass = 0; pass < sales.Length - 1; pass = pass + 1)
{
    for (int i = 0; i < sales.Length - 1 - pass; i = i + 1)
    {
        if (sales[i] > sales[i + 1])
        {
            // The elements are in the wrong order, need to swap them around
            int temp = sales[i];
            sales[i] = sales[i + 1];
            sales[i + 1] = temp;
        }
    }
}
```

Take a careful look at this code. The crucial statement is the one controlling the inner loop:

```
for (int i = 0; i < sales.Length - 1 - pass; i = i + 1)
```

This statement uses the value of pass to shorten the distance down the array that each pass travels. This simple change roughly halves the number of comparisons that the program does.

Question: Is the program doing more passes through the array than it needs to?

> **Answer:** The answer is probably. The outer loop has been written to handle the worst-case scenario, in which the smallest number is right at the bottom of the array and needs to be bubbled all the way to the top. If the smallest value is somewhere else in the array, the program will be making passes through the array when it is already sorted, which is a waste of computer time. It would be best if the sorting stopped as soon as the array was in the correct order. But how can the program detect that?

If the program makes a pass through the data and doesn't make any swaps, then the array must be in the correct order. We can add a flag to the program that is set when two elements are swapped. If this flag is still clear after a pass, it means that the array is in order:

```
for (int pass = 0; pass < sales.Length - 1; pass = pass + 1)
{
    // clear the swap flag for this pass
    bool doneSwap = false;

    // Make a pass down the array swapping elements
    for (int i = 0; i < sales.Length - 1; i = i + 1)
    {
```

```
            if (sales[i] > sales[i + 1])
            {
                // The elements are in the wrong order, need to swap them around
                int temp = sales[i];
                sales[i] = sales[i + 1];
                sales[i + 1] = temp;
                doneSwap = true;
            }
        }
        if (!doneSwap)
            // Quit the sort if we didn't do any swaps
            break;
    }
Ch07_10_BubbleSortPerformance
```

The program uses a Boolean variable called doneSwap. This variable is set to false before we make a pass through the data. It is set to true if a swap occurs. This flag is checked after the pass, and if it is still false, no swap happened, and the program breaks out of the loop that controls the passes through the array.

MAKE SOMETHING HAPPEN

Sort the party guests

The Bubble Sort algorithm works for strings as well as for integers, but a program needs a way of comparing two strings alphabetically. In C#, the string type provides a Compare method that compares two strings and produces an integer that is less than 0 if the first string precedes the second in alphabetical order. The integer returned is greater than 0 if the first string follows the second. If the two strings are the same, the Compare method returns 0. The following program shows how this works. It displays the message because "Rob" comes before "Simon" in an alphabetical list.

```
public static void StartProgram()
{
    string n1 = "Rob";
    string n2 = "Simon";

    if (string.Compare(n1, n2) < 0)
    {
        SnapsEngine.DisplayString(n1 + " is first");
```

```
    }
}
Ch07_10_StringCompare
```

See if you can make your party-guest program display the guest names for your party in alphabetical order. You could use this program anytime you want to use sorting to put some words (or anything) in order.

Our program also needs to display sales data in the order highest to lowest. Implementing this request turns out to be quite easy. We just need to change the greater-than operator to the less-than operator in the statement in the middle of the loop that compares values as the loop works through each of the elements.

```
if (sales[i] < sales[i + 1])
{
    // The elements are in the wrong order, need to swap them round
    int temp = sales[i];
    sales[i] = sales[i + 1];
    sales[i + 1] = temp;
    doneSwap = true;
}
```

Finding the highest and lowest sales values

Another request the customer made was for the program to find the highest and lowest sales in the set of results. Before you write the code to do this, it's worth thinking about the algorithm to use. In this case, the program can implement an approach very similar to one that a human would use. If you gave me some numbers and asked me to find the highest value, I would compare each number with the highest value I had seen so far and replace the current highest value each time I found a larger one. In programming terms, this algorithm would look a bit like the following. (This is not C# as such; a description like this is sometimes called *pseudocode*. It looks something like a program, but it is there to express an algorithm, not to run inside a computer.)

if(new value > highest I've seen), highest I've seen = new value

When the program starts, we can set the "highest I've seen" value to the value of the first element in the array (since this is the highest we've seen at the start of the process). We can then use the counter in a `for` loop to index each element of the array and test each value in turn. Programmers have given a name to this process of working through each item in a collection. They call this behavior *enumeration*. Humans do this, too. When we go shopping, we enumerate—that is, we work through each item in our shopping list. C# provides an additional kind of loop that can be used to enumerate items in an array. It's called a `foreach` loop.

```
int highest = sales[0];
foreach (int sale in sales)
{
    if(sale > highest)
        highest = sale;
}
```

The `foreach` construction enumerates each element of an array in turn, and the array must contain elements of the type given. In the preceding code, the first time around the loop, the variable `sale` holds the sales value at the start of the array. Next time around, it holds the value of the next element, and so on to the end. The largest value is compared with each successive sales value, and the highest is found. **Figure 7-8** shows the general structure of this type of loop.

Figure 7-8 The general structure of a `foreach` loop.

The `foreach` construction is a lot easier to write than code that creates and manages a counter. However, it can be used only to read items out of an array; it is not possible to store values in an array by using `foreach`. The loop will always go through the array from the start to the end.

We can use the same approach to find the smallest value. This time, we're looking for values that are smaller than the smallest one we have seen so far.

```
int lowest = sales[0];
foreach (int sale in sales)
{
    if (sale < lowest)
        lowest = sale;
}
```

But since we are already making a pass through the array to find the largest value, we can make the program slightly more efficient by using the same loop to find the highest and lowest in a single pass through the data. (Note that at the start of the loop, the initial element in the array is both the highest and lowest value.)

```
int highest = sales[0];
int lowest = sales[0];
foreach (int sale in sales)
{
    if (sale > highest)
        highest = sale;
    if (sale < lowest)
        lowest = sale;
}
Ch07_11_HighestAndLowest
```

Working out the total and the average sales

To work out the total of the sales, the program must add up all the elements in the array. You can do this by using another foreach loop—or by adding code to the loop that we also use to find the highest and lowest sales values.

```
int total = 0;
foreach (int sale in sales)
{
    total = total + sale;
}
Ch07_12_TotalSales
```

Once we have the total sales, we can calculate the average sales value. Of course, the average of a set of numbers is the total of the numbers divided by the count of how many numbers. With the total number of sales calculated, working out the average is very easy.

```
if (command == "Average sales")
{
    SnapsEngine.SetTitleString("Average sales");
```

```
    int total = 0;
    foreach (int sale in sales)
        total = total + sale;

    float average = total / sales.Length;

    SnapsEngine.DisplayString("Average sales " + average);
}
```

The code to work out the total is the same as the code you have already seen. The floating-point variable average is set to the total sales divided by the number of sales values, which we can get from the length of the sales array.

This code looks fine, so we run it with some test data. To keep things simple, we just use three data values:

- Stand 1 - 50

- Stand 2 - 30

- Stand 3 - 20

The total number of sales is 100. This means that the average should be 100 divided by 3, which is the value 33.33333. But when we run the program, we don't see that value appear, as shown in **Figure 7-9**.

Figure 7-9 The average here is represented as an integer.

The integer portion of the result is there, but the fractional part is missing. We've encountered this problem before. The C# language has versions of operators for different types of operands. If you use the + operator between integers, it adds the values together. If you use the + operator between two strings, it concatenates them. If you use the / operator between two integers, it produces an integer result, which is why the average sales value is 33 and not 33.33333. To get a floating-point result, we have to change the code so that at least one of the operands is a floating-point value. We can do this by using casting:

```
float average = (float)total / sales.Length;
```

Here, the value of `total` is converted to a floating-point value before the average is calculated. The program now gives the right result, as you can see in **Figure 7-10**. There are probably more decimal places there than we really want, but the answer is a lot more accurate.

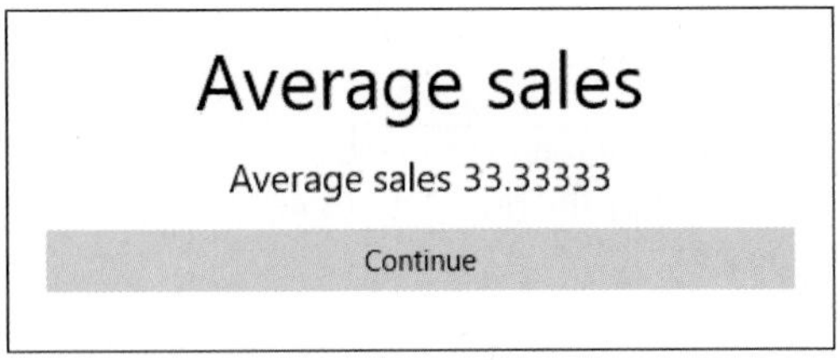

Average sales

Average sales 33.33333

Continue

Figure 7-10 After casting, the correct average is displayed.

Completing the program

We now have all the features we need to create the finished application, but we still need to complete the logic. At this point, we can go back to the storyboards that we created with the customer. They give us the sequence that we want. Essentially, the program breaks down into two loops, an outer and an inner one. The outer loop runs forever. When it starts running, it first allows the user to enter some data. Once the program has some data to work with, it performs the inner loop. This loop repeatedly reads in a command and acts on it. If the user selects the command to enter more data, this causes the inner loop to end, and the program goes back to the outer loop and reads in some more data. The following code shows the structure of the nested loops.

```
while(true)
{
    // Enter some sales data

    while(true)
    {
        // Read in a command from the user
        // Act on the command
        // If the command is "Enter Figures"
        //    break out of this while loop
```

```
        }
    }
}
Ch07_13_CompleteProgram
```

Multiple dimensions in arrays

All the arrays we have created up to this point have been one dimensional—in other words, they have only a length. However, sometimes a program needs to store more than one dimension of data. For example, let's say that the customer for the ice-cream sales analysis program has come back and told you how pleased she is with the code and that she's thought of some improvements. She would like to be able to store sales for different days of the week so that she can keep track of sales over time. She has drawn out a table that shows how the data would look.

	MONDAY	TUESDAY	WEDNESDAY	...
Stand 1	50	80	10	
Stand 2	54	98	7	
Stand 3	29	40	80	
...				

You can think of the program you've written to this point as one column in the table (for example, the sales for Monday). The user can enter sales figures for that day, but what the customer now wants is a way for the program to store successive columns of sales figures for subsequent days.

One way to do this would be to have multiple arrays, called Monday, Tuesday, Wednesday, and so on. However, this arrangement seems a bit like using individual variables for each sales figure, the problem we addressed earlier by using a one-dimensional array. Working with the data in this way would be difficult. For example, it would be very hard for a program to find the highest sales for the week. Fortunately, C# lets a program create a two-dimensional array by using a statement such as this:

A comma indicates two dimensions.

First dimension: day of the week; second dimension: number of stands

```
int[,] weeklySales = new int[7, 10];
```

You can think of a two-dimensional array as a grid. The first dimension specifies the number of columns (you can regard this as the x value if you like), and the second dimension specifies the number of rows (you can regard this as the y value). With a two-dimensional array, a program must give two index values to specify the required element. This statement would set the Monday sales for stand 1 to 50. (Remember that array indexes always start at 0.)

```
weeklySales[0, 0] = 50;
```

CODE ANALYSIS

Dodgy index values

Question: Which of the following statements would fail when the program runs?

```
Statement 1: weeklySales[0, 0] = 50;

Statement 2: weeklySales[8, 7] = 88;

Statement 3: weeklySales[7, 10] = 100;
```

Answer: Statement 1 is completely correct (as it should be; it is used in the text). Statement 2 will fail because the first index (the day of the week) has the value 8. The array, however, contains seven elements, with index values that go from 0 to 6, so this statement is trying to access a nonexistent element. Statement 3 is also invalid. Because elements are indexed starting at 0, this statement attempts to go beyond both dimensions, and the program will fail as a result. If we want to access the element at the bottom-right corner of the array, we should access element weeklySales[6,9].

Using nested for loops to work with two-dimensional arrays

At the start of this chapter, we wrote some C# code such as the following, which reads a single set of sales figures:

```
for (int stand = 0; stand < 10; stand = stand + 1)
{
    // User likes to count from 1, not zero
    int displayCount = stand + 1;
    sales[stand] = SnapsEngine.ReadInteger("Enter the sales for stand " +
                                    displayCount);
}
```

This code uses a for loop construction to work through the array, storing the sales values. The variable stand is used to count each sales stand. To read a whole week's worth of figures, we simply need to run this code inside another loop that is executed for each day of the week:

```
using SnapsLibrary;

class Ch07_14_WeeklySalesProgram
{
    public void StartProgram()
    {
        int[,] weeklySales = new int[7, 10];
        for (int day = 0; day < 7; day = day + 1)
        {
            for (int stand = 0; stand < 10; stand = stand + 1)
            {
                // User likes to count from 1, not zero
                int displayCount = stand + 1;
                weeklySales[day, stand] =
                    SnapsEngine.ReadInteger("Enter the sales for stand " +
                                    displayCount);
            }
        }
    }
}
```

Using a loop like this is called *nesting*. (We've put loops inside one another before, which is how the program repeatedly reads and acts on commands.) Here we have an outer loop that goes around seven times (once for each day) and an inner loop that is performed 10 times (once for each ice-cream stand). When the loop has completed, the program will have put all the values into the array.

Loop counting

Question: How many times will the statements inside the two loops be obeyed?

Answer: They will be obeyed 70 times. The outer loop is obeyed 7 times, the inner loop is obeyed 10 times. To get the total number of times around the loop, you multiply one by the other, giving 70 times around the loop.

Question: How would you change this program so that it could handle more than a week's worth of sales?

Answer: We can add more days to the array. From the point of view of the table, this would be equivalent to adding more columns.

Question: How would we work out the total sales for the entire week?

Answer: To do this, we would have to work through all the elements and add them together, using code like this:

```
int totalSales = 0;                                        Set the total sales to zero.
for (int day = 0; day < 7; day = day + 1)                  Loop for each day
{
    for (int stand = 0; stand < 10; stand = stand + 1)     Loop for each stand
    {
        totalSales = totalSales + weeklySales[day,stand];  Add to the total.
    }
}
Ch07_15_WeeklySalesProgramTotal
```

To work through all the elements in the array, we use the same nesting technique we used to read the values in. The `totalSales` variable starts at 0, and then each sales value from the array is added to this.

Making test versions of programs

When I wrote the program to read in the sales values, my heart sank a little bit because I knew I'd have to test the total sales calculation and that would mean typing in 70 numbers. What's worse, if I found a fault in the program, I'd have to type the values in all over again. And if I got a test value wrong, my total would be wrong, and I'd probably have to do it a third time.

Fortunately, I've acquired a bit of cunning in the time I've been writing programs, so I slightly changed the program that reads in the data by adding a Boolean value that can be set to make the program automatically generate a test value for the sales figures rather than reading in the values from the user.

```
int[,] weeklySales = new int[7, 10];

bool testMode = true;                                          Test flag

for (int day = 0; day < 7; day = day + 1)
{
    for (int stand = 0; stand < 10; stand = stand + 1)
    {
        // User likes to count from 1, not zero
        int displayCount = stand + 1;
        if (testMode)                              If the test flag is set,
            weeklySales[day, stand] = day;        use the day of the
        else                                       week as the sales.
            weeklySales[day, stand] =
                SnapsEngine.ReadInteger("Enter the sales for stand " +
                                        displayCount);
    }
}
Ch07_16_WeeklySalesProgramTotalTest
```

The test value at the moment is just the number that corresponds to the day of the week—in other words, all the sales for Monday will be 0, all the sales for Tuesday will be 1, and so on to the end of the week. This gives me some data that I can use to test the addition behaviors with.

Finding the length of an array dimension

A program can get the number of elements in a one-dimensional array by using the Length property of the array. Here is the code we originally used with a single set of figures in the array called sales.

```
for (int count = 0; count < sales.Length; count = count + 1)
{
    // Count through the elements in the array
}
```

You can use a similar technique to get the length of the two dimensions in the weekly-Sales array:

```
for (int day = 0; day < weeklySales.GetLength(0); day = day + 1)
{
    for (int stand = 0; stand < weeklySales.GetLength(1); stand = stand + 1)
    {
        // Count through the elements in the array
    }
}
Ch06_17_WeeklySalesProgramTotalAutoSize
```

The GetLength method is given the dimension that the program wants the length of. In C# programing tradition, this number starts from 0, so the length of the first dimension (the number of days in a week) is obtained by calling GetLength(0). You can use the GetLength method to ensure that a program works correctly with arrays of different sizes.

More than two dimensions

If you ever need to represent a large number of tables, you can move up to a three-dimensional array. The best way to visualize this type of array is as a pile of pages, with one page for each week. The third dimension would be the number of the page containing the results for that week.

The next statement shows how the 3-D array would be created. You need to add another comma to specify that the location of an element is specified by three index values. Then you need to give dimensions for each of these values when you create the array itself. The code here creates an array that can hold 52 weeks of data.

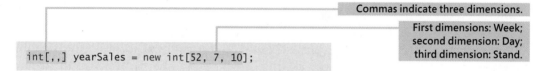

Commas indicate three dimensions.

First dimensions: Week;
second dimension: Day;
third dimension: Stand.

```
int[,,] yearSales = new int[52, 7, 10];
```

If the customer wants to keep track of different weeks of data, you might think this would be a good time to use a three-dimensional array like this, but I'm not convinced. I think it would be much more sensible just to extend the two-dimensional array so that it can contain more columns:

```
int[,] yearSales = new int[365, 10];
```

This would create a two-dimensional array that can hold a set of readings for each day in the year.

PROGRAMMER'S POINT

Keep your dimensions low

In all my years of programming, I've never had to use anything more than three dimensions, and I've only ever used three dimensions a couple of times (and one of those occasions was to create a 3-D Noughts and Crosses game).

If you find yourself having lots of dimensions in your arrays, I would suggest that you are trying to do things the wrong way and that you should step back from the problem and think about how your data fits together. Later in the book, you'll see ways to build structures that contain a number of related data items. It is often much easier to make a one-dimensional array from such structures rather than move into multiple dimensions.

The computer is quite happy to work in very large numbers of dimensions as long as it doesn't run out of memory. However, I've found that the same can't be said for programmers.

Using arrays as lookup tables

Now that you know how to store the data in the program, you can discuss with the customer again how the program is supposed to be used. The customer is quite impressed with the data-storage plans, but she raises an interesting issue. She is concerned that when the sales figures are entered, the program doesn't show the user the day the sales figures are for. The program will work perfectly correctly, but it might be confusing to use. What she would like is for the program to show the day that is being entered, as in **Figure 7-11**.

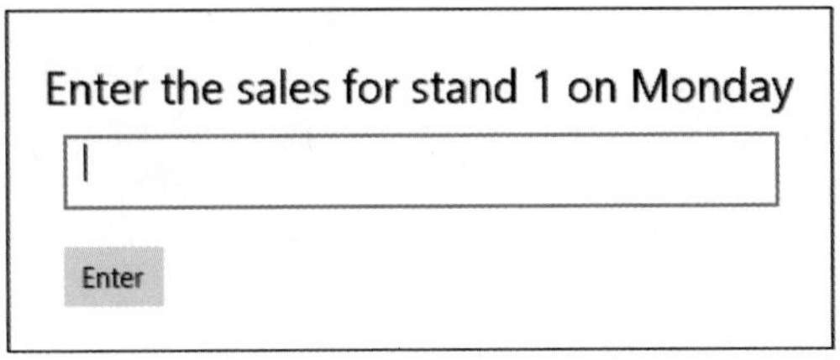

Enter the sales for stand 1 on Monday

|

Enter

Figure 7-11 The program improved to show the day of the week.

To do this, the program must display a message that identifies the day of the week. The program uses a variable called day to count through the days as they are read. The variable starts at 0 for Monday and then counts to 6 for Sunday. We could display the day number, but the user has specifically asked for the name of the day. You might use a collection of if conditions to convert the day number to a string:

```
string dayName;
if (day == 0) dayName = "Monday";
if (day == 1) dayName = "Tuesday";
if (day == 2) dayName = "Wednesday";
if (day == 3) dayName = "Thursday";
if (day == 4) dayName = "Friday";
if (day == 5) dayName = "Saturday";
if (day == 6) dayName = "Sunday";
```

This code would work fine, but it would be tedious to type in, and there is a good chance that you would make a mistake. C# provides a much easier way to do this through a feature that we haven't seen yet. You can create a preset array and use it as a lookup table.

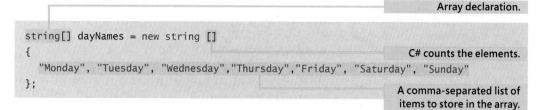

```
string[] dayNames = new string []
{
    "Monday", "Tuesday", "Wednesday","Thursday","Friday", "Saturday", "Sunday"
};
```

Array declaration.

C# counts the elements.

A comma-separated list of items to store in the array.

When the program runs, the array is created with the preset contents. There will be an element for each day of the week, as shown in **Figure 7-12**.

Figure 7-12 Name array for lookups.

The program can now directly convert a day value in the range 0–6 to the matching day.

```
for (int day = 0; day < 7; day = day + 1)
{
    for (int stand = 0; stand < 10; stand = stand + 1)
    {
        // User likes to count from 1, not zero
        int displayCount = stand + 1;
        weeklySales[stand,day] =
            SnapsEngine.ReadInteger("Enter the sales for stand " +
                displayCount + " on " + dayNames[day]);
    }
}
Ch07_18_DayNames
```

Look up the day in dayNames.

Lookup tables are very useful. They can be used to make *data-driven* applications—programs that work by using built-in data rather than hard-wired behaviors.

What you have learned

In this chapter, you've learned how to store large amounts of data in a C# program through the use of arrays. An array is an area of computer storage of a fixed size. A programmer can create an array of any C# type. The array contains a particular number of elements. Each element is equivalent to a single variable of the same type as the array. In other words, you can regard an integer array as a large number of integer variables held in one place.

A program can specify which particular element is to be used by adding an index value to the array. The element at the start of the array has the index 0, and successive elements are numbered sequentially up to the limit of the array. For example, a five-element array would have elements numbered 0,1,2,3,4. The index of an array element can be expressed as a fixed value or by using the value of a variable. This makes it easy to use a loop construction to work through the elements in an array. The array provides a `Length` property that can be used in a program to determine the number of elements in the array. The C# language provides an additional loop construction, called `foreach`, that can be used to enumerate the elements in an array.

Arrays can have multiple dimensions. A one-dimensional array has size only in one direction. A two-dimensional array can be visualized as a table of values. One index of a two-dimensional array can be regarded as specifying the row in the table and the other index the column. The C# language is capable of supporting arrays of many dimensions, although in general programming, it is very unlikely that more than three dimensions will be used.

Here are some points to ponder about arrays.

Do we really need arrays?

Yes. There are many situations where it would be impossible to create the program if arrays were not available. Very simple programs can use single variables, but to process large amounts of data you need to have an array.

How does an array actually work?

When the program creates an array, a block of memory is reserved that is just the right size for all the data elements in the array. When a program accesses an array element, the program first checks to see whether the requested element is in that memory block (that is, it makes sure that you are not trying to use an element that does not exist). If the element can't be found, the program is terminated with an exception. If the element is inside the array's bounds, the program finds the base of the array block and then moves down the block to find the selected element.

Why can't array index errors be detected before the program runs, when it is being compiled?

The compiler can only perform *static* analysis of the program code. This means that the compiler can make a few assumptions based on the program that you have written, but it can't know everything that will happen to values in variables when the program runs. For example, the compiler has no idea what number a user might type in when the program runs. Since array accesses happen when the program runs, there is no chance that the compiler can flag these errors.

Part 2

Advanced programming

In Part 1, you learned that the basic behavior of a program is to take data in, do something with it, and output it again. You saw how programs store different kinds of data, how a program can make decisions based on the values that data has, how to use loops, and how to use lists and arrays to store large amounts of data. These are really the only things you need to know to write every program you can imagine.

In Part 2, you'll build on the programming abilities you've learned so far by exploring some advanced features of the C# language that make it easier to create larger programs and fit a program to a specific problem. You'll also find out how the Snaps framework is constructed and how you can add your own elements to customize it.

8

Using methods to simplify programs

What you will learn

Methods are an essential part of program design. You can use methods to break a large solution into individual components and to create libraries of behaviors that your programs can use. The programs we've created to this point have worked with methods in the Snaps library (the `DisplayString` method, for example) to interact with users. In this chapter, you will learn how to create and use methods of your own. You'll find out how to give methods data to work on and how a program can receive results from a method's work. Methods are a great way to make programs more concise and easier to manage.

What makes a method?

A method is a block of C# code that you give a name to. When the C# compiler finds a method, it takes the statements that define the method and stores them away, ready for use. Take a look again at the declaration of the `StartProgram` method that we examined in Chapter 3. The declaration of a method is also known as the method's *header*. Compare it to **Figure 8-1**, which describes the general structure of a method's header.

```
public void StartProgram()
```

public	void	StartProgram	()
method modifier	return type	method identifier	parameters

Figure 8-1 The structure of a method header.

Let's examine these elements in turn:

The *method modifier* `public` means that the method is available outside the class in which it's declared. You make methods in a class public when you want programs outside the class to be able to use them. The `StartProgram` method must be public because it needs to be called to start the program running. (If the `StartProgram` method were not visible outside the class, there would be no way to start the program.) Later in the book, we will look at the way a programmer can control the level of access to methods and other elements in a class.

The method's *return type* is identified as `void` in this case. This means that the method doesn't return any information when it is called. Some methods return values, while others just perform a task—the `StartProgram` method is one that just performs a task. The Snaps `ThrowDice` method is an example of a method that returns a value. In the following example, you can see how `ThrowDice` is declared as a method that returns an integer value—the keyword `void` has been replaced with the type `int` to indicate this.

```
public int ThrowDice()
```

The *method identifier* is the name given to the method. Methods are often named as verbs because they describe an action that the method will perform.

The *parameters* to a method define the data the method needs to do its work when it runs. In the method header, the method's parameters are enclosed in parentheses. The StartProgram method doesn't accept any parameters because it doesn't need any information to do its job. If there are no parameters, the parentheses are empty.

The Snaps SpeakString method is declared as a method that accepts a string that contains a message. The parentheses after the method identifier now contain the definition of this parameter—a string named message.

```
public void SpeakString(string message)
```

A method also has a *body*. The body of a method is a block of statements enclosed in curly brackets. These statements run when the method is called. Here's a simple method that says "Hello." The body of this method calls the Snaps method SpeakString.

```
void SayGreeting()
{
    SnapsEngine.SpeakString("Hello");
}
```

Adding a method to a class

A program can make use of many methods. You can add another method to a class simply by declaring it above the StartProgram method, as you see here:

```
using SnapsLibrary;

class Ch08_01_GreetingMethod
{
    void Greeting()                               Method header
    {                                             Start of method body.
        SnapsEngine.SpeakString("Hello");
    }


    public void StartProgram()
    {
        Greeting();                               Call the Greeting method.
    }
}
```

The class Ch08_01_Greeting now contains two methods, one named Greeting and the other named StartProgram. We place the new method in the Ch08_01_Greeting class and then call it from the StartProgram method. If you run this program, you'll hear the program say "Hello". If you use the Visual Studio debugger to step through the code, you will find that when the call to the Greeting method is reached within the body of StartProgram, the execution of the program transfers to the Greeting method.

CODE ANALYSIS

Program pathfinder

It is perfectly correct C# for one method to call another, as you've seen in some earlier examples similar to this one:

```csharp
using SnapsLibrary;

class Ch08_02_ProgramPathfinder
{
    void M1()
    {
        M2();
        SnapsEngine.SpeakString("cat");
        M3();
        SnapsEngine.SpeakString("mat");
    }

    void M2()
    {
        SnapsEngine.SpeakString("The");
    }

    void M3()
    {
        SnapsEngine.SpeakString("sat on");
        M2();
    }

    public void StartProgram()
    {
        M1();
    }
}
```

Question: What would this program display when it runs?

Answer: The best way to determine this is to work through the program a statement at a time, just like the computer does when it runs the program. Remember that when a method is complete, the program's execution continues at the statement following the call of that method. The output from this program is exactly what you would expect—"The cat sat on the mat."

Question: What happens if a method calls itself; for example, if the StartProgram method called StartProgram?

Answer: The effect is similar to what you see if you arrange two mirrors so that they face each other. In the mirrors, you see reflections going off into infinity. When the Start-Program method calls itself, your computer will go very quiet for a few seconds and then produce an error message indicating that it has run out of "stack space." The stack overflow is caused because each time a method is called, it stores the return address (the place it must go back to) on a data structure inside the computer (called a *stack*). When a running program reaches the end of a method, it grabs the address on top of the stack and heads back to where the address points. This means that as methods are being called and returned, the stack grows and shrinks.

However, when a method calls itself, the program repeatedly adds return addresses on the stack. Each time the method calls itself, another return address is added to the top of the stack. Eventually the stack grows too large for the memory space it was allocated, and the program is halted.

Computer scientists have a name for a method that works by calling itself. They call it *recursion*. It is occasionally useful in programs, particularly when the program is searching for values in large data structures. However, I've been programming for many years and have used recursion only a handful of times. I advise you to regard recursion as strong magic that you don't need to use just now. You should hardly ever need to use recursion. It is usually best to use a loop to repeat blocks of code

Feeding information to methods by using parameters

The Greeting method shows how methods can be used, but it isn't really that useful—it simply has the computer speak "Hello" each time it's called. To make a method truly useful, we need to give the method some data to work on. You've already seen lots of methods that are used in this way. The SpeakString method and the DisplayString method accept a string that the methods speak or display, respectively. Let's build on this to create a method that can both speak and display a message on the screen.

Making an Alert method with a single parameter

If we want to make a program that displays and speaks a message, we could do this by calling the `DisplayString` method and the `SpeakString` method one after the other, like this:

```
SnapsEngine.DisplayString("Reactor going critical.");
SnapsEngine.SpeakString("Reactor going critical.");
```

These two statements mean that the rather important message is both spoken and displayed on the screen, but it would be hard work to keep using both statements each time we wanted to send a message. To make things easier, we can create a method named `Alert` that displays and speaks the string it's given by using a parameter:

```
void Alert(string message)
{
    SnapsEngine.DisplayString(message);
    SnapsEngine.SpeakString(message);
}
```

Remember that the parameters that a method accepts are given in the parentheses that follow the method identifier. The `Alert` method accepts a string as its parameter and then displays and speaks that string. You can think of a parameter as a variable that is set to a particular value when the method is called. The method uses the value in the parameter to do its job. When a program calls the `Alert` method, it must include the string that the method will work on. This string is called an *argument* to the method call and is passed to the method just as we have passed strings to other methods we've used.

Here is a complete program with the `Alert` method in place:

```
using SnapsLibrary;

class Ch08_03_Alert
{
    void Alert(string message)                       ──── Alert method with a
    {                                                      single parameter.
        SnapsEngine.DisplayString(message);          ──── Display the alert message.
        SnapsEngine.SpeakString(message);            ──── Speak the message.
    }
```

```
public void StartProgram()
{
    Alert("Reactor going critical.");
}
}
```

Call Alert to deliver the
message.

Methods let you create layers in your programs

If you think about it, using a method like this gives you a lot of flexibility. If you want to
change the program so that the user can select whether alerts are spoken or displayed, you
can put this behavior into the Alert method, and all the other parts of the program that
use the method will just keep working. If you have a need to save alerts in a log file, you
could add some code to the Alert method that will save the alerts.

You can think of the Alert method as providing a connection to an *alert layer* that takes
alerts and does things with them. If the alert handling has to change, you can achieve this
by modifying the method that implements the behavior for that layer.

Methods with multiple parameters

The Alert method is given a single item to work on—the string that contains the alert
message. Sometimes we want to write methods that can work on more than one item
of data. For example, you might want to add an urgent flag to our alerts. If the alert is
an important one, the method is designed to play a warning sound before speaking
the message. You can write methods to use any number of parameters, depending on
what information the method needs to complete the task it's been written to perform.

```
void Alert(string message, bool urgent)
{
    if (urgent)
        SnapsEngine.PlaySoundEffect("ding");
    SnapsEngine.DisplayString(message);
    SnapsEngine.SpeakString(message);
}
```

Method header for the Alert method.

Test the value of the urgent parameter.
If urgent is true, play the alert sound.

The new Alert method has two parameters. The first is the string that specifies the
alert text. The second parameter is a bool value that indicates whether the alert is an

urgent one. When you design a method, you need to decide what inputs it must work on and create parameters to receive these inputs.

By defining the `Alert` method with two parameters , you can use it as follows. Here, the first call of the method displays just the message, and the second call plays the sound effect first:

```
Alert("Time for a coffee break.", false);     ——— Message is not that important, no alert.
Alert("Reactor going critical.", true);       ——— Message is very important, play the alert.


Ch08_04_AlertLevel
```

The C# compiler matches the order in which arguments are given with the order of the parameters defined in the method. For the `Alert` method, that's how the compiler knows which value is for the message and which is for the sound effect. But this can lead to problems if you make a mistake. Consider this method call:

```
Alert(false, "Donuts have arrived");
```

This call has the arguments in the wrong order, which confuses the compiler and produces errors when the program is compiled.

```
Error 2    Argument 1: cannot convert from 'bool' to 'string'

Error 1    Argument 1: cannot convert from 'string' to 'bool'
```

The first error says essentially, "You've given me a Boolean value, and I wanted a string." The second error says the reverse. You would get similar errors if you tried to make incorrect calls to Snaps methods.

One way to avoid this problem is not to put the parameters in the wrong order. Another way is to use *named arguments*, like this:

```
Alert(urgent:false, message:"Donuts have arrived");     ——— Named arguments make
                                                            the method call clearer.
```

In this version of the call, I added the name of each argument before the value. This approach has two big advantages. First, now it doesn't matter in which order I give the arguments. Second, it means that the program is much clearer to someone reading it. It is very obvious from the method call what values the method will be using when it runs.

CODE ANALYSIS

Parameters as values

When a method is called, the value of the argument is passed into the method parameter. This is a great thing to say, but what exactly does it mean?

Consider the following program. It contains a method with the interesting name WhatWould-IDo. The method accepts an integer as a parameter. The method doesn't do much; it just sets the value of the parameter to 99 and then returns. The method is then called using the value of a variable named test as an argument.

```
using SnapsLibrary;

class Ch08_05_WhatWouldIDo
{
    void WhatWouldIDo(int input)
    {
        input = 99;
    }

    public void StartProgram()
    {
        int test = 0;
        WhatWouldIDo(test);
        SnapsEngine.DisplayString("Test is: " + test);
    }
}
```

Question: What would the program display when it runs? 0 or 99?

Answer: When the code runs, it follows this sequence:

1. Sets the value of test to 0.

2. Calls the WhatWouldIDo method, passing the *value* of test as an argument.

3. When the WhatWouldIDo method starts, the parameter called input is assigned this value (0).

4. The WhatWouldIDo method sets the value of the parameter called input to 99.

5. The WhatWouldIDo method now ends, and execution returns to the calling statements.

6. The value of test is displayed on the screen.

Remember that an argument is the item actually fed into the method call. If the argument is a value, this means that when we use a variable as an argument, the value of that variable is used, not the variable itself. So the value that is displayed by this program is 0.

Returning values from method calls

As I mentioned earlier, a method can return a value. You have seen this in many of the programs that we've written. Here's an example that uses the ReadString method from the Snaps library. The method accepts an argument (the prompt to be shown to the user) and returns a value (the string that the user types in). :

```
string guestName = SnapsEngine.ReadString("What is your name?");
```

Now take a look at this method header:

```
int GetValue(string prompt, int min, int max)
```

This method is named GetValue. It has three parameters: a string that gives the prompt to be displayed for the user and two int parameters for the minimum and maximum values of the number that GetValue can return. The method itself is of type int, which means that somewhere in the method there must be a statement that returns an integer result.

```
int GetValue(string prompt, int min, int max)          Method header for GetValue.
{
    return 1;                                           This version of the method
}                                                       always returns 1.
```

This version of GetValue is pretty simple—it always returns the value 1. However, it also shows you how return is used.

Methods and return

Let's take a closer look at how `return` is used in a program.

```
int GetValue(string prompt, int min, int max)
{
    return 1;
    return 2;
}
```

Question: What would this version of `GetValue` return?

Answer: It would return the value 1. The second `return` statement would not be reached because execution of a method ends when it reaches a `return` statement.

Question: Can a method contain multiple `return` statements?

Answer: Yes. The program will return when it reaches the first `return` statement.

Question: Must the `return` keyword return a value?

Answer: If the method has a type (in other words, if it is not void), then the method must use the `return` keyword to return a value of that type. It is also possible to use `return` in a `void` method. In this case, the `return` statement does not contain a value to return, and `return` is just a way of making an early exit from a method.

Now take a look at the complete `GetValue` method. It repeatedly reads integers until supplied with one that is in the required range—in other words, a value of `result` that is less than `min` or larger than `max` will cause the loop to repeat. The loop ends when a valid value is entered, at which point the `return` statement is reached and the method returns.

```
int GetValue(string prompt, int min, int max)          ── Method header
{
    int result;                                        ── Variable to hold
                                                          the method result.
    do                                                 ── Start a loop.
    {
        result = SnapsEngine.ReadInteger(prompt);      ── Get an integer, and
    } while (result < min || result > max);               store it in result.
                                                       ── Loop while the result
                                                          is too low or too high.
```

```
        return result;                                        ──────        Return the result.
    }
```

We can use this method to make programs much simpler. These two statements get
the age and the height of a person.

```
int age = GetValue(prompt:"Enter your age in years", min:0, max:100);
int height = GetValue(prompt:"Enter your height in inches", min:30, max:96);
Ch08_06_GetValue
```

PROGRAMMER'S POINT

Designing with methods

Methods are a very useful part of the programmer's toolkit and form an important part of
the development process. Once you have worked out what a customer wants the application to do, you can start thinking about how you are going to break down the program into
methods. Often you find that as you write the code, you repeat a particular action. If you
do this, you should consider taking that action and turning it into a method. There are two
reasons why this is a good idea: first, it saves you writing the same code twice; second, if a
fault is found in the code, you have to fix it in only one place.

Programmers call this kind of change *refactoring* a program. Refactoring occurs during
development because your understanding of your program will improve as you write it.
You might think of a better name for a variable, for example, in which case you can use the
refactoring tools in Visual Studio to rename the variable for you.

Making a tiny contacts app

Let's put what we've learned about methods to use by building an application. You'll
learn more about how to use methods to help design an application and about how
parameters and arguments are used. You'll also learn a bit about how to store data for
when a user needs to retrieve that data from storage.

You are now gaining a reputation as a person who gets things done. Your friend the
lawyer gets in touch because she needs someone to create a personal, confidential
contacts app. All your friend wants is a quick way of storing contact details—names,
addresses, and telephone numbers—for her super-important clients. She's keen for

you to write the program because she trusts you. As usual, you start by drawing up a storyboard for the program and settle on the first screen that the program will display, shown in **Figure 8-2**.

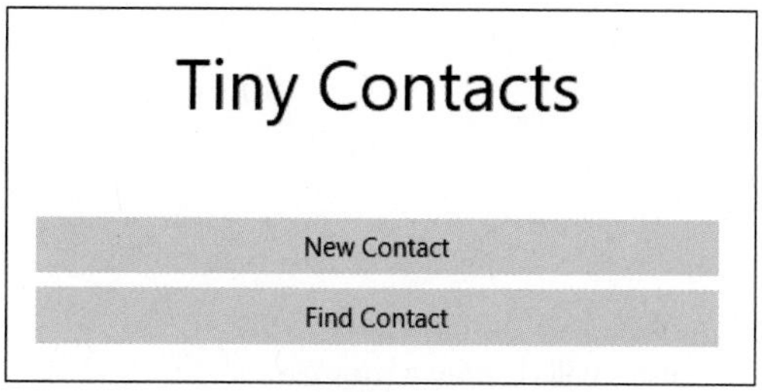

Tiny Contacts

New Contact
Find Contact

Figure 8-2 The Tiny Contacts start screen.

If the user selects **New Contact**, the program asks for the contact's name, address, and phone number by using three successive screens. **Figure 8-3** shows the screens used to get these items.

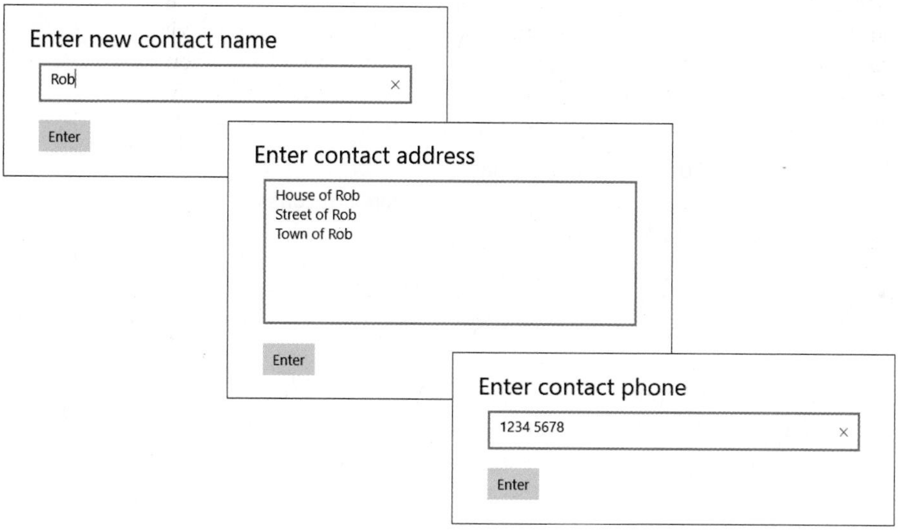

Enter new contact name

Rob ✕

Enter

Enter contact address

House of Rob
Street of Rob
Town of Rob

Enter

Enter contact phone

1234 5678 ✕

Enter

Figure 8-3 Contact data-entry screens

If the user selects **Find Contact**, the program displays the screens shown in **Figure 8-4**. The program asks her to type in the name of the contact, and then the details for that contact are displayed.

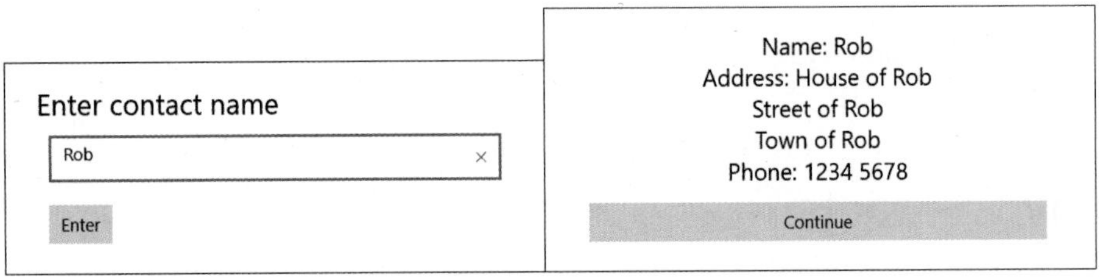

Figure 8-4 Searching for and displaying contact details.

When the user has read the details, she can use the **Continue** button to return to the main menu. If the contact details are not found, the program will display a message (shown in **Figure 8-5**), and the user can press the **Continue** button to return to the main menu.

Figure 8-5 This message is displayed if a contact can't be found.

The lawyer agrees that the program can work like this, and you start building it. The first thing the program needs to do is determine whether the user wants to enter a new contact or find an existing one. You can use the `SelectFrom2Buttons` method from the Snaps library to set up this screen:

```
string command = SnapsEngine.SelectFrom2Buttons("New Contact", "Find Contact");
```

The `command` string will hold either the text "New Contact" or "Find Contact" once the user has selected what she wants to do. If the command selected is **New Contact**, the program must get the name, address, and phone number for the new contact. We can put these behaviors in a method named `NewContact`, which will actually do the work.

```
if (command == "New Contact")
{
    NewContact();
}
```

This is a first-class example of designing with methods. Now we just have to fill in the `NewContact` method. (Note that the name of the method and the name of the command are essentially the same. This is not accidental. It means that anyone who reads the program's code has a good chance of being able to find the parts of the program that make it work.)

Reading in contact details

The `NewContact` method must get the contact's details from the user, but it also needs to store these details for when the user searches for the contact later. The Snaps method `ReadString` can be used to read a single line of text, and a single line is fine for the name and the phone number of the contact. For the address, however, we need to read multiple lines.

Fortunately, the Snaps library contains the `ReadMultiLineString` method, which will read a string that contains more than one line. **Figure 8-3** earlier shows the display produced when the method is called.

```
string address = SnapsEngine.ReadMultiLineString("Enter contact address");
```

A user can press the Enter key to mark the end of each line of text as she types in an address. The `ReadMultiLineString` method then returns a string that contains *control characters* that mark the end of each line. To understand how this works, you have to learn a little more about how string and characters work in a C# program.

Strings and characters

C# provides the `string` type to hold text. The C# language also provides a type named `char`, which can hold a single character.

```
char ch = 'R';
```

The previous statement would create a character variable called `ch`, which contains the letter *R*. The compiler can tell that the value 'R' is a character and not a string through the use of single quotation mark characters (') to identify the start and end of the value.

You can think of a string as containing a collection of `char` values. The string "Rob Miles" contains nine characters. Note that the space between "Rob" and "Miles" is also a character, even though nothing appears on the screen when it is displayed.

Many of the characters that can be held in a `char` are visible—for example letters, numbers, and punctuation—but some are *control characters*, which are not visible but instead control the behavior of the display. Individual lines of an address read by `ReadMultiLineString` are separated from each other by two control characters. The first is a carriage return, which moves the display position back to the start of the line. The second control character is a line feed, which moves the display position down one line.

C# represents a control character by using the backslash character followed by a letter. This is called an *escape sequence*. The backslash means "escape from the normal rules of character values and use a new set of rules." The escape sequence \r means *carriage return*, and \n means *new line*. The address entered in **Figure 8-3** could be written in a program as follows:

```
address = "House of Rob\r\nStreet of Rob\r\nTown of Rob" ;
```

You can use the sequence \r\n in a string if you want to insert a new line at that point.

Storing contact information

Once the NewContact method has acquired the name, address, and phone number strings, it needs to store these strings for this particular contact. Here again we can use methods to help us build our program. In the following code, the NewContact method reads in the contact information and then calls a method named StoreContact to store the contact details.

```
void NewContact()
{
    SnapsEngine.DisplayString("Enter the contact");
    string name = SnapsEngine.ReadString("Enter new contact name");
    string address = SnapsEngine.ReadMultiLineString("Enter contact address");
    string phone = SnapsEngine.ReadString("Enter contact phone");
    StoreContact(name: name, address: address, phone: phone);
}
```

PROGRAMMER'S POINT

Placeholder methods can be a great idea

At the moment, we don't know how to make the StoreContact method, but you can always add an empty method to a program so that you can still test the rest of the code. You could make this method display a message to tell you that it is not available yet:

```
void StoreContact(string name, string address, string phone)
{
    SnapsEngine.DisplayString("Store contact to be completed");
}
```

The program will build and run perfectly, but if the user tries to store a contact, the message tells him that the feature is not available yet. Programmers talk about adding ToDo comments to their programs in this situation. Methods that are incomplete are called *placeholder methods* or *method stubs*. They are a great way to get something running that you can show to the customer to make sure that you are building the program in the way the customer likes.

Using Windows local storage

Up until now, the data in our programs has existed only while a program actually runs. As soon as the program stops, the data disappears. But to make the StoreContact method work, we need to store and retain data when the program stops so that it can be retrieved later.

The Windows 10 operating system provides *local storage* as a way for us to save data such as contact details. Windows assigns each application an area of local storage on the host device. You don't need to know precisely how this works, but local storage does provide a place where a program can store things. I've created two Snaps methods that deal with local storage. One saves a string in local storage, and the other fetches it back.

The Snaps method SaveStringToLocalStorage is given two parameters. One is the name of the item to be stored, and the other is the actual string of text to be stored.

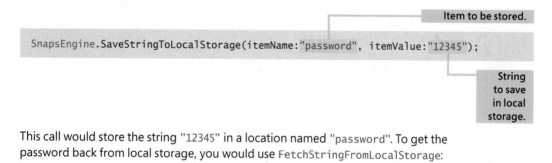

Item to be stored.

```
SnapsEngine.SaveStringToLocalStorage(itemName:"password", itemValue:"12345");
```

String to save in local storage.

This call would store the string "12345" in a location named "password". To get the password back from local storage, you would use FetchStringFromLocalStorage:

```
string myPassword = SnapsEngine.FetchStringFromLocalStorage(itemName:"password");
```

When the FetchStringFromLocalStorage method runs, Windows finds the "password" item in local storage and returns the contents of that item. This would result in the variable myPassword being set to 12345.

Storing a contact in local storage

We need to store the address and phone number for each contact listed in the contact app, and each stored item needs a name to identify it. The program can use the name of the contact being stored as an item name. The following statement shows how this works:

```
SnapsEngine.SaveStringToLocalStorage(itemName: name + ":address",
                                     itemValue: address);
```
Construct the item name for the address.

Remember that the name and address of the contact have been entered by the user of the program, and this statement is using the name of the contact to create the name of the stored item. If the name entered is "Rob", then the address would be stored in the location called "Rob:address".

Here is the method that I created to save a contact. It's given the name, address, and phone information to be stored. Note that the program doesn't need to store the name of the contact; the user will enter the name when they want to find the contact details. The name will then be used to create the item names that the system must find.

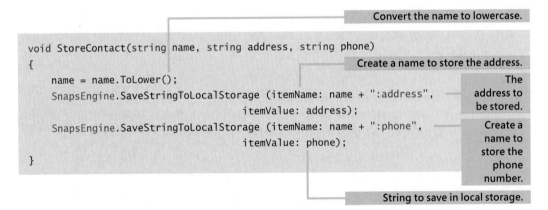

Convert the name to lowercase.

Create a name to store the address.

The address to be stored.

Create a name to store the phone number.

String to save in local storage.

```
void StoreContact(string name, string address, string phone)
{
    name = name.ToLower();
    SnapsEngine.SaveStringToLocalStorage (itemName: name + ":address",
                                          itemValue: address);
    SnapsEngine.SaveStringToLocalStorage (itemName: name + ":phone",
                                          itemValue: phone);
}
```

Loading contact details from local storage

When the user enters the name of the contact, the program can construct the item to search for by using that name. The following statement builds up an item name to look for by adding ":address" to the end of the name of the contact. The FetchString-FromLocalStorage method then finds the address information that was stored in this location. The method can do the same thing to obtain the contact's phone number.

```
address = SnapsEngine.FetchStringFromLocalStorage(itemName: name + ":address");
```

Using reference parameters to deliver results from a method call

The StoreContact method will save a contact in local storage. The program also needs a FetchContact method that will fetch the address and phone number for a contact. FetchContact will have three parameters: the name of the contact to search for, the address of that contact, and the phone number of that contact. An early version of such a method might look like this:

```
void FetchContact(string name, string address, string phone)
{
    address = SnapsEngine.FetchStringFromLocalStorage(itemName: name +
        ":address");
    phone = SnapsEngine.FetchStringFromLocalStorage(itemName: name + ":phone");
}
```

The method is given the name of the contact to search for and sets the address and the phone number parameters to the address and phone number fetched from local storage. A program might try to use the FetchContact method like this:

```
string contactAddress;
string contactPhone;
string name = SnapsEngine.ReadString("Enter contact name");
FetchContact(name: name, address: contactAddress , phone: contactPhone );
```

This code snippet uses the ReadString method to get the contact name from the user and then calls the FetchContact method to get the address and the phone number for that contact and set them to the values of the parameters contactAddress and contactPhone. Unfortunately, this doesn't work. The contactAddress and contact-Phone variables will never be updated by FetchContact. The reason is that in C#, each method parameter is passed *by value*. This means that when the FetchContact method is called, it's given copies of the values of the name, contactAddress, and contactPhone arguments and then uses those copies in the method body.

But the program must use parameters in a different way. Rather than giving the FetchContact method the value of a parameter variable, we want to give the method a *reference* to that variable.

Humans use references all the time. When someone brings you a cup of coffee, you say something like "Put it over there, please," pointing to a clear, flat surface (which might be your mouse pad). You are effectively making a reference. In C# terms, a reference parameter refers to a variable in the program. When that reference is used, the program follows the reference to the variable the reference indicates.

We can turn the address and phone parameters into reference parameters by adding ref in front of their names when the method is declared:

```
void FetchContact(string name, ref string address, ref string phone)
{
    address = SnapsEngine.FetchStringFromLocalStorage(itemName: name +
        ":address");
    phone = SnapsEngine.FetchStringFromLocalStorage(itemName: name + ":phone");
}
```

When the code in the method makes an assignment to the address and phone parameters, this now changes the value of the variable given as an argument. When we make a call to the FetchContact method, we now have to pass references into the method call rather than the values themselves. We do this by putting the keyword ref in front of the arguments in the call:

```
FetchContact(name: name, address: ref contactAddress, phone: ref contactPhone);
```

When FetchContact is called, it is passed references to the address and phone variables. After the method completes, it will have set the address and phone variables to the values it has loaded.

CODE ANALYSIS

References and parameters

The use of references is one of the hardest things to get your head around, so let's consider some questions about it.

Question: If you look closely at the definition of FetchContact, you will notice that only the address and phone parameters are reference parameters. Why is the name parameter to the FetchContact method not a reference parameter?

Answer: The reason is that the method does not change the name of the contact it is fetching. The method just needs the name to perform the search.

Question: When should I use a reference parameter?

Answer: You should use a reference parameter only if you want to allow the method to make changes to a variable. In the case of FetchContact, the method must find the address and phone number information and deliver those values to the caller, so it is appropriate to use reference parameters.

Question: Reference parameters seem a lot more flexible than ones passed by value. Why can't I use them all the time?

Answer: There's no technical reason why not. The C# compiler will not complain. However, I use references only when I have to because they give the method slightly more control over the variables passed as parameters. If I pass a parameter by value, all that a method can do is read that value. But if I pass the parameter by reference, the method can change the value of that variable, and I might not want that to happen.

Using out parameters

A reference parameter lets a method have full access to the parameter that is supplied. However, the designers of C# decided to define a slightly more fine-grained level of control when using references. They added an *out* type of parameter. A method must store a value in a parameter declared as an out parameter.

If you think about it, there is no reason why the FetchContact method should ever read the contents of the address and phone numbers that it is being asked to set. It is also very important that both the address and phone numbers are set by the method. Flagging a parameter as an out parameter, which is shown in the next code example, means that the compiler will refuse to compile the method if the parameter is not set. The compiler will also produce an error if the method tries to read the contents of the variable.

```
void FetchContact(string name, out string address, out string phone)
{
    address = SnapsEngine.FetchStringFromLocalStorage (itemName: "addr" + name);
    phone = SnapsEngine.FetchStringFromLocalStorage (itemName: "phone" + name);
}
```

When FetchContact is called, the arguments to the call must now be marked as outputs from the method:

```
FetchContact(name: name, address: out contactAddress, phone: out contactPhone);
```

When you design methods and parameters, you should decide how the method is going to use the information that is being delivered to the method and choose whether to pass in the value or pass in a reference.

Method headers

Just to build your understanding of these parameter types and method headers, here are a few scenarios that you might like to consider.

Question: I've written a method that will generate two integer dice throw values for use in a board game. What kind of parameter should I use?

> **Answer:** Each of the two parameters should be out parameters, which can be set by the method when it is called. The method itself will not return a value.

```
void ThrowTwoDice(out int dice1, out int dice2)
```

Question: How would I call ThrowTwoDice?

> **Answer:** When the program calls the method, it must provide out references to integer variables as parameters.

```
int d1, d2;

ThrowTwoDice(out d1, out d2);
```

Question: I want to provide my age to a method that will then decide whether I am old enough to see a movie. What should the method header look like?

> **Answer:** The method only needs the value of my age, so I can pass the age as a value. The method could return a bool value that indicates whether I can see the movie or not:

```
bool AllowedToSeeMovie(int age)
```

Reading a nonexistent contact

The principle of the contacts app should be that the user stores something before they try to load it back. However, we need to consider what would happen if the user tries to fetch a nonexistent item. This will happen in the case where the user types in the name of a contact that is not stored in the app.

It turns out that C# provides a value just for this purpose. The value is called *null*. The value null is a setting that we can give a C# variable if it is not sensible for the variable to refer to anything. For example, the following statement sets the string variable name to refer to the string "Rob" :

```
string name = "Rob";
```

If we want to represent the situation where the name has not been set, we can write the following:

```
string name = null;
```

If a program tries to use a null reference, it will fail with an exception. Here are some statements that try to display a string that has been set to null. When they run, the program will be abandoned, and the exception in the following screenshot will be generated.

```
string name = null;

SnapsEngine.DisplayString(name);
```

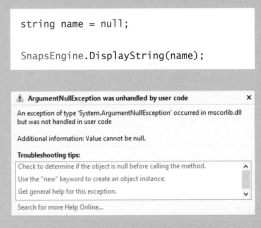

Whenever you create a behavior in a program, it is very important that you consider how it could fail and the best thing for it to do if it does. In the case of FetchStringFromLocalStorage, the method returns null if it's asked to find an item that does not exist. This means that if the user of our contact app tries to look for a name that does not exist, she runs the risk of seeing an exception like the one above, which would be bad. You can address this by making the FetchContact method return a Boolean value that indicates whether or not it was able to fetch a contact. If either the name or the address for a contact is not found, the method can return false to indicate this:

```csharp
bool FetchContact(string name, out string address, out string phone)
{
    address = SnapsEngine.FetchStringFromLocalStorage(itemName: name +
        ":address");
    phone = SnapsEngine.FetchStringFromLocalStorage(itemName: name + ":phone");

    if (address == null || phone == null) return false;

    return true;
}
```

When the FetchContact method is used, the value it returns should be checked to make sure that data was found:

```csharp
if (FetchContact(name: name, address: out address, phone: out phone) == true)
{
    // Got the contact - display it
}
else
{
    // Display an error message
}
```

This sequence of statements shows how the result of FetchContact should be used.

PROGRAMMER'S POINT

Make good use of the values that methods return

There is no obligation for a programmer to write code that checks on the value returned by a method. The C# compiler would be quite happy if our program ignored the value of FetchContact. However, I would not be. Ignoring the result of FetchContact means that the program will fail with an exception if it ever tries to use the address and phone details that FetchContact was supposed to deliver. The program won't commit the ultimate sin, which is displaying invalid data to a user, but it does crash in front of the user. A good programmer makes sure that no information is lost by a program, and this includes making proper use of the values that methods return when they run.

Displaying the contact details

The `FetchContact` method is used by the `FindContact` method, which runs when the user wants to find a contact. The `FindContact` method calls `FetchContact` to get the contact details and displays them if they are available. If the details can't be found, the `FindContact` method displays an appropriate message.

```
void FindContact()
{
    // Get the name of the contact to search for
    string name = SnapsEngine.ReadString("Enter contact name");     // Ask the user
                                                                     // for the name to
                                                                     // search for.

    // Variables to hold the address and phone number being fetched
    string contactAddress, contactPhone;

    if (FetchContact(name: name, address: out contactAddress, phone: out
        contactPhone))                                              // Fetch the contact.
    {
        // Got the contact details - display them
        SnapsEngine.ClearTextDisplay();                             // If the contact is
                                                                     // found, display it.

        SnapsEngine.AddLineToTextDisplay("Name: " + name);
        SnapsEngine.AddLineToTextDisplay("Address: " + contactAddress);
        SnapsEngine.AddLineToTextDisplay("Phone: " + contactPhone);
    }
    else
    {
        // Tell the user the name was not found
        SnapsEngine.DisplayString("Name not found");               // Tell the user that the
                                                                     // name was not found
    }

    // Give the user a chance to view the details
    SnapsEngine.WaitForButton("Continue");                          // Wait for the Continue
                                                                     // button to be pressed

    // Clear the display
    SnapsEngine.ClearTextDisplay();
}
```

Input sanitizing

This contact application is so simple that your mother could use it. Although she might not like it very much if the program doesn't always find people that she knows are in the list. One reason for this might be that she is trying to find contact information for "Rob" when the information was stored under the key "rob". Remember that C# regards these two strings as completely different (even though a human would work out that they are the same person). The user has to enter the name exactly as it was originally entered, otherwise the program fails to find the contact.

You can fix this by using something we've seen before. You can ask a string to return a version of itself converted to lowercase by using a method named ToLower. The ToLower method converts any alphabetic characters in a string to their lowercase version so that contact details will now be found successfully.

```
name = name.ToLower();
```

At this point, you're rather proud of your program, so you show it to your younger brother and invite him to try and break it—and he succeeds. He finds a way to enter a name that looks okay, but the name can't be found by the program. You both know there is a contact stored for this person, but the program doesn't find it. You ask him to show you how he does it, and he shows you the following search screen.

Enter new contact name

| Rob   × |

| Enter |

If you look carefully at the screenshot, you'll see that your brother broke the program by adding a space in front of "Rob", so the program is searching for " Rob", with a leading space in front of the *R*. C# is a stickler for accuracy, so these searches will fail. Fortunately, we can use another method to attack this problem. You can ask a string to "trim" itself by removing any leading and trailing spaces. This would change " Rob" to "Rob" and make the program work.

The best way to solve these problems is to write a helper method that will use Trim and ToLower to tidy up text that the user enters:

```
string TidyInput(string input)
```

```
{
    input = input.Trim();
    input = input.ToLower();
    return input;
}
```

The TidyInput method takes in a string and cleans it up ready for a search. It trims off any leading and trailing spaces and then converts any letters in the string to lowercase text. The StoreContact and the FetchContact methods can use this method to tidy up any strings that they are asked to store or search for:

```
void StoreContact(string name, string address, string phone)
{
    name = TidyInput(name);

    SnapsEngine.SaveStringToLocalStorage(itemName: name + ":address",
                                         itemValue: address);
    SnapsEngine.SaveStringToLocalStorage(itemName: name + ":phone",
                                         itemValue: phone);
}

bool FetchContact(string name, out string address, out string phone)
{
    name = TidyInput(name);

    address = SnapsEngine.FetchStringFromLocalStorage(itemName: name +
                                                      ":address");
    phone = SnapsEngine.FetchStringFromLocalStorage(itemName: name + ":phone");

    if (address == null || phone == null) return false;

    return true;
}
```

Creating the TidyInput method is a really good idea. It makes our program slightly shorter, but it also means that all the tidying up of names takes place in one part of the program. Otherwise, I could make a mistake such as using ToLower in the StoreContact method and ToUpper in the FetchContact method. Furthermore, if we decide to make changes to the tidy-up behavior—for example, to use only the first 10 characters of a name as the search item—we have to change the behavior only once in the program.

Professional programmers call this part of a program *input sanitizing*. It's the process of making sure that what the user types cannot be used to upset the proper behavior of the program. As a budding developer, you need to remember that whenever you give the user a chance to type something into your program, you are giving them a chance to break it, and you should treat all inputs with a proper amount of suspicion.

Storing contact information in the cloud

Your lawyer customer is very impressed with the contact manager application and promptly installs it on all her Windows devices. And then she notices a problem. She discovers that she has to enter contact details on each device, and she frequently finds that the details she wants are on a device she doesn't have with her. What she really wants is a way to synchronize contact details over all the Windows devices she owns.

This sounds like a really tricky thing to do, and it is. But fortunately, it's also my favorite kind of problem—one that somebody else has already solved. The Windows system provides what is called *roaming* storage. This is managed by the operating system in each Windows device. An amount of networked storage is linked to each Windows account, and each time the user of that account logs in to a Windows device, his or her roaming information is downloaded to that machine from Microsoft server systems.

This is a very good example of what is called the *cloud*. The Microsoft systems are somewhere "out there in the Internet," and the Windows operating system connects to them and makes the storage available to programs that run on Windows devices.

To make an application store things in the cloud, you simply have to use different Snaps methods to save and load the strings that make up the contact information. Rather than using `SaveStringToLocalStorage`, the program has to call `SaveStringToRoamingStorage` instead. There is a corresponding `FetchStringFromRoamingStorage` method to bring the data back.

The roaming storage mechanism works very well. It can take a little while for the storage to synchronize, and if a machine is not connected to the network, the synchronization can't take place. There are also some limitations placed on the amount of data that can be stored in roaming storage. It is fine for a program to store a small amount of information, such as a small number of contacts or settings information, but this is not a good way to synchronize your music collection across multiple machines.

This kind of storage is organized on a per-application basis, which means that if you create two different applications, they will not be able to view the contents of each other's storage. Your lawyer friend is a bit concerned about the security of the data that is held, but the data is sent securely between devices and the cloud.

Improve the Tiny Contacts app

The Tiny Contacts application can be used as the basis of any application that needs to store and retrieve text. You could use it to store recipes or just as a general purpose note jotter. Here are some things you could do to make it even more interesting:

- Improve the application so that users can edit the details of the contacts. A user could activate the edit behavior after he has viewed a contact.

- Add a password to the program. You could even add a menu option to let the user set the password. The password could be stored along with the contact information.

- Make the program speak the information as well as display it, or allow users to choose which form of output they want.

- Change the program to use roaming storage so that contact information is synchronized across all your Windows devices.

Adding IntelliSense comments to your methods

Modern software is rarely written by one person alone. One person might write the first version of the code, but many other programmers follow in that person's footsteps, adding features and tracking down bugs. As you've learned, comments add a huge value to a program. They make it easier for other programmers to understand how the code works.

You can also add special comments to a code file that can be displayed by Visual Studio and greatly improve the experience of developers. The feature you use to do this is called IntelliSense. You may have already seen how IntelliSense can help you when you write a program. For example, when I was writing the `TidyInput` method, I could point to the name of a C# method, and a description of the method would appear, as shown in **Figure 8-6**. It turns out that it is really easy to add comments to our methods to enable this behavior.

```
string TidyInput(string input)
{
    input = input.Trim();
    input = input.ToLower();
    return input;
    ┌─────────────────────────────────────────────────┐
}   │ ⊗  string string.ToLower()                      │
    │    Returns a copy of this string converted to lowercase. │
    └─────────────────────────────────────────────────┘
```

Figure 8-6 Intellisense displayed for the ToLower method.

You start by finding the line above the method header and typing the forward slash character (/) three times. Visual Studio takes a look at the method header and builds a template for adding comments to the method:

```
/// <summary>
///
/// </summary>
/// <param name="input"></param>
/// <returns></returns>
string TidyInput(string input)
{
    input = input.Trim();
    input = input.ToLower();
    return input;
}
```

The template is written in a language called XML (for Extensible Markup Language), which you can use to format a comment that describes what the method does. You can now add some details to this template:

```
/// <summary>
/// Tidies up a contact name for use in a search
/// </summary>
/// <param name="input">name to be tidied up</param>
/// <returns>tidied contact name</returns>
string TidyInput(string input)
{
    input = input.Trim();
    input = input.ToLower();
    return input;
}
```

The clever thing that happens next is that Visual Studio will use the text you enter to offer help if you start to use the method later in the program. Whenever you use the TidyInput method in a program, you'll get back the comment information that you entered, making it much easier to use. You can add these comments to every method in your program. The comments also provide information about the number and type of the parameters to the method and any values that are required, as you can see in **Figure 8-7**.

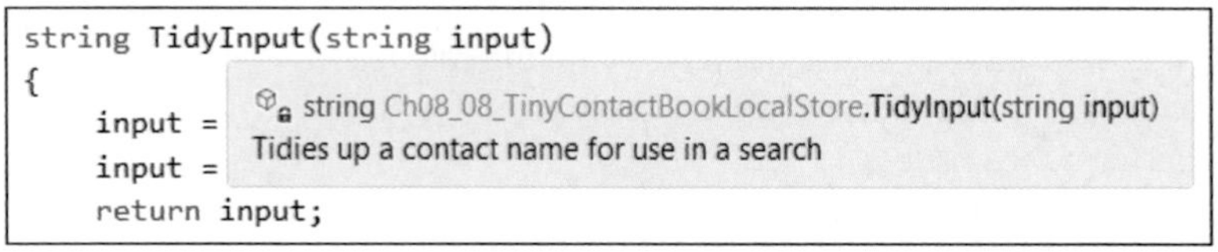

```
string TidyInput(string input)
{
    input =      ⊕ₐ string Ch08_08_TinyContactBookLocalStore.TidyInput(string input)
    input =         Tidies up a contact name for use in a search
    return input;
```

Figure 8-7 Intellisense for TidyInput parameters.

I think there is something quite magical about the way that code you create suddenly becomes part of the system. Whenever I create a method, I add these comments as a matter of course, and I'd like to think that you will too. In the BeginToCodeWithCSharp solution, if you open the final version of the Tiny Contacts manager (in the **Chapter 08** folder, the file **Ch08_08_TinyContactBookLocalStore.cs**), all the methods are properly commented and will show up in IntelliSense when you use Visual Studio.

What you have learned

In this chapter, you have learned how to take a block of code and turn it into a method that can be used from other parts of the program. You've seen that a method contains a header, which describes the method, and a block of code that is the body of the method. The method header gives the name of the method and specifies what type of data the method returns, if any. The header also gives the names and types of any parameters that are accepted by the method. When a method is called, the programmer supplies an argument that matches each parameter.

Parameters are items that the method can work on. They are usually passed by value, in that a copy is made of the argument given in the method call. If the method body contains statements that change the value of the parameter, this change is local to the method body.

A method can return a single value, which can be of any type. If a method must return multiple values, it can make use of reference parameters. A reference parameter is connected to the variable used as an argument, and it allows code in the body of the method to read and write the parameter variable. If the method is only required to output values into a parameter, there is a variant of the reference parameter called an out parameter. Code in the body of the method can only write to an out parameter, and it must set a value in the parameter before the method body completes.

Here are some questions that you might like to ponder about the use of methods in programs:

Does using methods in a program slow the program down?

Not normally. There is a certain amount of work required to create the call of a method and then return from it, but this is not normally an issue. The benefits of methods far outweigh the performance issues.

Can I use methods to spread work around a group of programmers?

Indeed you can. This is a very good reason to use methods. There are several ways that you can use methods to spread work around. One popular way is to write placehoder methods and build the application from them. A placeholder method will have the correct parameters and return value, but the body will do very little. As the program is developed, programmers fill in and test each method in turn.

How do I come up with names for my methods?

The best methods have names that are given in a verb-noun form. `FetchContact` is a good name for a method. The first part indicates what it does, and the second part indicates what it works on. I find that thinking of method names (and variable names, for that matter) can be quite hard at times. The good news is that you can use Visual Studio (and other tools) to rename the methods in your program if you think of better names for them later. This process is called *refactoring,* which is an important part of programming.

9

Creating structured data types

What you will learn

Programs can work with many different types of data, including integers, floating-point numbers, and strings of text. They can also create arrays of a particular data type. However, the data that programs need to work with is often more complex than single values. In this chapter, you'll learn how to build structured data types that can bring together a number of related items into a single variable. Knowing how to do this lets you design data storage that matches the specific needs of an application.

Storing music notes by using a structure

You can use Snaps to make music with the `PlayNote` method. You give the method a number that identifies the pitch of the note to be played and another number that sets the duration of the note in seconds. **Figure 9-1** shows the numbers for the notes that are available. There is an octave of notes to work with, providing 13 possible values for a pitch.

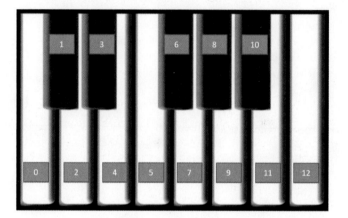

Figure 9-1 Numbered keys to use with the `PlayNote` method.

When a program performs the following statement, it plays the note with pitch 0 (C) by using the speaker for your device. The note will be played for 0.4 seconds.

```
SnapsEngine.PlayNote(pitch:0,duration:0.4);
```

After the note has been played, the program continues to the next statement. A program can play a sequence of notes by making a sequence of calls to the `PlayNote` method. When the following program runs, the second note plays for twice as long as the first one.

```
using SnapsLibrary;

class Ch09_01_PlaySomeNotes
{
    public void StartProgram()
```

```
    {
        SnapsEngine.SetTitleString("Play Three Notes");
        SnapsEngine.PlayNote(pitch:0,duration:0.4);  ———————— Play C for 0.4 seconds.
        SnapsEngine.PlayNote(pitch:2,duration:0.8);  ———————— Play D for 0.8 seconds.
        SnapsEngine.PlayNote(pitch:4,duration:0.4);  ———————— Play E for 0.4 seconds.
    }
}
```

From the point of view of this program's data, we can say that a note in a tune is represented by two values: the pitch of the note that we play and the duration of the note.
If we want to store a larger number of notes so that we can play a more complicated
tune, we can use arrays to hold the pitch and duration values. One array would hold
the pitch value, and another the duration of the note.

```
int [] notePitches = new int[3];             ———— Array to hold the note values.
double [] noteDurations = new double[3];     ———— Array to hold the duration values.

notePitches [0] = 0; noteDurations [0] = 0.4;   ⎫
notePitches [1] = 2; noteDurations [1] = 0.8;   ⎬  Statements that set pitch
notePitches [2] = 4; noteDurations [2] = 0.4;   ⎭  value and duration.
```

I've put two statements on each line of the program above. Each line sets the pitch
and the duration for one note.

We can use a for loop to work through the pitch and duration arrays and play each
note in turn. We could create a longer tune just by adding more elements to the note
and duration arrays.

```
for (int i = 0; i < 3; i = i + 1)  ————————  Loop around each element in the array.
{
    SnapsEngine.PlayNote(pitch: notePitches [i], duration: noteDurations[i]);
}                                                ———— Play the corresponding note.
Ch09_02_PlayNotesWithArrays
```

This tune-storage mechanism relies on the two arrays remaining "in step"—in other
words, notePitches[2] must match up with noteDurations[2]. If the arrays get out
of step, the tune will sound wrong as notes are played for the wrong lengths. What we
really want is a way for a program to create a single variable type that holds both data
items required to make a note. C# provides a way to do this—it is called a *structure*.

Creating and declaring a structure

A *structure* brings together a number of separate data items. Each data item is called a *field* or *member* of the structure. You design the composition of the structure, and the compiler can then create variables of the structure's type. In other words, making a structure adds a new data type to your programs. We could create a SongNote structure like this to hold information about one note in a song:

```csharp
public struct SongNote
{
    public int NotePitch;
    public double NoteDuration;
}
```

You've seen the public modifier before when you looked at methods in Chapter 8. Later in this chapter, you'll see how the C# language provides security for members of a structure by declaring them as private. This lets a programmer protect objects and their contents from other code. You could use this object security to protect the NotePitch and NoteDuration values, and you could also make the SongNote structure itself usable only in certain parts of a program. But for now, we're going to make everything public.

It's important to remember that we have not stored any note data to this point. What we have done is told the C# compiler how to make a SongNote structure when we declare a variable of that type. We do that by using a statement such as the following, which creates a variable named myNote of type SongNote.

```csharp
SongNote myNote;
```

When the C# compiler sees the name of a type (for example, int or string or Song-Note), it goes off and looks in the list of "things I know how to make" for instructions on how to make this particular type of variable. When the compiler finds the instructions, it creates the variable. In the case of a SongNote variable, the compiler will reserve space for two values: an integer NotePitch and a double precision NoteDuration. (The names of structures, like other C# elements, are case sensitive. You'll get an error if you type songNote instead of SongNote.)

Programs can extract the members of a structure variable and use them as they would any other variable of that type. The following statements set up a SongNote variable that represents C (note number 0) being played for 0.4 seconds.

```
SongNote myNote;
myNote.NotePitch = 0;
myNote.NoteDuration = 0.4;
```

Using structure variables

Structure variables are a new way of holding data. It is worth thinking about how they work in some detail.

Question: What does the period character do in a statement like `myNote.NotePitch = 0;`?

Answer: The period separates the name of the variable (`myNote`) from the name of the member (either `NotePitch` or `NoteDuration` in this case) of the variable of that structure. This is how a program can access elements inside an object.

Question: Is there anything special about members of a structure value?

Answer: No. They can be used in the same way as variables of that type. In other words, a program can use the `NoteDuration` member of a `SongNote` value as a double-precision floating-point value.

Question: What are the initial values of the members of a brand-new structure variable?

Answer: The compiler will complain if a program tries to use a variable before it has been given a value. The following code will not compile:

```
int newInt;
int i = newInt;
```

The error "Use of unassigned local variable 'newInt'" would be produced because the program is trying to use the value of the variable before it has been assigned one. Structures behave in the same way. The initial values of all of the items they hold are set to "unassigned."

```
SongNote newNote;
int r = newNote.NotePitch;
```

These statements would also fail to compile because the value of `NotePitch` in the `newNote` variable has not been assigned.

Question: What happens when I assign one structure variable to another?

Answer: When structures are assigned, the program copies the value of each member of the structure into the destination.

```
SongNote originalNote;
originalNote.NotePitch = 0;
originalNote.NoteDuration = 0.4;
SongNote noteCopy = originalNote;
```

In the code above, the variable noteCopy would end up with a NotePitch value of 0 and a NoteDuration of 0.4

Creating arrays of structure values

We started using structures because we wanted a way of safely storing song information. The SongNote structure gave us a way to bring together the information needed to play a note by holding both the note number and the duration the note should play for.

Remember that the SongNote structure is a new type of data. You can use a SongNote (or another structure you define) everywhere you use other C# types. This means that a program can contain arrays of SongNote values.

In Chapter 7, you saw that when a program creates an array, each element is set to the default value for that type. This behavior extends to the elements of the song array, which means that the NotePitch member of each element would be set to 0, as would the NoteDuration. This statement creates an array that can hold three song notes.

```
SongNote[] song = new SongNote[3];
```

A program can then use an index value to get hold of a particular note in the array and access the NotePitch and NoteDuration values held within it. These statements set the note and duration values for the note at the start of the array.

```
song[0].NotePitch = 0;
song[0].NoteDuration = 0.4;
```

The next program creates an array of SongNote values and then plays the tune stored in them. Because each note is now stored in a structure, there's no chance that the

`NotePitch` and `NoteDuration` properties of a note can get out of step because the two values are stored inside a single item.

```
using SnapsLibrary;

class Ch09_03_PlayNotesFromStructureArray
{
    public struct SongNote
    {
        public int NotePitch;
        public double NoteDuration;
    }

    public void StartProgram()
    {
        SongNote [] notes = new SongNote[3];
        notes[0].NotePitch = 0; notes[0].NoteDuration = 0.4;
        notes[1].NotePitch = 2; notes[1].NoteDuration = 0.8;
        notes[2].NotePitch = 4; notes[2].NoteDuration = 0.4;

        for (int i = 0; i < 3; i = i + 1)
        {
            SnapsEngine.PlayNote(pitch:notes[i].NotePitch,
                duration:notes[i].NoteDuration);
        }
    }
}
```

Structures and methods

The value of a structure variable can be used as a parameter to a method call. You use the type of the structure as a parameter in the same way that you passed strings to the `Alert` method in the previous chapter. Here, the method `PlaySongNote` accepts a `SongNote` as a parameter. When the method is called, it extracts the pitch and duration values from the parameter supplied to the call and plays the note.

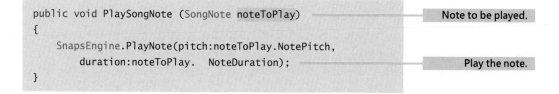

```
public void PlaySongNote (SongNote noteToPlay)                    Note to be played.
{
    SnapsEngine.PlayNote(pitch:noteToPlay.NotePitch,
        duration:noteToPlay.  NoteDuration);                     Play the note.
}
```

A program can call PlaySongNote and pass it a SongNote as a parameter. These statements create a note and then call PlaySongNote to play it.

```
SongNote myNote;
myNote.NotePitch = 0;
myNote.NoteDuration = 0.4;
PlaySongNote(myNote);
```

Structures as method parameters

Question: What would happen if PlaySongNote changed the pitch of a note passed as a parameter?

Answer: In Chapter 8 you saw that unless you specify otherwise, parameters to a method are passed by value—in other words, the value of an argument is copied into the method when it is called. Exactly the same thing happens with structures. In the example above, if the PlaySongNote method changed the NotePitch of the myNote passed into it as a parameter, the NotePitch member of the myNote variable would not be changed. In this respect, structure values behave exactly as integers or any other type.

A method can also return a structure as a result. The RandomSongNote method shown next is of type SongNote. It returns a SongNote value that is set to a random pitch and duration. It uses the dice value (which returns a number between 1 and 6) to pick a random pitch and another dice value to select a random duration for the SongNote that it returns.

```
public SongNote RandomSongNote()
{
    SongNote result;
    result.NotePitch = SnapsEngine.ThrowDice();          Pick a note between 1 and 6.
    result.NoteDuration = SnapsEngine.ThrowDice() / 10.0;          Pick a duration.
    return result;
}
```

We can use this method to play random note sequences. Here's a program that uses both the RandomSongNote and PlaySongNote methods to play a twenty-note random song that sounds almost exactly like a cat walking along a piano keyboard.

```
for (int i = 0; i < 20; i = i + 1)          ──── Go around the loop 20 times.
{
    SongNote note = RandomSongNote();       ──── Pick a random note and play it.
    PlaySongNote(note);
}
Ch09_04_RandomMusic
```

Improve the keyboard cat alarm

You can use the random music code to make a really annoying alarm that plays a sequence of notes randomly when it goes off. The notes will continue until the user taps the screen:

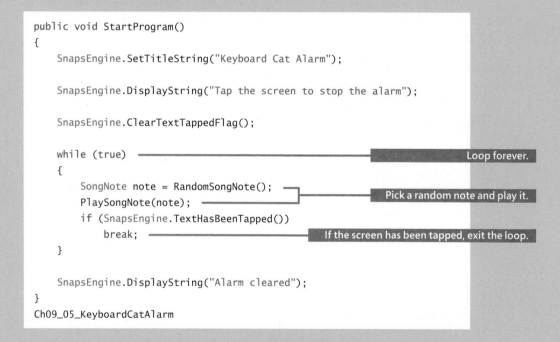

```
public void StartProgram()
{
    SnapsEngine.SetTitleString("Keyboard Cat Alarm");

    SnapsEngine.DisplayString("Tap the screen to stop the alarm");

    SnapsEngine.ClearTextTappedFlag();

    while (true)                              ──── Loop forever.
    {
        SongNote note = RandomSongNote();     ──┐ Pick a random note and play it.
        PlaySongNote(note);                    ─┘
        if (SnapsEngine.TextHasBeenTapped())
            break;                            ──── If the screen has been tapped, exit the loop.
    }

    SnapsEngine.DisplayString("Alarm cleared");
}
Ch09_05_KeyboardCatAlarm
```

The program uses the screen-tap methods introduced in Chapter 6 to detect when the user taps the screen to silence the alarm. You can improve the program by adding a delay so that it waits a few minutes before sounding. You can further improve it by making the program flash the screen in random colors as it plays each note.

Constructing structure values

Structures can contain methods as well as data members. This means that structure types can contain code that will perform tasks, and one of the tasks that it can perform is to set itself up.

So far in our tune-playing program, we are setting the values of structure variables "the hard way." A program needs to use three statements to create a new SongNote and set its NotePitch and NoteDuration members:

```
SongNote note;
note.NotePitch = 0;
note.NoteDuration = 0.4;
```

Fortunately, C# provides a way of creating a new structure object and setting its values at the same time. You do this by giving the SongNote type a *constructor method*. A constructor is a method that is itself a member of a structure. The constructor method for an object has the same name as the object, in this case SongNote. An object can have lots of different constructors, each of which reflect a different way of setting the initial values in that structure.

```
public struct SongNote
{
    public int NotePitch;                              ──────  Data members
    public double NoteDuration;

    public SongNote(int pitch, double duration)  ──── Constructor method member
    {
        NotePitch = pitch;                             ──────  Copy parameters
        NoteDuration = duration;                                to the members of
    }                                                              the structure.
}
```

This constructor for the SongNote takes pitch and duration parameter values and uses them to set up the members of the structure. We can use the constructor when we create a new SongNote value:

```
SongNote note = new SongNote(pitch: 0, duration: 0.4);
```

This single statement creates a new SongNote and then sets the variable note to this value. The note and the duration are set by the constructor when it is called. I've used named arguments to the constructor to make it clear which value is the pitch and which is the duration.

This is a much cleaner way to create a SongNote value. It ensures that when a variable is created, it holds values for all the members of the structure. It also provides a way for us to ensure that our notes contain valid information.

Programs never actually call the constructor method; it is called automatically when a note is created. In the following example, I've added a message that is displayed by the SongNote constructor.

```
using SnapsLibrary;

class Ch09_06_ConstructingSongNotes
{
    static SnapsEngine snaps;

    public struct SongNote
    {
        public int NotePitch;
        public double NoteDuration;

        public SongNote(int note, double duration)
        {
            NotePitch = note;
            NoteDuration = duration;
            SnapsEngine.DisplayString("Hello from the SongNote constructor");
        }
    }

    public void StartProgram()
    {
        SongNote note = new SongNote(note: 0, duration: 0.4);
    }
}
```

When this program runs, the message appears when the new SongNote value is created. Note that you would not normally do this; a constructor should just run silently.

What's special about the constructor method?

Question: We've seen methods in objects before, but there's something special about the constructor method for the SongNote structure. What's special about it?

> **Answer:** It doesn't have any return type. When we've considered methods before, we saw that C# insists that a method return a value—for example, the GetNumber method returns an integer—or we have to use the void keyword to explicitly state that a method does not return anything. The constructor doesn't seem to have any information about the type of a result it might return. This is because the method doesn't ever return anything. The constructor method is called automatically, just as an object is coming into existence. When the constructor is complete, the object has been created.

Invalid data in a constructor call

The **Snaps** framework uses pitch numbers that range from 0 to 12. A pitch value outside that range can't be played. However, there's nothing stopping a programmer from trying to construct a SongNote that contains invalid values:

```
SongNote note = new SongNote(pitch: -99, duration: 0.4);
```

This creates a SongNote with a pitch value of –99, which is outside the allowed range. If this note is ever played, it will not work correctly. You might wonder why someone would try to create a note like this. One reason is to attack our system. The word "hacker," once an honorable term describing someone who is good at making things work, now also means someone who tries to break into computer systems. One way to break into a system is to use invalid inputs and see what happens. If the hacker is lucky, the program might crash or otherwise misbehave when it is given invalid data.

To counter this problem, a constructor can check the values that are being used to set up the object, and it can reject any invalid values that it finds. The constructor can reject invalid values by throwing an exception.

Throwing exceptions in constructors

You first encountered exceptions in Chapter 6 when you saw that if a program tries to access a nonexistent element in an array, an exception is thrown that prevents this. The constructor for the SongNote object is going to create and throw an exception to stop the program because it would not be sensible to continue and make an invalid SongNote value.

The C# keyword throw is used to throw an Exception object. The exception can be given a message that describes what has gone wrong.

```csharp
throw new Exception("Invalid note pitch value");
```

As the name implies, exceptions should be thrown only in exceptional circumstances. If a user enters invalid data, for example an age of 1,000, this is not exceptional; it is more likely that the user pressed a key more times than he meant to. You have seen how to deal with errors like this; a program can use a loop to repeatedly ask for values until the user enters one that is valid. However, if a constructor detects an invalid input, there is nothing it can do. The constructor must not allow a SongNote that contains an invalid pitch value to be created.

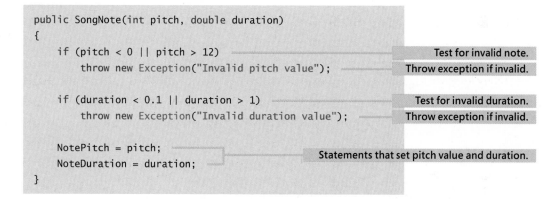

```csharp
public SongNote(int pitch, double duration)
{
    if (pitch < 0 || pitch > 12)                    Test for invalid note.
        throw new Exception("Invalid pitch value");    Throw exception if invalid.

    if (duration < 0.1 || duration > 1)              Test for invalid duration.
        throw new Exception("Invalid duration value");  Throw exception if invalid.

    NotePitch = pitch;
    NoteDuration = duration;                          Statements that set pitch value and duration.
}
```

This version of the SongNote constructor method will refuse to create a SongNote that has an invalid pitch number or a duration of less than one-tenth of a second or greater than 1 second. If anyone tries to make an invalid SongNote, they will find that their program is stopped by an exception. I call this technique *defensive programming*. I try to make sure that my programs can't be upset, even by invalid inputs. I also try very hard to make sure that my programs fail at the point the mistake is made rather than later on. This program should fail when it tries to create an invalid SongNote, not some time later when it tries to play one. Later in the book you will discover how to catch and deal with exceptions.

The Exception type?

Question: What is the purpose of the Exception type?

> **Answer:** The Exception type contains a description of the state of the program at the point at which the error occurred, along with a description of the error itself. You will see later that a program can catch this information and use it to provide information to the user (and the programmer) about what has gone wrong.

Question: Where does the Exception type come from?

> **Answer:** The Exception type is defined in the System namespace. (You first saw namespaces in Chapter 3 when you learned that all the Snaps methods are defined the Snaps-Library namespace.) To directly access types from the System namespace, a program must contain a using directive to tell the compiler to look in the namespace for those types. This means that a program that uses both Snaps and System types must contain two using directives.

```
using SnapsLibrary;
using System;
```

Making a music recorder

Earlier, you saw how an array can hold a set of ice-cream sales figures. Next you are going to use an array to hold a tune as an array of SongNote values. The program will repeatedly ask the user for pitch and duration values, use them to create new note values, and store them in an array called tune.

```
SongNote[] tune = new SongNote[100];            The tune can contain up to 100 notes.

int tuneLength = 0;                             Holds the length of the tune entered by
                                                                                  the user.

for (int tunePos = 0; tunePos < tune.Length; tunePos = tunePos + 1)   Loop to read and
{                                                                       store notes.

    string command = SnapsEngine.SelectFrom2Buttons("New Note", "Play Tune");
                                                                Ask the user what to do.

    if (command == "Play Tune")                                 Check if Play Tune
    {                                                              is selected.

        tuneLength = tunePos;              Record how far user got through the loop.
```

```
        break;
    }

    int notePitch = SnapsEngine.ReadInteger("Note Pitch");
    float noteDuration = SnapsEngine.ReadFloat("Note Duration");

    SongNote newNote = new SongNote(pitch: notePitch, duration: noteDuration);

    tune[tunePos] = newNote;
}
```

If we get here, we are entering a new note, so get the pitch

Get the note duration.

Create a new note.

Store the new note in the tune.

This loop could sit in the middle of a music-recorder program. The user can enter as many notes as he wants up to the size of the array. Each time around the loop, the program asks whether the user wants to add a new note or exit the loop. If the user wants to enter a new note, the program requests the pitch of the note to play and the duration value. These are then used to create a new note that is copied into the array. When the user has finished entering the tune, he selects the **Play Tune** button and the program stops recording notes and plays the entire tune. Here is the code that will play all the notes that the user has entered.

```
// Play the tune
for (int tunePos = 0; tunePos < tuneLength; tunePos++)
{
    SnapsEngine.PlayNote(pitch:tune[tunePos].NotePitch,
        duration:tune[tunePos].NoteDuration);
}
Ch09_07_MusicRecorder
```

Work through each note up to the end of the tune.

Play the note.

CODE ANALYSIS

Examining the music recorder

Question: How does the music-recorder program know how long the tune is?

Answer: The recording program uses a counter variable called tunePos to keep a record of where in the array to place the next note to be stored. Each time around the storage loop, the value in tunePos is increased by one. When the user selects the **Play Tune** command, the program records the value of tunePos in a variable called tuneLength, which is then used to control the for loop that plays the tune.

Question: What would happen if the user entered an invalid pitch or duration value into the note recorder?

Answer: The constructor for the note would throw an exception and the note-entry program would stop. This is not very friendly behavior for the music recorder. You might like to think about changing the program so that it checks the pitch and duration values before it tries to create the note.

Creating preset arrays

You could use the music recorder program to enter and play the notes of your favorite song, perhaps "Twinkle, Twinkle Little Star." However, it would soon become tedious to enter all the values each time you wanted to hear the same song. What you might like to do is create a preset array of notes for this song.

In Chapter 7, you saw how to create preset arrays. The ice-cream sales program used a preset array that contained the names of each day of the week so that it could convert a day number into the name of that day. We can also create a preset array of notes. This allows us to build song data into our program. Many programs have data built into them in this way. A game might have preset data that describes the various levels of the game; a currency conversion program could have the names of the different kinds of currency it works with. A program can also create preset structure values. The `twinkleTwinkle` array of `SongNote` values is created as shown here.

```
SongNote[] twinkleTwinkle = new SongNote[] {              Start of the array initializer.
    new SongNote(pitch:0, duration:0.4), new SongNote(pitch:0, duration:0.4),
    new SongNote(pitch:7, duration:0.4), new SongNote(pitch:7, duration:0.4),
    new SongNote(pitch:9, duration:0.4), new SongNote(pitch:9, duration:0.4),
    new SongNote(pitch:7, duration:0.8), new SongNote(pitch:5, duration:0.4),
    new SongNote(pitch:5, duration:0.4), new SongNote(pitch:4, duration:0.4),
    new SongNote(pitch:4, duration:0.4), new SongNote(pitch:2, duration:0.4),
    new SongNote(pitch:2, duration:0.4), new SongNote(pitch:0, duration:0.8)
};                                       The note values to put into the new array.
```

We can then use a loop to work through each note in the array and play it. This will work for an array of any length.

```
foreach(SongNote note in twinkleTwinkle)                      Fetch each note in turn
{
    SnapsEngine.PlayNote(pitch:note.NotePitch), duration:note.NoteDuration);
}                                                                  Play the note.
Ch09_08_PresetMusic
```

Examining the preset tune

Question: How does the `foreach` loop play the preset tune?

Answer: A program uses `foreach` to work through each item in an array. Each time around the loop, the variable `note` is set to the next successive item in the `twinkleTwinkle` array.

Question: How would you add extra notes to the tune?

Answer: The program will automatically accommodate extra notes if they are added to the program text.

Objects and responsibilities: Making a **SongNote** play itself

At the moment, the program is using the SongNote structure just as a way of bringing together the note and duration values that describe a note in a song. However, users of the SongNote structure need to know what a SongNote structure contains to use it. In other words, if I want to write a program that plays songs, I need to know how the NotePitch and NoteDuration members of the SongNote are used with the Snaps methods that play music.

It would be much easier if we could just ask a SongNote value to play itself. It turns that you can do this because structures can contain methods.

```
public struct SongNote
{
    public int NotePitch;
    public double NoteDuration;

    public void Play()
    {
        SnapsEngine.PlayNote(pitch:NotePitch, duration: NoteDuration);
    }
}
```

The Play method is part of the SongNote structure. In the same way that we can access data members of a structure, a program can also call methods that the structure contains:

```
foreach (SongNote note in tune)
{
    note.Play();
}
Ch09_09_NotePlay
```

This version of the song playback loop asks each note to play itself by calling the Play method inside the SongNote structure. This means that other programmers can use the SongNote structure to play tunes without knowing how the note works. This is an extremely powerful feature.

PROGRAMMER'S POINT

Self-contained objects are a good thing

A coder using the SongNote structure will know she has to specify a NotePitch and a NoteDuration to create a note, but she won't need to know how to use the PlayNote method in the Snaps framework to play the note. This is because the SongNote structure provides a Play method that takes care of how the music is played. It's a bit like driving a car with an automatic transmission versus a manual transmission. In the automatic car, you just have to press a pedal to make the car go faster. In the manual car, you have to know how to select gears, when to shift gears, and so on. When designing the elements that are going to make up a complex system, try to make each element as self-contained and as easy to use as possible.

Protecting values held in a structure

As you've seen, we made the SongNote structure's values public so that our program can store data in the note. The public in front of the declarations of the NotePitch and NoteDuration members means that these members are visible to programs that use the SongNote structure:

```
public struct SongNote
{
    public int NotePitch;
    public double NoteDuration;
}
```

This is how we created and set up our first SongNote value:

```
SongNote note
note.NotePitch = 0;
note.NoteDuration = 0.4;
```
Put values into the NotePitch and NoteDuration members of the structure.

The note is declared, and then the values in it are set. However, the fact that these values have been marked with public means that they can be changed by the program at any point in the future. In the case of a SongNote, this is probably not a problem; it just means that a nasty programmer could make a tune sound wrong. However, if we were writing a program for a bank, it would be much more dangerous if programmers were able to change the amount of money in an account.

The C# language lets you mark members of a structure as private. A private member of a structure is not visible to code running outside the structure:

```
public struct SongNote
{
    private int notePitch;
    private double noteDuration;

    public void Play ()
    {
        SnapsEngine.PlayNote(notePitch, noteDuration);
    }

    public SongNote(int pitch, double duration)
    {
        notePitch = pitch;
        noteDuration = duration;
    }
}
```
Make the notePitch and noteDuration members private.

This code can use the member variables because it is part of the SongNote structure.

Sets the initial values of the note.

The preceding code shows a more secure version of the SongNote structure. The notePitch and noteDuration values have been made private, which means that only statements in methods that are members of the SongNote structure are able to use these variables. Once we have created a SongNote value, it is not possible for any program to change the value or duration of that note.

```
SongNote note
note.notePitch = 0;
```
This statement would not compile because notePitch is now private.

CODE ANALYSIS

Public and Private

Question: Look closely at the code for the more secure and the original SongNote structures and you should notice something slightly different. What is different about the more secure version of SongNote?

Answer: The two data members, notePitch and noteDuration, now have identifiers that start with a lowercase letter: for example, NotePitch has become notePitch. This is a C# convention that coders use to make programs easier to understand. If an identifier starts with an uppercase letter, the member is public and can be seen by code running outside the structure. If an identifier starts with a lowercase letter, it is private.

Question: Can we make member methods private, too? What would happen if we made the Play method in SongNote private? Would this be a good idea?

Answer: It is possible to make methods private. The effect of doing so is that the method can't be called from code outside the structure. This would not be a sensible thing to do in the case of Play because it is used by code external to the structure. If Play were private, the external code would not be able to call it, and the note could not be played.

PROGRAMMER'S POINT

Consider "active" and "passive" safety in your program design

A data member of a class that is public can be regarded as a potential failure point. This is because you have no control over the value in that variable. Another program could change the value at any time. When you design a large program, you should decide how you are going to make sure that all the values that the program works with are valid at all times.

This is part of making software of good quality. Car designers talk about "active" and "passive" safety. Active safety features (good brakes and steering) help prevent a driver from getting into trouble, and passive ones (airbags and seat belts) help prevent a driver from being injured if there is trouble. Likewise, good software has active and passive elements. Private and public elements contribute to active safety—they make it harder for values in the program to be damaged by mistakes in the code. (You can't corrupt the settings for a note in a song because the data members have been made private.) Exceptions in programs contribute to passive safety. If a program detects that it is dangerous to continue, it can throw an exception and fail in a managed way.

Making a drawing program with Snaps

A program like the one shown in **Figure 9-2** seems like a complicated thing, but let's try to build one anyway. You'll learn more about data structures as we go!

Figure 9-2 A drawing program in the hands of an expert.

The user of this program will be able to draw on the screen with a finger, mouse, or pen. The first version of the program will be simple. It will find out where the pen is and then draw a colored dot at that position. If the program repeats these two actions in a loop, we have a simple drawing program. We'll add more advanced features, such as color selection, once the basics are in place.

Drawing dots on the screen

Before we code our program, we have to work out how we're going to express the drawing positions we're going to use. In computer graphics, the position values for drawing are frequently expressed in *pixels*. A pixel is an addressable dot on the screen of the device that you are using. Display manufacturers talk about displays that are 1280 pixels by 768 pixels, for example, and the resolution of a digital camera is also expressed in pixels. The more pixels a screen has, the more details it can show, although this is, of course, affected by the size of the screen, too.

As shown in **Figure 9-3**, for a given position on the screen, the value of X specifies how far the position is from the left edge, and the value of Y specifies how far down the screen from the top edge. A specific location is expressed as (X, Y).

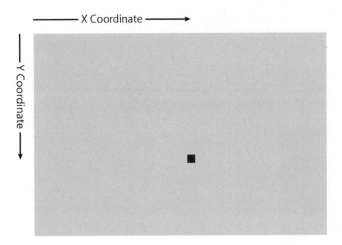

Figure 9-3 Screen coordinates.

CODE ANALYSIS

Making sense of coordinates

Question: Where on the screen is the coordinate (0,0)?

    Answer: This position is sometimes called the *origin* of the coordinate system. When we draw on a computer screen, the origin is usually the top-left corner of the screen. Note that this is different from most graphs you draw on paper, which have their origin at the bottom-left corner.

Question: If I increase the value of Y, which way do I move my position on the screen?

    Answer: This is very important. Increasing the value of Y moves the position down the screen, not up, because the origin of the screen is the top-left corner.

Using the DrawDot Snap to draw a dot on the screen

The DrawDot method lets a program draw a dot on the screen. When the method is called, it is given the position and the width of the dot to draw:

```
using SnapsLibrary;

class Ch09_10_DrawADot
{
    public void StartProgram()
    {
        SnapsEngine.DrawDot(x:100, y:200, width:10);
    }
}
```

If you run this program, a 10-pixel-wide dot will appear on the screen. The dot will be 100 pixels from the left edge and 200 pixels down from the top edge. The color of the dot will be a rather unimpressive gray, as you can see in **Figure 9-4**.

Figure 9-4 Drawing a dot.

This version of the DrawDot method accepts two integers that express the drawing position (in the form of X and Y values). However, the Snaps framework contains a much better way to manage screen positions: the SnapsCoordinate structure.

The SnapsCoordinate structure

The drawing program we are going to create needs to manipulate positions on the screen. The Snaps framework contains a data structure I created to make this possible. In fact, the Snaps framework contains a set of types I created so that it can work with different types of data. These are held in the **Snaps Types** source code. In Visual Studio, use Solution Explorer to open the **SnapsCoordinate** source code, as shown in **Figure 9-5**.

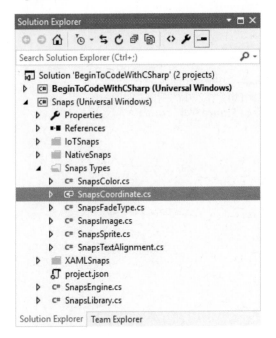

Figure 9-5 Finding the Snaps types.

Take a look at the design of this structure:

```
namespace SnapsLibrary
{
    public struct SnapsCoordinate
```

```
    {
        public int XValue;
        public int YValue;


        public SnapsCoordinate(int x, int y)
        {
            XValue = x;
            YValue = y;
        }
    }
}
```

Data values held in the coordinate.

Constructor method for the coordinate.

I'll say more about the namespace keyword later, when we start creating large programs. For now, focus on the SnapsCoordinate structure, which contains two data members that specify a position on the screen. It also provides a constructor that we can use to create a coordinate with a particular pair of X and Y values. We can create our own values of the structure if we like:

```
SnapsCoordinate dot = new SnapsCoordinate(x:100,y:200);
SnapsEngine.DrawDot(pos:dot,width:10);
```

The first statement creates a variable named dot, which is a SnapsCoordinate. The coordinate describes a position 100 pixels from the left edge and 200 pixels down the screen. This coordinate is then used to draw a 10-pixel-wide dot on the screen at that position. Note that the program uses an *overloaded* version of the DrawDot method. A program overloads a method by providing multiple versions of the method, each of which can accept a different set of arguments. In the case of DrawDot, we can specify a dot position either by using separate X and Y values (which is sometimes useful) or by using a SnapsCoordinate value (which is also sometimes useful).

CODE ANALYSIS

Method overloading

The idea behind method overloading is that you can decide on a sensible name for the task that the method performs and then create versions of the method that are used in different ways, depending on the needs of the program using the method. In the case of DrawDot, it is useful to be able to call the method with integers or coordinates. However, overloading can also lead to confusion. Consider the following two methods:

```
public static void m1 (int x)
{
    SnapsEngine.DisplayString("integer method");
}

public static void m1(float x)
{
    SnapsEngine.DisplayString("floating method");
}

public static void m1(string title, int x)
{
    SnapsEngine.DisplayString("string and int overload");
}
```

All the methods are named m1 and have different parameter types.

Question: Will this code compile correctly?

> **Answer:** Yes. The compiler says that they are all different methods because they have different parameter types. The name m1 is being *overloaded*.

Question: Which method will be called by the following statement?

```
m1(x:3);
```

> **Answer:** This will run the first version of the m1 method because the parameter is of type integer. However, this form of overloading is potentially confusing because someone reading the code might assume that the floating-point version will be used. I suggest that each overloaded version of a method should have a different number of arguments, as in the third version of the method. Then there is no potential for this kind of confusion.

Using the GetDraggedCoordinate Snap to detect a drawing position

The next step is to find out where the user is drawing on the screen. The Snaps library provides a method that will do this for us. You can use the GetDraggedCoordinate Snaps method to find out where on the screen the user wants to draw something:

```
SnapsCoordinate draggedCoordinate = SnapsEngine.GetDraggedCoordinate();
```

The method will wait until the user performs a drawing action on the screen. If the user has a touchscreen, the method waits for the user to touch the screen. If the user has a pen, it waits for the user to move the pen across the screen. If the user has a mouse, the user can click the left mouse button and move the mouse to draw on the screen.

The result from `GetDraggedCoordinate` is the value of a structure variable of type `SnapsCoordinate`. The coordinate values exactly match those that are used by the `DrawDot` method. This means that a program can get a position from the user and immediately use it to draw a dot on the screen.

Get the draw position.

```
SnapsCoordinate draggedCoordinate = SnapsEngine.GetDraggedCoordinate();
SnapsEngine.DrawDot(pos: draggedCoordinate,width:10);
```
Draw a dot there.

These two statements are the heart of our drawing program. The first one waits for the user to indicate where he wants to draw, and the second statement draws a dot there. This is like me waiting for my wife to tell me where on the wall she wants me to hang a picture. She says, "Two feet from the wall and five feet up," and then I hold the picture against the wall so that she can take a look. Then she will say, "Actually, I'd prefer it six inches higher," and we then adjust the height until we find a position that we agree on.

To let the user draw freehand on the screen, we can just put these two statements in a loop. This tiny program uses an infinite loop that lets the user draw on the screen by dragging a finger, pen, or mouse across it. (You have to hold down the left button to draw with the mouse.)

```
class Ch09_11_SimpleDraw
{
    public void StartProgram()
    {                                                        Repeat the loop for ever
        while (true)
        {                                                    Get a dragged coordinate
            SnapsCoordinate draggedCoordinate = SnapsEngine.GetDraggedCoordinate();
            SnapsEngine.DrawDot(pos: draggedCoordinate, width: 10);    Draw a
        }                                                             dot on the
    }                                                                 screen at
}                                                                  the dragged
                                                                      position
```

Running out of dots

Play with the **Ch09_11_SimpleDraw** Snaps app. You'll notice that after you draw for a while, the program starts to erase dots from the screen. The dots that are erased are the first ones that were drawn. The reason for this is that the **Snaps** framework's drawing routines work by adding dot objects to the display. The display has a limited capacity for dots, and after 3,000 have been drawn, it starts to erase the older ones. This is purely a limitation of the way I coded the framework.

Using the `SetDrawingColor` Snap to set the drawing color

At the moment, the drawing is performed in the default color (that rather boring gray). The **Snaps** library provides a method that you can use to set the color to be used by all subsequent drawing operations. It can be used just like the `SetBackgroundColor` method that we've used before. You supply the method with three arguments: the amount of red, green, and blue to be used to set the color. This statement sets the drawing color to red (remember that the maximum value for any color is 255):

```
SnapsEngine.SetDrawingColor(red:255, green:0, blue:0);
```

Colors and dots

```
using SnapsLibrary;

class Ch09_12_MysteryImage
{
    public void StartProgram()
    {
        SnapsEngine.SetBackgroundColor(red: 100, green: 100, blue: 100);
        SnapsCoordinate pos = new SnapsCoordinate(100, 200);
        SnapsEngine.SetDrawingColor(red: 255, green: 255, blue: 255);
```

```
        SnapsEngine.DrawDot(pos: pos, width: 100);
        SnapsEngine.SetDrawingColor(red: 0, green: 0, blue: 0);
        SnapsEngine.DrawDot(pos: pos, width: 80);
        SnapsEngine.SetDrawingColor(red: 0, green: 0, blue: 255);
        SnapsEngine.DrawDot(pos: pos, width: 60);
        SnapsEngine.SetDrawingColor(red: 255, green: 0, blue: 0);
        SnapsEngine.DrawDot(pos: pos, width: 40);
        SnapsEngine.SetDrawingColor(red: 255, green: 255, blue: 0);
        SnapsEngine.DrawDot(pos: pos, width: 20);
    }
}
```

Question: The above statements draw something on the screen. Any idea what it is?

Answer: The first thing that happens is that the screen is changed to a gray color. Then an image is drawn on the screen. The image is made up of a sequence of dots. They are all drawn at the same position, which is set at the start: (100, 200). Each successive dot is drawn smaller than the one before it and is displayed on top of the others. If you are keen on archery, you'll know exactly what the program has drawn: an authentic archery target.

Question: What would happen if the program drew the white circle last rather than first?

Answer: All you would see would be a large white dot, because it would obscure the circles underneath. We can use program code to create drawings by overlaying circles of different colors.

Question: Can I stop the Snaps selection page from being displayed when my program stops?

Answer: Yes. The display of the target is spoiled by the appearance of the Snaps program menu when the program finishes. You can ask the Snaps framework not to display this menu by setting a Snaps control flag:

```
SnapsEngine.DisplayControMenuAtProgramEnd = false;

Ch09_13_MysteryImageNoControlMenu
```

This flag is normally true. If the flag is set to `false`, the user has to use Windows controls to close the program, and he will not be able to select another Snaps program.

Using the `ClearGraphics` Snap to clear the screen

So far we haven't been able to clear the screen and start a new drawing, but the **Snaps** framework provides a method for doing so, named `ClearGraphics`. We can write a drawing program that clears the graphics when the user clicks or taps in the top-left corner of the screen. The key to the behavior of this program is the `if` condition in the middle. It uses two conditions that are combined by using the `&&` (AND) logical operator. If the X position is less than 10 pixels from the edge *and* the Y position is less than 10 pixels from the top, the graphics are cleared away. (Using 10 pixels seems to work okay, but it can be a bit tricky to clear the display if you are using touch input.) If the drawing action is not in the top-left corner, the `else` part of the condition is obeyed, which draws a dot on the screen.

```
using SnapsLibrary;

class Ch09_14_DrawingClear
{
    public void StartProgram()
    {
        while (true)                                                    Get the draw position.
        {
                                                                        If the
            SnapsCoordinate drawPos = SnapsEngine.GetDraggedCoordinate();   position
            if (drawPos.XValue < 10 && drawPos.YValue < 10)             is in the
                SnapsEngine.ClearGraphics();                            top-left
                                                                        corner,
            else                                                        clear the
                SnapsEngine.DrawDot(pos: drawPos, width: 20);           graphics.
        }
    }                                                                   Else, draw the dot.
}
```

The SnapsColor structure

Up until now our graphics programs have manipulated color as three values that represent the red, green, and blue intensity values. However, it's often useful to be able to manipulate a color as a single value, and I created the SnapsColor structure to allow this:

```
namespace SnapsLibrary
{
    public struct SnapsColor
    {
        public byte RedValue;
        public byte GreenValue;
        public byte BlueValue;

        public SnapsColor(byte red, byte green, byte blue)
        {
            RedValue = red;
            GreenValue = green;
            BlueValue = blue;
        }
    }
}
```

The SnapsColor structure contains three byte values: the intensity of the red, green, and blue values that represent the color being stored. We can construct new values by giving the amounts of each color:

```
SnapsColor pink = new SnapsColor(red: 255, green: 192, blue: 203);
```

The constructor method for the SnapsColor structure accepts the red, blue, and green values and then stores them in the object.

There are overloaded versions of all the color-selection methods that accept a **Snaps** color rather than three integer values. This would set the drawing color to pink:

```
SnapsEngine.SetDrawingColor(pink);
```

Creating enumerated types

Structures are very useful when we want to design data storage that can hold a set of related values. But sometimes, rather than increasing the capacity of a data-storage element, you want to restrict the range of possible values that a variable can have. For example, we could improve the drawing program to let the user draw with different shaped pens or even with an erasure pen that draws with the background color. One way to address this would be to map some integer values onto the different kinds of pens that are available:

```
int penType;
if (penType == 1)
{
    // round pen
}
if (penType == 2)
{
    // square pen
}
if (penType == 3)
{
    // erase pen
}
```

The variable penType is an integer. The code above uses the values 1, 2, and 3 to mean round pen, square pen, and erase pen, respectively. Each time a drawing operation is performed, the program can select the appropriate action based on the value in the variable. This would work fine, but from a programming point of view, it's a bit dangerous. There's nothing to stop a programmer from putting an invalid value into the variable:

```
penType=99;
```

This would break the program. What we really want is to create a new data-storage type that can hold only three possible values. It turns out that C# provides just this, the *enumerated type*:

```
enum PenModes                              Create an enum called PenModes.
{
    RoundPen,
    SquarePen,                                  List of possible values
    ErasePen
};
```

The **enum** keyword is followed by the name of the enumerated type being created.
That name is followed by a block containing a list of the possible values that this type
can hold. The **PenModes** type contains three entries, but you can use as many as you
need.

Once we have created the new type, we can create some variables of that type:

```
PenModes  penType;
```

The variable **penType** can be set to any of the values available for this type:

```
penType = PenModes.SquarePen;
```

The statement above sets the value to represent drawing with the square pen. Enumerated types can be used in a C# program in the same way as other types. They can
be used as parameters to methods or return values from them. But it is not possible to
do arithmetic with them. The idea of adding 1 as a **PenMode** value does not have any
meaning. A program can test the value of an enumerated type by using a condition.
This code tests whether the pen type is set to the square pen:

```
if(penType == PenModes.SquarePen)
{
    // draw with the square pen
}
```

Another useful side effect of using enumerated types is that code becomes easier
to understand. If the program compares **penType** with the value 3, the reader has to
know, or find out, that 3 means erase. But if the program compares **penType** with **Pen-
Modes.ErasePen**, what's going on is very obvious to someone reading the code. This is
a good thing!

Making decisions with the **switch** construction

Our drawing program could use a sequence of `if` conditions to select the required drawing behavior, but it turns out that C# has a much better way of using enumerated types when making decisions. The enumerated value can be used in a `switch` condition:

```
switch(penType)                                    Start of the switch that specifies
{                                                              the control value
    case PenModes.RoundPen:                                    Case option
        SnapsEngine.SetDrawingColor(drawColor);
        SnapsEngine.DrawDot(drawPos, 20);
        break;                                                    break that
                                                               ends this case

    case PenModes.SquarePen:
        SnapsEngine.SetDrawingColor(drawColor);
        SnapsEngine.DrawBlock(drawPos.XValue, drawPos.YValue, 20,20);
        break;

    case PenModes.ErasePen:
        SnapsEngine.SetDrawingColor(backgroundColor);
        SnapsEngine.DrawBlock(drawPos.XValue, drawPos.YValue, 20, 20);
        break;
}
Ch09_15_DrawEnum
```

The code above shows how the `switch` would be used. It is part of a drawing program that displays a palette from which the user can select how they want to draw on the screen. The `penType` value is used as the control value for the `switch`, and the program will select the case that matches the control value. If the round pen is being used, the program will set the drawing color and then draw a dot. If the square pen is being used, it will set the drawing color and draw a block by using the Snaps `DrawBlock` method. Finally, if the erase pen is being used, it will set the drawing color to the background color and draw a block that will erase the drawing on that part of the screen.

You can put as many statements as you like in a particular case, but you must make sure that the last statement in the case is the `break` keyword, which ends the execution of the code for that case.

You can also use the switch statement with strings and integer numbers; it can be a convenient way of selecting a particular option. A case statement can also have a default behavior, which is obeyed if none of the cases match the selection value. This program would display an "Invalid Command" message because the value of the command variable does not match any of the cases in the switch:

```
int command=0;

switch(command)
{
    case 1:
        SnapsEngine.DisplayString("Command One");
        break;
    case 2:
        SnapsEngine.DisplayString("Command Two");
        break;
    default:
        SnapsEngine.DisplayString("Invalid Command");
        break;
}
```

You can also have multiple elements to select a particular case. The following switch statement selects a method depending on the command that is entered. The command strings "Delete", "Del", and "Erase" all result in the doDelete method being called.

```
string commandName = readCommand();

switch(commandName)
{
    case "Delete":
    case "Del":
    case "Erase":
        doDelete();
        break;

    case "Print":
    case "Pr":
    case "Output":
        doPrint();
        break;
```

```
    default:
        doInvalidCommand();
        break;
}
```

Extra Snaps

Here are a few more **Snaps** you can use to make interesting graphics.

GetTappedCoordinate

GetTappedCoordinate is similar to GetDraggedCoordinate, but it returns the position
where the user tapped rather than the position where the user dragged the screen.
The position is returned as a coordinate. The **TapDraw** program shows how this
works, drawing a dot on the screen at each position the user taps.

```
using SnapsLibrary;

class Ch09_16_TapDraw
{
    public void StartProgram()
    {
        while (true)
        {
            SnapsCoordinate tappedPos = SnapsEngine.GetTappedCoordinate();
            SnapsEngine.DrawDot(tappedPos, 20);
        }
    }
}
```

DrawLine

The DrawLine method does exactly what you would expect: it draws a line. It accepts a start position and an end position and draws a line between them. The sample code draws an X made up of a red line in one direction and a blue line in the other:

```
using SnapsLibrary;

class Ch09_17_DrawLineDemo
{
    public void StartProgram()
    {
        SnapsEngine.SetDrawingColor(red: 255, green: 0, blue: 0);
        SnapsEngine.DrawLine(x1: 0, y1: 0, x2: 100, y2: 100);
        SnapsEngine.SetDrawingColor(red: 0, green: 0, blue: 255);
        SnapsEngine.DrawLine(x1: 0, y1: 100, x2: 100, y2: 0);
    }
}
```

There are two versions of the DrawLine method. One of them is given the start and end positions of the line as separate X and Y values, as you can see above. The other is given the start and end positions as a coordinate, which makes DrawLine more flexible. Programs can call the method that works best for them. The program below shows how this works. It draws a line from the top-left corner (0,0) to the position on the screen tapped by the user. This is another example of method overloading. The name of the method (in this case DrawLine) is used to represent a number of different methods, each of which accepts a different set of parameters.

```
using SnapsLibrary;

class Ch09_18_TapLine
{
    public void StartProgram()
    {
        SnapsCoordinate origin = new SnapsCoordinate(x: 0, y: 0);

        SnapsEngine.SetDrawingColor(red: 255, green: 0, blue: 0);
        while (true)
        {
            SnapsCoordinate lineEnd = SnapsEngine.GetTappedCoordinate();
            SnapsEngine.DrawLine(p1: origin, p2: lineEnd);
        }
```

```
        }
    }
```

GetScreenSize

Your programs may have to run on a variety of different devices: a desktop PC, a tablet PC, a mobile device, or maybe even a Raspberry Pi. Each of these will have a different display resolution; the width and height of the screen will be different. The GetScreenSize method returns a Snaps coordinate with the X value set to the width of the screen and the Y value set to the height.

The **StarMaker** program shown next gets the screen size and then uses this to work out the center of the display. The user can then draw a star by tapping different places on the screen. The program draws a line from the center of the screen to the position of each tap.

```
using SnapsLibrary;

class Ch09_19_StarMaker
{
    public void StartProgram()
    {
        SnapsEngine snaps = new SnapsEngine();

        SnapsCoordinate screenSize = SnapsEngine.GetScreenSize();
        SnapsCoordinate center;
        center.XValue = screenSize.XValue / 2;
        center.YValue = screenSize.YValue / 2;

        SnapsEngine.SetDrawingColor(red: 255, green: 0, blue: 0);

        while (true)
        {
            SnapsCoordinate lineEnd = SnapsEngine.GetTappedCoordinate();
            SnapsEngine.DrawLine(center, lineEnd);
        }
    }
}
```

PickImage

In Chapter 5, you saw how to use `DisplayImage` to display images in your programs. A program can use `PickImage` to select and display an image. The program will display a file-selection menu so that the user can pick an image for display, and the image will then be fitted to the screen.

```
using SnapsLibrary;

class Ch09_20_PickImage
{
    public void StartProgram()
    {
        SnapsEngine.PickImage();
    }
}
```

What you have learned

In this chapter you've learned how to design and create new data types that act as containers for a number of data members. These new types can be used in the same way as data types that are built into the C# language. Programs can create variables of these new types—for example, descriptions of musical notes—and these variables can be passed into methods and returned as the result of a method call. A structure can have a constructor method that is used to create a new structure and set the initial values of the members inside the structure.

The data members inside a structure can be accessed individually, and they can also be made private or public. Public data members can be used by program code outside the structure. Making data public means that programs can have easy access to the contents of a structure, but it also means that the structure cannot control the content of the values that it holds. A program can contain arrays of structure values, which can be preset inside the program. The structures themselves can also contain methods that will allow a structure value to perform actions when requested.

You've seen a variety of contexts in which structures can be used to good effect. You've seen how the data required to represent graphical coordinates, colors, and even musical notes can be stored inside a single object. These structures can also contain methods that allow a structure object to behave in a cohesive manner. For example, a musical note structure can contain a method that can be used to make the note play itself. We've also taken a look at the way that graphical displays and user interfaces are created by computer programs in terms of how graphical objects are displayed on the screen and how a program can be made to respond to a user's actions.

You have discovered how to make new types—enumerated types—that have a limited number of particular values. You can use these in your programs to reduce program errors because you are ensuring that the variable of an enumerated type cannot be set to a meaningless value. Finally, you've seen how to use the C# `switch` construction to select a particular option from a given range, and you've learned that switches work extremely well with enumerated types.

Here are some questions to ponder about the topics in this chapter:

Does using structures in programs slow the program down?

We considered a similar question when looking at methods in Chapter 8. Structures are similar to methods in that they make it much easier to manage large programs that work on complex items of data. There is some processor overhead in working with structures, but I think this is better than all the effort required to write a program without structured data.

When should I use `private` in a structure?

Structures (and indeed objects) work best if they have total control over the data that is stored within them. When you write programs, you should be concerned about situations where your program starts to work with invalid data. We know that a music program that contains invalid note information will sound wrong when it tries to play those notes, so we make the data inside the notes private so that the data cannot be changed by program code outside the note. You can also create a constructor method that will not allow a note (or other data) to be created that contains invalid information. This means that a given note value is guaranteed to have integrity, in that there is no way the system can create an invalid note or corrupt an existing one.

Can structures contain other structures?

Indeed they can. This can be the basis of very good design. A graphics application might have a need for a "dot" data structure that contains the coordinate where the dot is to be drawn and the color of the dot. We could use values of color and coordinate structures inside the dot structure. This would make our program easier to write and also, because we would be using objects that had already been created and (we hope) tested, make the program more reliable.

Should we store the color values as an enumerated type?

This is a good question. I think the answer is no. There are two reasons for this. The first is that there are lots of possible color values because there are many millions of ways of combining the possible values of red, green, and blue. There are a few particular colors that we might think of as special: for example, pure red, green, and blue, along with black and white. However, many other colors exist for which we don't have specific names. The second reason why it would not be sensible to represent a color as an enumerated type is that you can regard a color value as being made up of red, green, and blue values, but an enumerated type holds only one value.

Do we have to use the `switch` construction in our programs?

The `switch` construction is definitely useful, but you can write successful programs without using it. Programmers call this *syntactic sugar*. It's something nice, but it doesn't make possible anything that you couldn't already do.

10

Classes and references

What you will learn

In the previous chapter you saw how a programmer can create custom designs for variables. If a program needs to manipulate musical notes, graphical coordinates, or color values, you can create data structures for these types of data and use those structures in the same way that you do the built-in data types provided by C#.

In this chapter, you will expand on this knowledge and learn how to design classes, which build on the abilities of structures and on the way a program can work with very large and complex data items. You'll find out how to use properties to manage access to data held inside objects and how C# uses references to reduce the need to move data objects around in memory. You'll wrap up this chapter by learning how to store data using classes.

Making a time tracker

Programs have a habit of growing bigger. Sometimes this occurs because you underestimate the scope of the problem (which is bad), but it can also happpen because your customer likes your first program and comes back to you with additional requests (which is good). In this chapter, the news is good. We heard back from our friend the lawyer, who's been using the tiny contact book we created in Chapter 8. She now asks you to add to the program the capability to track the amount of time she spends with a client so that she has this information handy for billing. She would also like to be able to discover which customers occupy most of her time.

Creating a structure to hold contact information

A good start would be to improve the way that contact information for an individual is stored. In the previous Tiny Contacts program, the information was stored in a number of different strings—one for each data item. For the updated program, we can design a structure to hold contact information and then store a collection of objects built from the structure.

Here is my design for a structure named `Contact`. The structure contains four member values, which hold the name, address, phone number, and time spent with a specific contact. The name, address, and phone number items are held as strings, and the number of minutes spent with the contact is held as an integer. The structure also contains a constructor method that a program can use to set up the values in the contact. Note that the `MinutesSpent` value is set to 0 when the contact is created.

```
struct Contact
{
    public string ContactName;
    public string ContactAddress;
    public string ContactPhone;
    public int ContactMinutesSpent;

    public Contact(string name, string address, string phone)
    {
        ContactName = name;
        ContactAddress = address;
        ContactPhone = phone;
        ContactMinutesSpent = 0;
    }
}
```

This code gives us a template for the `Contact` structure, which the program uses when it declares a variable of type `Contact`, like this:

```
public static void StartProgram()
{
    Contact rob = new Contact(name: "Rob", address: "Rob's House",
                              phone: "Rob's Phone");

    SnapsEngine.SetTitleString("Contact Structure Demo");

    SnapsEngine.ClearTextDisplay();
    SnapsEngine.AddLineToTextDisplay("Name: " + rob.ContactName);
    SnapsEngine.AddLineToTextDisplay("Address: " + rob.ContactAddress);
    SnapsEngine.AddLineToTextDisplay("Phone: " + rob.ContactPhone);
    SnapsEngine.AddLineToTextDisplay("Minutes: " +
                                     rob.ContactMinutesSpent.ToString());

}
Ch10_01_ContactStructure
```

This program creates a new `Contact` value and uses the constructor method in the structure to set the name, address, and phone number properties. These are then displayed as you see in **Figure 10-1**.

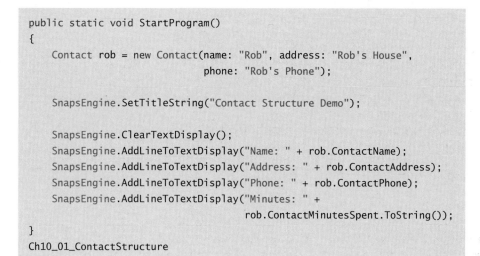

Figure 10-1 Contact structure demonstration.

Using the `this` reference when working with objects

The constructor method for the `Contact` structure has a set of parameters that are passed into the method when it's called. The parameters make it very easy to set the contents of a new `Contact` structure value.

```
Contact rob = new Contact(name: "Rob", address: "Rob's House",
                          phone: "Rob's Phone");
```

The parameters to the constructor are called `name`, `address`, and `phone`, which makes sense. However, these are very similar to the names of the member values stored in the contact, which are called `ContactName`, `ContactAddress`, and `ContactPhone`. There is a danger that a developer might confuse the constructor parameters and the members of the object and create a program that doesn't work properly.

It would be useful if there was a way that code running inside an object could explicitly specify when it wants to use variables that are members of the object. It turns out that we can do this by using a C# keyword that is confusingly called `this`.

```
public Contact(string name, string address, string phone)
{
    this.ContactName = name;
    this.ContactAddress = address;
    this.ContactPhone = phone;
    this.ContactMinutesSpent = 0;
}
```

In the preceding code, the keyword `this` makes it explicit that the members of the structure are being initialized by using the constructor parameters.

CODE ANALYSIS

Broken constructor problems

The best way to understand how `this` works is to take a look at a situation where it is not used properly. The `CupCake` structure has been designed to hold cupcake recipes for a baker. It holds the name, ingredients, and recipe.

```
struct CupCake
{
    public string Name;
    public string Ingredients;
    public string Recipe;

    public CupCake(string Name, string Ingredients, string Recipe)
    {
        Name = Name;
        Ingredients = Ingredients;
        Recipe = Recipe;
    }
}
```

Question: The constructor method shown above is supposed to use the values of its parameters to set the data members inside the CupCake value that is being created. Unfortunately, this code is not correct and won't compile correctly. What's wrong?

> **Answer:** The parameters to the constructor have the same names as the data members inside the structure. This is quite legal C#. Within the CupCake constructor, the identifier Name means the parameter to the method, not the Name property of cupcake. This is called *hiding* because the member called Name has been hidden by the parameter with the same name.
>
> There is nothing to stop a programmer from "hiding" a member variable in this way. However, in the constructor above, the result is that the data members of the structure are not assigned by the constructor, which means that the compiler will refuse to compile the code. We can fix this by using the this keyword to specifically identify the data members inside the object as the target of the assignment.

```
struct CupCake
{
    public string Name;
    public string Ingredients;
    public string Recipe;

    public CupCake(string Name, string Ingredients, string Recipe)
    {
        this.Name = Name;
        this.Ingredients = Ingredients;
        this.Recipe = Recipe;
    }
}
Ch10_02_CupCakeStructureWithThis
```

The compiler is now much happier. The parameter values are being copied into the data members in the structure and the use of `this` has removed all ambiguity.

Managing lots of contacts

The original Tiny Contacts manager stored details in special local storage on the device. This works fine for storing individual items, but the lawyer wants to be able to manipulate contact information as a whole—she wants the program to sort the list of contacts by the amount of time she spends with them.

We have seen that we can use arrays to store collections of information. Our program can contain an array of contacts such as this:

```
Contact[] contacts = new Contact[100];
```

This statement will create an array of "empty" contact structures. When C# makes an empty structure variable, it sets numbers in the structure to the value 0 and strings in the structure to a special value called *null*. We saw in Chapter 8 that the value null is a way that a program can explicitly represent the situation where a variable does not contain a value.

```
bool storeContact(Contact contact)
{
    // work through each element in the array using  a for loop
    for (int position = 0; position < contacts.Length; position = position+1)
    {
        if (contacts[position].ContactName == null)
```

If the name is null, this element is empty . . .

```
        {
            contacts[position] = contact;
            return true;
        }
    }
    return false;
}
```

...copy the contact
into the array

The `storeContact` method is given a `contact` value to put in the array. It searches for an empty element in the array to store the contact in. An empty element has a `ContactName` member that is set to `null`. When the method finds an element with a null `ContactName` member, the method copies the contact being stored into the array at that position and returns the Boolean value `true` to mean that the contact was stored successfully.

CODE ANALYSIS

Filling up the array

Question: What happens when the array is completely full?

Answer: Each time a contact is stored in the array, the `ContactName` value in that array element is no longer null. If the program continues to add items, at some point there are no elements with an empty name. In this case, the loop that is searching for an empty element will run to completion and the method will continue to the statement after the `for` loop. This returns the value `false` so that the code that called the method can detect that the save action failed and display an appropriate message:

```
Contact newContact =
    new Contact(name: name, address: address, phone: phone);
if(StoreContact(newContact))
{
    SnapsEngine.DisplayString("Contact stored");
}
else
{
    SnapsEngine.DisplayString("Storage failed");
}
```

The preceding code creates a new contact and attempts to store it. If the contact is stored correctly, a message is displayed. If the StoreContact method returns false, the code will display a different message—"Storage failed."

Question: Why doesn't the StoreContact method throw an exception if the storage fails? That would guarantee that a programmer would have to deal with the situation where the program runs out of storage space.

> **Answer:** This is a very good question. My code is making the assumption that the programmer who is storing a contact will make sure that the program deals with the situation when there is no room to store the contact. It seems obvious to me that a programmer would do this, so I don't feel the need to stop the program if this foreseeable mistake is made. Of course, there is an element of risk in this choice because if a programmer does ignore the return from StoreContact, it means that there is a chance the user might think that something has been stored successfully when it hasn't.

Making test data

To test the Time Tracker, we are going to need a few contacts to track. I could add these individually, but this is not really a good use of my time, particularly because I could easily write a bit of code that will make the contacts for me.

```
void makeTestData()
{
    string [] testNames = {
    "Rob", "Mary", "David", "Jenny",
    "Simon", "Kevin", "Helen", "Chris",
    "Amanda", "Sally" };

    // the number of minutes for contacts
    int minutes = 0;

    foreach (string name in testNames)
    {
        Contact newContact = new Contact(name: name,
            address: name + "'s house",
            phone: name + "'s phone");
        newContact.MinutesSpent = minutes;
        minutes = minutes + 30;
        storeContact(newContact);
    }
}
```

The method `makeTestData` creates 10 contacts. It works through the array of names and creates a contact for each of them. It uses the name of the contact to create fake address and phone data and then adds the new contact to the array of contacts. A contact is also given a particular number of minutes of contact time, each getting 30 minutes more than the previous one.

PROGRAMMERS POINT

You can get a lot of credibility by making good test data

Over the years I've watched a lot of demonstrations of software. Quite often someone will show me a system that is designed to handle many thousands of customers, but their demo will show only five or six because they "didn't have time to enter lots of test data." I find it very hard to take such demonstrations seriously. I'm much more impressed by a demonstration that contains thousands of customers. You can create lots of names by combining first names and surnames. Twenty first names and twenty surnames will give you four hundred people to work with.

Our program can create a set of test data when it starts running. Of course, we will need to be careful not to release the software with the test data in it. Later on in the book, I'll describe ways that you can instruct the compiler to ignore sections of source text in a program file when it builds the program.

Designing the Time Tracker user interface

Now that you know how to store data in the Time Tracker, we can design the way that the user will interact with the system. As usual, you sit down with the customer and work out what the new program should look like when it runs. The program will need four menu options. Two of them are the same as the previous contact-manager application, but we now have time-tracking features that the user can select. These are activated by using two new buttons on the main menu, as shown in **Figure 10-2**.

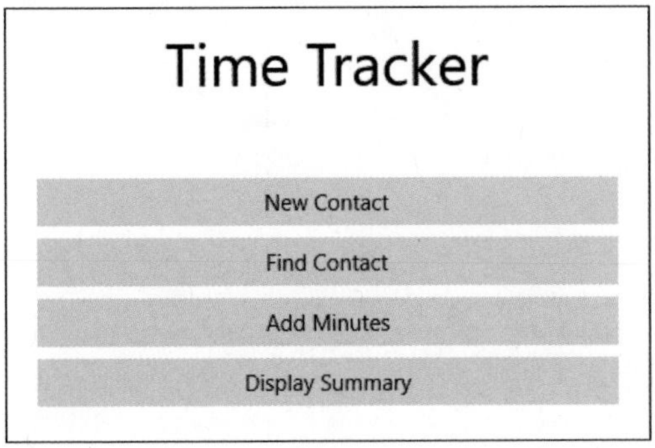

Figure 10-2 Time Tracker main menu.

Structuring the Time Tracker program

You have seen before that a good way to design a program is to create the user interface and then create methods for each of the button behaviors. At the start of development, the methods are empty, and the creation of the program boils down to filling in the methods that perform each of the behaviors. In the case of the Time Tracker, we have four methods to implement; newContact, findContact, addMinutes and displaySummary.

```
void newContact()
{
    SnapsEngine.SetTitleString("New Contact");
    SnapsEngine.WaitForButton("Continue");
}
```

This is the starting code for the newContact method. All the others have the same format. We will fill out each of these methods to perform the required task. The program uses a switch construction to select the method to run, depending on which command the user selects:

```
while (true)
{
    SnapsEngine.SetTitleString("Time Tracker");

    string command = SnapsEngine.SelectFrom4Buttons("New Contact", "Find Contact",
        "Add Minutes", "Display Summary");

    switch (command)
    {
        case "New Contact":
            newContact();
            break;

        case "Find Contact":
            findContact();
            break;

        case "Add Minutes":
            addMinutes();
            break;

        case "Display Summary":
```

```
            displaySummary();
            break;
    }
}
```

PROGRAMMER'S POINT

Filling in the blanks is a good way to build systems

This is a really good way to build software. It means that right from the start you have a program that does something. It might just show you the name of the selected function, but at least it runs. I much prefer this to an approach where you write a thousand lines of code and then run it to find out what it does. Once you have the empty methods, you can decide which one to create first and then work through and implement each in turn.

Creating a new contact

The first method we should write is the one that creates a new contact. We've already written the method that will store the contents of a contact in the array. Now we just have to create a method that reads the information from the user and then stores it.

```
void newContact()
{
    SnapsEngine.SetTitleString("New Contact");
    string name = SnapsEngine.ReadString("Enter new contact name");
    string address = SnapsEngine.ReadMultiLineString("Enter contact address");
    string phone = SnapsEngine.ReadString("Enter contact phone");

    Contact newContact = new Contact(name: name, address: address, phone: phone);
    if (storeContact(newContact))
    {
        SnapsEngine.DisplayString("Contact stored");
    }
    else
    {
        SnapsEngine.DisplayString("Storage failed");
    }
}
```

This is the full implementation of the `newContact` method. It is called when the user selects the command to create a new contact. It asks the user for content details, creates a new contact, and then adds the contact to the array.

Finding customer details

Now that we have a set of customers to work with, we can write the method that finds the details of a customer and displays them:

```
void findContact()
{
    SnapsEngine.SetTitleString("Find Contact");

    string name = SnapsEngine.ReadString("Enter contact name");

    bool foundAContact = false;

    SnapsEngine.ClearTextDisplay();

    foreach (Contact contact in contacts)
    {
        if (contact.ContactName == name)
        {
            SnapsEngine.AddLineToTextDisplay("Name: " + contact.ContactName);
            SnapsEngine.AddLineToTextDisplay("Address: " + contact.ContactAddress);
            SnapsEngine.AddLineToTextDisplay("Phone: " + contact.ContactPhone);
            SnapsEngine.AddLineToTextDisplay("Minutes: " +
                                    contact.ContactMinutesSpent.ToString());
            foundAContact = true;
            break;
        }
    }

    if (!foundAContact)
        SnapsEngine.AddLineToTextDisplay("Contact not found");

    SnapsEngine.WaitForButton("Continue");
    SnapsEngine.ClearTextDisplay();
}
```

The `findContact` method is called when the user wants to view the details of a contact. It asks for the name of the contact and then works through the array of contacts to find the one with the matching name. If it finds a matching contact, it will display the contact details and set a flag, called `foundAContact`, to indicate that the contact has been found. After the loop has completed, the value of `foundAContact` is checked, and if it is false (that is, no contact was found) a message is displayed.

WHAT COULD GO WRONG

Duplicate names

There is actually a serious bug in the system that we've created. It is possible to create a new contact with the same name as an existing one. And because the "duplicate" contact will be stored further down the array than the original one, it will never actually be used. The program will always find the original contact first. This would result in one of our array elements being wasted. You might like to consider how you could modify the program so that it doesn't have this problem.

PROGRAMMER'S POINT

Look for problems when you are defining the specification

When you talk to the lawyer about the Time Tracker application, there is no guarantee that problems such as duplicate contact names will be discussed. It is the job of the programmer to consider the ways a system can go wrong and add the extra behaviors to deal with these. There are a number of different ways to handle duplicate account names. You could number names to create "Rob Miles1" and so on. You could make the system ask "Are you the Rob Miles from Hull?" when searching for an account, or you could create a contact number that is unique for each contact. Giving items in a system a unique name means that they can be managed much more precisely and also can be used to handle situations where the name of an item might change.

You need to find out how the lawyer wants to handle the problem. The worst thing you can do in a situation like this is to assume you know what the customer would like the system to do. This will almost certainly mean your solution will behave incorrectly when things go wrong.

Of course, you must also make sure that your system can manage the situation when your solution fails. Using a unique number for each contact is a great idea, but you will also need to add a way of dealing with the situation when the lawyer forgets the number for a particular contact.

Adding minutes to a contact

Now that we know how to make the program store and display contact details, we need to write the method that will add the minutes that the lawyer spends with a particular customer. If the **Add Minutes** option is selected, the program allows the lawyer to select a contact and then add a value to the number of minutes spent working for that contact. **Figure 10-3** shows the screen used to add minutes once we have found a contact.

Figure 10-3 Adding minutes to a contact's details.

Once the user has added the minutes for that customer, the program displays a dialog box to confirm what it has done, as shown in **Figure 10-4.**

Figure 10-4 Confirmation message that minutes have been added.

We might want to revisit this design in the future. The customer might ask for an option to review the changes that are about to be made, but for now this looks like a workable sequence.

We can implement this by using a method structure similar to the `findContact` method, except in this case we won't display the customer details but instead update the `minutesSpent` value of the customer that we find.

```
void addMinutes()
{
    SnapsEngine.SetTitleString("Add Minutes");

    string name = SnapsEngine.ReadString("Enter contact name");
    int minutes = SnapsEngine.ReadInteger("Enter contact minutes");

    bool foundAContact = false;

    SnapsEngine.ClearTextDisplay();

    for (int position = 0; position < contacts.Length; position = position + 1)
    {
        if (contacts[position].ContactName == name)
        {
            SnapsEngine.AddLineToTextDisplay("Added " + minutes + " minutes\n" +
                "to " + name);
            contacts[position].ContactMinutesSpent =
                            contacts[position].ContactMinutesSpent + minutes;
            foundAContact = true;
            break;
        }
    }

    if (!foundAContact)
        SnapsEngine.AddLineToTextDisplay("Contact not found");

    SnapsEngine.WaitForButton("Continue");
    SnapsEngine.ClearTextDisplay();
}
```

The first thing the addMinutes method does is request the name of the contact and
the number of minutes to be added. Then the method uses a loop to work through
the Contacts array, searching for a contact with the selected name. If the contact is
found, the MinutesSpent value is updated. The method uses the same flag technique
we used for the findContact method to display "Contact not found" if the contact
is not found. Note that, as you saw in Chapter 7, a foreach loop lets a program work
through the items in a collection, but the code in the loop is not allowed to change
the contents of the item that is extracted from a collection by the loop. This means
that the addMinutes method uses a conventional for loop with a counter to find the
contact that needs to be updated. To go into more detail about the reasons for this
behavior would fill up the rest of this chapter, so I'd be most grateful if you could be
happy with that explanation and just remember that if you want to work through

an array and make changes to the elements in it you have to use a `for` loop with a counter variable.

Display a summary

The final option we have to add is one that lets the user see how much time has been spent with each contact. The **Display Summary** menu option allows the lawyer to view how much time she has spent with each of her contacts. **Figure 10-5** shows a summary of the contact times.

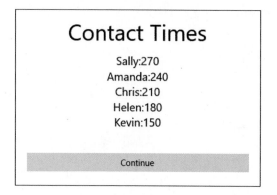

Figure 10-5 Summary of minutes spent with contacts.

We provide this behavior in the final method, which is named `displaySummary`. This method displays the names of the top five clients and the time that they have spent with the lawyer. We can create this output by sorting the `contacts` array into descending order of minutes spent and then displaying the first five elements in the array. The sorting can be performed by using a bubble-sorting routine that repeatedly swaps elements in the array if they are in the wrong order:

```
for (int pass = 0; pass < contacts.Length - 1; pass = pass + 1)
{
    for (int i = 0; i < contacts.Length - 1; i = i + 1)
    {
        if (contacts[i].ContactMinutesSpent < contacts[i + 1].ContactMinutesSpent)
        {
            // the elements are in the wrong order, need to swap them round
            Contact temp = contacts[i];
            contacts[i] = contacts[i + 1];
            contacts[i + 1] = temp;
        }
    }
```

```
    }
}
```

We first used bubble sorting in Chapter 7 when we sorted ice-cream sales figures. This is not a very efficient version of the sort, but it will put the largest values at the top. The next thing to do is build a display of those values:

```
SnapsEngine.SetTitleString("Contact Times");

SnapsEngine.ClearTextDisplay();

for (int position = 0; position < 5; position = position + 1)
{
    if (contacts[position].ContactName == null)
        break;
    SnapsEngine.AddLineToTextDisplay(contacts[position].ContactName +
        ":" + contacts[position].ContactMinutesSpent);
}

SnapsEngine.WaitForButton("Continue");

SnapsEngine.ClearTextDisplay();
```

This code looks at the first five elements in the array and adds them to a results string that is then displayed. The code also checks to be sure that it is displaying a valid contact by looking for a nonnull name at that position in the array. If it finds a null name, it abandons the display.

MAKE SOMETHING HAPPEN

Fix the Time Tracker program

The program that we have created works, but it is not all that good. I can think of several ways in which it is less than perfect:

- The program allows the user to enter two contacts with the same name.

- When updating the minutes-spent value for a customer, if the user enters a contact name that is not in the contact array, the program still asks for a number of minutes for that contact, even though adding the minutes is bound to fail.

- If the user enters a negative number of minutes, the program will add this to the number of minutes and cause that value to go down.

- The program does not give the user a chance to confirm the action that is to be performed.

Fix the program so that it works correctly. You might like to add a new command that also clears out the contacts list. You can find a version to start from in **Ch10_03_TimeTracker**.

Structures and classes

We are now approaching the most important part of this chapter, where you'll learn the difference between structures (which we have been using for a while now) and classes (which you are about to discover how to use). Structure variables are managed by *value*, and class variables are managed by *reference*. In Chapter 8 you saw values and references in the context of method parameters; now you are going to explore them in the context of object design.

Sorting and structures

The updated time-tracking program is nearly finished. When you show it to the lawyer, she's very impressed, but then she makes another request. She'd like to be able to see a summary list of her clients sorted in order of their names. From a programming perspective this is not a hard thing to do. We can use the Bubble Sort technique to perform the sort and compare the names of the contacts. However, you need to think hard about the effect that sorting has on the data.

When you sort an array that contains the values of structure variables, the computer has to do quite a lot of work. Here are the statements that swap the content of two adjacent elements in the contacts array.

```
// The elements are in the wrong order, need to swap them round
Contact temp = contacts[i];
contacts[i] = contacts[i + 1];
contacts[i + 1] = temp;
```

Each time one contact is assigned to another, the entire contents of that contact object are moved from one part of memory to another—and the program will perform all the moving around of data each time we sort the contacts by name or by the minutes spent.

In the case of the time-tracking program, this is not a huge problem because the contact structures are quite small and there are not very many of them to be sorted. But if we were working with lots of large data items, perhaps medical records or bank accounts, this swapping process would be very slow, which would be a problem. Each time we wanted to reorder data—for example, sort on customer name rather than the amount of money in each account—the computer would have a lot of work to do.

Sorting and references

What we want is a more efficient way of moving variable values around in memory. To understand this problem, consider how money used to be managed on the Pacific Island of Yap. The currency on this island was once based on stones that were 12 feet high and weighed several hundred pounds each. The value of a "coin" in the Yap currency was directly related to the number of men who died in the arduous boat journey bringing the rock to the island. The bigger and harder a rock was to move, the more it was worth.

When you paid someone with one of these stones, you didn't actually pick it up and give it to them because the stone was too heavy. Instead, you said to them, "The stone by the road on top of the hill is now yours." In other words, the people on Yap used references to manage objects that they didn't want to have to move around. We can also use references in our programs.

Figure 10-6 shows what happens when the Bubble Sort algorithm swaps adjacent elements in an array until they are all in the right order. Remember that the program has to move a lot of data around during the sorting as the values "bubble" into their correct positions. When the sort has completed, the elements have been moved into order.

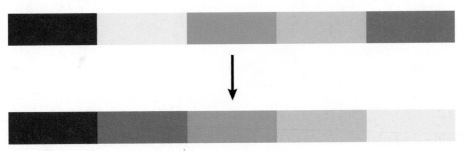

Figure 10-6 Sorting by moving objects around

Figure 10-7 shows how we could sort the information by using references. The objects themselves never move. Instead, we have an array of references. Each reference in the list refers to one object in memory, and during the sort we only have to exchange the values of the references themselves, which are much smaller and easier to move around in memory than the objects that they refer to.

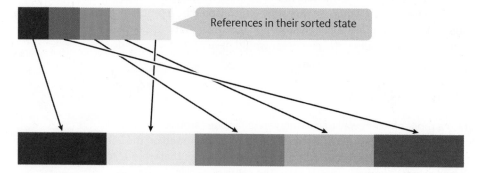

Figure 10-7 Sorting by using references.

References get even more useful when you consider the possibility of multiple lists of references that order the data items in different ways. To satisfy the requirements of the updated contact app, we could have two lists—one ordered on customer name and another ordered on the minutes spent.

Reference and value types

It is very important that you understand the distinction between reference and value types because the distinction has a huge impact on the way that variables are used. Consider this code:

```
struct ContactStruct
{
    public string ContactName;
    public string ContactAddress;
    public string ContactPhone;
    public int ContactMinutesSpent;
}
```

This is the `Contact` structure we've been using. A program can create a variable of type `ContactStruct` simply by declaring something of that type:

```
ContactStruct structRob;
structRob.ContactName = "Rob";
SnapsEngine.DisplayString(structRob.ContactName);
```

These statements create a structure variable named structRob and then set the ContactName property of the variable to the string "Rob". When the statements are performed, they do exactly what you would expect: the name "Rob" is displayed in relation to the variable structRob. You can use the other data members of the ContactStruct object in the same way because the ContactStruct structure contains space to hold each data member.

Now let's make a small change to the program and convert the contact structure to a class:

```
class ContactClass
{
    public string ContactName;
    public string ContactAddress;
    public string ContactPhone;
    public int MinutesSpent;
}
```

The contact information is now being held in a class rather than a structure. You might think that you can use ContactClass in exactly the same way as ContactStruct:

```
ContactClass classRob;
classRob.Name = "Rob";
```

But when we compile the program, we get an error:

```
Error CS0165: Use of unassigned local variable 'classRob'
```

What's going on? To understand, you need to know what operation the following line performs:

```
ContactClass classRob;
```

This statement looks like a declaration of a variable of type ContactClass named classRob. However, what this statement creates is not the same as when a program declares a variable of a structure type. What you actually get when the program obeys the preceding statement is a *reference* named classRob. Such references are allowed to refer to instances of `ContactClass`. You can think of a reference being like a luggage tag, in that it can be tied to a suitcase with a piece of rope or twine. If you have the tag, you can follow the rope to the object it is tied to.

But when you create a reference, you don't actually get one of the things that the reference can refer to. The compiler knows this, so it displays an error, because the line

```
classRob.ContactName = "Rob";
```

is an attempt to find the object that is tied to the `classRob` tag and set the `ContactName` property to "Rob". But because the tag is not currently tied to anything (and the compiler knows this), the program is not allowed to run. The compiler says, in effect, "You are trying to make a program follow a reference that has not been set to refer to anything. Therefore, I am going to give you a 'variable undefined' error."

You solve this problem by creating an instance of the class and then connecting a tag to it. You use a statement such as the following to do this:

```
ContactClass classRob;
classRob = new ContactClass();
classRob.Name = "Rob";
```

The highlighted statement creates a new `ContactClass` instance that is referred to by the reference named `classRob`. This relationship is shown in **Figure 10-8**.

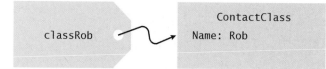

Figure 10-8 Creating a new object.

You have seen the new keyword before. We used it to set up structure values by calling the constructor for the structure. What the new keyword creates is an object, and an object is an instance of a class. Let me repeat that on its own line:

An object is an instance of a class.

It is very important that you understand this.

Remember from Chapter 3 that a class definition provides the *design* of an object. The new keyword asks that the class information be used, like a blueprint, to actually make an object in the memory of your program, this object *is* the instance of the class.

Note in **Figure 10-8** that I named the object `ContactClass` not `classRob`. I did this because the object instance does not have the identifier `classRob`; that instance is simply the one that `classRob` is connected to at the moment. Which particular object a reference refers to can change as the program runs. This happens, for example, when a program assigns a new value to a reference.

References and assignments

Using references to manage objects changes the behavior of the assignment operator—the operator that programs use to change the value of variables. Consider the following statement:

```
ContactStruct s1;                   Create contact structure s1
ContactStruct s2;                   Create contact structure s2
s1.ContactName = "Rob";             Set the name of s1 to Rob
s2 = s1;                            Set the value of s2 to the value of s1
s2.ContactName = "Jim";             Set the name of s2 to Jim
```

We can regard the two variables (`s1` and `s2`) as named boxes in memory, with each box holding a particular value. When we perform an assignment, the program copies the value from one box to the other. These statements would complete with two contact structures, one containing the name "Rob" and the other the name "Jim".

However, when the program starts using references, the situation changes.

```
ContactClass c1 = new ContactClass();      Create a contact class reference called
ContactClass c2 = new ContactClass();      c1 referring to a new contact
c1.ContactName = "Rob";                     Create a contact class reference called
c2 = c1;                                     c2 referring to a new contact
c2.ContactName = "Jim";          Set the name of the contact referred to by c1 to "Rob"
                                 Make c2 refer to the same object as c1
                                 Set the name of the contact referred to by c2 to "Jim"
```

This sequence of statements does exactly what the ones we just saw do. However, these work with variables of type `contactClass`. At the end of the statements, we have an arrangement such as is shown in **Figure 10-9**. Both of the tags are now tied to the same object in memory, and the object originally assigned to c2 has nothing tied to it at all. The name of the contact is now "Jim" because the final assignment overwrote the value of "Rob" that was set earlier.

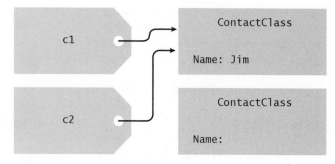

Figure 10-9 Assigning references.

C# does not have a problem with programs that attach multiple reference tags to a single object. But they do have an effect on what happens when the program runs.

When you work with references, you have to remember that the assignment operator now works in this way. Rather than moving data from one variable to another, it makes two references refer to the same object in memory. This is very useful if your program has good reason to do this—for example, so that two documents in a word processor can share a single dictionary—but it is also very confusing if you don't plan for it.

Objects that have no references to them

One other situation we need to consider is when an object in memory can end up having nothing referring to it. We saw this in **Figure 10-9**, where the reference originally assigned to c2 ended up "hanging" in space, with nothing referring to it. As far as making use of data in the instance is concerned, it might as well not be there.

The C# language implementation has a special process called the *garbage collector* that is given the job of finding such useless items and disposing of them. Note that the compiler will not stop us from writing code that releases references to objects; this all happens when the program runs, not when it is compiled.

You should also remember that you can get a similar effect when a reference to an instance goes out of scope:

```
{
    ContactClass localVar;
    localVar = new ContactClass();
}
```

The variable `localVar` is local to the block. When the program execution leaves the block, the local variable is discarded. This means that the only reference to the `ContactClass` is also removed, meaning another job for the garbage collector.

PROGRAMMER'S POINT

Try to avoid making work for the garbage collector

While it is sometimes reasonable to release items you have no further use for, you must remember that creating and disposing of objects takes up processor time. When I work with objects, I worry about how much creating and destroying I am doing. Just because the objects are disposed of automatically doesn't mean that you should abuse the facility. One way to improve performance is to have a "free list" of objects that are not currently in use. When the program needs a new object, it gets it from the list rather than by creating a new one from scratch. Unwanted objects are put in the free list rather than discarded. The Windows operating system itself makes use of this programming trick to manage many of the objects that keep the system going.

CODE ANALYSIS

Value types vs. reference types—Fight!

Given their confusing nature, you might think that using references is a bad idea. They add complications to your program that you'd rather not have. But in the great tradition of video games, let's take a look at how value types and reference types can work together to solve programming problems.

Value types

A value type is the kind of thing you'll find holding the height of a football player, the amount of money you have in the bank, the color of a pixel, or the date you were born. These are just values that describe something. We never want to share these objects. They just represent values that a program is interested in.

Value types: Special skills

- When assigned, all the content of the value type is copied to the destination.

- When you pass a value type into a method, the method is given a copy of the value and can't mess with the original.

- When a method returns a value type result, this is just a value and the user can't mess with the original.

Value types: Weaknesses

- It can be hard to move value types around in memory. A very large structure (which will be managed by value) will take a lot of effort to copy when it is moved from one location to another.

- If you want to make a method that changes the content of a value type, you have to copy the contents of the value into the method when it is called and then copy the changed version back into your program afterward, which is slow.

Reference types

A reference type refers to things like your bank account details. It is useful when a program includes something that you really don't want to move around much and you want programs to be able to share. This can be something that is effectively read-only—for example, the image file for a corporate logo that is used in lots of documents or a sound file that is played to alert a user. A reference can also refer to a large data object—for example, a huge customer account record—that you'd prefer not to move around in memory.

Reference types: Special skills

- Changing a reference so that it refers to a different object is very quick and is performed at the same speed regardless of the size of the object.

- Using a reference to an object as a parameter is also very fast because only the location of the object is passed into the method.

- Methods can return huge objects very quickly because they just have to return the reference.

- A program can contain multiple lists of object references that give different views of the data. For example, one list of bank accounts could be ordered by name, another by account balance.

Reference types: Weaknesses

- Programmers need to be aware that creating a reference and creating the object that it is connected to are two different steps.

- Programmers need to understand the effect of assigning one reference to another.

- If I give another program a reference to my object, I lose control of what happens to that object. The other program can change that object in ways I might not expect, which might lead to faults in my software that are hard to diagnose.

- To use references, we need some mechanism of tidying up objects that no longer have references to them. This garbage collection can slow a program down or result in unpredictable changes in performance as memory is tidied up during program execution.

Reference vs. value

I'm making a Space Invader game. I've designed an object that contains data of different types that I'm going to create to manage the game. Which of the new types in the SpaceAlien class should be value types and which should be reference types?

```
public class SpaceAlien
{
    public Coordinate Position;  // position of the alien on the screen
    public Damage Damage;        // damage taken by the alien
    public Sound KillSound;      // sound made when alien is killed
    public Image Image;          // image of the alien
}
```

- Position   Each alien will have its own unique position on the screen. There's no benefit in sharing position values among aliens, so the Position type should be a value type, in this case a structure.

- Damage   Each alien will have a Damage value that tracks how many hits they've had and the number of hits that it takes to kill the alien. This should be a value type because each alien will have its own specific amount of damage.

- KillSound   This is the sound that an alien will make when it is destroyed. The sound information is quite a large lump of data. We might have up to 100 aliens on the screen at any time and we don't want to store the sound information inside each alien. This means that KillSound should be a reference type. Each SpaceAlien will have a variable that holds the sound that it makes when it is destroyed. Note that this doesn't mean that each alien must have the same kill sound, but if two aliens do have the same kill sound, this sound is stored only once in the game.

- Image   This is the image of the alien. Just like the sounds, there are only a few images that are to be shared for all the aliens, so this should be a reference type, too.

The fight over the SpaceAlien ends as a draw, with two data members each.

Should the SpaceAlien itself be a value type or a reference type? I would say that the game will want to work with these objects in many different ways. It might want to make a list of dead aliens that have been removed from the game during gameplay. It might also want to organize the aliens in different attack waves, which will mean placing them in lists. So a reference type would make sense to me. Chalk up a win for reference types on this fight.

Classes and constructors

Classes can have constructors in the same way that structures do.

```csharp
class Contact
{
    public string ContactName;
    public string ContactAddress;
    public string ContactPhone;
    public int ContactMinutesSpent;

    public Contact(string name, string address, string phone)
    {
        this.ContactName = name;
        this.ContactAddress = address;
        this.ContactPhone = phone;
        this.ContactMinutesSpent = 0;
    }
}
```

This class-based Contact object has the same constructor code as the structure-based version that we saw earlier. And we can make a new instance of a Contact by constructing it in exactly the same way:

```csharp
Contact rob = new Contact(name: "Rob", address: "Rob's House",
                          phone: "Rob's Phone");
```

After you have given a class a constructor method, that is the *only* way that a program can create instances of that object. In other words, the compiler will complain if you write the following statement:

```csharp
Contact rob = new Contact();
```

The compiler will insist that to create a new Contact, you must provide name, address, and phone number arguments that match the parameters of the constructor method.

This is a very powerful feature of the C# language because it gives a programmer control of exactly how an object is created and what information must be provided to create one. We'll take a more detailed look at constructors in classes a little bit later in the book.

Arrays of class references

We can create an array of class references in the same way as we create any other kind of array:

```
Contact[] contacts = new Contact[100];
```

If the Contact type is a class, this statement will create an array that can hold 100 references to Contact objects. Note that in the same way that we didn't create any instances when we created a single class reference, creating a 100-element array of references doesn't create any objects. Each reference in the array is set to null, meaning that it is empty.

To change the time-tracking program so that it uses classes rather than structures, we have to change the storeContact method so that it looks for an array element that contains a null reference rather than an empty name:

```
Contact[] contacts = new Contact[100];

bool storeContact(Contact contact)              ──── Parameter to storeContact is
{                                                      now a reference to a class
    for (int position = 0; position < contacts.Length; position = position + 1)
    {
        if (contacts[position] == null)         ──── If the reference is null,
        {                                              this element is empty.
            contacts[position] = contact;
            return true;
        }
    }
    return false;
}
```

Note that although the method looks very similar to the storeContact method that we used to store a structure, there is one crucial difference. The parameter passed into the storeContact method is a *reference* to the contact that is being stored because Contact is now a class. Previously, the storeContact method was given the *value* (that is, a copy) of the structure as a parameter.

CODE ANALYSIS

Class references as parameters to a method call

Question: What would happen if the storeContact method changed the value of the parameter?

```
bool storeContact(Contact contact)
{
    contact.ContactName = "I'm a chicken";
    return true;
}
```

This is a very silly implementation of the storeContact method, but the question remains: What will be the effect of this code?

> **Answer:** A "chicken coded" version of a storeContact that works on a class would corrupt the name of any Contact object passed as a parameter.

```
Contact rob = new Contact(name: "Rob", address: "Rob's House",
                          phone: "Rob's Phone");
storeContact(rob);
```

In the preceding code, the Name property of the contact referred to by the variable rob would be changed to "I'm a chicken" by the call of storeContact. This would not happen if the Contact type was a structure because in that situation a copy of the contents of rob would be passed into the call.

Question: Which is faster, a structure parameter or a class parameter?

> **Answer:** When a structure is used as an argument to a method, the method actually receives a copy of the values in the structure. This copying takes time. In the case of a reference, the size of the argument is much smaller, as it just has to tell the method the location of the object in memory. So it is much faster to pass classes into method calls.

From arrays to lists

Arrays are great for storing a particular number of items. They are less useful when you don't know how many items you want to store at the time the program is being built. For example, if your program used an array to store the names of guests arriving at a party, you'd have to make the array really big. This statement creates an array that can store 100 strings:

```
string [] guestNames = new string[100];
```

This will work fine, right up to the point that guest number 101 arrives, at which point the array will run out of space and the program will fail. You could address this by making the upper limit really, really big:

```
string [] guestNames = new string[100000];
```

Now we have space for 100,000 guests. However, we might also waste computer memory by doing this, particularly if we have a lot of arrays in the program. What we would really like is an "elastic" array that can grow automatically.

The designers of C# wanted one of these, too, so they created a class named `List` that will look after lists for us. A list holds a collection of references to objects of a particular type, and it can grow as required. `List` is one of a number of *helper classes* that are provided to help programs manage collections of data.

The full name of the `List` class is `System.Collections.Generic.List`. This name is called a *fully qualified name* and provides a unique name for this particular class. Fully qualified names are useful because they prevent confusion. If another programmer creates a class named `List` (which is actually quite likely), that class cannot be confused with the one that is part of the system because the class will have a different fully qualified name.

We use a similar mechanism when we store files on our computer.

c:\2015\Jan\sales.txt

c:\2015\Feb\sales.txt

These files are both called sales.txt, but this does not cause a problem for the file system because they are stored in different folders. When we organize files, we use the complete path to specify a particular file. The C# language uses something similar to allow programmers to identify specific classes. The C# mechanism is called a *namespace*. When you create a class, you can place it in a particular namespace, and one namespace can contain another. We will look at creating namespaces later in the book.

We can use the fully qualified name for the `List` class, but this is rather tedious. Instead we can tell the compiler to look in a particular namespace for things it can't find in our program. We do this by adding a `using` statement at the top of the program.

```
using System.Collections.Generic;
```

In effect, this statement says, "If you can't find something with a particular name, add the namespace prefix System.Collections.Generic to the name and look again." Now we can write *List* in our program, and the compiler will automatically look for `System.Collections.Generic.List`. You saw this in Chapter 9 when we wanted to use the `Exception` object in the `System` namespace.

The statement that creates a `List` is similar to the statement that creates an array. Note that a `List` is actually a list of *references,* so all the items in the list will be managed by reference.

```
List<string> guestNames = new List<string>();
```

When you create a `List`, you ask for a list of a particular type, in this case `string`. You can use the `List` mechanism to hold lists of any C# type, including classes and structures that you create. The type of list that you want is given between the < and > characters. If we want to store the contact information for the Time Tracker, we would write this:

```
List<Contact> contacts = new List<Contact>();
```

The construction is exactly the same, only the type of the list has been changed.

When you create a list you don't specify how many items the list will store. You can add elements to the end of the list at any time.

```
void storeContact(Contact contact)
{
    contacts.Add(contact);
}
```

This is the code for the `storeContact` method when a `List` is used to store the contact information. It has suddenly become a lot simpler. The original version of the method would return `true` or `false` to indicate whether the contact was saved correctly. This version does not need to return a result because the store operation will always work correctly.

PROGRAMMER'S POINT

Single-line methods are still a good idea

You might wonder why we still bother with a `storeContact` method now that it is only one statement long. The program might as well use the contacts list to store a data item rather than call this method. However, I think that a single-line method is sometimes a very good idea. If someone reading my program finds a call to a method with the name `storeContact`, she is going to have a good idea about what is happening. But if she sees `contacts.Add`, she has to know that we are storing our data in a list called `contacts`.

Furthermore, using a method like this gives me a lot of flexibility. If I decide to use a different mechanism for storing the contact information—perhaps a database—then I can just change the `storeContact` method and everything else would still just work.

Working through lists of data

A program can work through a `List` just as it works through an array. The `List`-based version of the Time Tracker application uses the same code for the `findContact` method as the array-based version does.

A program can find out how many elements a list contains by using the `Count` property of the `List`. This program snippet prepares a string that tells how many contacts are present in the list.

```
string contactNumbers = "There are " + contacts.Count + " contacts";
```

Count vs. Length

If you have a good memory, you'll recall that a program can find out how many elements an array contains by asking the array for its Length property. But with a list, the same information is supplied as a Count property.

Question: Why have the designers of C# made things difficult by changing the name?

>   **Answer:** I think this is quite clever. In an array, the number of elements can never change. So, when the array is created, the length is a fixed value. But when you use a list, the number of elements can change at any time. This means that you are not getting a fixed size (as with an array), you are counting the elements in the list at a specific time. Since the behavior is different, the designers of C# decided to make the name different, too.

Question: What would be the count value for a brand-new List?

>   **Answer:** A brand-new list would return a count of zero.

Lists and the index value

You use an index value to specify which particular element of an array you want to work with. You can also access elements of a list by using an index value:

```
Contact startContact = contacts[0];
```

This statement sets the variable startContact to contain the name of the first contact to be added to the list. If no contacts have been stored and the list is empty, the statement would cause the program to fail with an "index out of range" exception. This is the same error you get if your program falls off the end of an array by using an invalid index value.

Lists of structures

Lists are much easier to use than arrays. However, they do have one or two interesting foibles, particularly if you use a List to hold a collection of value types such as a structure. Because structures are managed by value and everything in a List must be managed by reference, a C# program does some fancy footwork to make the structure values into reference types. The effect of this footwork is that structure values held in a `List` are effectively read-only in that their contents cannot be changed.

My advice is to use a `List` in preference to an array if you are using classes, but to think carefully about using lists with structures. The sample program **Ch10_04_Time-TrackerClass** holds a version of the Time Tracker program that uses a class for the contact information and a `List` to hold the data.

Storing data using JSON

You have seen before that variables in programs hold their value only while the program is running. When the user stops running the program, all its variables are discarded. The Tiny Contacts application used local storage in Windows to store the strings of text that made up the contact information. But the Time Tracker has a list of objects to store. We need something that takes data that we don't know how to save—the list of contacts—and converts it to something that we do know how to save, such as a string of text. It turns out that we have exactly this technology at our fingertips in the form of the JSON serialization library from Newtonsoft.

Serialization is a process that takes a collection of data and converts it to a sequence of data items. This sequence can then be stored or sent to another computer and *deserialized* to recover the data. It is a process that is used all over the Internet. The data used by the Snaps method that delivers weather information is sent over the Internet in the form of a serialized string. There are a number of ways to perform serialization. Two popular ones are XML (Extensible Markup Language) and JSON (JavaScript Object Notation). We are going to first use JSON in this chapter. We'll take a look at XML a little later.

JSON is very popular as a way of moving information between websites and programs that run inside your Internet browser. You can see how it works by taking a look at the output it produces. The following statement creates a new `Contact` instance:

```
Contact rob = new Contact(name: "Rob", address: "Rob's House",
                          phone: "Rob's Phone");
```

If we convert this object into JSON, we get the following string:

```
{"ContactName":"Rob","ContactAddress":"Rob's House",
"ContactPhone":"Rob's Phone","ContactMinutesSpent":0}
```

The JSON conversion process creates a string that contains the value of each of the members of the class, identifying the values by the names of the class members. The curly brackets ({ and }) mark the start and end of the object, and the double quotation marks (") mark the start and end of the names of each member of the class and the strings that form part of the data in the class. Note that the `ContactMinutesSpent` member, which is a number, is stored as an integer value rather than a string of text.

WHAT COULD GO WRONG

Data and special characters

You might wonder what happens if the data you are storing contains double quotation marks or curly brackets itself. The designers of JSON thought of this, too. If you look at the following JSON, you can see that inside the address string ("House of Quotes"), the quotation mark characters are preceded by an escape character—"\.

```
{"ContactName":"Rob",
"ContactAddress":"\"House of Quotes\"",
"ContactPhone":"Rob's Phone","ContactMinutesSpent":0}
```

This is the same technique that's used in writing a program in which you want to include a double quotation mark inside a string. We can allow users of the Time Tracker to include any strange characters that they like, and these are always converted into safe versions.

PROGRAMMER'S POINT
Be aware of the possibility of injection attacks

So-called injection attacks occur when special characters like these are injected into program inputs. These attacks have resulted in many security breaches over the years. Whenever you create a solution that uses characters that have a special meaning, you must make sure that the solution can handle these characters if they appear in the data the program is processing.

The Newtonsoft JSON library

Now that you know a bit about how JSON works, you need to find a way of converting program objects into JSON strings. It turns out that there is a library of classes that will do this for us. We've already used one library in this chapter. The `List` class was supplied as part of the C# library, and we're using it to store all the customer information in the Time Tracker.

The JSON library we want to use to help store the customer information was written by James Newton-King, a programmer from New Zealand who has achieved worldwide fame by writing some terribly useful software and sharing it with the world. Visual Studio contains a tool that you can use to obtain shared libraries like this (called NuGet), but the SnapsDemo solution already contains the Newtonsoft library, so for now we just have to include the namespace where the library is located:

```
using Newtonsoft.Json;
```

To store a single contact, we can use the `SerializeObject` method provided by the `JsonConvert` class, which is part of the Newtonsoft library:

```
Contact rob = new Contact(name: "Rob", address: "Rob's House",
                          phone: "Rob's Phone");
string json = JsonConvert.SerializeObject(rob);
```

These statements create an object and then make a JSON string from it. We can store the string on our Windows computer or transfer it over the network to a remote machine. If we want to convert a JSON string back to an object, we can use a method that reverses this process:

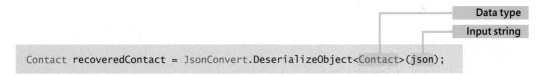

```
Contact recoveredContact = JsonConvert.DeserializeObject<Contact>(json);
```

The `DeserializeObject` method is a *generic* method in that it works for a particular type of object that is to be deserialized. In this case we want it to deserialize a `Contact` object, so this type is added to the method call. The statement would create a `Contact` from the contents of the string `json`.

You can experiment with the serializer (and even try it out with strange names and addresses) by taking a look at the example in **Ch10_05_JsonDemo**.

Invalid JSON strings

You might wonder what happens if the string that is being deserialized doesn't contain valid JSON. In this situation, the `DeserializeObject` method does the only thing it can do, which is to throw an exception. Of course, if the string was valid JSON, it is still possible that the content has no meaning—for example, the `MinutesSpent` value could be -100000. In the next chapter, we'll take a look at how we can make sure that our objects are always sensible.

Storing and recovering lists

It's easy to store a single `Contact` item by using JSON, but what about our list of contacts? Well, it turns out that JSON can take this in stride. The following statement makes a string called `json`, which contains all the contacts in the list.

```
string json = JsonConvert.SerializeObject(contacts);
```

And here is how a JSON string can contain multiple objects; they are stored as a comma-separated list of objects inside square brackets:

```
[{"ContactName":"Rob","ContactAddress":"Rob's house",
"ContactPhone":"Rob's Phone","ContactMinutesSpent":0},
{"ContactName":"Mary","ContactAddress":"Mary's house",
"ContactPhone":"Mary's Phone","ContactMinutesSpent":30},
{"ContactName":"David","ContactAddress":"David's house",
"ContactPhone":"David's Phone","ContactMinutesSpent":60},
{"ContactName":"Jenny","ContactAddress":"Jenny's house",
"PhoneContactPhone":"Jenny's Phone","ContactMinutesSpent":90}]
```

When the program wants to read back the collection, it can use the same method as before, except that the destination type is now a list of `Contact` objects rather than a single `Contact`:

```
contacts = JsonConvert.DeserializeObject<List<Contact>>(json);
```

The `SerializeObject` and `DeserializObject` methods can be used to store a list of any kind of object. The save and load methods for the Time Tracker program turn out to be very simple.

```
string SAVE_NAME = "TimeTracker.json";                    Name used to save the data.

List<Contact> contacts = new List<Contact>();

void storeAllContacts()
{
    string json = JsonConvert.SerializeObject(contacts);       Create the string.

    SnapsEngine.SaveStringToLocalStorage(itemName: SAVE_NAME, itemValue: json);
}
                                                    Save the string in local storage.
```

This is the `storeAllContacts` method. It creates a JSON string and then saves the string in local storage.

```
void loadAllContacts()                         Fetch the string from local storage.
{
    string json = SnapsEngine.FetchStringFromLocalStorage(SAVE_NAME);

    if (json == null)                     If the string is null, no contacts were found
    {
        // If we get here, there is no string in local storage
        SnapsEngine.WaitForButton("Created empty Time Tracker store");
        contacts = new List<Contact>();          Create an empty list and tell the user.
    }
    else
    {                                     Deserialize the contacts from the string
        contacts = JsonConvert.DeserializeObject<List<Contact>>(json);
    }
}
```

The `loadAllContacts` method has to be slightly more complicated because it needs to deal with the possibility that the contacts information might not be available. This will be the case the very first time the program runs. This version of the method creates an empty list and tells the user that is what it has done.

You can explore how these methods are used in the **Ch10_06_TimeTrackerJson** sample program, which uses a JSON-formatted string as storage for a fully working Time Tracker application.

You can use JSON to add data storage to any of the applications that we have written so far. Any data that is held as a list of class instances can be stored and retrieved using serialization.

MAKE SOMETHING HAPPEN

Add data storage to the Pizza Picker

We wrote the pizza picker a while back. It lets a bunch of people decide what pizza toppings they want by pressing the matching button. Pressing the **Show Totals** button shows the total number of orders for each kind of topping. .

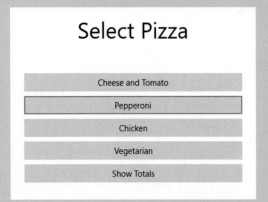

One problem with this application is that it doesn't "remember" the previous count values. If the program is restarted, the counts for each topping are reset to 0. It works this way because at the time we wrote it we didn't know how to store the values. But now we do.

```
class PizzaDetails
{
    public int CheeseAndTomatoCount=0;
    public int pepperoniCount=0;
    public int chickenCount=0;
    public int vegetarianCount=0;
}
```

We can create a class named `PizzaDetails` to hold a value for each type of topping. These are initially set to 0. Then, when the program starts, we can load an instance of this class from a JSON string:

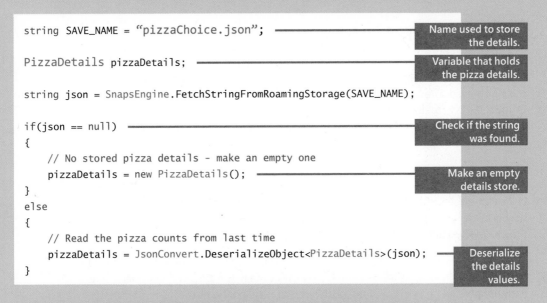

```
string SAVE_NAME = "pizzaChoice.json";                          Name used to store
                                                                    the details.

PizzaDetails pizzaDetails;                                      Variable that holds
                                                                 the pizza details.

string json = SnapsEngine.FetchStringFromRoamingStorage(SAVE_NAME);

if(json == null)                                                 Check if the string
{                                                                     was found.
    // No stored pizza details - make an empty one
    pizzaDetails = new PizzaDetails();                          Make an empty
}                                                                details store.
else
{
    // Read the pizza counts from last time
    pizzaDetails = JsonConvert.DeserializeObject<PizzaDetails>(json);   Deserialize
}                                                                        the details
                                                                          values.
```

This sequence of statements tries to fetch a pizza-choice JSON string from roaming storage.
If there is no string found (this will happen when the program runs for the first time), an
empty details object is created. If the string is located, it is used to restore the pizza count.

After each command, the program can store the pizza-choice values:

```
json = JsonConvert.SerializeObject(pizzaDetails);              Create the JSON string.
SnapsEngine.SaveStringToRoamingStorage(itemName: SAVE_NAME, itemValue: json);

                                                               Save the string in roaming
                                                                               storage.
```

There is a version of the pizza-picking program that uses storage in **Ch10_07_PizzaPicker**.
You can use this pattern to add data storage to many applications.

Fetching data using XML

JSON is a great way to convert complex objects into a simple string of text. XML is
another technology that is very popular for this type of work. As noted above, XML is
the abbreviation for Extensible Markup Language. You can use XML to design a language that represents whatever data you want to work with. Unlike JSON, which is just
a lightweight way of representing the contents of a class, XML can be used to create

structured XML documents. The design of a document can be expressed in an XML schema, which formally expresses the information that the document must contain. For example, the schema for the contact information in the Time Tracker system could express the requirement that the name of a contact must be present but the address can be omitted. The language of the World Wide Web—HTML, or Hypertext Markup Language—is actually based on the design of XML, and I could spend the rest of this book explaining how to structure and format XML documents (but I really don't want to do that).

XML is used to encode lots of information that we can download from the Internet. The XML schema used for lots of news and blog sites is known by the name RSS, which stands for either Really Simple Syndication or Rich Site Summary. Many information sites provide what is called an *RSS feed*, which is really a web address from which the XML-formatted data can be obtained.

The RSS schema defines an object called `channel` that contains a number of items. You can think of a `channel` as a list of items. An `item` contains a number of members. One member of `item` is the `title` of the post, another is called the `description`. In the case of a blog post, the `description` contains the post itself. All these items are strings.

My blog host exposes an RSS feed that you can find at the address **www.robmiles .com/?format=rss**. If you point your browser at this URL, you'll get back a document that contains a large chunk of XML. We can use the Snaps method `GetWebPageAs-String` to fetch this text from my website:

```
string rssText =
    SnapsEngine.GetWebPageAsString("http://www.robmiles.com/?format=rss");
```

This statement creates a string called `rssText` that contains the RSS feed from my blog. What we'd like to do next is convert this block of XML into an object that we can work with to extract XML elements and work with them. We need the XML equivalent of the Newtonsoft library that we used to convert JSON strings.

C# has a feature named *Language Integrated Query*, or LINQ (rhymes with "think"), that will do this job for us. LINQ can be used for lots of jobs, but for now we are going to use it to convert a string of XML text into an XML element that our program can work with. To get easy access to the LINQ classes, we first need to add the LINQ namespace:

```
using System.Xml.Linq;
```

Now our program can use a LINQ class that will read a string of XML and create an XML element that holds that text:

```
XElement rssElements = XElement.Parse(rssText);
```

This statement takes the text that was obtained from my blog and converts it into an XElement object that represents the blog's structure. Now we can navigate down the elements to find the title of the blog post:

```
string title =
    rssElements.Element("channel").Element("item").Element("title").Value;
```

This rather complicated statement drills down through the channel, item, and title elements to get the value of the title element, which in this case is a string that provides the title of the blog post.

```
using SnapsLibrary;
using System.Xml.Linq;

class Ch10_08_RSSReader
{
    public static void StartProgram()
    {
        snaps = new SnapsEngine();
        string rssText =                                    Get the contents of the RSS feed.
            SnapsEngine.GetWebPageAsString("http://www.robmiles.com/?format=rss");

        XElement rssElements = XElement.Parse(rssText);        Convert the RSS feed
                                                                into an XElement.
        string title =
            rssElements.Element("channel").Element("item").Element("title").Value;

        SnapsEngine.SetTitleString("Headline from Rob");
        SnapsEngine.DisplayString(title);
    }
}
```

This is the complete program that displays the title of my latest blog post. You can use this program to get headline information from any RSS feed. Just replace the address of my blog with a different website. Although I've no idea why you'd want to do this.

If you take a look at a complete RSS feed, you'll discover that a `channel` actually contains a sequence of items rather than just one. You can use a `foreach` loop to work through these:

```
using SnapsLibrary;
using System.Xml.Linq;

class Ch10_09_RSSTitles
{
    public static void StartProgram()
    {
        snaps = new SnapsEngine();
        string rssText =
            SnapsEngine.GetWebPageAsString("http://www.robmiles.com/?format=rss");

        XElement rssElements = XElement.Parse(rssText);

        SnapsEngine.SetTitleString("Headlines from Rob");

        SnapsEngine.ClearTextDisplay();

        foreach ( XElement element in
            rssElements.Element("channel").Elements("item"))
        {
            SnapsEngine.AddLineToTextDisplay(element.Element("title").Value);
        }
    }
}
```

Get all the item elements.

Display each title on the screen.

This program uses the `Elements` property of the `channel` to get each `item` in turn. It then uses the Snaps method `AddLineToTextDisplay`, which makes it easy to build up multiline displays. When the program runs, it displays the headlines shown in **Figure 10-10**.

Headlines from Rob

Adventures in 3D Printing #4: Pen Holder
Get get-iplayer
Happy New Year at the C4DI
Adventures in 3D Printing #3: Panic Button
Adventures in 3D Printing #2: Jack
Adventures in 3D Printing #1: Tape Dispenser
Folly Lake Cafe Scones Rock
Star Wars - the Force Awakens
Robot Drawing
Merry Christmas from me and the Robot
Full Moon on Christmas Eve Eve
Taking a look at the Photon
Nice Weather for Pictures - Mostly
Robot Visitor
What use is an old, cheap lens?
Global Game Jam Hull - Registration Site
now Live
Enter FameLab - I have
Making Useful Software is Hard
Tiny Christmas Bash
Fun and Games at the Black Marble Event

Figure 10-10 Blog titles gathered through an RSS feed.

My blog host shows only a limited number of items. Some feeds provide a lot more of
them.

MAKE SOMETHING HAPPEN

Read some feeds

It is very easy to make a program that can read feeds in this way. If you dig into the format of
the document, you can also extract the description text. You might even be able to make a
program that uses speech output to read you the news each morning. Here are some feeds to
get you started.

- http://feeds.bbci.co.uk/news/rss.xml

- http://www.nasa.gov/rss/dyn/breaking_news.rss

- http://www.theguardian.com/world/rss

What you have learned

In this chapter, you have learned the difference between structures, which are managed by value, and classes, which are managed by reference. You know that when using a value type, all the data in a variable is copied from one object to another when assignment takes place, whereas when working with references, an assignment will cause two references to refer to the same object.

You have seen how you can use value types to hold specific values about a particular object—for example, the position of a space alien in a game. You have also seen how reference types make it easy for programs to work with very large objects without having to move them around in memory—for example, a reference to a very large object that holds all the bank account information for a customer or an image to be shared by many elements in a computer game.

You have also discovered the List class, which is part of a set of resources that are supplied alongside the C# language. Lists work with reference types to provide a much more flexible way of storing objects than arrays. You have seen how C# namespaces allow programmers to give unique names to the objects that they create, and how the List class is part of the Collections namespace.

Finally, you saw how JSON serialization makes it very easy to convert a list of objects into a string of text that can be easily stored on the computer and how XML works in a similar way to encode and transfer data.

Here are some questions that you might like to ponder:

Is it possible to write programs without using references?

References are one of the hardest things to understand when you are writing programs. At least I found them to be that way. It is tempting to "stay with what you know" and try to write everything using structures. This is possible, but you will find that your programs are harder to understand and sometimes slower and larger than they need to be. Both references and value types have their place, and you need to understand how and when they are to be used. Think of a value as being something "about" an object—for example, the amount of money that is in a bank account. Think of a reference as pointing to something that you'd rather not move around or something you want to share—for example, a large sound effect that is being used for the engine noise by many different spaceships in a game. If you make explicit choices during the design stage of your application, you will find that these are much easier to understand.

Does a namespace affect where your program files are stored?

A namespace is a "space where names have meaning." In this way, you can think of it as being structured a bit like a file store, where every file has a unique path that can be used to locate the file on a physical storage system somewhere. However, a name in a namespace is not physical. It is logical in that it exists only in the mind of the programmer and the C# compiler. Elements in a namespace can be spread across many files in a C# application. We use namespaces to organize how we identify things, not precisely where they are stored on a disk. It is important to start to think about things in terms of their physical and logical properties when you create systems. A telephone has a physical number that is hard-wired into the circuitry, but we prefer to refer to a particular telephone as "Dad's phone" rather than "0121 23432 3983". To make this work, the telephone contains a layer of software that looks up the physical number of "Dad's phone" whenever we need to call it. In the same way, the C# compiler will search all the C# source files and libraries to find a class from a particular namespace. As a programmer, you don't have to know precisely where the code lives, you just have to use the logical name of the item that you want to work with.

Can writing software really make you rich and famous?

Yes. We all know about Bill Gates and Mark Zuckerburg, who have built empires starting with their software smarts, but there are also a lot of people who have achieved fame and some fortune from their code-writing skills. Many systems that are used every day by millions of companies have their roots in software that was written by "ordinary" developers who started coding at home and gave their software away. One of the best ways to start making a name for yourself is by contributing to an open-source project run by volunteers. This might not lead to riches, but it is a great way to practice and start to make a name for yourself. After all, you don't need everyone to recognize your genius, just the person who will give you that job you really want.

11

Making solutions with objects

What you will learn

You now know enough about programming to be useful—and dangerous. If this book were teaching you how to drive, you would know how to steer the car, what most of the pedals do, and how to start and stop, but you wouldn't yet know the rules of the road—how to drive safely and economically with regard for other drivers.

In this chapter, you are going to learn some "rules of the code" (sorry about that) that will allow you to create solutions that are more secure, robust, and flexible. You'll discover how to use the features of C# that let you provide integrity to the objects that you use in your programs. You'll also discover quite a few new C# features, including ones that let you create programs that can manipulate dates and times and store photographs.

Creating objects with integrity

Integrity in a person is a prized quality. We prefer it when people turn up when they say they are going to, remember that they owe us five dollars, and generally tell us the truth. It's the same with software objects. Programmers prefer objects that always contain valid values—and don't suddenly say that our bank balance has just become $8,388,607.

The designers of C# also prize integrity in objects, and they provided some language features that you can use to ensure that the classes and structures you create can be made to behave with a degree of reliability. In this section, you'll find out how these features can be used to make objects that always hold values that make sense. We'll start by adding some integrity to the Time Tracker application.

Protecting data held inside an object

For the Time Tracker application, we needed to store four items about each contact: name, address, phone number, and number of minutes the contact has spent with the lawyer. To meet these requirements, we created a Contact object that contains a data member for each of these items. The name, address, and phone number elements can be stored in strings. The number of minutes spent with the contact is held in an integer, which is set to 0 when the contact is created.

Each time the lawyer spends time with a contact, the number of minutes should be increased to reflect this. It is very important to the lawyer that the minutes-spent value is correct at all times. If these minutes are not properly recorded, it costs her money. So what happens in our program when we run code such as this?

```
using SnapsLibrary;

class Ch11_01_PublicMenace
{
    class Contact
    {
        public string ContactName;
        public string ContactAddress;
        public string ContactPhone;
        public int ContactMinutesSpent;

        public Contact(string name, string address, string phone)
        {
```

```
            this.ContactName = name;
            this.ContactAddress = address;
            this.ContactPhone = phone;
            this.ContactMinutesSpent = 0;
        }
    }

    public void StartProgram()
    {
        Contact insecure = new Contact("Rob", "Rob's House", "Rob's Phone");
        insecure.ContactMinutesSpent = -99;
        SnapsEngine.DisplayString("Minutes are " + insecure.MinutesSpent);
    }
}
```

This example demonstrates a dangerous defect in our design. Up until now we have been marking all the members of our objects as `public`. However, the fact that these elements are public means that their contents can be made invalid very easily.

When this example runs, it creates an instance of the `Contact` class and then modifies the `ContactMinutesSpent` member of that object:

```
Contact insecure = new Contact("Rob", "Rob's House", "Rob's Phone");
insecure.ContactMinutesSpent = -99;
```

The first statement simply creates a contact entry for Rob, but the second statement does something fairly dangerous. It sets the number of minutes spent for the contact to –99, which is obviously invalid. The problem is that our solution doesn't "know" that it is impossible to spend –99 minutes with someone. As we have seen, programs just follow the instructions that we give them, whether the instructions are sensible or not.

PROGRAMMER'S POINT

Build common sense into your objects

You might think that I'm worrying more than I should about my objects. After all, nobody would be foolish enough to try to set the minutes-spent value to –99? Unfortunately, my experience is that people are known to do this kind of thing. If you are working as part of a team, the objects that you create may be used by many programmers over time. Some of these programmers might use the objects incorrectly. This can happen through ignorance of the way that the objects work, but there is also the threat of *malware*, which is code written specifically to find and exploit weaknesses in other programs.

I'm a strong believer in *defensive programming*, which is making sure that, where appropriate, you take steps to ensure that your objects have some common sense built in. If I'm writing a computer game, I tend to be fairly relaxed about the integrity of my objects. But the Time Tracker program is quite different. Any corruption of the value of Contact-MinutesSpent in the contact information could have a serious effect on the business of my customer, so I'm going to be sure that I protect the integrity of this value to the best of my ability.

The C# language lets you mark members of objects as public or private. You saw this first in Chapter 9, when we made the data elements of our song notes private to protect them from unwanted changes. You know that public means that code outside the class can access the member. If the member of a class is marked private, code outside the object is no longer allowed access to it.

How you do this is as simple as changing the method modifier public to private:

```csharp
class Contact
{
    public string contactName;
    public string contactAddress;
    public string contactPhone;
    private int contactMinutesSpent;

    public Contact(string name, string address, string phone)
    {
        this.contactName = name;
        this.contactAddress = address;
        this.contactPhone = phone;
        this.contactMinutesSpent = 0;
    }
}
```

Class member marked as private.

Once a member of a class has been made private, it can be used only by code running inside the class.

```csharp
Contact secure = new Contact("Rob", "Rob's House", "Rob's Phone");
secure.contactMinutesSpent = -99;
```

If we try to compile these two statements with the contactMinutesSpent value marked private, the compiler will generate an error:

'Contact.contactMinutesSpent' is inaccessible due to its protection level

This compilation error protects the `MinutesSpent` value from being changed by code running outside the `Contact` object. As the creator of the object, you now have complete control over how and when this data member is used.

Protection inside objects

Question: Why is it that the statement in the constructor for the `Contact` object can set `MinutesSpent` but the other assignment statement can't?

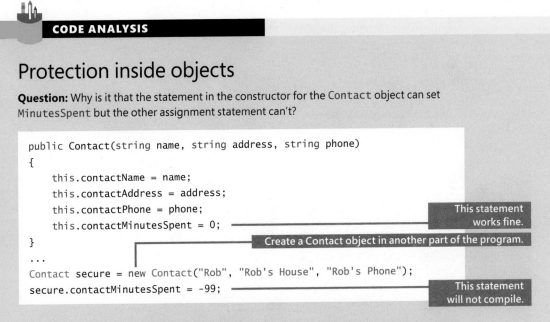

```
public Contact(string name, string address, string phone)
{
    this.contactName = name;
    this.contactAddress = address;
    this.contactPhone = phone;
    this.contactMinutesSpent = 0;                         This statement
                                                          works fine.
}
...                                 Create a Contact object in another part of the program.
Contact secure = new Contact("Rob", "Rob's House", "Rob's Phone");
secure.contactMinutesSpent = -99;                         This statement
                                                          will not compile.
```

Answer: This is all about context. Any piece of C# code will execute in a particular context. In the case of code running within the constructor method for the `Contact` object, this code runs in the context of the object itself and is therefore trusted, in that code running inside an object is considered part of the object. The second statement is running in a different context, perhaps inside the `StartProgram` method, which is *not* inside the `Contact` class. Because the code is not running in the context of the object, it is not allowed access to private members of that object.

Providing Get and Set methods for private data

We now have protection around the precious data stored in the `MinutesSpent` variable, but this level of protection is actually too strong. There is no way that any code outside the `Contact` class can use the value that is stored there. You can solve this problem by creating methods in the Contact class that are public and provide access to the MinutesSpent value.

The following version of the Contact class contains two new methods, one called GetMinutesSpent and one called SetMinutesSpent. They manage access to the data.

```
class Contact
{
    public string ContactName;
    public string ContactAddress;
    public string ContactPhone;

    private int contactMinutesSpent;

    public int GetMinutesSpent()                    Method to get the value.
    {
        return this.contactMinutesSpent;
    }

    public void SetMinutesSpent(int newMinutesSpent)    Method to set the value.
    {
        this.contactMinutesSpent = newMinutesSpent;
    }
}
```

The next group of statements shows how the methods can be used. The program sequence gets the number of minutes that Rob has spent with the lawyer, adds 10 to that value, and then stores the result back in the object. At no time is code outside the Contact object able to interact directly with the contactMinutesSpent variable, but it can call the public methods in the object that provide the access.

```
Contact moresecure = new Contact("Rob", "Rob's House", "Rob's Phone");
int robsMinutes = moresecure.GetMinutesSpent();          Get the value.
robsMinutes = robsMinutes + 10;                          Add 10 minutes to the value.
moresecure.SetMinutesSpent(robsMinutes);                 Set the value.
```

As it's written so far, however, the SetMinutesSpent method does not stop a program from setting an invalid ContactMinutesSpent value. It simply copies the value supplied as a parameter into the Contact object. However, we can change the method so that it performs some validation:

```
public void SetMinutesSpent(int newMinutesSpent)
{
    if(newMinutesSpent > 0)
        // Only set a value that is greater than 0
        this.contactMinutesSpent = newMinutesSpent;
}
Ch11_02_PrivateMinutesSpent
```

This version of the SetMinutesSpent method ensures that a Contact never contains
a value of minutesSpent that is less than 0. If a program tries to set a value that's less
than 0, the new value will be ignored.

What happens if you leave off public and private?

Question: A programmer is not forced to mark a member of a class as public or private.
What happens if you leave them out?

>**Answer:** In C#, the default protection of class members (that is, the protection that you
>get if you don't specify what you want) is private.

Providing methods that reflect the use of an object

Providing get and set methods allows a programmer to control the changes that
can be made to the elements in an object. But for the Time Tracker application, it is
probably more sensible to create a method that allows a program to add minutes to
a contact than it is to provide a set behavior that can be used to put a new value into
the minutes-spent value.

```
public class Contact
{
    private int contactMinutesSpent;

    public int GetMinutesSpent()
    {
        return contactMinutesSpent;
```

```
    }

    public void AddMinutes(int timeValue)
    {
        contactMinutesSpent = contactMinutesSpent + timeValue;
    }
}
```

Now all that users of the Contact class can do is add time. Our lawyer customer will like this feature a lot because it means there is no way that a badly behaved program can lose minutes that she has spent with a contact.

This statement adds 30 minutes to the time spent with Rob. This approach could be the basis of a more secure solution—the only way to change the number of minutes spent is to call the method that adds time to it:

```
rob.AddMinutes(30);
```

Using methods like this is a very popular programming pattern. The data in the object (the values we really care about) is held in members that are private. This means that the data items are not directly accessible to code that's not running inside the object. However, the methods that control access to the data are made public so that they can be used to change the data and read the value back. Programmers love having control, and this design pattern gives them control when changes are being made to variables in the program.

WHAT COULD GO WRONG

Feeding invalid values into a method

The AddMinutes method is a good start at managing access to the minutes value, but it is not quite perfect.

Question: What would be the effect of the following statement?

```
rob.AddMinutes(-30);
```

Answer: This would add the value –30 to the minutes spent for rob, which would reduce the minutes value by 30 (which might save rob some money).

Question: How do we prevent this corruption of the minutes value?

Answer: One way is to modify the AddMinutes method so that it updates the contact-MinutesSpent value only if the value being added is positive.

```
public void AddMinutes(int timeValue)
{
    if(timeValue > 0)
        contactMinutesSpent = contactMinutesSpent + timeValue;
}
```

This version of the method contains a condition that tests the value of the parameter and adds the time only if the value being added is greater than 0.

PROGRAMMER'S POINT

You need to think of errors in the context of risk

You can use the public and private C# features to control what happens to a data member in an object, but you need to consider the broader implications of their use. It might seem very sensible to protect data in the way that you have just seen, but consider what would happen if the lawyer entered a minutes value that was extraordinarily large, perhaps because of problems with the keyboard. If the program was designed to prevent the minutes value for a customer only from being reduced, there would be no way to fix this problem.

This is all about managing risk. There is a risk that the user might enter an invalid minutes value, and there is also a risk that code in the application might attempt to set the value incorrectly. As a developer, you need to consider the impact of these events and act accordingly. This means asking the lawyer "What's the longest meeting you could ever have?" and then setting upper limits on the size of a session. It also means asking the question "How much effort do you want me to put into making sure that rogue programs can't damage this data?" The lawyer may be keen that this data is protected, but she will also be keen on getting her program written for the best possible cost.

You must also think about the ethical responsibility of a programmer toward his or her customers, which is a bit beyond the scope of this simple programming book but is something you really should think about whenever you write a program for a fee—even if the fee is paid in ice cream or cupcakes.

Using properties to manage access to data

You've seen that you can create methods to manage access to objects, and this can be made to work very well. It allows programs to reduce the chances for objects to contain invalid data. However, there is another technique that is used to manage access to data in objects, and that is the C# *property*.

A property lets a program gain control when a member in an object is being read or written to. Here's an example of how a property can be used to store the name of a contact:

```
using SnapsLibrary;

class Ch11_03_PropertyDemo
{
    class Contact
    {
        private string contactName;                     Private value managed
                                                            by the property.

        public string ContactName                       Start of property declaration.
        {
            get                                         Get behavior (property is read).
            {
                SnapsEngine.DisplayString("Getting the value of the name");
                return this.contactName;               Return the value.
            }

            set                                         Set behavior (program
            {                                              writes to the property).
                SnapsEngine.DisplayString("Setting the name to " + value);
                this.contactName = value;              Set the private value
            }                                              managed by the
        }                                                  property.
    }

    public void StartProgram()
    {
        SnapsEngine.SetTitleString("Name Property Demo");
        Contact rob = new Contact();
        rob.ContactName = "Robert";                    Use the set behavior to
                                                           set the name.
```

```
        SnapsEngine.WaitForButton("Continue");
        string name = rob.ContactName;                              Use the get behavior to
        SnapsEngine.WaitForButton("Continue");                           read the name.
    }
}
```

In this example, the value of the name is stored as a private string member called
contactName (note that the identifier for this variable starts with a lowercase c). This
variable is stored as a member of the Contact class, and because it is private, it cannot
be accessed by code that is not part of the Contact class.

The name is exposed to the outside world as a public property with the name ContactName (which starts with a capital C). Programs running outside the Contact object
can access this property, and when they do the set or get behavior runs, depending
on whether the program is assigning a value to the property or reading the value
back. The next two statements show how this works:

```
Contact rob = new Contact();
rob.ContactName = "Robert";
```

The first of these statements creates an instance of the Contact class. The second sets
the Name property of the class to "Robert". When the assignment is performed, the set
behavior inside the ContactName property will run:

```
set
{
    SnapsEngine.DisplayString("Setting the name to " + value);
    this.name = value;
}
```

The set behavior does two things. It displays a message so that we can watch it work,
and then it sets the value of the name member to whatever is being assigned to the
property. The set behavior uses a new C# keyword, value, which is the value that is
being assigned by the set operation. In the case of our sample program, the value
keyword is set to "Robert", since that is the value being assigned. You can think of the
value keyword as being a bit like a parameter to a method call; it is given the value of
whatever is being fed into the assignment. This version of the set behavior uses this
value to set the name immediately, but we could add some validation to reject invalid
names—in fact, we will be doing this later.

When the get behavior is used, the process reverses:

```
string name = rob.ContactName;
```

Reading from a property causes the get behavior to run. This behavior *must* return a value of the type of the property, in this case a string.

```
get
{
    SnapsEngine.DisplayString("Getting the value of the name");
    return this.contactName;
}
```

As with the set behavior, I added a statement to display a message that shows what is going on. In the final program, these messages would not be displayed, but you can run the sample program and see how execution flows through it.

If this is a little confusing, remember that we added the Name property to make it easy for other programs to get hold of the Name value of a contact, but we also wanted to keep control of how the text in the name is changed. For example, we could modify the set behavior so that it rejects names that are empty strings:

```
set
{
    if (value != "")
        this.contactName = value;
}
```

This version will set the name only if there is a name to set; otherwise, the value of the name is not changed. Users of the Contact class can read and write to the Name property very easily, but changes to the value of the name are controlled so that the Contact class always holds a name that can be regarded as valid.

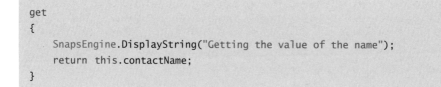 **WHAT COULD GO WRONG**

Detecting invalid changes

Using properties to protect values held in an object stops bad things from happening to the values. If we use the Name property set behavior shown above, we can be absolutely sure that users of the Contact object can't set the name of a contact to an empty string. However, the user of the object never knows that he's done something wrong. This statement would run without any problems. It wouldn't set the name correctly, but the program would continue without incident.

```
rob.ContactName = "";
```

I'm not a fan of this behavior. I don't want the users of a program to think that an action they performed has succeeded when, in fact, it has not. The snag here is that there is no way that a set property can indicate that the value it's been given is wrong. The only thing it can do is throw an exception:

```
set
{
    if (value == "")
        throw new Exception("Invalid name: " + value);
    this.name = value;
}
```

This is a set behavior with attitude. If the set behavior doesn't like the name value that is supplied, it rejects the value by throwing an exception. We first saw the Exception object in Chapter 9, where we threw exceptions to prevent the creation of invalid song notes. Here we are using it to reject invalid names. Throwing an exception has the result of stopping the program flow; later in the book, you will find out how a program can catch exceptions and deal with them, but for now we are going to regard exceptions as a way of preventing a program from continuing if it detects that something is going wrong.

Using properties to enforce business rules

If you think about the art of software creation (and you should), you are designing a system to behave in a way that makes sense to our lawyer customer. If you ask her, she will have an opinion on what constitutes a valid name for a customer. She might say something like, "A name cannot be an empty string," which is useful because that is what our Name property enforces.

I call these statements "business rules" because they are constraints that our system must enforce. One of the most important parts of any project you work on with a customer is to go out and find business rules and use them to build a specification for what you are doing.

Once you have the business rules, you can create software that enforces them. I use a particular pattern of methods to do this. My pattern starts with a validate method:

```
static public string ValidateName(string newName)
{
    if (newName == "")
```

```
            return "A name cannot be an empty string\n";

        return "";
    }
```

This method works on the basis that "no news is good news." It returns an empty string if it regards the input as valid and an error message ("A name cannot be an empty string") if it is asked to validate an empty name. Now any user of the Contact class can check to see whether a name is invalid without generating an exception.

The next thing I do is use the validate method in my set behavior:

```
set
{
    string message = ValidateName(value);
    if (message != "")
        throw new Exception(message);

    name = value;
}
```

If the validation fails, the set property behavior will throw an exception that contains the reason why the name was rejected. My theory is that the exception will hardly ever be produced because a thoughtful developer will use the ValidateName method first to make sure that his change is going to work. Here is how the program would read a valid name from the user by repeatedly asking for name values until the user enters one that is valid. The loop would complete only when the name validated correctly.

```
string errorMessage;
string name;

do                                                                    Start the loop.
{
    name = SnapsEngine.ReadString("Enter new contact name");    Read the name.
    errorMessage = Contact.ValidateName(name);                  Validate the name.
    if (errorMessage != "")
    {
        SnapsEngine.DisplayString(errorMessage);                If the name is
        SnapsEngine.WaitForButton("Try again");                 wrong, an error
        SnapsEngine.DisplayString("");                          occurs.
    }
} while (errorMessage != "");                                   Repeat while there
                                                               is an error.
```

Why is the `ValidateName` method static?

You might not have spotted this, but the `ValidateName` method was marked as a `static` method. This means that it is a member of the `Contact` class, not part of an instance of the class.

Question: Why is the `ValidateName` method static?

Answer: To understand this design choice, you first need to be sure that you know what `static` means. The `static` keyword makes a member of a class "always there." It is part of the class rather than part of an instance of a class. Methods such as `AddMinutes` can't be made static because a program would call `AddMinutes` to add some minutes to a particular instance of the `Contact` class. However, the `ValidateName` behavior is not specific to any particular `Contact` instance, and it is very useful to be able to use this method if you don't happen to have a `Contact` instance in your program. For example, a program might be acquiring the information it needs to build a new `Contact`, and it would be very useful to be able to do this without having another `Contact` instance around to perform the validation.

Managing the object construction process

The pattern I just described can be used to make sure that changes to the data in an object conform to the business rules required by the application. If the lawyer decides that only people with four-letter names are allowed to be stored, we can change the `ValidateName` method to enforce this requirement. However, there is one other place where we need to think about validation, and that is when objects are constructed:

```
Contact badNews = new Contact(name: "", address:"", phone: "");
```

The statement above would create a `Contact` value with completely empty name, address, and phone number members. This would be a bad thing and completely break all our business rules. The way to fix this is to use the validation behaviors in the constructor.

```
public Contact(string name, string address, string phone)
{
    // errorMessage contains the complete error message
    string errorMessage = "";
    // error contains the message produced by each validation
    string error;

    // validate the name
    error = ValidateName(name);
    // if the name is invalid, the error string holds the reason
    if (error != "")
        // if we get here, there is an error in the name
        errorMessage = error;

    // validate the address
    error = ValidateAddress(address);
    // if the address is invalid the error string holds the reason
    if (error != "")
        // if we get here, there is an error in the address
        // add it to the error report
        errorMessage = errorMessage + error;

    // validate the phone number
    error = ValidatePhone(phone);
    // if the phone number is invalid, the error string holds the reason
    if (error != "")
        // if we get here, there is an error in the phone number
        // add it to the error report
        errorMessage = errorMessage + error;

    // if the error message is not an empty string something went wrong
    if (errorMessage != "")
        // Abandon construction by throwing an exception
        throw new Exception(errorMessage);

    this.ContactName = name;
    this.ContactAddress = address;
    this.ContactPhone = phone;
    this.contactMinutesSpent = 0;
}
```

The constructor method for a class is called when a new instance of the class is being created. In the code just above, the constructor uses validation methods for each of the items being supplied to create a new contact. If any of the validation methods fail, the error that the validation created is added to a composite error message that will describe exactly why the construction failed. This error message is then thrown in an exception, to be picked up and used for error reporting by the program trying to create the new contact.

Catching and dealing with exceptions

I've discussed throwing exceptions as a way of stopping a program from running, but I have not yet covered how a program can deal with exceptions that may be thrown. The C# language provides a `try/catch` construction that can be used to catch exceptions. You can use it to display an appropriate message when creating a new contact.

```
static void newContact()
{
    SnapsEngine.SetTitleString("New Contact");

    string name = SnapsEngine.ReadString("Enter new contact name");
    string address = SnapsEngine.ReadMultiLineString("Enter contact address");
    string phone = SnapsEngine.ReadString("Enter contact phone");

    Contact newContact;

    try {                              Code that might throw an exception goes in the try block.
        newContact = new Contact(name: name, address: address, phone: phone);
        storeContact(newContact);
        storeAllContacts();
        SnapsEngine.DisplayString("Contact stored");
    }
    catch (Exception e)               Code that deals with the exception goes in the catch block.
    {
        SnapsEngine.SetTitleString("Could not create contact");
        SnapsEngine.DisplayString(e.Message);          Use the Message
    }                                                  property to get the
    SnapsEngine.WaitForButton("Continue");           reason for the exception.
}
Ch11_04_CatchingExceptions
```

If the user types in valid contact information, the constructor for the Contact class doesn't throw an exception and the program does not obey any of the statements in the catch block. Instead, it goes straight to the call of SnapsEngine.WaitForButton at the end of the method. However, if one of the values passed into the constructor is invalid, the exception is thrown, and execution transfers *immediately* to the block after the catch keyword.

Why isn't the contact always stored?

A programmer on your team is keen to find out how exceptions work and has been studying the code for the newContact method. She has a particular problem with the following part of the code, however:

```
try
{
    newContact = new Contact(name: name, address: address, phone: phone);
    storeContact(newContact);
    storeAllContacts();
    SnapsEngine.DisplayString("Contact stored");
}
```

She thinks this program is wrong because if the name, address, or phone information supplied to the constructor is invalid, the constructor will throw an exception. However, once the exception has been dealt with, the program will then continue on to the next statement and store an invalid contact.

Question: Why is your colleague wrong?

> **Answer:** Once an exception has been thrown, *all* the statements after the point at which the exception occurred are skipped. The program will transfer execution to the first statement of the catch block, and when the catch block completes, the program will move on to the next statement after the catch.

> You explain to your teammate that an exception prevents the execution of any further statements in a try block, but then she asks another question about the methods that store a contact after a new one has been added.

Question: What happens if the storeContact or storeAllContacts method throws an exception?

> **Answer:** If either of these methods throws an exception, the program will transfer execution to the catch block. The exception handler can use the Message property of the exception to deliver a message that should describe what went wrong. For example, if the storeContact method is not able to store the contact for some reason, it could generate an exception that describes this situation. The message would then be picked up by the exception handler and displayed for the user to see.

```
throw new Exception(message: "Contact could not be saved");
```

Your colleague is happy with this explanation, but then asks one final question.

Question: How can the exception handler know what has caused the exception?

Answer: It's not possible for the exception handler to "know" what caused the exception that it is catching. In the case of the `newContact` method, there are three possible causes for an exception to be thrown. The name, address, or phone number for the new contact might be invalid; it might not be possible to store the new contact in memory; or it might not be possible to store all the contacts. The `catch` code is currently dealing with this problem by just displaying the message inside the exception that is thrown. If you want the program to take specific actions for different exceptions, you have to put each statement in its own `try` block and catch the exceptions that it produces.

Creating user-friendly applications

At the moment, our contact-creation process makes sure that we never create an invalid contact in the Time Tracker store. But it is not going to make many of its users happy because if they enter an invalid name for the contact, they don't find out until they have entered all the other data as well. They would much prefer to be told they have made a mistake at the time they make it. To achieve this, we can use a loop that will repeatedly read a value:

```
string errorMessage;
string name;

do
{
    name = SnapsEngine.ReadString("Enter new contact name");      Read a new name.
    errorMessage = Contact.ValidateName(name);                    Validate the name.
    if (errorMessage != "")                                       If the name is
    {                                                             invalid, add the
        SnapsEngine.DisplayString(errorMessage);                 error message.
        SnapsEngine.WaitForButton("Try again");
        SnapsEngine. ("");
    }
} while (errorMessage != "");                                     Loop again if there is an error.

Ch11_05_TimeTrackerFriendly
```

The only way to exit this loop is to enter a valid name. You can use the same program structure to read in valid address and phone items, which can then be used to create a contact. Of course, because we validate the items before we create the contact, there is no need to handle exceptions that the `Contact` constructor might produce—there can never be any. I think this is the correct way to write programs. You try to avoid causing exceptions to be thrown by making sure that input is valid before you pass it onto other methods.

Saving drawings in files

The data that our programs has stored to this point has been based on C# variables. We have stored integers, floating-point numbers, and strings in this way. However, a picture is a much larger and more complex object, which is usually stored in a file.

The Snaps framework provides methods that a program can use to store a drawing as an image. The image is stored in a file in the same way that your digital camera stores a picture when you take it. The graphics file format used is PNG (short for portable network graphics). A number of programs can work with PNG files.

Let's look at some methods that you can use to store the graphics from a drawing program. By using these methods, you could start to create a drawing diary.

SaveGraphicsImageToFileAsPNG

The `SaveGraphicsImageToFileAsPNG` method saves the current drawing in a file on the user's computer. The user is prompted where the file should be stored.

The following program draws a gray dot and then saves the picture on the host computer. The user is then asked where the file should be stored by using the standard File Save dialog box, shown in **Figure 11-1**, where you can see the results from some of my tests.

```
using SnapsLibrary;

class Ch11_06_SaveGraphics
{
    public void StartProgram()
    {
        SnapsEngine.DrawDot(x: 100, y: 100, width: 50);
        SnapsEngine.SaveGraphicsImageToFileAsPNG();
    }
}
```

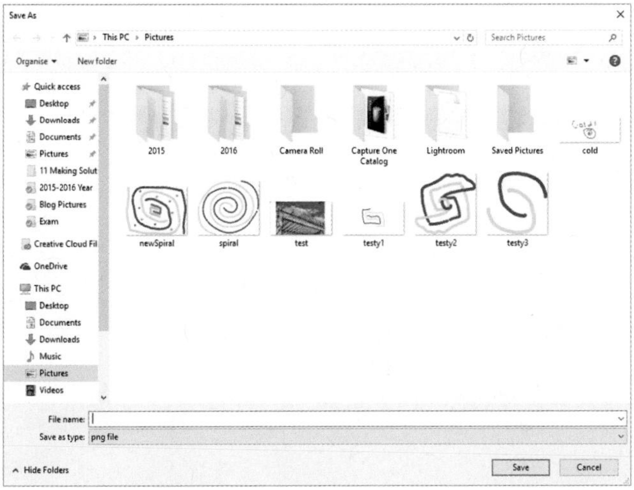

Figure 11-1 Drawing files saved by using the Save As dialog box.

You can use the SaveGraphicsImageToFileAsPNG method if you want to store individual drawings, but the idea behind a drawing diary is that the program will automatically store files without the user having to select a destination. To do this, you have to use a method that works with local storage.

SaveGraphicsImageToLocalStoreAsPNG

A Universal Windows Application, like the ones we have been writing, has its own private space in the file store on the host computer. An application can write as many files as it likes to this private storage area, but this storage area is specific to that one application and not visible to any other programs on the device. In addition, an application is not allowed to directly interact with files in any other part of the computer.

The Snaps library includes a method that stores the currently displayed graphic in a file in local storage. The method, SaveGraphicsImageToLocalStoreAsPNG, is given the name of the file to be created. Here's a statement that saves an image in a local file with the name **test.png**.

```
SnapsEngine.SaveGraphicsImageToLocalStoreAsPNG("test.png");

Ch11_07_SaveGraphicsLocal
```

The user will not be able to find this file in the normal file store on their computer, but this isn't a problem because the drawing application has access to these files and is able to display them when required.

LoadGraphicsPNGImageFromLocalStore

When a Snaps application wants to display the contents of a local image, it uses the LoadGraphicsPNGImageFromLocalStore method:

```
if (!SnapsEngine.LoadGraphicsPNGImageFromLocalStore("test.png"))     Try to load an
{                                                                      image from local
                                                                       storage.
    SnapsEngine.DisplayDialog("Image not found");         Display an error message if
}                                                          the image isn't found.
Ch11_08_LoadGraphicsLocal
```

This program snippet opens the image in the file **test.png** and displays the image on the screen. If the image cannot be found, the method returns the value false. In this program, we use the return value to trigger an error message. If you run this program before you run **Ch11_07_SaveGraphicsLocal**, or use a file name different from **test.png**, you'll see the error behavior in action.

These methods provide the basics for how a drawing diary application can save and view simple drawings, but each drawing to be saved needs to have a file name. One good way to assign a unique file name is to use a data structure that we haven't seen before—the `DateTime` structure. This structure provides lots of useful behaviors that you can use to work with dates and times. If you associate each drawing with the date and time that it was made, you can find drawings that you made on particular days.

The `DateTime` structure

Lots of programs need to work with dates and times, so the designers of C# created a structure that can represent a particular day and time. The structure provides day, month, year, hour, minute, and second properties that a program can use.

CODE ANALYSIS

Structures vs. classes: Repeat

Question: It's important for you to understand the difference between a structure and a class and when each should be used. Why is the `DateTime` object a structure and not a class?

> **Answer:** A `DateTime` object should always be manipulated in terms of its value, not as an object that is managed in terms of references. A given `DateTime` value describes a unique point in time and will often be a property of another object—for example, the date and time of an appointment or the date and time when a photograph was taken. We don't want these values to be managed by reference; they should be part of the object they are helping to describe. The designers of C# made `DateTime` a structure to reflect this. When you make your own objects, you need to think about this, too. Don't make everything a class. Think about how the values are going to be used.

The `DateTime` structure lives in the `System` namespace. Whenever you want to use the structure, you can use the fully qualified name (`System.DateTime`), but it is simpler to include a `using` statement to tell the C# compiler that you want to use the `System` namespace:

```
using System;
```

Getting the current date and time

The DateTime structure provides a static property named Now that returns the current date and time as a DateTime object. You can use this property to create a Snaps program that displays a digital clock:

```
using SnapsLibrary;
using System;

class Ch11_09_DigitalClock
{
    public void StartProgram()
    {
        SnapsEngine.SetTitleString("Snaps Clock");

        while(true)
        {
            DateTime currentDateAndTime = DateTime.Now;          Get the current
                                                                 date and time.
            SnapsEngine.DisplayString(currentDateAndTime.ToString());   Display
                                                                        the date
                                                                        and time
            SnapsEngine.Delay(1);                                       as a string.
        }                                                        Wait for a second.
    }
}
```

This program contains a while loop that will never end. Inside the loop, the program reads the date and time and displays it on the screen. It uses the ToString method to ask a DateTime value for a string that describes the contents of the date and time value being displayed.

The loop also contains a call of the Snaps Delay method. This call delays the program for one second each time the loop goes around. If there was no delay, the program would go around the loop as fast as it could, which would provide quite a bit of work for the computer running the program. Since the time display shows the ticking of the seconds value, there is no point in updating the display more rapidly than once a second. The program uses the Delay method to allow other programs to run until the time needs to be updated. This means that the clock program does not cause the computer to do more work than it needs to.

Fading date and time displays

If you run the clock program shown above, you will notice that, unless you specify otherwise, the Snaps DisplayString method will gently fade in the text that is being displayed. This is fine in most situations because users don't like sudden changes in the display. However, if you want to display a ticking clock, you need the new date and time to be displayed immediately rather than fade in. We can call a different version of the DisplayString method and ask it not to fade in the text:

```
SnapsEngine.DisplayString(message:currentDateAndTime.ToString(),
    alignment: SnapsTextAlignment.center,
    fadeType: SnapsFadeType.nofade,
    size: 50);
Ch11_10_DigitalClockNoFade
```

This is an overloaded version of the DisplayString method that accepts another three parameters that allow us to specify the alignment of the text, the fade type to use, and the size of the text.

If you run the sample program **Ch11_10_DigitalClockNoFade**, you will find that the seconds tick by in a most impressive manner. The text size of 50 gives a nice size for the display, too, as you can see in **Figure 11-2**.

Figure 11-2 A simple digital clock built with Snaps.

Using the date and time to make a file name

We want to use the date and time to create a unique file name for our drawings. This is something that a digital camera does every time you take a picture. Unfortunately, the ToString method provided by the DateTime structure returns a string description of the time that contains colon characters, which are illegal in file names. Instead, you can ask a DateTime value to give you a number that denotes that date and time. The DateTime structure provides a method named ToFileTime that returns a long integer value that is made up of the date information encoded as a single value. (The To FileTime method is so-named because the format of the time data is the same as that used in the Windows operating system to hold time stamps on files held in the file store.) It's not really important how the value is constructed; all you need to know is that if you convert this value to a string, you can use the string as the name of a file you want to store.

```
DateTime fileTime = DateTime.Now;                          Get the current date and time.
string filename = fileTime.ToFileTime().ToString();         Create a file name string.
```

Creating a Drawing class

After creating a file name and saving each drawing, we next have to consider how to get a saved file back again. One way to do this is to make a Drawing class that will contain the DateTime value for a given drawing. The class could also manage saving and loading drawings.

```
class Drawing
{
    public DateTime date;                                   DateTime of this
                                                            drawing.

    private string fileName
    {
        get
        {                                                   Property used in
                                                            the Drawing class to
            return date.ToFileTime().ToString();            get the file name.
        }
    }

    public void StoreGraphicsNow()
    {
        date = DateTime.Now;                                Method that
        SnapsEngine.SaveGraphicsImageToLocalStoreAsPNG(fileName);   saves the
    }                                                       drawing and
                                                            sets the time
                                                            stamp.
    public void ShowStoredGraphics()
    {                                                       Method that
        SnapsEngine.LoadGraphicsPNGImageFromLocalStore(fileName);   shows the
    }                                                       picture on the
}                                                           screen.
```

The Drawing class contains one data member, which is the DateTime value for this drawing. The Drawing class has two public methods. One saves the current drawing, and the other method is used to display a save drawing on the screen.

Here is how a program would create a new `Drawing` and then use it to store the graphics.

```
Drawing record = new Drawing();
record.StoreGraphicsNow();
```

When the program wants a drawing to be displayed, it just has to call the `ShowStored-Graphics` method.

```
record.ShowStoredGraphics();
```

CODE ANALYSIS

Looking at the Drawing class

Question: How are we going to use the `Drawing` items to store pictures?

> **Answer:** You can think of each `Drawing` item as a bit like a `Contact` in the Time Tracker application. It contains a member that identifies a particular drawing. You could store a list of drawings in a JSON string and use this to find drawings—like you stored a list of contact items in the Time Tracker applications.

Question: If you are so concerned about the protection of data in objects, why is the `date` member of the `Drawing` class not private?

> **Answer:** If we want to use the JSON serializer to store the `Drawing` values, we have to allow the date and time to be set during the serialization process. This means that the data member has to be made public so that its value can be set when it is loaded. If I was really serious about security, I'd use one class (perhaps called `DrawingJson`) to manage saving and loading behaviors and another class (perhaps called `SecureDrawing`) that had full protection of the data held inside it.

Question: Why is the file name of the drawing a property of the class? Wouldn't it be quicker to create the file name string from the `date` property each time it's needed?

> **Answer:** Experienced programmers try to make sure that they do a particular task in one place only. This is not to improve performance but so that if we need to change the behavior (perhaps to fix a bug), we have to make the change only in one place.

Creating a list of drawings

Storing a single drawing is great, but a drawing diary needs to account for many drawings. We can do this by creating a list of `Drawing` values. Each time a new drawing is saved, it is added to the list of drawings held in the program. A program can locate each drawing in turn by working through the list.

```
List<Drawing> drawings;
```

The previous statement creates the list of drawings. When the program starts running, this list is loaded into memory:

```
void LoadAllDrawings()
{
    string json = SnapsEngine.FetchStringFromLocalStorage(SAVE_NAME);     Fetch
                                                                          the JSON
                                                                          string.
    if (json == null)
    {
        // If we get here there is no string in local storage
        SnapsEngine.WaitForButton("Created empty Drawing store");     If no string,
        drawings = new List<Drawing>();                              create an empty
                                                                    drawing store
    }                                                               and tell the user.
    else
    {
        drawings = JsonConvert.DeserializeObject<List<Drawing>>(json);
    }                                                               Create the
}                                                                  drawing list from
                                                                   the JSON string.
```

The `LoadAllDrawings` method loads all the drawings. The first time the method runs, there will be no drawings. If this happens, the program shows a message to the user and then creates an empty list.

The program also needs a corresponding method to save all the drawings:

```
string SAVE_NAME = "MyDrawings.json";

void StoreAllDrawings()
{
    string json = JsonConvert.SerializeObject(drawings);     Create the JSON
                                                            string...
```

```
        SnapsEngine.SaveStringToLocalStorage(itemName: SAVE_NAME, itemValue: json);
}
```

Save the string in
local storage.

Making the drawing diary methods

Now that we have the methods to store and load graphics and drawings, we can create the rest of the methods we need to save and display drawings.

The StoreDrawing method creates a new Drawing value, uses it to store the drawing,
and then clears the graphics screen ready for the next drawing.

```
private void StoreDrawing()
{
    Drawing record = new Drawing();
    record.StoreGraphicsNow();
    drawings.Add(record);
    StoreAllDrawings();
    SnapsEngine.ClearGraphics();
}
```

Ask the new drawing to store the graphics.

Add the drawing to the list.

Store the drawing.

The DisplayDrawings method works through the list of drawings, asking each one in
turn to display itself. It pauses for a second between each drawing. When the drawings have been displayed, the method clears the graphics screen, ready for the next
drawing.

```
void DisplayDrawings()
{
    foreach (Drawing d in drawings)
    {
        d.ShowStoredGraphics();
        SnapsEngine.Delay(1);
    }
    SnapsEngine.ClearGraphics();
}
```

The DisplayHelp method does just what the name implies. It tells the user how to use
the program. The idea here is that the user draws his drawing on the screen and then
touches the top-left corner when he wants to perform a command.

```
void DisplayHelp()
{
    SnapsEngine.SetTitleString("Drawing Diary");
    SnapsEngine.DisplayString("Touch the top-left corner to display the menu");

    SnapsEngine.Delay(3);

    SnapsEngine.SetTitleString("");
    SnapsEngine.DisplayString("");
}
```

The `DrawDotsUntilDrawInLeftCorner` method is very similar to the drawing method that we used in Chapter 9. It waits for the user to draw by touching the screen or clicking with the mouse. It then draws a dot at the draw position. If the user draws in the top-left corner of the screen (within 50 pixels of the corner), the method returns.

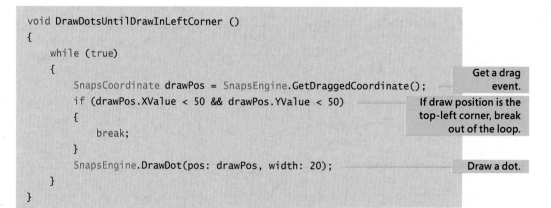

```
void DrawDotsUntilDrawInLeftCorner ()
{
    while (true)
    {
        SnapsCoordinate drawPos = SnapsEngine.GetDraggedCoordinate();    ──── Get a drag event.
        if (drawPos.XValue < 50 && drawPos.YValue < 50)                  ──── If draw position is the
        {                                                                     top-left corner, break
            break;                                                            out of the loop.
        }
        SnapsEngine.DrawDot(pos: drawPos, width: 20);                    ──── Draw a dot.
    }
}
```

The `ProcessCommand` method takes a command from the user and calls the required method to perform the command. The user can clear the screen, store the graphics image as a drawing, and play all the current drawings.

```
void ProcessCommand()
{
    string command = SnapsEngine.SelectFrom3Buttons("Clear", "Save", "Play");

    switch (command)
    {
        case "Clear":
            SnapsEngine.ClearGraphics();
            break;
```

```
        case "Save":
            StoreDrawing();
            break;
        case "Play":
            DisplayDrawings();
            break;
    }
}
```

Here is the complete program. It starts by loading the drawings, setting the drawing color, and then repeatedly lets the user draw and enter commands. The final program uses lots of tiny methods. I think this is a really good way to structure the code. It makes it very easy to navigate. If a client asks you to add an extra command, perhaps to allow her to select different drawing colors, it is obvious where that code should go. Each of the methods has a sensible name that makes it very easy for another programmer to find their way around the program.

```
public void StartProgram()
{
    LoadAllDrawings();

    SnapsEngine.SetDrawingColor(SnapsColor.Blue);

    DisplayHelp();

    while (true)
    {
        DrawDotsUntilDrawInLeftCorner();

        ProcessCommand();
    }
}
Ch11_11_DrawingDiary
```

🚀 **MAKE SOMETHING HAPPEN**

Make a Mustache Maker Rogues Gallery

You can now use what you learned to create a mustache editing program that lets you load pictures that you have taken and annotate them, perhaps to add a mustache or even a full beard. You can use the program to save the picture and provide a slide show of "wanted" people. It would be really nice if you were able to use the camera on your device from your Snaps application. It turns out that this is really easy:

```
SnapsEngine.TakePhotograph();
```

The TakePhotograph method will open the camera dialog box on your Windows 10 device and allow you to take a photograph. When you've taken the photograph, it's displayed on the screen. If the program performs any drawing actions, these will be added to the image and stored when the image is stored.

I've put a Mustache Maker program in the sample code for this chapter. You can find it in the demo file **Ch11_12_MustacheMachine**. One thing you may find surprising is just how similar it is to the drawing diary. Go ahead and add a "take picture" command to the drawing diary.

What you have learned

In this chapter, you've taken some solid steps toward becoming a "professional" developer. You've seen how to use C# constructions to allow programs to manage access to elements and behaviors held within objects. You have seen that by making data private and providing public get and set methods, you can create an object that will always hold valid content in the context of the business rules that apply to the program.

You've also discovered C# properties, which make it very easy for others to have access to data managed by an object but also allow you to ensure that the data held inside the object always has integrity. You've also taken a look at exceptions and dis-covered how a program can deal with exceptions that are thrown as a program runs.

You also built an entirely new application from scratch. In the Drawing Diary, you've explored the relationship between data held in objects and that which is held in files on the host computer. It also shows how to break a fairly complex program into a set of small, easy to understand methods.

Here are some questions that you might like to ponder:

Do we really need to protect data held in our objects?

It depends on the context of the program. If you are writing a trivial game or a program that only you will ever use, you can probably dispense with data protection and make everything in your program public. However, if you are working with other programmers or creating something that will be used by other programmers, I think you should pay attention to the integrity of your program objects. In my experience, if someone does something foolish with one of your software objects that causes bad things to happen, it will be seen as your fault if an application fails as a result. Saying "That was a silly thing to do" is not a valid defense in this situation.

Which are better, properties or `get` and `set` methods?

We know that we can stop uncontrolled changes to the elements in an object by making the member data private. However, once we have done that, we now have to allow the outside world access to this member data in some way; otherwise, the data is useless. There are essentially two ways to provide this access. You can create `get` and `set` methods for the data or hide the private data behind a public property. This is one of those subjects that people have strong opinions about. I like using `get` and `set` methods because the `set` method can tell you why it didn't like the value it was given without having to throw an exception. However, I also like the ease of use of properties.

However, in a given solution, I'd be more concerned about consistency of approach (always using one or the other) rather than the advantages or disadvantages of each.

What's to stop someone from changing the contents of an object of ours when it is saved?

This is a good question. A malicious programmer could change the `minutesSpent` value inside a contact record just by changing the text in the JSON string when it is stored in local storage. There are, however, a couple of ways that a program can stop this from happening.

The first way is to use some kind of encryption when you save the data. Encryption is a mechanical process that takes in data—for example, "Helloworld"—and converts it to data that is harder to understand—for example "Ifmmpxpsme". This is actually not very secure encryption because it just replaces each letter by the next one in the alphabet. There are much better encryption technologies than this that you could use to make it harder for someone to corrupt your data. When a program reads the data, it decrypts the information by reversing the encryption process and recovers the valid data.

The other way to deal with data corruption is to not perform any encoding, but to do something to detect when the data in an object has been changed. If we combine all the values in a `Contact` object in a particular way (for example, add up all the character codes and data values and multiply by a few magic numbers on the way), we can generate a *check code* that is stored with the data. If anyone changes the contents of a `Contact`, our program will notice because it will recalculate the check value when it loads the data and see whether the value matches the stored one.

If you think all this sounds like a game of cat and mouse, you are right. These games of encryption and data validation are being played out all over the world as network and computer designers battle hackers who are constantly trying to break and subvert the digital systems that so much of our lives are based on. It's a fascinating field, and one which is a great place to get some very interesting (and well paid) work.

Part 3

Making games

Games are a great place to develop your programming skills. They are fun and immediate, and you can create them to impress your friends. They also provide a fantastic framework within which you can build on the fundamental principles of object-oriented software development. You've already started using objects in your programs, so now let's find out how we can have some serious fun with them.

12
What makes a game?

What you will learn

Programmers have been creating games for as long as we've had computers. I think that you should try your hand at writing some games even if you don't intend to go into game development. For one thing, getting good at programing is all about practice, and games give you a great place to write lots and lots of code. But the main reason is that developing games let you "doodle" with code with no fear of failure.

When you create a game, you don't have to worry about meeting a specification or implementing the "right" way to solve a problem. You can just write something that might be fun and then find out whether it is. If it doesn't work as you expected, that can be interesting too. Writing games lets you experiment with coding, and that's a lot of fun.

In this chapter, you'll discover how games operate and start working with the software elements that make up gameplay.

Creating a video game

Today we are going to start writing a game. To keep things simple, we'll work in two dimensions—in other words, the objects in our game will be flat. Xbox One games such as Halo provide vast, three-dimensional worlds that players can explore and interact with. Our games will allow players only to work with images on a flat screen.

This is not actually a huge problem from a gameplay perspective. Some of the most popular games ever, from Pong to Space Invaders to Angry Birds, are two-dimensional. One of the lessons from this chapter will be just how compelling a simple game can be.

We'll start by drawing some game objects and getting them to move around and interact with one another. Then we can branch out into different forms of gameplay.

Games and game engines

A *game engine* is the program code that sits underneath a computer game and provides a platform for the game to use. Major game studios spend millions developing the game engines that underpin their products. The game engine is in charge of drawing the display the player sees and updating the state of the objects in the game. It performs drawing and update actions many times a second, giving players an engaging gaming experience.

There are many different game engines. For our purposes, I'm going to use a tiny game engine that I created that runs within the Snaps framework. It's not the most powerful engine in the world, but it will let you grasp the principles of game development. Once you've cut your gaming teeth with the Snaps engine, you can move on to other platforms. I'll give some helpful hints about a framework you might like to use at the end of this chapter.

The Snaps game engine does not run all the time. Instead, you turn it on when you want to play a game. When the game engine starts, it makes the game full screen (if requested) and sets up the input devices that are to be used. Here is the Snaps method a program calls to start the game engine running:

```
using SnapsLibrary;

public class Ch12_01_EmptyGame
{

    public void StartProgram()
```

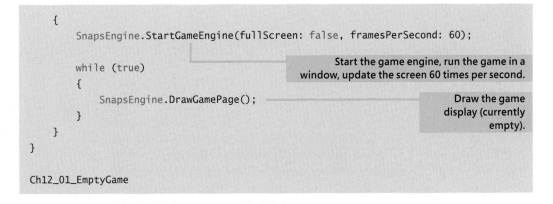

```
    {
        SnapsEngine.StartGameEngine(fullScreen: false, framesPerSecond: 60);

        while (true)
        {
            SnapsEngine.DrawGamePage();
        }
    }
}
```

Start the game engine, run the game in a window, update the screen 60 times per second.

Draw the game display (currently empty).

Ch12_01_EmptyGame

A game can run in full-screen mode or in a window on the display. The Start-GameEngine method is given a Boolean value to select which mode to use. The game engine is also given the number of frames per second that the game is to run at. If you run the **Ch12_01_EmptyGame** Snaps application, you won't see anything on the screen just yet. We'll add some objects to the game in a moment.

CODE ANALYSIS

Frames per second

The second parameter to the StartGameEngine method is the number of frames per second that the game should aim to run at.

Question: What does frames per second actually mean?

Answer: The clue is in the name. The frames-per-second value is the number of times that the screen should be redrawn each second. A game works by redrawing the entire screen at regular intervals. Images on the screen appear to be moving because they are drawn at different positions with each operation. If the time interval between successive redraws increases, the images on the screen appear to move in larger steps, creating a jerky display. Modern games usually try to run at 60 frames per second, although this figure will vary depending on how many items are on the screen at one time. You can experiment with this value to try and get a display that looks good to you. I find that 60 is a good number to start with.

The game loop

If you look at the code in **Ch12_01_EmptyGame,** you'll notice that it contains a loop that will run forever but doesn't seem to do much.

```
while (true)
{
    // Game update logic goes here
    SnapsEngine.DrawGamePage();
}
```

This loop is called the *game loop*. It runs continuously while the game is active. At the moment, the loop just contains one statement, which calls the `DrawGamePage` method in the Snaps library. This is the method that will update all the items on the screen. If any game element has changed position, the method will redraw the item in the updated position. This method also manages timing so that the game loop actually updates the screen at the frame rate that was selected when the game engine was created. At the moment, there is nothing on the screen, so I think we need to move on and display some items.

CODE ANALYSIS

Infinite loops

An infinite loop can be a bad thing for a program to perform because it means that the program will never stop. However, we have one in our program now, which probably deserves some discussion.

Question: When is an infinite loop a good thing?

Answer: An infinite loop is one that runs forever and doesn't have any way of exiting it. But for a game, this continuous update process is actually what you want. When you are playing the game, you want the display to be continuously updated. However, you don't need to worry that this loop will run very quickly and tie up the computer unnecessarily. The `DrawGamePage` method will pause the program so that the game updates only at the frame rate that's requested, which in this program is 60 times per second.

Games and sprites

We can call each element on the game display a *sprite*. A sprite contains an image and has a position and an orientation. If you are playing a space-shooter game, it uses sprites for the spaceships on the screen, the background picture, and the missiles flying through space. We are going to start with a very simple yellow ball sprite.

Adding a sprite image to a game

You can add an image to a Snaps application by dragging it from where it is stored on your PC to the Images folder in Visual Studio. This makes a copy of the image in the game. We did this in Chapter 3, when we added images to be displayed by using the Snaps method named `DisplayImageFromUrl`. **Figure 12-1** shows how Visual Studio lets you manage the ball image file (ball.png) in the Images folder for the sample code for this book.

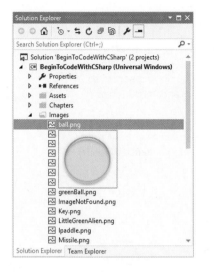

Figure 12-1 The ball image in the Images folder.

If you hover the mouse over one of the images in the Images folder, Visual Studio will show you a thumbnail preview of the image in that file. I'll be using this ball in my examples, but you can add images of your own to the games. This makes it a lot more interesting and personal.

MAKE SOMETHING HAPPEN

Make a game image of your own

You can add an image of your own to the game by dragging it into the Images folder of your Snaps Visual Studio project. The image can be a JPEG, GIF, or PNG image. I prefer to use PNG files because these files support transparent images—in other words, parts of a PNG image can be made to show another image behind them. You will see this when we start to use the ball in our games. The image of the ball is a rectangular picture, but only the round part of the ball obscures the image underneath. The rest of the ball image is transparent.

You can have a lot of fun working with images. If you need a good, free image editor that supports layers and transparency, I would suggest you take a look at Paint.NET, which you can download from www.getpaint.net.

The Snaps ImageSprite class

Now that we have an image file in our project, we need to attach it to a software object that will manage the image within the game. By now you should be familiar with the idea that a programmer can create a software object to represent things that their program will work with. We have created and used objects to represent musical notes and address book contacts, to name just two.

Our games need a sprite on the screen that can display an image. I created an Image-Sprite class that will represent an image on the screen. In your programs, you can create a new ImageSprite instance at any time:

```
ImageSprite ball = new ImageSprite(imageUrl: "ms-appx:///Images/ball.png");
```

There is a constructor for the ImageSprite class that accepts a single parameter, which is a string giving the location of the image to be displayed by the sprite. Once this statement has completed, it has created a reference named ball that refers to an ImageSprite instance that will produce the ball image when drawn in the game. The ball on its own will not do much—it has to be added to the game engine so that it can be displayed. The game acts as a container for all the sprites and manages how and when they are drawn on the screen.

If you'd rather make sprites in your games from images on the Internet, you can do this:

```
ImageSprite ball = new ImageSprite(imageURL:
"https://farm9.staticflickr.com/8713/16988005732_7fefe368cc_d.jpg");
```

You can think of the `ImageSprite` as a kind of carrier for an image. You can tell the `ImageSprite` to place the image on the screen at any location you like. You can also use it to scale and rotate the image in a variety of ways.

Adding an ImageSprite to the game engine

The game engine keeps a list of sprites that are currently in use. When you create an `ImageSprite`, you have to tell the game engine to add the new sprite to this list.

```
SnapsEngine.AddSpriteToGame(ball);
```

This statement adds the ball to the game. Now, when the game loop runs, the sprite will be drawn on the screen. If you reach a point in the game where a particular `Image-Sprite` is no longer needed (perhaps the player has gone from level 1 to level 2), you can remove the sprite by using the `RemoveSpriteFromGame` method.

Here is the simplest possible game:

```
using SnapsLibrary;

public class Ch12_02_BallSprite
{

    public void StartProgram()                                    Start the game engine.
    {
        SnapsEngine.StartGameEngine(fullScreen: false, framesPerSecond: 60);

        ImageSprite ball = new ImageSprite(imageUrl: "ms-appx:///Images/ball.png");
                                                              Create a new ImageSprite
        SnapsEngine.AddSpriteToGame(ball);                    using the ball image.

                                                              Add the ImageSprite to
        while (true)                                          the game.
        {
            SnapsEngine.DrawGamePage();
        }
    }
}
```

Actually, this is more an image-display program, in that nothing happens to the sprite each time the game updates, so it doesn't do anything—it just shows a nice large ball on the screen. **Figure 12-2** shows the ball as it is drawn when the **Ch_12_02BallSprite** program runs.

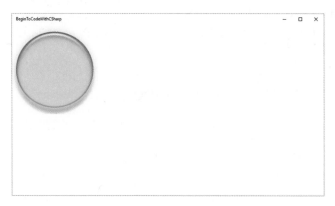

Figure 12-2 Displaying the ball sprite.

The ball image is about 260 pixels in size and is being drawn with that dimension, which is a bit large for our game. We need to find a way of making a ball that is a better size.

Changing the size of an `ImageSprite`

In Chapter 11 you saw how a class can contain property behaviors that can be used to manage access to data held inside the object. The `Contact` class had a `Name` property that allowed a program to manipulate the name of the person the `Contact` value was holding. The `ImageSprite` class provides properties that let a program manipulate the width and height of a sprite when it is displayed.

```
using SnapsLibrary;

public class Ch12_03_SquishyBall
{
    public void StartProgram()
    {
        SnapsEngine.StartGameEngine(fullScreen: false, framesPerSecond: 60);

        ImageSprite squishyBall = new ImageSprite(imageURL:
                                       "ms-appx:///Images/ball.png");
```

```
SnapsEngine.AddSpriteToGame(squishyBall);

float maxWidth = 500;                              Maximum ball width.
float minWidth = 100;                              Minimum ball width.
float currentWidth = 100;                    Current ball width (start at 100).
float widthUpdate = 1;              Amount width changes each time around the
                                                            game loop.

while (true)
{
    currentWidth = currentWidth + widthUpdate;     Update the current width
    if (currentWidth > maxWidth)                   by the update amount.
        widthUpdate = -1;              If ball is wider than maximum width, change
    if (currentWidth < minWidth)        update value so width narrows.
        widthUpdate = 1;                        If the ball is narrower than
    squishyBall.Width = currentWidth;             minimum width, change
    SnapsEngine.DrawGamePage();                    the update value so it
}                                                          counts up.
}
                                              Set the width of the ball to
}                                             currently calculated width.
```

A program can set the width and height of a sprite by assigning values to the sprite's
Height and Width properties. Changing the size of the sprite doesn't instantly change
its size on the display, however; the size changes only when the DrawGamePage method
is called. When the preceding program runs, it makes a ball squish in and out, as you
can see in **Figure 12-3**.

Figure 12-3 Squished ball as a result of changing height and width.

A program can scale an image to any height and width, but when you scale a sprite,
you need to be careful to preserve the ratio of height to width so that the display
looks "right." If you get the ratio wrong, as I did above, you run the risk of objects
looking stretched in one direction or another.

When images go bad

When your program changes the size of an image, the Windows graphics system will scale it to fit the size that you requested. Making an image smaller will result in some detail being lost, but the image quality will still be good. However, if you take a very small image and try to make it very large, you will notice that the scaled image looks blurry, and you might start to see dots and other corruption of the picture. You can see this in the stretched ball in **Figure 12-3**, where the edges of the ball have "steps" in them as the original dots that make up the picture are expanded to fill the space.

When I make a game, I try to be sure that all my images are larger than they need to be so that when I scale them to fit on the screen, I am always making them smaller. This way I can be sure that the items on the screen always look their best.

Get your images squeezing

You can have a lot of fun changing the shape of images. You can use this technique to zoom in to an image or make it shrink to nothing. If you change the size of the update value, you can make the image grow very slowly or flick up and down. Try this with some pictures of your own. You can have quite a lot of fun "squishing" your family photos. Or at least, I did.

Scaling a sprite

We have seen the effect of getting the height and width of an image wrong, which makes it look squished. We can use this to comic effect if we want. However, what we really want is some way to scale a sprite and preserve its shape. It turns out that the ImageSprite provides methods that will do this for us. We can set the width or the height of a sprite, and the other dimension will be adjusted to keep the sprite looking sensible.

The ScaleSpriteWidth method sets the sprite's width as requested and automatically adjusts the height so that the shape of the sprite is correct and does not appear stretched. The ScaleSpriteHeight method does the same for the height of the sprite.

```
float maxWidth = 500;
float minWidth = 100;
float currentWidth = 100;
float widthUpdate = 1;

while (true)
{
    currentWidth = currentWidth + widthUpdate;
    if (currentWidth > maxWidth)
        widthUpdate = -1;
    if (currentWidth < minWidth)
        widthUpdate = 1;                          ← "Squeezing" code used in the previous example.
    scaledCity.ScaleSpriteWidth(currentWidth);   ← Scale the sprite to the
    SnapsEngine.DrawGamePage();                     calculated width.
}

Ch12_04_ScaledCity
```

This program snippet changes the width of a city picture between 100 and 500 pixels. If you run the program, you will notice that the shape of the picture, shown in **Figure 12-4**, is preserved so that it looks right in both sizes.

Figure 12-4 Scaled city photograph.

The formal term for the relationship between the height and the width of an image is the *aspect ratio* of the image, which is the ratio of the height and width of the picture. You see this term used in discussions about video displays. A wide-screen video is usually displayed with an aspect ratio of 16:9 (16 units wide to 9 units high), whereas an older display, and some tablet PCs, have an aspect ratio of 4:3 (4 units wide to 3 units high). One of the challenges for game developers is to make sure that their games work on displays of any size and shape.

What do the height and width values actually mean?

We have been using numbers to specify the dimensions of our screen objects, and you may have noticed that, quite sensibly, when the numbers get bigger, the objects on the screen get bigger. But we need to consider just what these numbers mean and how they are used.

Question: What do the size values actually mean?

> **Answer:** The position and size values are specified in pixels. In the first days of video games, a pixel exactly equaled a single dot on the display. This would mean that the stretched ball image in **Figure 12-3** would be exactly 400 dots wide and 100 dots high. Today, there are many different sizes and resolutions for displays, and it is not sensible to work in dots anymore. On a Windows 10 display, a pixel is equal to around one ninety-sixth of an inch, so the ball I showed earlier would be displayed slightly larger than an inch in size, irrespective of the type of display on the device that is running the program.

If you intend to run your game only on one computer, you can use sprite sizes that work for the display on that machine. However, if you want to make your game available for many users, perhaps via the Windows Store, you need to be sure that players get a good experience irrespective of the device they are using.

A ball size of around one inch would be perfect for a large-screen computer, but it would be a very bad idea for a small tablet PC or a Windows Mobile device. The way to solve this is to adapt the size of your sprites to fit the machine that the game is running on.

Adapting sprite size

We want to make the game adapt to different screen sizes. Snaps provides you with properties that tell a program the dimensions of the *viewport* that the game is presently using. You can think of a game as being drawn on an infinitely large space. The viewport is that part of the space that is visible to the person playing the game. The top-left corner of this viewport is at coordinate 0,0, and the position of the bottom and the edge at the right depends on the width of the viewport. Anything that is not visible in the viewport is not drawn.

For a particular game, I might want the ball to be one-twentieth of the width of the viewport. The following statements use the `GameViewportWidth` property to get the width of the viewport and then calculate a value that is one-twentieth of this to use as the ball's width. There is also a corresponding height property.

Create the sprite from the image.

```
ImageSprite scaledBall = new ImageSprite(imageUrl: "ms-appx:///Images/ball.png");

SnapsEngine.AddSpriteToGame(scaledBall);                    Add the sprite to the game.

double ballWidth = SnapsEngine.GameViewportWidth / 20.0;   Calculate one-twentieth of
                                                            the width of the viewport.
scaledBall.ScaleSpriteWidth(ballWidth);                    Set the width of the sprite to this value.

Ch12_05_BallSpriteTwentieth
```

Figure 12-5 shows a ball that is one-twentieth of the width of the screen. Most games work by setting the size of the game's objects when the game starts.

Figure 12-5 A smaller ball, drawn to scale.

CODE ANALYSIS

Viewport widths and screen sizes

Question: If you are thinking I've told you about screen sizes before, you're right. In Chapter 9, when we worked on the drawing program, we used a Snaps method named GetScreen-Size, which a program can use to determine the width and height of the screen. The method returns a SnapsCoordinate value that has the X value set to the width of the screen and the Y value set to the height. Why do we have two versions of getting the screen size?

Answer: The GetScreenSize method returns the size of the window that the program is running inside of. However, when we make a game that runs in full-screen mode, the game takes over the entire screen display, and the window-size value is not correct in this situation. So we have two size methods.

Filling the screen with a sprite

If you want to make an image fill the entire screen, you can set the width and height values of the sprite to match the screen dimensions. Here's how:

```
scaledBall.Width = SnapsEngine.GameViewportWidth;
scaledBall.Height = SnapsEngine.GameViewportHeight;

Ch12_06_BallSpriteFullScreen
```

Set width and height of the sprite to reflect viewport.

In the case of the ball image, filling the screen results in the image being badly stretched out of shape. However, this technique is a great way to make a background sprite that fills the entire screen. If the sprite contains a pattern—for example, a field of grass or a concrete floor—rather than a recognizable object, it is unlikely that the player will notice that the image is slightly distorted.

Positioning a sprite on the screen

The ImageSprite class provides properties that can be used to manage the position of a sprite on the screen. These two statements place the ball at the top-left corner of the screen:

```
ballSprite.X = 0;
ballSprite.Y = 0;
```

Set the X and Y values of the sprite position to 0.

The values of X and Y give the position of the top-left corner of the sprite. In other words, if we draw with both X and Y set to 0, the ball is drawn at the top-left corner of the page. Unless you specify otherwise, the X and Y positions of an ImageSprite are set to 0 when it is created, which is why all the sprites we have drawn so far have been drawn at the top left.

A program can place a sprite anywhere on the screen by changing the values of X and Y. As with the size of the sprite, the position of the sprite changes on the screen only when the DrawGamePage method runs.

Making a sprite move

What we really want is a game in which elements move around on the screen. To do this, the game can make changes to a sprite's position during the game loop. To understand how this works, take a look at the following code.

```
while (true)                                          Repeat the loop forever.
{
    ball.X = 0;
    ball.Y = 0;                                       Set the X and Y position of
    SnapsEngine.DrawGamePage();                            the sprite to 0.
    SnapsEngine.Delay(0.5);               Update the game display and wait half a second.
    ball.X = 500;
    ball.Y = 500;                                     Reset the X and Y position.
    SnapsEngine.DrawGamePage();
    SnapsEngine.Delay(0.5);               Update the game display and wait half a second.
}

Ch12_07_FlickingSprite
```

When you run the program, the ball appears to flick between two different positions on the screen. Of course, it isn't really moving—it's that your brain is fooled into thinking that it has moved from one place to another. If we update the sprite more frequently, and we don't move quite as far with each step, we can create the appearance of smooth movement. Here's some code that shows how this would work:

```
double XBallSpeed = 1;
double YBallSpeed = 1;                      Set the speed across (X direction) and down
                                                      (Y direction) the screen.

while (true)                                                        Loop forever.
{
    ball.X = ball.X + XBallSpeed;
    ball.Y = ball.Y + YBallSpeed;           Update the X and Y positions by the speed.
    SnapsEngine.DrawGamePage();                     Draw the game on the screen.
}

Ch12_08_MovingSprite
```

This is a classic game loop. The first two statements in the game loop update the ball position, and then the screen is drawn. The loop then repeats. If you run this program, you will see the ball move smoothly down the screen. You see this structure in just about every game you play.

The ball moves steadily because the pixel values are being increased by a ball-speed value of 1 each time the loop goes around. The DrawGamePage method has been told to draw new frames at a rate of 60 per second, so in one second, the ball moves slightly more than half an inch over the screen (remember that there are around 96 pixels in an inch). If you want the ball to move twice as fast, you just have to change the values of xBallSpeed and yBallSpeed to 2.

Sprite movement

This code repays careful study and also raises some interesting questions.

Question: Why does the sprite move down the screen when Y is increased?

> **Answer:** In computer graphics, the origin of the display (the point with the coordinate 0,0) is always the *top left* of the screen. This may have something to do with the way that hardware displays are mapped into memory from the top of the screen, but I must admit I'm not sure. For the purpose of this chapter, I think the answer has to be "because it does," and we just have to move on from this.

Question: What happens if the program tries to draw an image off the screen area?

> **Answer:** The Windows management system doesn't care if your program tries to draw something that is not on the screen. You can regard the screen as a *viewport* onto an infinitely large area that contains the objects being displayed. Windows will draw those parts of the objects that are visible through the viewport; anything else is clipped. One way to make an `ImageSprite` "disappear" is to move it off the visible area, but it is more efficient to use the `Hide` method, which stops the sprite from being drawn at all.

Question: What would happen if we set one of the speed values to zero?

> **Answer:** The program expresses the direction the ball is moving in terms of two values: how far across the screen to move, and how far down the screen to move. If one of these values is 0, it means that there was no movement in that direction. For example, if `YBall-Speed` was 0, the ball would move horizontally but not vertically. If both speed values were 0, the ball would be stationary.

Question: What would happen if we set one of the speed values to a negative number?

> **Answer:** Negative speeds are perfectly okay; they make the ball move in the opposite direction. On the X axis (left to right), a negative speed moves toward the left. In the Y axis (up and down), a negative speed moves the ball upward.

Making a bouncing sprite

We now have movement, but it is not very useful movement. The ball travels down the viewport and then vanishes off the bottom. What we would like is for the ball to bounce off the bottom, top, and sides of the viewport.

If the ball tries to go off the bottom of the screen, the game must make the ball change direction and move up. If the ball tries to go off the top of the screen, the game must make it move down. The game must also make sure that the ball doesn't go off the left and right edges by making similar tests. We can express the algorithm for our bouncing ball as follows:

"If the ball reaches the bottom of the viewport, it should bounce up. If the ball reaches the top of the viewport, the ball should bounce down. If the ball reaches the left of the viewport, it should bounce right, and if the ball reaches the right of the viewport, it should bounce left."

When something bounces, the direction of movement changes. Our program must detect when the ball is moving out of the viewport and make the appropriate change to direction. The ImageSprite class provides a Bottom property that gives the Y coordinate of the bottom of the sprite. If this value ever exceeds the height of the viewport, the ball must change its direction of movement and bounce upward. Here is the code that makes the ball bounce off the bottom of the screen:

```
if(ball.Bottom > SnapsEngine.GameViewportHeight)                    Has bottom of
{                                                                 the sprite moved
    // ball is going off the bottom edge                          beyond viewport?
    if(YBallSpeed > 0)                          If we have gone beyond the bottom and are
    {                                              still going down, we need to reverse.
        // ball is moving down the screen
        // because the speed is positive
        // make it bounce back into the viewport
        // make the speed negative
        YBallSpeed = -YBallSpeed;                The - operator negates a value in a variable.
    }
}

Ch12_09_BouncingSprite
```

There is also a Top property that gives the Y coordinate of the top of the sprite. If the Top value ever becomes less than 0, the ball must bounce down. This is the second test that must be made to make the ball bounce off the top.

```
if (ball.Top < 0)
{
    // ball is going off the top edge
    if (YBallSpeed < 0)
    {
        // ball is moving up the screen
        // because the speed is negative
        // make it bounce back into the viewport
        // make the speed positive
```

```
        YBallSpeed = -YBallSpeed;
    }
}
```

There are also `Left` and `Right` properties that provide the X coordinate of the left and right edges of an `ImageSprite`.

The sample code in **Ch12_09_BouncingSprite** has conditions that test for the ball moving off the four edges. We can now make a ball bounce around the screen. What we need next is a paddle to hit the ball with. But that's in the next chapter.

MAKE SOMETHING HAPPEN

Get some pictures bouncing around the screen

Now that you know how to scale images and position things on the screen, you can have some serious fun with images. You can slowly pan around a sprite by moving it around the viewport, or zoom in by changing the size of the sprite. Or you can just make your brother's or a friend's face bounce around the screen. There is a lot of fun to be had combining multiple images like this.

PROGRAMMER'S POINT

Sometimes very simple behaviors need quite a bit of code

Bouncing is something that seems very simple. After all, if a rubber ball can do it, how hard can it be for a computer program? However, as you have seen, we actually have to do a fair bit of work to get the bouncing behavior to work correctly. Fortunately, modern computers can perform thousands, if not millions, of such instructions every second, so it is not a problem for our game to repeatedly test the position of the ball and update the speed directions when required.

What you have learned

In this chapter you have learned the fundamentals of computer games, what a game is, and how it actually runs. You've seen that a game works by repeatedly updating the objects that make up the game environment and then redrawing these objects in their new positions. You have also discovered that the fundamental element of a two-dimensional game of the kind we are going to make (one in which all the game objects are flat) is the *sprite* and that a sprite is a container for an image that can be positioned and scaled by the game. Changes to the size and position of the sprite give the player the impression of movement. The Snaps framework provides a game engine and an `ImageSprite` class that can be used to manage sprites.

You have also learned more about how the coordinate system of computer displays works, with the origin (the point where the values of X and Y are 0) at the top-left corner of the screen. You now know that dimensions on a Windows display are expressed in pixels and that there are 96 pixels to the inch. This can lead to problems if a game is to run correctly on a range of devices, so you have also seen that there are Snaps methods that can be used to scale `ImageSprites` so that their shape is preserved correctly.

Finally, you have found out that playing around with images and moving them around the screen is a lot of fun.

Here are some questions that you might want to ponder about game development?

Do I really need a very powerful computer to run these games?

Not in my experience. The Snaps game engine has been tested on the most powerful Surface Book and also on a lowly seven-inch tablet. In both cases it seems to work fine. The key consideration is the number of sprites on the screen at any one time. It seems that the system can cope with up to 500, which is plenty for the kinds of games that we are going to write. The only device that does seem to struggle with the Snaps game engine is the Raspberry PI device. The games actually run, but they update very slowly. This is due to the fact that at the time of writing, the embedded version of Windows 10 that runs on a Raspberry Pi does not support the graphics acceleration that is needed to provide a good update speed.

Do all game engines work like the Snaps game engine?

The Snaps engine is massively simplified, and it actually runs on top of the graphical environment that underpins Universal Windows Applications. That it works as well as it does is a tribute to the skill of many engineers. Most games engines are much more closely coupled to the underlying hardware, which means they can provide much, much better performance.

This game development thing looks like fun. Where can I find a proper game engine?

My favorite C# engine for writing games is called MonoGame. It is easy to learn and use, makes good use of the C# language, and can be used to write games for Windows 10, Android, and even Apple iOS. Once you have mastered the techniques in this book, I strongly advise you to look for MonoGame in your favorite search engine.

13
Creating gameplay

What you will learn

In this chapter, you'll write your first proper game, with a beginning, a middle, and an end. You'll find out how a game gets input from players and uses it to control objects in the game. You'll also discover how games detect when objects on the screen interact and how you can use these interactions to generate gameplay. Games are not just about images, though, so we'll also consider how a game can produce sound output and display text messages for its players. At the end of the chapter, we'll take a look at a complete game and consider how to use randomness, one of the greatest allies of the computer gamemaker, to add interest to gameplay. All the way through, I'll highlight jumping-off points where you can take the sample code we're looking at and use it to make your own creations, whether they are animated mood messages or games of your own. Computers are one of the most creative devices you can work with, and I think games are one of the best ways you can explore this potential for creativity.

Creating a player-controlled paddle

At the end of Chapter 12, we had a ball sprite that could bounce around the screen. Now we're going to add the player control that will be used to interact with the ball. I've provided a purple paddle that you can use to hit the ball. (You can find the image for this sprite—paddle.png—in the Images folder in the BeginToCodeWithCSharp project. You can also add an image of your own.)

The following statements load the paddle sprite into the game and set it up. Its size is set to one-tenth of the width of the viewport, and the bottom of the paddle is placed 10 pixels from the bottom of the screen. **Figure 13-1** shows the paddle's position.

Load the paddle image into the sprite.

```
ImageSprite paddle = new ImageSprite(imageUrl: "ms-appx:///Images/paddle.png");
SnapsEngine.AddSpriteToGame(paddle);
double paddleWidth = SnapsEngine.GameViewportWidth / 10.0;
paddle.ScaleSpriteWidth(paddleWidth);
paddle.Bottom = SnapsEngine.GameViewportHeight - 10;
paddle.CenterX = SnapsEngine.GameViewportWidth / 2;
```

Add the sprite to the game.

Calculate and set the paddle width.

Position the paddle.

Ch13_01_SpriteAndPaddle

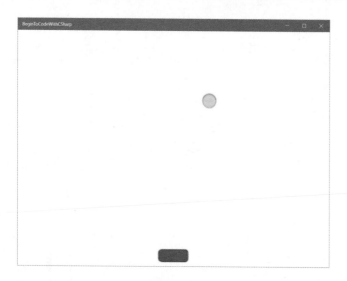

Figure 13-1 Ball and paddle together but without any interaction.

If we add these statements to the bouncing-ball program we wrote at the end of Chapter 12, we can see the ball and paddle on the screen together. Now we need to allow the player to move the paddle. This turns out to be quite easy.

The Snaps gamepad

The Snaps framework provides methods that can be used to get the status of a "gamepad" that is managed by the Snaps game engine. To control the game, players can work with the Snaps gamepad in a variety of ways—with the keyboard, the touchscreen, a mouse, or even an Xbox One or Xbox 360 controller.

The Snaps gamepad can detect five actions—Left, Right, Up, Down, and Fire. The directions are mapped to the arrow keys on your keyboard, and the fire action is mapped to the Spacebar. If you are using a controller, the directions are mapped to the d-pad, and the fire action is the A button.

When the game is running, an on-screen gamepad is also displayed for mouse and touchscreen use, as shown in **Figure 13-2**. You can activate the panels by resting the mouse pointer on the one that you want to trigger or by touching a panel on your touchscreen if you have one.

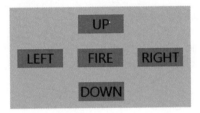

Figure 13-2 The on-screen gamepad.

The game can read the settings of the Snaps gamepad and update the objects in the game appropriately. For example, the XPaddleSpeed variable holds the speed that the paddle moves when the player moves it. I've made it 15 in the following statement, which is quite a bit faster than the corresponding ball speed of 10. This is fair because it gives the player a chance to catch up with the ball. The closer this speed is to the speed of the ball, the more skillful the player must be.

```
double XPaddleSpeed = 15;
```

Of course, if you make the paddle move more slowly than the ball, the game becomes unplayable because the player will never be able to catch up with the ball. This is a rather nasty thing to do to a player, but it might be fun to try.

A game program can check to see whether a player has triggered a particular gamepad action by using one of five methods, which are named `GetRightGamepad`, `GetLeftGamepad`, `GetUpGamePad`, `GetDownGamePad`, and `GetFireGamepad`. These methods return `true` as long as the corresponding action is being selected. Note that unlike keystrokes and mouse clicks, which detect events, these methods detect levels—in other words, they don't detect when a key on the keyboard is pressed; instead, they let a game check whether the key is up or down.

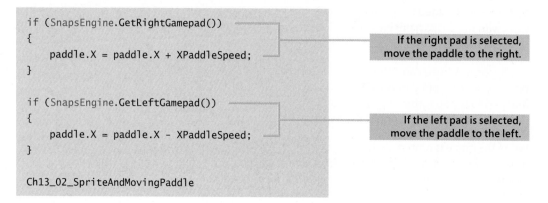

```
if (SnapsEngine.GetRightGamepad())
{
    paddle.X = paddle.X + XPaddleSpeed;
}
```
If the right pad is selected, move the paddle to the right.

```
if (SnapsEngine.GetLeftGamepad())
{
    paddle.X = paddle.X - XPaddleSpeed;
}
```
If the left pad is selected, move the paddle to the left.

```
Ch13_02_SpriteAndMovingPaddle
```

The preceding code shows how a program can read the Snaps gamepad and update the position of the paddle. If the `GetRightGamePad` method returns `true`, the program moves the paddle to the right by the amount of the paddle speed. If the `GetLeftGamePad` method returns `true`, the program moves the paddle toward the left by the amount of the paddle speed. (Remember that increasing the value of the X coordinate moves items toward the right of the viewport.) This is all we need to allow the player to move the paddle left and right.

CODE ANALYSIS

Paddle movement

Question: Why does the paddle move continuously when the test is performed only once?

Answer: Looking at the statements above, it looks like the test for the paddle movement is made only once in the program, but remember that this code is inside the game loop and is repeated many times a second. This means that the paddle will move when the player selects a direction and then stop when the player lets go. This turns out to offer a very realistic and playable feel to the controls.

Question: How would I make the paddle move up and down the screen?

Answer: You can use the same technique to allow players to move the paddle all over the screen. A game can use the `GetUpGamepad` and `GetDownGamepad` methods to detect when the player has selected Up or Down. It can then update the Y position of the paddle to reflect the change.

Question: What happens if the player selects left and right movements at the same time?

Answer: Try it! The paddle moves to the left because Left is selected and then moves to the right because Right is selected. The result is that the paddle doesn't move at all, which is just what should happen.

Question: How fast should the paddle move?

Answer: This is something you have to find out by trial and error. I've made the gamepad move at a rate of 15 pixels per update, whereas the ball in my game moves at 10 pixels per update. This gives players the edge because it means that they can always catch the ball if they move the paddle fast enough. One very popular trick in game design is to increase the speed of the objects in the game as the game progresses. Perhaps when a player reaches a certain score, you could increase the ball speed to 12 and the paddle speed to 16. This speeds up the game and makes more demands on the skill of the player. Game companies use armies of "playtesters" who are employed to play games before release to make sure that any progression like this does not make the game unplayable. If you are thinking of making a game available for sale, it is a very good idea to enlist as many friends as you can to make sure that your game is fun to play as well.

Stopping the paddle moving off the screen

You might be quite happy moving the paddle left and right to chase the ball, although at the moment the two objects don't interact. However, you might have noticed one flaw in the gameplay. It is very easy to move the paddle completely off the side of the viewport. If you just hold down the Left arrow key, the paddle moves to the left margin and then vanishes. This happens because, unlike for the ball, nothing in the program stops the paddle from moving off the margins of the screen. Fortunately, we can add some code to our game loop to fix this:

```
if (paddle.Left < 0)
{
    // Trying to move off the left edge - pull the paddle back
    paddle.Left = 0;
}

if (paddle.Right > SnapsEngine.GameViewportWidth)
{
    // Trying to move off the right edge - pull the paddle back
    paddle.Right = SnapsEngine.GameViewportWidth;
}
```

These two conditions are performed after the game has updated the position of the paddle. They make sure that the paddle never leaves the viewport by resetting the paddle's position to the edge of the viewport when it goes beyond it. This is a very common practice in video games. It is called *clamping*. A value is clamped inside a particular range and not allowed to go outside it.

Hitting the ball with the paddle

At the moment, the ball and the paddle don't interact; the ball just passes through the paddle. What we want is to provide a behavior that causes the ball to bounce off the paddle when the two objects intersect. The ImageSprite class provides a method that can be used to check whether another sprite intersects with a particular sprite:

```
if (paddle.IntersectsWith(ball))                          Test whether ball and paddle are
{                                                                        intersecting.

    if(YBallSpeed > 0)                                    Test to be sure that
    {                                                     the ball bounces
                                                          only if it is going
        // ball is going down, make it bounce off the paddle   down the screen.
        // and go up
        YBallSpeed = -YBallSpeed;                         Reverse direction.
    }
}

Ch13_04_HittingTheBall
```

When the ball and the paddle intersect, the game reverses the direction of the Y speed, which causes the ball to appear to bounce off the paddle. The player of our game can now "hit" the ball with the paddle. If you play with this for a while, you'll notice that sometimes the ball seems to hit the paddle when it really shouldn't. **Figure 13-3** shows what is going on here.

The IntersectsWith method shown in the preceding code uses the width and height of the objects on the screen to draw a box around each. If the boxes intersect, the method returns true. In **Figure 13-3**, the paddle and the ball aren't actually touching, but the boxes around them intersect, so the ball is made to bounce off the paddle even when it shouldn't. Some games solve this problem by testing the intersection area (the tiny rectangle that is shared by the ball and the paddle) to see whether any of the pixels in each of them actually overlap. If they do, the sprites have collided.

Other games solve the problem by making all the sprites rectangular so that they actually seem to collide.

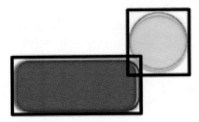

Figure 13-3 Ball and paddle boundary box.

> **PROGRAMMER'S POINT**
>
> ## Games are a great place for cheating
>
> The wonderful thing about writing a game is that you control the entire game universe. In this case we have a problem, which is that sometimes the ball and the paddle collide when it doesn't look like they should. We could write some fancy extra code to solve this problem by checking to see whether pixels overlap, or we could change the shape of the ball and the paddle so that they are rectangular. Another way would be to continue to use rectangles to detect collisions around the sprites but make the rectangles smaller so that the ball has to go a little farther into the paddle before it collides with it.
>
> In this case, we are going to ignore the problem and hope that when the action is moving quickly, players are so caught up in the game that they won't notice. Games are full of small cheats like this. The key test is whether the compromises you make get in the way of a good gaming experience.

Adding sound to games

Sound effects can add a great deal to a game. The Snaps game engine contains a special sound-effects method that you can use to play back sounds during gameplay.

```
if (paddle.IntersectsWith(ball))
{
    if (YBallSpeed > 0)
    {
        // ball is going down, make it bounce off the bat
        // and go up
```

```
        YBallSpeed = -YBallSpeed;

        // Play a sound
        SnapsEngine.PlayGameSoundEffect("ding");
    }
}


Ch13_05_HittingTheBallWithSound
```

Play a sound when the player hits the ball.

Remember that you can add your own sounds to a game. To refresh your memory about adding sounds to a program, look back at Chapter 5, where we first saw the PlaySoundEffect method.

Games and sounds

Question: Why do we need a special sound-effect method for games?

Answer: I've created a special sound-effect method for games because it is possible that a game will try to play lots of sounds at once. This can have a bad effect on the way that programs use memory and can cause the gameplay to "stutter" when this memory is recovered as the program runs. The PlayGameSoundEffect method restricts the number of sound channels that a game uses by reusing sounds. This means that some sounds might not play to completion, but it does ensure that the gameplay remains good.

MAKE SOMETHING HAPPEN

Get some gameplay going

Now you can take all the images that you've been playing with and use them to create gameplay. Perhaps you could move a soccer ball up the screen. Add some up and down movement so that players can chase objects up the screen. You could use the gamepad controls to change the draw position of an ImageSprite so that the player can pan around a picture or change the image size so that the player can zoom into an image.

Displaying text in a game

Any game needs to display text messages. The Snaps framework provides a special kind of sprite that can be used to display text.

```
TextBlockSprite tinyTextSprite = new TextBlockSprite(        Create a new
    text: "Hello. I'm Tiny Text in the default font",        TextBlockSprite.
    fontSize: 20,
    color: SnapsColor.Blue);                                 Specify text to
                                                             display and the text
                                                             size and color.

SnapsEngine.AddSpriteToGame(tinyTextSprite);                Add the sprite to the game.
```

You can use a `TextBlockSprite` everywhere you can use an `ImageSprite`. The major difference between text and image sprites is how their size is set. For an image sprite, you set the width and height values, but for a `TextBlockSprite` you have to use the `FontSize` setting when the sprite is created. The `FontSize` value is the height of the font in pixels. In this case, the height means the distance between the top of the tallest character (perhaps the top of an A) and the bottom of the lowest character (perhaps the bottom of a g). I usually use trial and error to get type sizes that look right.

If you don't specify a font family, text is drawn using the default font, which is Segoe UI. I like this font, but if you prefer a different one you can add a `FontFamily` string that gives the name of a family of font designs. The `giantTextSprite`, shown next, uses the Impact font family at the rather impressive size of 200 pixels.

```
TextBlockSprite giantTextSprite = new TextBlockSprite(
    text: "I'm Giant",
    fontSize: 200, fontFamily: "Impact",
    color: SnapsColor.Red);
SnapsEngine.AddSpriteToGame(giantTextSprite);
```

And here's a program that displays the two text blocks on the viewport. You can see how the text blocks appear in **Figure 13-4**.

```
using SnapsLibrary;

public class Ch12_13_DisplayingText
{

    public void StartProgram()
    {
        SnapsEngine.StartGameEngine(fullScreen: false, framesPerSecond: 60);

        TextBlockSprite tinyTextSprite = new TextBlockSprite(
            text: "Hello. I'm Tiny Text in the default font",
            fontSize: 20, color: SnapsColor.Blue);
        SnapsEngine.AddSpriteToGame(tinyTextSprite);

        TextBlockSprite giantTextSprite = new TextBlockSprite(
            text: "I'm Giant",
            fontSize: 200, fontFamily: "Impact",
            color: SnapsColor.Red);
        SnapsEngine.AddSpriteToGame(giantTextSprite);

        while (true)
        {
            tinyTextSprite.Top = 10;
            tinyTextSprite.CenterX = SnapsEngine.GameViewportWidth / 2.0;

            GiantTextSprite.Bottom = SnapsEngine.GameViewportHeight - 10;
            GiantTextSprite.CenterX = SnapsEngine.GameViewportWidth / 2.0;

            SnapsEngine.DrawGamePage();
        }
    }
}

Ch13_06_DisplayingText
```

Figure 13-4 Displaying text in two sizes and positions.

A program can change the content of a TextBlockSprite at any time. The text displayed will change the next time the display is updated. Changing the content might cause the width and height of the sprite to change, but you can easily center text or position it on the left or right side of the display. This statement sets the center position of tinyTextSprite to the center position of the display.

```
tinyTextSprite.CenterX = SnapsEngine.GameViewportWidth / 2.0;
```

For this positioning to work, it must be performed in the game loop so that the position can be updated if the width or height of the text sprite changes.

Rotating text

If you want to display text going up the screen, have your words appear at an intriguing angle, or even make messages spin on the screen, you can set the RotationAngle property of a TextBlockSprite. The angle is given in degrees:

```
GiantTextSprite.RotationAngle = 90;
```

This statement rotates the angle of the GiantTextSprite by 90 degrees clockwise. You can update the rotation angle of a sprite during the game loop to make some awesome displays.

```
using SnapsLibrary;

public class Ch13_07_HypnoticText
{

    public void StartProgram()
    {
        SnapsEngine.StartGameEngine(fullScreen: false, framesPerSecond: 60);

        TextBlockSprite hypnoticTextSprite = new TextBlockSprite(
            text: "You are feeling sleepy",
            fontSize: 20, color: SnapsColor.Red);
        SnapsEngine.AddSpriteToGame(hypnoticTextSprite);

        double maxTextSize = 500;
        double minTextSize = 10;
        double textSizeUpdate = 0.2;
        double textSize = minTextSize;

        while (true)
        {
            hypnoticTextSprite.CenterX = SnapsEngine.GameViewportWidth / 2.0;
            hypnoticTextSprite.CenterY = SnapsEngine.GameViewportHeight / 2.0;
            hypnoticTextSprite.RotationAngle =
                hypnoticTextSprite.RotationAngle + 1;
            hypnoticTextSprite.FontSize = textSize;

            textSize = textSize + textSizeUpdate;
            if (textSize > maxTextSize || textSize < minTextSize)
            {
                // reverse the direction of the size update
                textSizeUpdate = -textSizeUpdate;
            }

            SnapsEngine.DrawGamePage();
        }
    }
}
```

Maximum and minimum size of the text.

Rate at which the text's size changes.

Keep track of current text size.

Center text in the viewport.

Rotate text one degree clockwise.

Set the font's size to currently calculated value.

Update font size.

Check maximum and minimum limits.

Ch13_07_HypnoticText

The preceding program is similar to the squishy-ball program (**Ch12_03_SquishyBall**) that you saw in the previous chapter. But rather than make a ball squish back and forth, this program displays a rotating hypnotic message that zooms in and out of the screen. It does this by changing the font size of the text each time the game updates. Run the program to see these effects.

Make some awesome message displays

You can have great fun playing with the hypnotic text display program. Changing the rate at which the text changes size is interesting, but you might also like to try displaying two messages at the same time and have them change size at different rates. You could use the gamepad to let the player change the speed of the message movement or select different ones.

You should also remember that your program can move a TextBlockSprite around the screen in the same way it does an ImageSprite (and you can rotate ImageSprites, too). You could replace the ball and the paddle with words if you want to. You might display an enormous message and then scroll it slowly across the viewport. You can also give text some real impact by drawing multiple color versions of the same message on top of each other to produce a shadow effect. I'll demonstrate that effect in the next section for the title of our first complete game.

Missing fonts can make your games look silly

A great way to make a game distinctive is to display game messages in an interesting font. But don't make the mistake of thinking that everyone has the same fonts available on their computer as you do. Programs such as Microsoft Office and Adobe Photoshop add extra fonts when they are installed. Some players of your games might not have these programs, so they won't have the fonts. A game won't actually fail to run if it tries to use a font that is not available on the host computer, but it might look rather silly. All the sample programs make use of fonts that are supplied with Windows 10.

Making a complete game

You know how to do just about all the things needed to make a simple sprite-based game. Now let's fit these elements together and make a playable game. The game will be a simple "keep up" game in which the player has to bounce the ball off the paddle as many times as he or she can. Players get a point each time they bounce the ball. If they miss the ball, however, and it hits the bottom of the screen, they lose a life. And if the player loses three lives, the game is over.

To make the gameplay develop, we can also move the ball up the screen each time the player scores a point, giving them less time to react. This game can form the template for lots of other games that you might like to write. You can find the entire game in the chapter's demo code in the file **Ch13_08_KeepUpGame**. **Figure 13-5** shows what the game looks like when it is played by a particularly skillful player (me).

Figure 13-5 The Keep-Up! game being played.

Here is the complete game program. I've broken the code down into methods to make it easier to understand. The game loop is in the middle of the program and continues until the player has lost all of his or her lives. Each method plays its part in making the game work, but they all use the behaviors that you have already seen. When the player loses the game, the score is displayed for 10 seconds and the game then restarts.

```
public void StartProgram()
{
    setupGame();

    while (true)
    {
        waitForGameStart();
        resetGame();
```

```
    while (true)
    {
        positionMessages();
        updateBall();
        updateGamepad();
        updateScoreDisplay();
        SnapsEngine.DrawGamePage();

        // If we have no lives left, we break out of the game loop
        // and end the game.
        if (lives == 0)
            break;
    }

    // When we get here, the game is over
    displayGameOver();

    SnapsEngine.Delay(10);
    }
}

Ch13_08_KeepUpGame
```

Have a go at the game

It might seem strange for a book about programming to actually encourage you to have a go at playing a game, but I really think that in this case it's a good idea. I want you to understand that really simple gameplay principles can make quite compelling games, particularly if you are playing with a few friends around. The challenge of "beating the high score" and avoiding that nasty sound you hear when you lose a life makes the game fun for at least a few minutes.

There is a market for disposable games such as this one, particularly if they are a bit silly. One way to make them silly is to change the artwork, so the next thing I suggest you do is change the images and messages and maybe add a background picture.

Adding some randomness to Keep Up!

At the moment, the Keep Up! game is very predictable. When the game starts, the ball and the paddle are always in the same place, the top-left corner of the viewport. It would make the game more interesting if there was a bit of variation, and one way to add this is to make the ball begin in a different position each time the game starts. To do this, we need to get a random number that is used to position the ball, and for this we need to take a more detailed look at how to get random numbers into our game.

We considered randomness in the past when we used the Snaps `ThrowDice` method to return a value in the range 1 to 6. Now we can take a look at how the `ThrowDice` method works, with a view to using the same techniques to make random numbers of our own.

Here is the `ThrowDice` method code from the Snaps library. You can find it in the **NativeSnaps** folder in the **Snaps** project.

```
using System;

namespace SnapsLibrary
{
    public static partial class SnapsEngine
    {
        static Random rand = new Random();

        public static int ThrowDice()
        {
            return rand.Next(1, 7);
        }
    }
}
```

The SnapsEngine class holds all the Snaps methods.

This is the Snaps random-number generator.

The Next method returns a value in the range given.

The `ThrowDice` method uses a class named `Random` that is located in the `System` namespace. The class provides a variety of methods that return random numbers for use by programs. The `ThrowDice` method uses the `Next` method. The `Next` method is provided with two numbers—a minimum value and an *exclusive* maximum value. This means that the user of `ThrowDice` will get at least a 1, but the largest number they will get will be 6 because the exclusive maximum is 7.

The `Next` method that's used by `ThrowDice` can be used to generate an integer in any range that you want. You just specify the required start and end values, but remember that the end value is *exclusive* in that you will never actually get that value.

Taking a look at ThrowDice

There are some interesting questions raised by this look inside the Snaps framework.

Question: Why is the SnapsEngine class marked as a partial class?

> **Answer:** Up until now, we have written all our classes as one single entity in the program file. However, C# lets you spread the contents of a class over a large number of source files. If you do this, each element of the class must be marked as partial to tell the compiler that it needs to assemble the whole class from all the separate elements.
>
> Making parts of the class partial has no effect on how the class works, but it can make it much easier for programmers to find their way around a very large program. Rather than having to look through lots of files to find the ThrowDice method, they just have to look through some files. It's a good idea to do this for a class as large as the SnapsEngine class, which provides all the Snaps behaviors.

The science of random-number generation

Although you might not think so, computers are not very good at truly random behavior. The best that a program can do is start with a value (which is called the *seed*) and then apply some cunning calculations to this number to compute the next number in the sequence. This process is repeated to provide each successive random value in turn. The Next method is therefore aptly named, in that it provides the next number in the sequence of random numbers managed by this random-number generator. This technology is called a *pseudo-random number generator* because the numbers you get will appear random, but they are actually completely predictable—as long as you know the seed value and the cunning calculations that are being used.

At this point you might be asking yourself, "If the computer can't make truly random numbers, how does the random-number generator get the first seed number?" The answer is that it uses the system clock for the host computer, which is constantly updated many times a second. A program reads the time from the clock and uses this as the seed value for the random-number generator. Each time a player runs the program, she gets a different sequence of random numbers.

A program can also set a particular value as the seed for the random-number generator, like this:

```
Random repeatable = new Random(1);
```

This statement would result in a random-number generator that produces exactly the same sequence of values each time it is used. This is a very useful facility. I happen to know (because I've tried it) that if you use a seed value of 1, as in the code above, the first throw of the dice will produce the value 2.

Some computer games use a technique known as *procedural generation* for parts of their game worlds. For example, instead of having the game remember which parts of the grass are green and which parts are brown, a fixed sequence of random numbers is used, which means that the ground looks the same each time the program runs, but the amount of data storage required is minimal. I've also used this technique to make game characters behave in a manner that repeats each time the game is played, which lets the players make progress by learning what the characters do. If we used a fixed seed for our random positioning, it would mean that the start positions of the ball would follow the same sequence each time the game was played. This might be a good thing to do because it encourages the players to practice the game and learn the sequence.

Generating a random ball start position

The Keep Up! game contains a method named resetGame that sets everything up for a new game.

```
public void resetGame()                              Resets the game, ready for another player.
{
    lives = 3;                                        Give the player
    score = 0;                                        three lives, and set
    XBallSpeed = 10;                                  score to 0.
    YBallSpeed = 10;
    ball.Top = 0;                                     Set the ball's speed
    ball.Left = 0;                                    and position.
    paddle.Bottom = SnapsEngine.GameViewportHeight - 10;
    paddle.CenterX = SnapsEngine.GameViewportWidth / 2;   Position the
    XPaddleSpeed = 15;                               paddle, and set its
}                                                    initial speed.
```

At the moment, this method sets the left edge of the ball to 0 so that the ball is in the left corner of the screen at the start of the game. But we can use a random-number generator to use a starting position that is less predictable.

```
Random ballPosition = new Random(1);
```

This is the random-number generator for the ball's position. I've given it a fixed seed so that the sequence of initial ball positions is the same each time the game is played. Inside the `resetGame` method, we can use this random-number generator to calculate a new start positon each time.

Calculate the width of the screen available.

NextDouble generates a random value between 0 and 1.

```
double availableWidth = SnapsEngine.GameViewportWidth - ball.Width;
double randomStartPosition = ballPosition.NextDouble() * availableWidth;
ball.Left = randomStartPosition;
```

Set the left edge of the ball to the calculated position.

Ch13_09_RandomStartKeepUpGame

We don't want the game to place the ball over the edge of the screen, so the range of possible positions is actually the width of the screen minus the width of the ball. Once we have the available width, we can calculate a random width value by multiplying this by a random number between 0 and 1, which is what the `NextDouble` method provides. This then gives a starting position for the ball.

There are lots of other places you could add some randomness. You could make the paddle start in a different positon for each game, or you could add some randomness to the speeds of the paddle and the ball.

MAKE SOMETHING HAPPEN

Make a "mash up" of Keep Up!

You can use the Keep Up! game as the starting point of a game of your own. The first step could be to change the images that the game uses and perhaps add a background picture. You could change the way that the ball and the player interact so that the player can hit the ball in one direction or another depending on which part of the paddle the ball hits. You could add a second ball that the player must avoid or lose the game instantly if they touch it. The ball could appear once the player has achieved a particular score. You could make the paddle shrink as the game progresses, or make it grow larger and have the player lose a life if the paddle hits the edge of the screen. You can change the speed of the paddle and the ball so that the paddle moves more slowly as the game progresses. You can take a look inside the Keep Up! code and find the secret of creating an impressive score (like the one in **Figure 13-5**). There are lots of things you can do to make the game yours.

Remember that you can use all the other Snaps methods in your game, too, so you can make it speak messages about the status of the gameplay when a game ends, or even run more slowly (or change the screen color) later in the day.

What you have learned

In this chapter you have learned how to make gameplay using a program, and how even very simple game behaviors can create something fun and competitive to play. You have discovered how to get user input into a game and use this to control the position of an object within a game environment. You have seen the importance of "clamping" to make sure that objects stay within particular boundaries and how objects can be made to interact by detecting when two of them intersect. And you can now add sounds to games to make the gameplay even more enjoyable.

You also discovered how to create and display text messages and use these as game objects in themselves. And you have investigated how computers generate random numbers and how these can be used in programs to create either random or predictable experiences for the game player.

Here are some questions that you might want to ponder about game development.

Is this all about games?

Absolutely not. To give just one example, the text manipulation that you saw in this chapter will serve you well in a lot of situations that have nothing to do with games. You could use this technique to display animated messages in any program. Users now expect animated behaviors in the user interface, and what you have learned provides a solid grounding in how a computer program can manipulate objects within a graphical environment. This is something you can build on if you start to create user interfaces with XAML (Extensible Application Markup Language) , which I introduce in Chapter 16.

Does a game always have to look pretty?

There is no doubt that nice artwork makes a game more enjoyable to play. But it is an undeniable fact that visuals alone do not make a game fun. The first computer games had the smallest possible number of graphical elements, and they were played by millions of people. And the history of computer games is littered with graphically beautiful creations that nobody liked much because they weren't very enjoyable.

How do I make a great game?

My strong suggestions are to make something that works and then tinker with it. Always have a working version of your game for people to try, and listen carefully to their comments. Instead of waiting until you finish creating all fifteen levels of your game, get some people to play it when the first three are complete and then change the rest of the game in line with what they say. And don't rely just on the opinions of your friends and your family. They're going to say they like your game because they like you. If your worst enemy has to concede that your game is quite fun to play, that's when you know you have a winner on your hands. And keep on trying.

14

Games and object hierarchies

What you will learn

Over the past few chapters, our focus has changed from "how to tell the computer to do stuff" to "how to manage complexity." We started by considering the actions a program can perform and then moved on to working with collections of data and creating structures and classes that help encapsulate data into meaningful objects. In this chapter, you'll expand your knowledge of object-oriented techniques by building a game. The techniques you'll learn can be applied far beyond games, but games are very useful place to explore them.

We'll first look at *inheritance,* a technique that can save you from repeating code elements inside classes. Then we'll explore how complex games can be created from a collection of cooperating objects.

Games and objects: Space Rockets in Space

In this section, we'll start building a new type of space-shooter game—Space Rockets in Space. We'll be ambitious and aim to include a moving star field in the background, rockets, different kinds of attacking aliens, and all kinds of other things. This might sound like a lot of work, but we'll have fun and learn some new programming techniques from doing it.

As you've learned, you can use objects to help manage large and complicated software projects. Because our new game may turn out to be rather large and complicated, we are going to use objects to make things a lot easier.

So far, we haven't used objects in our game programs. In the Keep Up! game we created in Chapter 12, the two game elements—the ball and paddle—were managed as a collection of different variables. As a quick review, the ball is managed in terms of the ImageSprite and the X and Y speed values that control the movement of the ball:

```
public ImageSprite sprite;
public double xSpeed, ySpeed;
```

If we wanted to put 20 balls on the screen, the program would have to store 20 image sprites and 20 of each of the speed values. These details would be hard to manage even if we used lists of each sprite element. Instead, we can keep these items together by creating a class, which I've called MovingSprite, to contain them. The Moving-Sprite class contains the image to be drawn (spriteValue) and the X and Y speed values (xSpeedValue and ySpeedValue). You can think of a MovingSprite as a container that will be used to move an ImageSprite around the viewport. The intention is to use it for aliens, rockets, and even falling stars—we can use it for any sprite that has movement.

```
public class MovingSprite
{
    public ImageSprite spriteValue;
    public double xSpeedValue, ySpeedValue;
                                                            Constructor for the sprite.
    public MovingSprite(ImageSprite sprite, double xSpeed, double ySpeed)
    {
        spriteValue = sprite;                   Set the sprite to the image for this sprite.
        xSpeedValue = xSpeed;
        ySpeedValue = ySpeed;                       Set the X and Y speed for the sprite.
```

```
        }

    public void Update()  ──────────────────────   Update the sprite and make it move
    {
        spriteValue.X = spriteValue.X + xSpeedValue;    ┐   Update the X and Y
        spriteValue.Y = spriteValue.Y + ySpeedValue;    ┘   position of the sprite by
                                                            adding speed values.
    }
}
```

The `MovingSprite` class contains two methods. The first is the constructor, which is used when a new `MovingSprite` is created. We use it to set up the `MovingSprite`. The second method is the `Update` method, which is called in the game loop each time the game updates. This method moves the sprite around the screen. As you can see in the preceding code, when `Update` is called, it adds the speed values to the position of the image, causing it to move.

PROGRAMMER'S POINT

Sometimes it's okay not to worry about security

When we've created classes that hold important information, I've mentioned the need to think about the security of the data the classes hold. We've used private data elements and public methods to control access to the data and ensure that it is always valid. However, in the case of a game, I reckon it's okay to make the elements in the game classes public. This lets you write the code more quickly and makes the objects easier to use.

Whenever you create an application, you need to think about the context of the code. If you are writing a silly space game for a customer, they might not appreciate having to pay for the time you spend making all the classes in the game completely bulletproof by adding `get` and `set` behaviors and an audit log of all the changes to the game objects. However, if you are writing a system to manage bank accounts, you'll find that the customer would be very happy to pay for these features.

Constructing a star sprite that moves

The first sprite we are going to create contains a star for the background of the game. Stars take no part in the game; they are just there to make the game look good and give the player the impression that their rocket is flying through space.

We'll start by creating a `MovingSprite` that displays a single star, get the sprite moving down the screen, and then look at how we can create the impression of many stars zooming past the player. **Figure 14-1** shows the image of the star we'll use. This will be scaled down so that it is very small on the screen. The background of the image is partly transparent so that a black background will show through it.

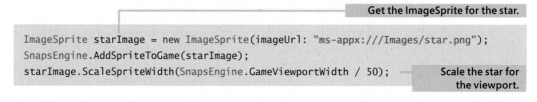

Figure 14-1 Star image that will be used as the game background.

The `MovingSprite` class's constructor sets up the contents of the object. When we create a `MovingSprite`, the program must give it the `ImageSprite` that will form the display, the start position of the sprite on the screen, and the speed that the sprite should move in each direction.

The following statements create the `ImageSprite`. It's scaled to one-fiftieth (1/50) of the width of the display and is added to the game so that it will be displayed on the viewport. This program doesn't set the X and Y values for a new `ImageSprite`. They are left at 0, which means that the star is placed at the top-left corner of the screen, at coordinate 0,0.

Get the ImageSprite for the star.

```
ImageSprite starImage = new ImageSprite(imageUrl: "ms-appx:///Images/star.png");
SnapsEngine.AddSpriteToGame(starImage);
starImage.ScaleSpriteWidth(SnapsEngine.GameViewportWidth / 50);
```

Scale the star for the viewport.

The next statement creates a `MovingSprite` called `star`.

Construct a moving sprite.

```
MovingSprite star = new MovingSprite(sprite: starImage, xSpeed: 0, ySpeed: 1);
```

The `ySpeed` value (the vertical speed) is set at 1, which means the sprite will move one pixel down the viewport each time the `Update` method is called. (Remember that the sprite moves down the screen because the top-left corner of the viewport is the position where the Y value is 0, and increasing the Y value moves an object down the viewport.) The xSpeed value is set to 0 so that the star will not move across the viewport. Instead, it will fall straight down the screen.

Updating a MovingSprite

The MovingSprite class's Update method controls what happens to the sprite when it's updated. When the game is running, the Update method will be called at regular intervals.

```
public void Update(SnapsEngine snaps)
{
    sprite.X = sprite.X + speedX;
    sprite.Y = sprite.Y + speedY;
}
```

In the case of the MovingSprite, the Update method moves the sprite by updating the X and Y positions with their respective speeds, which makes the sprite move in the directions set by the speed values. The following program shows how the Moving-Sprite is used. If you run the program, a single star will move down the viewport and disappear off the bottom.

```
public void StartProgram()
{
    SnapsEngine.SetBackgroundColor(SnapsColor.Black);

    SnapsEngine.StartGameEngine(fullScreen: false, framesPerSecond: 60);      Start the
                                                                              game
                                                                              engine.

    ImageSprite starImage = new ImageSprite(imageUrl:
                                "ms-appx:///Images/star.png");
    SnapsEngine.AddSpriteToGame(starImage);
    starImage.ScaleSpriteWidth(SnapsEngine.GameViewportWidth / 50);
    MovingSprite star = new MovingSprite(sprite: starImage, xSpeed: 0, ySpeed: 1);

                                                    Create a MovingSprite that
    while (true)                                    moves 1 pixel per update.
    {
        star.Update();                                         Update the star.
        SnapsEngine.DrawGamePage();                        Draw the game page.
    }
}

Ch14_01_MovingSprite
```

A MovingSprite on its own is not very interesting, but it can serve as the basis for all the moving objects on the screen. A MovingSprite object can move in any direction; you just have to set the respective speed values and it will move that way. But we also know that after a while, a MovingSprite object will move off the viewport and disappear. To address this, we can create other classes that build on the simple abilities of MovingSprite, which is what we'll do next.

Creating a FallingSprite based on a MovingSprite

We want a moving star field behind the game's action. The stars should fall continuously down the screen as the game is played, giving the impression of stars whizzing past the viewport. When a star moves off the bottom of the screen, it will place itself back at the top, ready for another pass down the screen. We can use this trick to make a rocket look like it is flying through a packed star field when in fact we just have a fixed number of stars that are making repeated passes down the screen.

We will create a FallingSprite class to do the job for us. You can think of a FallingSprite as much like a MovingSprite, but when a FallingSprite gets to the bottom of the viewport, it moves back to the top at a random position and then falls down the viewport again.

To create the FallingSprite class, we will use a programming technique called *inheritance*, where a new type of object (a *child*) is created based on an existing type (a *parent*). The child object inherits all the behaviors and properties of the parent and can add new behaviors and customize existing ones as needed. This action is known as *extending* the parent class.

> **PROGRAMMER'S POINT**
> ## Inheritance is all about making things less abstract
>
> It is important that you understand what we are doing here. We have started with a fairly abstract idea of a "sprite that moves," and now we are making more-refined versions of this sprite to play specific roles in the game. A falling sprite is a specialized moving sprite that falls down the screen. The rocket sprite (when we create it) will be a specialized moving sprite that the player can steer around the screen. The alien sprite will be a moving sprite that chases the player, and so on.
>
> The technique of inheritance works by making a fairly abstract parent class and then creating child classes that contain specific behaviors that fit the context of their use. In business, for example, if you were building classes to implement a banking system, you would create a class called Account, which would hold all the general details of a bank account—like the name and address of the account holder and perhaps the balance value of the account. Then you would create more specialized child classes—such as checking account, credit

card account, and mortgage account—that would contain the extra data and behaviors for their particular purposes. All of these accounts would use the core behaviors of the parent. If you find a bug in the code that manages the address of an account holder, you have to fix that bug only in the parent Account class, and all the child classes that use that behavior will be fixed as well.

If you find yourself confused about some of the terms and explanations, just keep coming back to the reason why we are doing this. We want to implement shared behaviors in a parent class and then have each child class provide a set of behaviors that are specific to its purpose.

Here is how you make a class that is a child of a parent. The child class is Falling-Sprite, and the parent class is MovingSprite. A FallingSprite can do all the things a MovingSprite can do, plus it has the extra functionality that makes it return to the top of the screen when it falls off the bottom. This is why we say that the FallingSprite class extends its parent class.

```
public class FallingSprite : MovingSprite
{
}
```

The colon is followed by the name of the class being extended.

But unfortunately, all that our shiny new child class can do at the moment is generate errors when we try to compile it:

```
Error CS7036 There is no argument given that corresponds to the required
             formal parameter 'sprite' of MovingSprite.MovingSprite
             (ImageSprite, double, double)'
```

The error doesn't make the issue very clear, but the problem is all about object construction. Because the FallingSprite object is based on a MovingSprite, the process of constructing a FallingSprite *must* involve constructing a MovingSprite first. This means that the FallingSprite class must have a constructor that constructs a MovingSprite. And to make a MovingSprite, we need to supply an ImageSprite and the speed the sprite is to move at.

If you find this confusing, then consider it from the point of view of baking. You can think of the parent class as a bit like a cake, and the child class as icing you put on the cake. We can't have the icing on its own; we have to have a cake to put the icing on. In the same way, constructing a FallingSprite must involve making a MovingSprite first. We can do this by writing a constructor that creates a FallingSprite but also calls the constructor in the parent class, MovingSprite.

The constructor for the FallingSprite will be supplied with the information that is needed to create a FallingSprite, and it will use this information to construct the MovingSprite object that it is based on. The MovingSprite needs to know the ImageSprite that is being moved, plus the X and Y speeds of movement. The Falling-Sprite needs to know the ImageSprite that is being moved and the speed that the sprite is falling down the screen. This information can be fed to the constructor for the FallingSprite object.

The following version of the FallingSprite class allows the program to compile correctly. It contains a constructor that calls the constructor of the parent class.

```
public class FallingSprite : MovingSprite
{
    public FallingSprite(ImageSprite sprite, double ySpeed) :
        base(sprite: sprite, xSpeed: 0, ySpeed: ySpeed)
    {
    }
}
```

Constructor for the falling sprite.

The base keyword makes a call to the parent class's constructor.

C# calls the parent of a class its *base* class. The C# language provides a keyword, base, that you can use to gain access to the constructor of the parent class. This is how we make the cake in our baking analogy. The content of the FallingSprite class (which is presently empty) is where the program configures any icing.

CODE ANALYSIS

The base keyword and construction

Question: We've not used the base keyword before now, so it's worth considering some questions about it. When the program runs, what happens when it reaches the base keyword?

Answer: When the program reaches the base part, it runs the constructor in the parent class. In this case, because FallingSprite extends MovingSprite, the MovingSprite constructor runs and sets up the MovingSprite contents.

Question: What do the arguments mean in the call base(sprite: sprite, xSpeed: 0, ySpeed: ySpeed)?

Answer: Here, the call of the base constructor method (the one that makes the MovingSprite that FallingSprite is based on) is given the incoming sprite and ySpeed values. Because the parameters have the same name in both the base and the parent constructors, it looks like some are being passed into themselves, but the values are actually being passed into the parent.

Question: Why is the xSpeed value sent to the base constructor set to 0?

Answer: A falling sprite falls straight down the screen, so it doesn't have any movement left or right, which is the movement that xSpeed would provide. The constructor for the FallingSprite tells the constructor for the base class (MovingSprite) that the xSpeed value is 0.

You can use a FallingSprite everywhere you can use a MovingSprite. This makes sense because the FallingSprite has inherited the abilities of its parent class. It contains X and Y speed values along with an Update method that can be called to update the state of the sprite.

The constructor for the FallingSprite must place the sprite at a random starting position somewhere on the screen. It does this by picking random values for the left edge and bottom of the sprite that is being created. Each new sprite is placed in a different position on the screen, giving a random star field when the game starts.

```
public class FallingSprite : MovingSprite
{
    static Random spriteRand = new Random();
    public FallingSprite(ImageSprite sprite, double ySpeed) :
            base(sprite: sprite, xSpeed: 0, ySpeed: ySpeed)
    {
        spriteValue.Left = (SnapsEngine.GameViewportWidth -
                            spriteValue.Width) * spriteRand.NextDouble();
        spriteValue.Bottom = SnapsEngine.GameViewportHeight *
                            spriteRand.NextDouble();
    }
}
```

FallingSprite constructor parameters.

Set the sprite's speed and position.

CODE ANALYSIS

The FallingSprite constructor's body

Question: What does the spriteRand variable do?

Answer: When the sprite is constructed, the spriteRand variable is used to pick a random position on the screen for the sprite to start in. The random-number generator is used again when the sprite is updated—when it picks a random position across the screen where the sprite reappears.

The technique I've used here is very similar to the one I used in the Keep Up! game, when we wanted to make the ball start at a different X position at the top of the screen each time the game is played. It uses a random-number generator to generate random X positions for the sprite.

Question: Why is the `spriteRand` variable static?

> **Answer:** Remember that static means "part of the class, not part of an instance." In other words, there is only one `spriteRand` value for the entire `FallingSprite` class to use. This actually makes very good sense. There is no need for each sprite to have its own random-number generator. All the sprites can share the same one.

Customizing the `FallingSprite` behaviors

Now that the `FallingSprite` has all the required information at its fingertips, we can create a customized `Update` behavior for falling sprites. We'll make a more specific (less abstract) version of the `Update` method that works for falling sprites. This is called *overriding* the method in a parent class.

The new `Update` method won't simply move the sprite around the screen; it will also pick the sprite up and put it back at the top when the sprite reaches the bottom. The `Update` method will use the `GameViewportWidth` and `GameViewportHeight` values that are provided by the Snaps library. C# allows an overriding method to call the method in the parent class (that is, the version of `Update` that just moves the sprite), and our new method will use this technique.

```csharp
public override void Update()          Overriding the method in the parent class.
{
    base.Update();                     Calls Update method in the parent class to move the star.

    if (spriteValue.Top > SnapsEngine.GameViewportHeight)
    {
        spriteValue.Left = (SnapsEngine.GameViewportWidth - spriteValue.Width) *
                    spriteRand.NextDouble();
        spriteValue.Bottom = 0;
    }                                          If sprite has gone off the screen,
}                                              place it at a random X position.
                                               Move sprite to the top of the screen.
```

Examining the Update method

Question: What does the `base.Update()` method call do?

Answer: It is often useful to call the method that is being overridden. In this case, the `Update` method in `FallingSprite` can call the `Update` method in `MovingSprite` to update the sprite position and then add its own behaviors after this has been performed.

Question: Why does the method check to see whether the top of the sprite has gone beyond the height of the viewport?

Answer: The `Top` property of the sprite is the Y coordinate of the top line of the sprite. The value of Y increases as we move down the screen. When the top of the sprite goes above the viewport's height value, this means that the sprite has just gone beyond the bottom of the viewport. At this point the sprite is no longer visible and can be placed at the top of the screen again.

Question: Why does the method set the bottom of the sprite to 0 when it places it again at the top?

Answer: Here, too, this is because the top of the screen has a Y coordinate of 0. We want the star to move into view from the edge of the screen, which places the sprite just above the top of the screen, ready to move down into view.

Allowing methods to be overridden

To allow overriding to work, we need to make a tiny change to the `MovingSprite` parent class. We have to make the `Update` method in the `MovingSprite` class a *virtual* method.

```
public virtual void Update()          ——————  Method flagged as virtual.
{
    spriteValue.X = spriteValue.X + xSpeedValue;
    spriteValue.Y = spriteValue.Y + ySpeedValue;   ——  Behaviors in MovingSprite to
}                                                        override in FallingSprite.
```

Adding the keyword `virtual` in front of a method declaration makes it possible for a method in a child class to override that method and provide a different version of it. And that's what we want to do—we want a sprite that moves, but it must move in a particular way, and we have created an `Update` behavior in a child class to get that form of movement.

Virtual methods

Inheritance seems to have brought with it a lot of new terms, and a couple of questions.

Question: What happens when a method is made virtual?

> **Answer:** As far as users of the method are concerned, there is no change to the way the method behaves. It works exactly the same. The difference occurs when the program is running and the method is called. If the system knows it is calling a virtual method, it will check to see whether there are any methods that might be overriding this method before it runs it.

Question: Why can't we make all our methods virtual for maximum flexibility?

> **Answer:** You could make all your methods virtual so that they can be overridden at any time by a child method. But there are a couple of reasons why you might not want to do that. First, it takes a little bit more time to call a virtual method because the system has to check for any overrides. Second, and more important, there may be some methods that you never want a child class to override. For example, in a Bank class, you would want to be sure that some methods, particularly those concerned with depositing and withdrawing funds, could not be replaced in child classes. We don't want programmers adding their own behaviors to methods as important as these.

If you run the sample program in **Ch14_02_SingleFallingStar,** you will see a single star fall down the screen. When it reaches the bottom of the screen, it is placed back at the top.

Creating a moving star field

Your friends, family, and other potential customers probably won't be that impressed by a game that features a single star moving down the screen. They'll want to see at least a hundred of them. It turns out that doing this is quite easy. We just need to create 100 falling stars and put them in a list:

```
List<MovingSprite> sprites = new List<MovingSprite>();          List to hold many sprites.

for (int i = 0; i < 100; i++)                                   Loop round creating 100 sprites.
{
    ImageSprite starImage = new ImageSprite(
                        imageURL: "ms-appx:///Images/star.png");
    SnapsEngine.AddSpriteToGame(starImage);
```

```
    starImage.ScaleSpriteWidth(SnapsEngine.GameViewportWidth / 75);
    FallingSprite star = new FallingSprite(sprite: starImage,ySpeed: 15);
    sprites.Add(star);
}
```
Make a falling star and add it to the list.

Once we have a list of moving sprites, we can then animate the list in the game loop.

```
while (true)
{
    foreach (MovingSprite sprite in sprites)
    {
        sprite.Update();
    }
    SnapsEngine.DrawGamePage();
}
Ch14_03_Starfield
```
Work through each sprite in the list.

Update one of the sprites in the list.

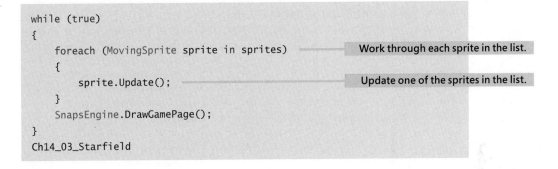

CODE ANALYSIS

Lists of moving sprites

Question: Why do we use a list of MovingSprites and not FallingSprites?

> **Answer:** If you understand the answer to this question, you are well on the way to under-
> standing class hierarchies and objects. We know that a child class can do everything
> that a parent class can do because it inherits all the parent's behaviors and properties.
> This means that a reference to a MovingSprite can also refer to a FallingSprite since
> they are both able to behave like a MovingSprite (although when the Update method
> is called on a FallingSprite, it will perform the Update method for that type, not the
> Update method for the MovingSprite).
>
> Next we are going to create a rocket sprite for the player to fly, and then we are going to
> create a chaser alien that will chase the player. These will also be based on the Moving-
> Sprite class, so they can also be added to a sprites list and updated by the game loop,
> but they will all have their own particular Update behaviors.

Question: How much code do I have to add to handle 200 falling stars?

> **Answer:** None. You only have to change the 100 value of the for loop limit to 200. This
> will make the loop go around 200 times and make 200 stars.

Have fun with particle effects

The moving star field is our first "particle effect," which refers to a game element that is created from lots of small particles that have a particular lifetime and behavior. You can think of each star as a particle that is created at the top of the screen, falls down to the bottom, and is then re-created at the top again. Many computer games use particle effects to produce things such as showers of sparks, smoke trails, and even fire. The particles are created with a particular behavior, run through that behavior, and are then reset to go around again. You could create a moving star field of your own face if you have an ego big enough.

You can also experiment with what are called "parallax effects." Put simply, this is what we experience when we are moving and objects close to us appear to move faster than those farther away. You can use a parallax effect to make a star field with stars of different sizes, where the larger stars move faster. This can provide a realistic effect of movement in three-dimensional space.

Creating a rocket based on a MovingSprite

Figure 14-2 introduces our rocket sprite against the field of stars we've created.

Figure 14-2 Rocket flying through stars.

Our players will use a `RocketSprite` object to control the game. In Keep Up!, we had a paddle that a player could move left and right, but for a rocket, we want the player to be able to move it all around the screen. The figure shows the effect we're looking for. The player can control the rocket with the gamepad as it flies over the star field.

We can make a rocket by using the same sequence we followed to make the falling sprite. First we need to work out what information the rocket needs to know. It turns out that all the rocket needs to know is the X and Y speeds for movement.

```
public class RocketSprite : MovingSprite
{
    public RocketSprite(ImageSprite sprite
        double xSpeed, double ySpeed ) : base(sprite:sprite,
                                     xSpeed:xSpeed, ySpeed:ySpeed)
    {
    }
}
```

Base constructor makes the MovingSprite the RocketSprite is based on.

This pattern is similar to the falling star, but because the rocket can move up and down and left and right, we need to give speed values for each direction.

```
public override void Update()
{
    if(snapsValue.GetUpGamepad())
        spriteValue.Y = spriteValue.Y - ySpeedValue;

    if (snapsValue.GetDownGamepad())
        spriteValue.Y = spriteValue.Y + ySpeedValue;
    if (spriteValue.Top < 0)
        spriteValue.Top = 0;

    if (spriteValue.Bottom > SnapsEngine.GameViewportHeight)
        spriteValue.Bottom = SnapsEngine.GameViewportHeight;
}
```

Update method for RocketSprite.

The `Update` method for the rocket works the same way as for the paddle in Keep Up! It uses the gamepad methods provided by the Snaps framework to determine which pads are active and then updates the position of the rocket sprite accordingly. It also uses the width and height of the viewport to clamp the rocket's position and stop it from moving out of the viewport. Note that the preceding code shows only the Y behavior. The same behavior is repeated for the X position of the rocket.

You don't have to use the base method

Question: There is no call of base.Update() in the Update method for the Rocket-Sprite class. Is this a mistake? Why doesn't RocketSprite use the Update method from MovingSprite?

> **Answer:** A MovingSprite is a sprite that moves, but this is a rather general term. A RocketSprite is more specialized because the rocket's movement is controlled by player input; the sprite doesn't move all the time. Sprites that must move all the time can use the Update method in MovingSprite and then add their own behavior to this. However, a RocketSprite should move only when the player selects the relevant direction on the gamepad. It can't use the "all the time" movement that the MovingSprite Update method provides.

Once we create our RocketSprite, the only thing left to do is add the rocket to our game. The sequence of these statements is the same as we used to add the moving star. The program must create the ImageSprite, add it to the game, set the size of the rocket to a sensible proportion of the screen, place it in the right place, and then use it to create the RocketSprite instance.

```
ImageSprite rocketImage = new ImageSprite(
                        imageUrl: "ms-appx:///Images/SpaceRocket.png");
SnapsEngine.AddSpriteToGame(rocketImage);
rocketImage.ScaleSpriteWidth(SnapsEngine.GameViewportWidth / 15);
rocketImage.CenterX = SnapsEngine.GameViewportWidth / 2.0;
rocketImage.CenterY = SnapsEngine.GameViewportHeight / 2.0;

RocketSprite rocket = new RocketSprite(sprite: rocketImage,
                                xSpeed: 10, ySpeed: 10);

sprites.Add(rocket);

Ch14_04_FlyingRocket
```

Adding some aliens

Your younger brother has asked for lots of alien sprites, and the game must have aliens with different personalities. He has already had ideas for six of them and is working on more. He thinks he is helping the game develop, but you are not so sure.

Having too many ideas can send you backward, not forward

I've spent a lot of time helping people write games. One of the most important lessons that a budding game developer needs to learn is that ideas are not always your best friends. When I'm chatting with teams that are developing games, I often have a conversation that goes like this:

ME: "How's the game coming along?"
TEAM: "It's going great, thanks. We've just had a meeting, and we've had six new ideas for the game. We're going to have rabbits with laser eyes, flying monkeys, and deadly cheese. It's going to be great."
ME: "How much of the game have you actually got working?"
TEAM: "Oh, nothing yet, but we can sort all that out later."

At that point, I mark the team as doomed and move on. The most important thing about writing a game (and many other types of applications) is to get something working that you can build on. This way, you have a program that you can discuss and show people. If you keep adding things to a game you're developing, all you do is increase the height of the mountain you are trying to climb. At some point you start to feel badly about having made nothing so far, give up on that game, and start having ideas for the next one.

Adding features and behaviors doesn't always make an application better. Some of the most popular games in the world are incredibly simple in design. And anyway, if a player is having a great time playing a version of your game, she isn't going to care about the lack of laser-eyed rabbits you intended to add. By all means have ideas, and by all means write them down for later, but once you have an idea of what you are going to build, my advice is to get that going and add to it later.

Given that we want different kinds of aliens, this is a good place to think more about class hierarchies. From discussions with your younger brother, you've discovered that all of his aliens have a target (the rocket they are trying to destroy) and they are either alive or dead. If we went ahead and added a full set of new alien sprite classes, we would repeat the target and status values for each of these types. Furthermore, we'd need to have separate lists for each alien type in the game. Instead, we can create an AlienSprite type that holds the information and behaviors that all aliens need:

```
public class AlienSprite : MovingSprite
{
    public bool AlienAlive = true;                      This flag is set to true when the
                                                        AlienSprite is still alive.
    public RocketSprite rocketValue;                   Rocket the AlienSprite is chasing.


    public AlienSprite(ImageSprite sprite, double xSpeed, double ySpeed,
                     RocketSprite target) :            Constructor for AlienSprite.
        base(sprite: sprite, xSpeed: xSpeed, ySpeed: ySpeed)
```

```
      {
          rocketValue = target;
      }

      public override void Update()
      {
          // don't do anything if the alien is dead
          if (!AlienAlive)
              return;

          // Update the position of the sprite
          base.Update();
      }
  }
```

Remember the rocket that we are chasing.

Override the Update method for the MovingSprite class

If we are still alive, update our position.

All our alien types can now extend the AlienSprite type to add any extra elements that they require. If we identify anything else that all aliens need, we can add that to the AlienSprite class and all the child classes will pick these things up as well. For example, you might decide later that each alien should be worth a particular number of points when it's killed. This property could be added to the AlienSprite class so that any class based on AlienSprite can now have a value.

PROGRAMMER'S POINT

Adding intermediate types is a very good idea

Quite often when you are designing types, you'll find a need for *intermediate* types like AlienSprite. For example, in a document-management system, you might have a parent *Document* class that is extended by an intermediate *Letter* class that holds the name and address of the recipient, the date it was sent, and so on. Underneath *Letter*, you can have *Order, Receipt, Statement,* and other kinds of letters that your system might need to work with.

Adding a chasing alien

The first alien we will create is similar to the rocket. But while the rocket moves when the player selects a movement direction, the alien moves all the time, and it chooses its direction of movement by using a very simple algorithm, like this:

- If the rocket is above us, accelerate up.

- If the rocket is below us, accelerate down.

- If the rocket is to the right, accelerate left.

- If the rocket is to the left, accelerate right.

If you are not sure what acceleration means, and about the difference between acceleration and speed, then let's have a look at some simple physics.

The speed of our alien is the distance it moves each time around the game loop. Each time the game updates, we add this speed value to the alien position value to update it. Speed changes distance over time. If we drive for an hour in a car doing 60 miles per hour, we'll travel 60 miles.

Acceleration is the rate at which speed is changing. If we press the accelerator in our car, our car speeds up over time (the speed changes over time). We might say that our car is traveling five miles per hour faster every 10 seconds. That would equate to a "0 to 60 miles an hour" time of 12 seconds.

We add an acceleration amount to the speed of the chasing alien to make it move in the direction of the target. You could say that we "press the accelerator" in the direction of the rocket. The interesting thing is the way that acceleration makes it possible for a player to dodge the alien.

The game will use these acceleration values, and the position of the rocket, when it updates during the game loop. There is also a friction value that slows down the alien. Each time around the loop, we multiple the speed of the alien by the friction value (which is less than 1) to dampen the movement a bit. This is the Update method that we'll use.

```
public override void Update()
{
    if (AlienAlive)
    {
        if (targetValue.spriteValue.CenterX > spriteValue.CenterX)    // Is the target on the right of the chasing sprite?
            xSpeedValue = xSpeedValue + xAccelerationValue;           // If the target is on the right, accelerate right.
        else
            xSpeedValue = xSpeedValue - xAccelerationValue;           // If the target is on the left, accelerate left.

        xSpeedValue = xSpeedValue * frictionValue;                    // Reduce the speed by the friction value.
        spriteValue.X = spriteValue.X + xSpeedValue;                  // Update the position by the speed.

        if (targetValue.spriteValue.CenterY > spriteValue.CenterY)
            ySpeedValue = ySpeedValue + yAccelerationValue;
        else
            ySpeedValue = ySpeedValue - yAccelerationValue;

        ySpeedValue = ySpeedValue * frictionValue;
```

```
            spriteValue.Y = spriteValue.Y + ySpeedValue;
    }
}
```

The alien will chase the rocket by accelerating toward it each time the game loop updates the sprite. Different values for the acceleration and friction values have a marked effect on the behavior of the sprite. You could, for example, make an alien that drifts slowly toward the player or one that attacks more quickly. These are new kinds of aliens that you can add with no programming effort at all; you just have to set different acceleration and friction values. You can spend many happy hours tuning the behavior of different kinds of chasing sprites and adding them to the game. When each alien is constructed, it must be given the acceleration and friction values that will control how fast it moves around the screen after the target. These values will be stored inside the alien and used to control how it behaves during the game.

Here is the constructor for a ChasingAlien instance. It stores the acceleration values that this particular alien is going to use.

```
public double xAccelerationValue;
public double yAccelerationValue;
public double frictionValue;

public ChasingAlien(ImageSprite sprite, RocketSprite rocket,
    double xAcceleration, double yAcceleration, double friction, int score) :
        base(sprite: sprite, xSpeed: 0, ySpeed: 0, target: rocket, score: score)
{                                                    Call the constructor for AlienSprite.
                                                         Set the initial speeds to 0.
    xAccelerationValue = xAcceleration;
    yAccelerationValue = yAcceleration;                       Store X and Y
    frictionValue = friction;                              acceleration and
}                                                             friction values.
```

Note that the constructor also sets the speed of the MovingSprite parent object to 0. It does this because when the ChasingAlien "wakes up," it will not be moving at all.

PROGRAMMER'S POINT

Use as much physics and artificial intelligence as you need in the game

The Update method in the chasing alien is a tiny "physics engine" inside our game. A true physicist will probably be deeply upset by the simplifications that we have made, but the great thing about this code is that it works, and it works very well. There is really no need for any more accurate physics simulation because what we have created makes for great gameplay. There is an important lesson here: start with something simple and, if that works, stop.

This is also the first time we have used artificial intelligence (AI) in a game. There is nothing special about AI in games. It is simply code to make the player think that the game is clever. If you play this game (and you should), you really could think that there is a little pilot inside the alien who is steering his craft toward you. You can even fool the opponent by letting him head toward you and then dodging out of his way at the last minute. There is no need to have the alien do anything more clever than the simplest possible behavior because that works well enough to give a good experience.

The following code shows the construction of a chasing alien. The amount the alien accelerates and the friction are values that I came up with from some testing. I think they work very well. The sprite seems to chase the rocket like an angry wasp.

```
ChasingAlien chaser = new ChasingAlien(sprite: chasingAlienImage,
    target: rocket,
    xAcceleration: 0.3, yAcceleration: 0.3,
    friction: 0.99, score: 100);

Ch14_05_ChasingAlien
```

MAKE SOMETHING HAPPEN

Fiddle with the physics in the game

If you look at the chasing alien code, you will find that it uses acceleration values of 0.3 and a friction value of 0.99. You might find it fun to change these values (not by too much to start with) and see what happens to the behavior of the alien as it goes after the player. For example, if you make the acceleration values bigger, the alien will chase more aggressively. You can create some really interesting gameplay by adding two aliens for the player to avoid and giving them different physics settings to make the aliens behave differently.

Another interesting addition would be to make one alien chase another. My chasing alien chases a rocket, but you could make another alien that follows aliens. If you add a number of these to the game, you can make a "snake" of aliens. If you make the first alien chase the player, you can develop some very interesting behaviors.

Adding a target sprite

As friends start playing your game, they like dodging the chasing sprite, but they also ask for some sprites to serve as targets that players can shoot at while they are dodging the nasty chasing sprite. We can use the following pattern to add these new elements to the game:

1. Create a new object that extends the parent we are basing it on.

2. Decide what the sprite needs to know to perform its behaviors.

3. Create a constructor for the new sprite type that receives and stores this information.

4. Decide what the sprite needs to do when it updates.

5. Add these behaviors to an Update method in the new sprite type.

6. Create the sprite and add it to the sprites in the game when the game starts.

Here's an example. The LineAlien moves slowly left and right between a maximum and a minimum position on the screen:

Positions the alien moves between.

```
public class LineAlien : AlienSprite
{
    public double xMaxValue, xMinValue;

    public LineAlien(ImageSprite sprite, double xSpeed, double ySpeed,
                RocketSprite target, double xMax, double xMin) :
        base(sprite: sprite, xSpeed: xSpeed, ySpeed: ySpeed, target: target)
    {
        xMinValue = xMin;
        xMaxValue = xMax;
    }

    public override void Update()
    {
        base.Update();

        if (AlienAlive)
        {
```

The max and min values are provided when the LineAlien is constructed.

Override Update method in the AlienSprite.

```
            if (spriteValue.X > xMaxValue)
            {
                spriteValue.X = xMaxValue;
                xSpeedValue = -xSpeedValue;
            }
            if (spriteValue.X < xMinValue)
            {

                spriteValue.X = xMinValue;
                xSpeedValue = -xSpeedValue;
            }
        }
    }
}
```

Check position and set movement.

The great thing about this code is how little there is to it. The only part we had to create from scratch is the `Update` method. Everything else is picked up from classes higher in the hierarchy.

A single `LineAlien` on its own is not that impressive, but we can use a `for` loop to create a row of them across the screen, as shown in the following code. **Figure 14-3** shows how the row of aliens looks in the work in progress. They move left and right in a manner similar to another very popular video game.

```
int noOfAliens = 10;
```

Change this value for number of aliens.

```
double alienWidth = SnapsEngine.GameViewportWidth / (noOfAliens * 2);
double alienSpacing = (SnapsEngine.GameViewportWidth - alienWidth) / noOfAliens;
double alienX = 0;
double alienY = 100;
for (int i = 0; i < noOfAliens; i = i + 1)
{
    ImageSprite alienImage =
        new ImageSprite(imageURL: "ms-appx:///Images/greenAlien.png");
    SnapsEngine.AddSpriteToGame(alienImage);
    alienImage.ScaleSpriteWidth(alienWidth);
    alienImage.CenterX = alienX;
    alienImage.Top = alienY;
    double xMin = alienX;
    double xMax = alienX + alienSpacing;
    LineAlien alien = new LineAlien(sprite: alienImage, xSpeed: 2, ySpeed: 0,
```

Calculate the width and spacing for alien sprites.

```
        target: rocket, xMax: xMax, xMin: xMin);
    sprites.Add(alien);
    alienX = alienX + alienSpacing;
}
```

Construct the alien with
our calculated values.

Move to the next alien
in the row.

Ch14_06_ChasingAndTargetAliens

Figure 14-3 A line of target aliens.

Designing a class hierarchy

Adding classes like LineAlien to our game is the basis of object-oriented design. We
can reuse and customize existing program elements as the program develops. However, it is probably best to have a design before you start building your classes. **Figure
14-4** shows the design for the game we've been building.

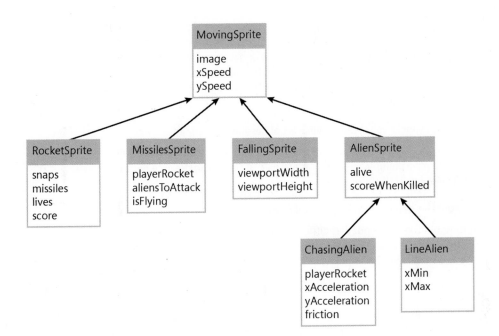

Figure 14-4 Game objects class diagram.

This is called a *class diagram*. It shows a kind of family tree of the objects in the game. Parent classes are at the top of the diagram, with child classes below them. The MovingSprite class is the parent class of all the game objects. It holds the image and position of the sprite. Each class beneath it builds on these items and adds extra data as required.

CODE ANALYSIS

Taking a look at class diagrams

Question: Which of the classes has the fewest abilities?

Answer: We've already considered this issue. The class at the top of the diagram is the one that has the fewest abilities, although this is a bit counterintuitive because most diagrams that show organizations put the most powerful person (the king or the boss) at the top, with the less powerful people underneath. However, the way that abilities accumulate as you move down the diagram means that the classes with the widest range of behaviors will be at the bottom.

Question: How does the missile know who it can attack?

Answer: These diagrams are very useful when you consider how the program will work and how objects in the system know enough to do their jobs. The missile contains a list of all the alien sprites that it can kill, and each time it is updated, it checks through this list of sprites to see whether it has hit any of them. If it has hit a sprite, it will call the `Kill` method on that sprite to kill it and find out how much it has scored. It then increases the score of the rocket that launched it.

Question: Why does the `RocketSprite` contain a list of missiles?

Answer: As the game progresses, you've been asked to add "power-up" elements that allow the player to have multiple missiles. This means that the `RocketSprite` must contain a list of missiles rather than just one.

Question: How would we handle different types of missiles?

Answer: It turns out that this is not that difficult to achieve. Just like we have an `Alien-Sprite` that provides the basis for all the aliens, we could have a `MissileSprite` that serves as the basis of all the missiles.

Figure 14-5 is a screenshot of the game as I've developed it so far. There are two kinds of aliens on the screen—the nasty purple chasing alien and a line of green aliens that just move back and forth. There is also a blue missile at the top of the screen that the player has just fired (and missed with). You can use this to make any kind of space shooter that you like.

Figure 14-5 Space Rockets in Space.

Make some games of your own

Now that you know how easy it is to add new game objects to a game, you can add sprites with different behaviors very easily. You could make a sprite that chases the player only when the player is close to the sprite or one that wakes up and starts chasing the player when they get too near. You can make sprites that change in size during the game so that they slowly take over the screen and become more difficult to dodge as time goes by. You could create a cowardly sprite that runs away from the player. (In this case, you might change the way the game works so that the aim of the game is for the player to catch things rather than avoid them.) You could make chasing sprites that bounce off the sides of the viewport or ones that "teleport" from one side to another. You can add randomness to the sprites to make them chase players only sometimes. There are lots of different kinds of behaviors to investigate.

What you have learned

In this chapter you've learned how to create objects that can underpin all the elements in a game. You have done this by creating a parent object that contains fundamental elements that all the game objects need and then child objects that extend this parent and provide more specific, less abstract behaviors. You have seen that by doing this, you can reduce the amount of code that you have to write to create a new type of game object—you can just focus on the difference between the parent and the child.

You discovered that in this kind of class hierarchy, the child objects that extend the parent objects are actually based on a parent instance and that the parent instance must be created during the construction of the child class. You have also seen that a method that has been marked as `virtual` in the parent can be overridden in the child class. The child can provide a version of the method that behaves in a way more specific to the role of the child. If it is useful, the child class can also make use of the method in the parent class by using the `base` keyword.

In our game, we used the `MovingSprite` type as the parent class for all the sprites in the game that move. Underneath this parent are `FallingSprite`, `RocketSprite`, and a number of other types of moving sprites. The game, which contains all the game objects, manipulates the sprites as though they are all `MovingSprites` and is unaware of the customized behaviors of each. The status of a sprite is updated when the game calls the `Update` method on that sprite. `Update` is a `virtual` method that is overridden in the child class to provide behavior that is relevant to that sprite type. This gives game developers the ability to make many different kinds of game objects, each of which has a behavior different from the others.

Here are some questions that you can ponder about class design.

Do I have to design all of my class hierarchy before I start?

Not necessarily. You should always attempt an initial design because this forces you to think hard about how the elements in your solution fit together, but as you build your program, you will get insights into how it should be structured. In many cases, it will be necessary to add new classes to a working system as new scenarios are identified during the lifetime of the project. One of the great benefits of an approach like this is how easy it is to insert new elements into the design.

Do I always need a class hierarchy?

You need a class hierarchy if your program needs to manipulate a large number of related items. For example, if you are creating a tool that collects evidence from the scene of a crime, it would be very useful to make some kind of class hierarchy based on a parent class called *Evidence*, which would hold the date, time, and location where the evidence was collected. Underneath that parent you could have child classes that contain images, sounds, details of samples collected, and so on. In that case you have a strong family of types of evidence that your system will want to collect. As technology advances, you might find different kinds of evidence that will need to be managed. These could be added as the system evolves.

However, if your program is concerned with something that is going to remain fundamentally the same and there are not going to be different kinds of this item, you don't need a class hierarchy. For example, if you write a program that plays cards, there is really only going to be one kind of playing card. The card will have a set of properties that denote its color, suit, and value, and this will never need to be extended because the program will never have to deal with new kinds of playing cards.

Is it possible to make bad designs using class hierarchies?

Oh, yes. There are a few common mistakes. The first is to have a very wide class hierarchy. This means that you end up with classes like *Car, SportsCar, PeopleCarrier, PickupTruck,* and so on. This breadth makes design very difficult. For example, is a sports utility vehicle (SUV) descended from *SportsCar* or *PeopleCarrier*? In this case, you really need only a *CarType* property in the *Car* object and you are good to go. But you'd probably have a class named *Truck* since trucks are very different from cars. When you are thinking about design, you need to consider whether the behavior of the class needs to be different for this particular type. If the answer is yes, you can think about making a new class; if the answer is no—if you are just storing something about this particular instance of the class—then instead you can add a property that holds this information.

Another mistake is to have a very deep class hierarchy. You create lots and lots of child classes "just in case" they might be useful. You might have *Car, TwoWheelDriveCar, FourWheelDriveCar, TwoWheelDriveConvertable, FourWheelDriveConvertable, TwoWheelDriveSportsCar,* and so on, all descending from each other. This makes the program slower because when it runs, it takes longer to find the overridden methods in the hierarchy. I try not to have more than three or four levels in my class designs.

The final mistake is to bring things into the class hierarchy that really should not be there. You might think about adding a new kind of car called *HiredCar,* which has the name and address of the person who hired the car stored inside the *Car* class. However, these items pollute the hierarchy by adding data to some class items that really should not be there. If you want to manage a car-hire business, you should work in terms of *Hire* objects that contain references to *Car* objects that are hired and *Customer* objects that hire them. The *Car* class should hold information directly relevant to cars and nothing else.

15

Games and software components

What you will learn

When you started to learn about programming, I said, "Anyone who can organize a party can write a program." You've now discovered that a lot of programming is actually all about organization, which is why good organizers tend to make good programmers. In the last chapter you saw how to create family trees of related objects to more easily organize complex applications. Instead of being made from scratch, a new version of an object has to provide only those behaviors that are different from the object it extends. This is an important principle that underpins many large-scale applications.

In this chapter, you are going to go further in understanding how objects are used in programs and start to think of them as components that you can fit together to form a solution. You are going to discover how objects can communicate by sending messages to each other and how an object can maintain a sense of its own state. Then you are going to move on to consider how to create template objects that can be used as the basis of complex designs and how to turn objects into reusable and flexible program elements by using software interfaces. At the end of the chapter, we'll have a fully playable space-shooter game as well!

Games and objects

The graphical elements for Space Rockets in Space are a good start. The game has an object the player can control (the rocket) and attacking aliens. But to develop a complete game, we need to let players shoot aliens, lose lives, and score points.

We've already created a set of objects that represent the game sprites on the screen, as shown in **Figure 15-1**. Now we need to make these objects work together to create a complete game experience. First we need to add some consequences for when aliens manage to catch up to the rocket. In our game, each time the rocket is hit by an alien, the rocket must lose one life. When the rocket has lost all its lives, the game is over. To do this, the first step is to discover how the aliens and the rocket can be made to interact.

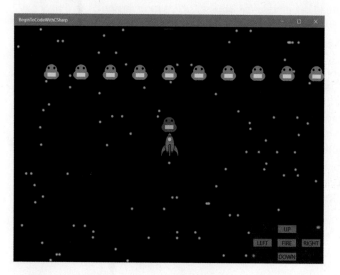

Figure 15-1 Space Rockets in Space.

Creating cooperating objects

In the terms of video games, the rocket must "take damage" when it's hit by an alien. From a programming point of view, you can think of this as an alien sprite sending a message to the rocket saying, "I just hit you." The rocket can then decide what effect this has.

When I was learning to program, I was very confused by what it meant for one object to send a message to another. But it actually turns out to be very simple.

- The RocketSprite class will contain a method named TakeDamage.

- The `AlienSprite` class will call this method.

So you can boil down "message passing" to an arrangement between objects in which one contains a method that receives the message, and the other calls this method to send the message. Programs use messages all the time. When you click the mouse, the active program receives a message to indicate that the mouse has been clicked. This message is delivered in the form of a method call. When you write Windows Presentation Foundation (WPF) applications in the next part of this book, you'll use this mechanism.

PROGRAMMER'S POINT
Message passing is important

Deciding how the objects in your system are going to interact is an important part of the design process. You might think that there is no need to send a message: perhaps the alien sprite could just reduce the value of a variable somewhere that counts the number of lives that the rocket has. However, "sending a message" is much better. The sender of the message just needs to call the method to deliver the message, but the sender doesn't need to know how the recipient actually deals with the message.

Furthermore, a method call can trigger an action in the other object—for example, the rocket could start an explosion animation, change its image to show that it's been damaged, or even send another message to the game to tell the game that the rocket has been destroyed.

If you think about this, it makes a programmer into something like an electrician. Once you have created your objects, you "wire them up" by connecting them via messages that are passed from one to the other.

In the following code, you can see the behavior of the `Update` method in the `AlienSprite` that detects whether the alien has hit the rocket. The `Update` method contains some statements that check whether the alien and the rocket intersect, using the `IntersectsWith` method that you saw in Chapter 13. When we wrote Keep It Up!, we used `IntersectsWith` to check whether the paddle and the ball had collided. In this game, we check whether the rocket and the alien have collided.

```
public class AlienSprite : MovingSprite
{
    // If false, the alien has no effect on gameplay
    public bool AlienAlive = true;

    // The rocket that the alien is chasing
```

```
    public RocketSprite rocketTarget;

    public AlienSprite(ImageSprite sprite, double xSpeed, double ySpeed,
                       RocketSprite target) :
        base(sprite: sprite, xSpeed: xSpeed, ySpeed: ySpeed)
    {
        rocketTarget = target;
    }

    // Called to tell the alien that is has been killed
    public void Kill()
    {
        // If we are already dead, we don't need to do anything
        if (AlienAlive)
        {
            // If we get here, we must kill ourselves
            // Set the flag to indicate we are dead
            AlienAlive = false;
            // Hide the sprite for this alien
            spriteValue.Hide();
        }
    }

    public override void Update()
    {
        // Don't do anything if the alien is dead
        if (!AlienAlive)
            return;

        // Update the position of the sprite
        base.Update();

        // See if the alien and rocket target sprites intersect
        if (spriteValue.IntersectsWith(rocketTarget.spriteValue))
        {
            // If we get here, the alien has hit the rocket
            // Kill ourselves
            Kill();
            // Tell the target that it must take damage
            rocketTarget.TakeDamage();
            return;
        }
    }
}
```

If the `IntersectsWith` method returns `true`, that means that the alien has hit the rocket. If this happens, the alien does a number of things. First, it calls a method called `Kill` to remove itself from gameplay. Next, the `TakeDamage` method on the `RocketSprite` is called to inflict damage on the rocket.

The code that follows shows the first version of the `TakeDamage` method, which is part of the `RocketSprite` class. When the rocket takes damage, the `Lives` counter is reduced by 1 and the method plays a sound effect.

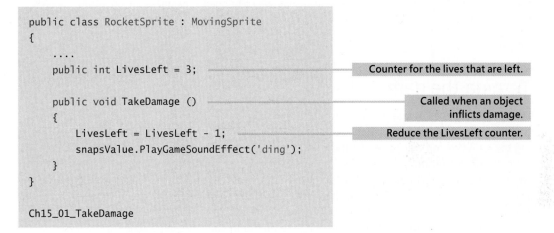

```
public class RocketSprite : MovingSprite
{
    ....
    public int LivesLeft = 3;                                  Counter for the lives that are left.

    public void TakeDamage ()                                  Called when an object
    {                                                          inflicts damage.
        LivesLeft = LivesLeft - 1;                             Reduce the LivesLeft counter.
        snapsValue.PlayGameSoundEffect('ding');
    }
}
```

Ch15_01_TakeDamage

If you run **Ch15_01_TakeDamage**, you'll find that aliens disappear (and you hear a ding sound) each time the rocket collides with an alien. If you look inside the program as it runs, you'll see that the `Lives` counter (the value of the variable `Lives` inside the rocket) is reduced each time a collision occurs. This version of the method doesn't end the game just yet, mainly because we don't know how the game should end. That's what we need to do next.

PROGRAMMER'S POINT

Think of each object in your program as a little person

If you were organizing a really large party, you'd probably put someone at the door to check tickets. You might say to them, "If someone you don't know turns up without a ticket, call me and tell me who it is. I'll tell you whether you can let them in." In programming terms, we have an object that receives the message "There's someone here with no ticket," and then knows what to do—"Call Rob and ask whether they can come in."

When you start to consider objects that are more active, as in the case of the sprites and other elements in the game we're writing, you can think of the objects as little people who are all cooperating to make the game work. Each person can be sent messages (for example, "Update yourself") and can generate other messages ("I've just caused you damage") when the program runs.

This principle builds on our understanding of a computer program as something that "takes something in, does something with it, and then sends out something else." You can now regard a large system as a collection of components that do just this by receiving and sending messages.

It helps to visualize what the program needs to do by putting yourself into the "head" of each of these little people and regard them as separate components that make the program work.

Turning the game into an object

We now consider all the game elements as items that take in messages, do something, and then produce other messages. We can apply this to larger objects, too, including the game we are writing. At the moment, all the gameplay has taken place in the StartProgram method, which is called when a Snaps program starts running. Inside this method, all the game elements are created and the game runs. However, if we want to be able to send the game itself messages (perhaps to tell it that the game is over), we need to create a game object. The game object contains all the sprites that the game uses, and it provides methods that we can use to start the game running.

```
public void StartProgram()
{
    SpaceRocketsInSpaceGame game = new SpaceRocketsInSpaceGame();

    game.PlayGame();
}

Ch15_02_GameClass
```

The preceding code shows how this works. The StartProgram method is called when a Snaps program starts to run. We have a new class, named SpaceRocketsInSpaceGame. When the program runs, it simply makes an instance of this class and then calls the PlayGame method on this instance. You can think of this as sending a message to the game to make it start playing. The PlayGame method creates all the sprites and then starts the game loop running—in other words, it does what the StartProgram method used to do.

One nice thing about this arrangement is that we can use it to create a program that lets a player choose from a menu of games. The StartProgram method could display this menu and then create an instance of the selected game.

If you run the example **Ch15_02_GameClass,** you will not notice any difference in the way the game works, but the program is now structured with the game in the form of a class.

Telling the game when the game is over

When the RocketSprite has lost its last life, the game has to end. The rocket doesn't actually know how to end the game, but that's fine. In fact, it is exactly how it should be. The only object that should know how to end a game is the game itself. The RocketSprite just has to generate the message to tell the game that it is now over. But for this to work—for the RocketSprite to deliver the message—the RocketSprite has to have a reference to the game that it is part of.

Here is the constructor for the rocket:

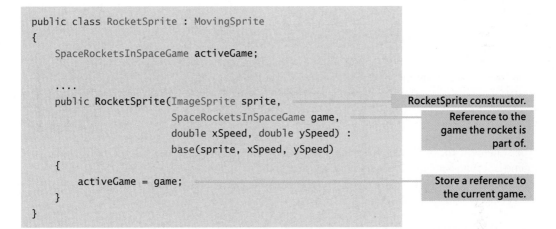

```
public class RocketSprite : MovingSprite
{
    SpaceRocketsInSpaceGame activeGame;


    ....
    public RocketSprite(ImageSprite sprite,                    RocketSprite constructor.
                    SpaceRocketsInSpaceGame game,             Reference to the
                    double xSpeed, double ySpeed) :           game the rocket is
                    base(sprite, xSpeed, ySpeed)                       part of.
    {
        activeGame = game;                               Store a reference to
    }                                                    the current game.
}
```

When the rocket is created, it's supplied with a reference to the Snaps game engine so that it can play sounds. It is also supplied with a reference to the game that contains the rocket. This is the game object that must be notified when the game is over.

Next is the TakeDamage method for the RocketSprite class.

```
public class RocketSprite : MovingSprite
{
    ....

    SpaceRocketsInSpaceGame activeGame;

    int LivesLeft = 3;
```

```
    public void TakeDamage()
    {
        LivesLeft = LivesLeft - 1;
        snapsValue.PlayGameSoundEffect('ding');
        if (LivesLeft == 0)                                    If no lives left, the
        {                                                          game is over.
            activeGame.EndCurrentGame();                       Tell the game that
        }                                                       the game is over.
    }
}
```

The TakeDamage method runs whenever our rocket takes damage. It reduces the number of lives the rocket has left, and if there are no lives remaining, it tells the game that the game is over by calling the EndCurrentGame method in the game the rocket is part of.

Here is the actual construction of the RocketSprite in the game.

```
rocket = new RocketSprite(sprite: rocketImage, snaps: snaps, game: this, xSpeed: 10,
                          ySpeed: 10);
```
Reference to the currently active game

The statement above is called from the SpaceRocketsInSpaceGame class when the game is setting itself up. The statement constructs the rocket that the player will control. The rocket needs to be given a reference to the game it is part of so that the rocket can tell the game that the game is over.

We have seen the this reference before. It is a reference to the object within which the code is currently executing. The statement above is running inside a method within an instance of the SpaceRocketsInSpaceGame class, so the value of this is a reference to the game class. This is exactly what the RocketSprite needs, so we pass the reference "this" into the RocketSprite when we call the constructor to make the RocketSprite.

CODE ANALYSIS

What does this mean again?

Question: What does the keyword this mean in the call to the RocketSprite constructor?

Answer: All this talk of objects, messages, and this can be confusing. The best way to deal with the complexity is to keep in mind what we are trying to do. We are making a game that involves a rocket and an alien. If the alien collides with the rocket, the rocket must take damage. If the rocket is destroyed, the game should end. So the alien needs a way of telling the rocket that it is causing damage, and the rocket needs a way of telling the game that the game is over. This is like me needing to know your phone number so that I can call you and ask you out for a coffee.

In the case of programs, we are talking about object references instead of phone numbers. The rocket needs a reference to the game so that it can tell the game that it is over. The programming keyword this in a human context means *my phone number*. If I want to let you know how to contact me, I have to give you my phone number. In the case of a method running inside an object, you can regard the reference this as a reference to the object the method is running inside of. So a method can pass this into another object to give that object a reference to (or the phone number for) itself.

Stopping the game from running

We now have a way to deliver a message to the game to tell it that the game is over. We also need a way to stop the game when it receives this message.

```
public class SpaceRocketsInSpaceGame          ——— Class that contains the entire game.
{

    ....

    bool gameRunning = true;                  ——— Flag set to true when game is active.

    public void EndCurrentGame()              ——— Method called to end the current game.
    {
        gameRunning = false;                  ——— When the method runs, set the flag to false.
    }
}
```

The game contains a flag named gameRunning that is true when the game is running. When EndCurrentGame is called to stop the game, it sets this flag to false. We can end the game at any time by calling the EndCurrentGame method.

The following code shows the PlayGame method in the game. It sets the game up and then repeatedly updates the game objects while the gameRunning value is set to true. As soon as this value becomes false, the while loop ends and the game completes.

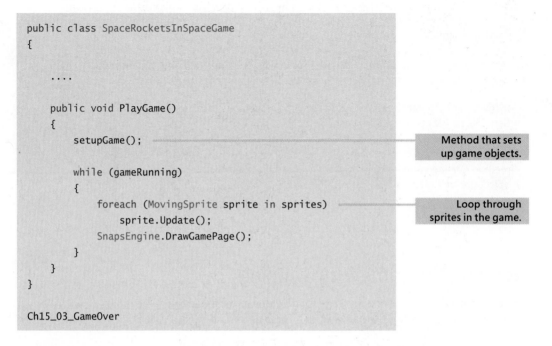

```
public class SpaceRocketsInSpaceGame
{

    ....

    public void PlayGame()
    {
        setupGame();

        while (gameRunning)
        {
            foreach (MovingSprite sprite in sprites)
                sprite.Update();
            SnapsEngine.DrawGamePage();
        }
    }
}
```

Ch15_03_GameOver

Method that sets up game objects.

Loop through sprites in the game.

If you play this version of the game, you will discover that as soon as the rocket has crashed into three aliens, the game will end. Now we need to make a game that can be played repeatedly so that players can try to improve their score. To achieve this, the game object can be made to occupy different states.

Objects and state

Everybody has their own favorite state of being. Mine is sitting in front of a computer writing programs, but I do have other states—for example, eating, sleeping, and (when I can't avoid it) working. It is often very useful to allow software objects to have a state, too. You have already seen that the aliens in Space Shooter have a state, in that they are either dead or alive. What we want to do now is extend the idea of state management into the game itself.

I've designed a title screen for the game, shown in **Figure 15-2**. I'm particularly proud of the instruction **Press SPACE to play**. This screen should be displayed until the player presses the Space bar (or the **Fire** button) to start the game. Then the game will run until the rocket is destroyed, at which point a **Game Over** screen will be displayed for a few seconds, and then the game should return to the title screen.

Figure 15-2 Space Rockets in Space title screen.

In other words, the game must have three different states:

1. Title screen

2. Playing the game

3. Game Over screen

The best way to handle this is for the `SpaceRocketsInSpaceGame` object that manages the game to contain a data member (a variable in the class) that holds the current state of the game. However, before we create the variable, we have to decide what type of variable will work best. Ideally, we want a variable type that can have only three possible values, one for each game state. We can use the C# enumerated type (see Chapter 9) to define a type that can hold the states that the game can have.

```
public class SpaceRocketsInSpaceGame
{
    ....
    enum GameStates
    {
        TitleScreen,
        GameActive,
        GameOver
    }

    GameStates state;
}
```

An enum type has particular values that we specify.

Variable that holds the state of the game

These statements show how to create and use an enumerated type called `GameStates`. Variables of this type can have one of three values, one for each state. The type is created inside the `SpaceRocketsInSpaceGame` class so that it can represent the state of the game. When the game is running, its behavior depends on the current state of the game.

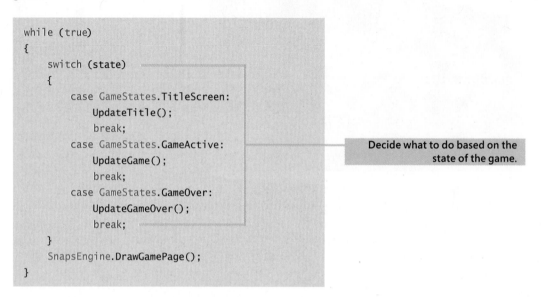

```
while (true)
{
    switch (state)
    {
        case GameStates.TitleScreen:
            UpdateTitle();
            break;
        case GameStates.GameActive:
            UpdateGame();
            break;
        case GameStates.GameOver:
            UpdateGameOver();
            break;
    }
    SnapsEngine.DrawGamePage();
}
```

Decide what to do based on the state of the game.

CODE ANALYSIS

Adding more game states

Just about all the objects in a program will have state of some kind that they will manage.

Question: How would we add a "High Score Display" state to the game?

Answer: The code for the game behavior is a really good template for the construction of a state-based game. We can add a new state by adding a value that represents the new state to the `enum`, adding a new method to update the game in that state, and then adding the case to the `switch` statement so that the method is called when the game is in that state.

Question: How would we add an extra level to the game?

Answer: Games like Space Rockets in Space often have several different levels, with different background screens and different kinds of attacking aliens. You might think that we could add more levels by adding more states to the game (for example, we could have a state called Level1Active and another called Level2Active and so on). However, this is not a good way to structure the code. A better way would be to add a property, perhaps called LevelNumber, which is the number of the level being played, and have the UpdateGame method deal with this. In other words, each of the methods that are called to manage their state could in fact be mini state machines themselves.

PROGRAMMER'S POINT
Messages and states go hand in hand

The state of an object will determine how it responds to a message that it receives. Some messages will cause a change in the state of an object, and some messages will be ignored in certain states. For example, if the game is not in the GameActive state, it will ignore any EndCurrentGame messages that come along because they are just not relevant. When you design a solution made up of cooperating objects, you can also design the states that the objects can occupy and the messages that will cause them to change from one state to another.

If we go back to our "party doorman" situation, we might tell the doorman that as soon as 50 people have arrived, he must put up a Party Full sign and stop allowing any new arrivals. In this case, the doorman will have changed state from "accepting arrivals" to "party full" and respond to "incoming person" in a different way.

The main game loop for this version of Space Rockets in Space now calls a specific update method for each of the possible game states.

```
public void UpdateTitle()
{
    if (SnapsEngine.GetFireGamepad())
    {
        StartNewGame();
    }
}
```

Above is the method that runs to update the title screen. It checks to see whether the **Fire** button has been pressed (this is the same as the Space bar on the keyboard). If the button has been pressed, UpdateTitle calls a method to start the game. The idea is that the StartNewGame method will then reset all the game objects and start the game running. But there's one problem: we don't know how to reset all the game objects.

Sometimes you get blindsided

We use *blindsided* to mean something that happens that you just did not see coming—like a friend of mine who carefully made two copies of all his files on two separate hard disks so he could be sure that he would not lose any data if one of his disks failed. Unfortunately, this did not help him much when his computer, with both drives inside it, was stolen.

You can get blindsided in software projects when you suddenly discover that there is a whole set of additional things that your program needs to do. I have had this happen to me a few times when I've been creating an application, and the problem usually occurs because I didn't work through my solution before starting to build it.

If we had worked through what happens when the game is played, we would have quickly discovered that we need a way of restarting the game, and to do this the game objects must be able to reset themselves. We need to add this behavior or we won't have a proper game.

You might think that if you carefully work through everything you will never get blindsided like this. Unfortunately, this is not always the case. I've been caught out by the customer forgetting to tell me about a whole bunch of things that the application needs to do, or experienced the unhappy discovery that the hardware that I've been told I must use doesn't actually go fast enough.

Every time I've been caught like this I've made a careful note of what happened, and in my next project I make sure that I do something to attack that problem, too. However, I still recognize that every now and then I'll have to deal with things I just wasn't expecting. It turns out that careful planning doesn't remove all the risk from a project, just like a carefully planned birthday party can be sent into turmoil if the birthday girl catches measles the day before the event. You just have to make sure that you have planned for the all the events that you can and be ready to respond to whatever else fate might send your way.

Game reset behavior and abstract classes

We just discovered an issue that we did not address in our design: what happens when a game finishes and we want to start a new one? We don't want to have to re-create all the sprite objects each time we start a new game because that would be very slow. What we need is to tell each sprite to reset itself to its starting position. We don't know precisely what a game object needs to do—for example, alien sprites will have to come back to life if they have died—but we do know that each object must do something.

We can use another C# feature to make this situation easier to manage: *abstract* methods. An abstract method is a statement of intent. It indicates a need for a behavior without saying exactly what that behavior should be. In a program, this requirement is expressed in the form of an "empty" method that is marked as abstract:

```
abstract public class MovingSprite
{
    public ImageSprite spriteValue;
    public double xSpeedValue, ySpeedValue;

    public MovingSprite(ImageSprite sprite, double xSpeed, double ySpeed)
    {
        spriteValue = sprite;
        xSpeedValue = xSpeed;
        ySpeedValue = ySpeed;
    }

    public virtual void Update()
    {
        spriteValue.X = spriteValue.X + xSpeedValue;
        spriteValue.Y = spriteValue.Y + ySpeedValue;
    }

    public abstract void Reset();
}
```

The MovingSprite class now contains an abstract method.

Defines an abstract method named Reset.

If the abstract method is in the class right at the top of the hierarchy, this effectively says, "Any class that extends the MovingSprite class must provide a Reset method if we are going to make an instance of that class." Abstract methods are a great design tool because they let you think about actions without having to describe exactly how those actions are going to be performed.

As an example, you might be implementing a system to manage different kinds of accounts for a bank. You know that the bank manages lots of different accounts—checking accounts, credit card accounts, saving accounts, and so on. A sensible way to address this would be to create a class hierarchy with an Account class at the top and more specific classes (CheckingAccount, SavingAccount, and so on) underneath, providing more specific behaviors. Every account must have some fundamental behaviors, such as paying in and withdrawing funds, checking the balance, and so on. These behaviors will be required by every account, but each account will perform them in its own way. What you want to do is define a requirement that these methods must be provided, without stating specifically how they are to be performed. You could do this by creating abstract methods for all the methods that you want the child classes to provide. These force the child classes to provide the required behaviors but without specifying how these behaviors will work.

Abstract methods and classes

Question: The Update method is virtual, and the Reset method is abstract. What's the difference?

> **Answer:** When we created the MovingSprite class, we decided that classes that extend the MovingSprite class might want to build on the Update behavior that makes a sprite move. Making a method virtual means that it can be overridden by a method in the child class. We've done this in lots of the classes. The RocketSprite overrides Update to provide a version that lets the player control the rocket, whereas the ChaserAlien class overrides Update to provide a version that moves the sprite toward the player at all times.
>
> Abstract is different. It says, "You need to do this in your own way. I don't know precisely what you need to do, but I do know that you need to do it." In the context of our game, the declaration of an abstract Reset method is expressing the need for every sprite to have some kind of reset behavior.

Question: Why is the MovingSprite class now abstract?

> **Answer:** The MovingSprite class is now abstract because the system can't ever make an instance of this class. If we did make an instance and somebody tried to use the Reset method on that object, the program would not know what to do.

Question: What does it mean if a class is made abstract?

> **Answer:** Abstract means that the program can never actually create a class of this type. The class now serves as a *template* for other classes, which will extend the abstract class and provide implementations of the abstract elements.

Question: Why didn't you just make a virtual Reset method that can be overridden?

> **Answer:** The Update method runs inside a sprite to update it in the game. We made the Update method virtual so that it can be customized in other classes that extend the MovingSprite class. However, there is not always a need for a class to override a method from a parent. In other words, there's nothing forcing a child class to provide an Update method. However, making a method abstract means that the child class *must* provide an implementation of the Reset method, forcing the object's developers to add one. I'm very keen that people don't forget the Reset method (like I did), so I'm forcing them to remember it.

Providing reset behaviors in objects

If we add an abstract Reset method to the MovingSprite class, this will have the effect of breaking the entire program. The compiler will now complain that none of the sprite classes in our game have a `Reset` method, so the program cannot be compiled anymore. There is nothing to do at this point but take a deep breath (and probably drink a cup of strong coffee), and then go through all the classes to add the required `Reset` behavior. For some of the objects, we will also need to change the constructor so that it stores the original position of the sprite when it was created. This way, the `Reset` method can use this position to put the sprite back on the screen in the same place.

The following code shows the `Reset` behavior for the `RocketSprite` class. When the sprite is created, the method stores the original X and Y values of the sprite. Then, when the sprite is reset, `Reset` moves the rocket back to this position and sets the lives and the score to the original values.

```
double originalXSpeed, originalYSpeed;
```
Storage for the original speed and position of the rocket.
```
double originalX, originalY;

public int LivesLeft, Score;

public override void Reset()
```
Reset method resets the rocket for a new game.
```
{
    xSpeed = originalXSpeed;
    ySpeed = originalYSpeed;
    spriteValue.X = originalX;
    spriteValue.Y = originalY;
    LivesLeft = 3;
    Score = 0;
}
```

```
public RocketSprite(ImageSprite sprite, SnapsEngine snaps, double xSpeed, double
                    ySpeed) :                              RocketSprite constructor
    base(sprite, xSpeed, ySpeed)
{
    originalXSpeed = xSpeed;
    originalYSpeed = ySpeed;
    originalX = sprite.X;
    originalY = sprite.Y;                      Store original rocket position
    snapsValue = snaps;                        for when the rocket is reset.
}
```

When the game wants to reset all the sprites, it simply has to do this:

```
public void ResetGame ()
{
    gameScore = 0;
    foreach (MovingSprite sprite in sprites)
    {                                                  Work through all
        sprite.Reset();                                the sprites and
    }                                                  reset them.
}
```

Ch15_04_CompleteGame

Remember that the variable sprites holds a list of all the sprites that the game is using. The loop you see above is exactly the same as we use in the Update method for each of the sprites. However, this time the Reset behavior is used. The Reset method that's called on each object is the one appropriate to that particular type. This method will still work even if you add lots of new sprites to the game because they will all be required to provide a Reset behavior that works for them.

The sample game **Ch15_04_CompleteGame** is a fairly complete game that uses the reset behaviors of the sprites each time the game is completed. It also displays the score and number of lives (which was borrowed from Keep It Up!) and will reset the aliens each time they are all destroyed.

Make your own complete game

You can use **Ch15_04_CompleteGame** as the basis for almost any sprite-based game that you would like to make. You can modify the behaviors of the sprites or just change the art-work. You can add more sounds to the game or make it completely silent. You can change the way the game works so that you have to capture falling raindrops while being chased by an angry wasp.

Interfaces and components

In the Space Rockets in Space game, all the sprites are based on the MovingSprite type and all the objects on the screen are held in a list of sprites.

```
List<MovingSprite> sprites = new List<MovingSprite>();
```

The list contains references to all the stars, aliens, rockets, and missiles. This works because MovingSprite is the parent for all these object types and a MovingSprite reference can refer to any of them. Each time we add a new type of sprite to the game, it is a child of the MovingSprite class and we can just add it to this list. Then, when we want to update the game, we can update all the sprites by just working through all the objects in the sprite list:

```
foreach (MovingSprite sprite in sprites)
    sprite.Update();
```

This works well, but it can be inflexible if we want to use other components in our game. For example, a fellow developer might have made a set of game objects that manipulate the game's background images, and we want to use these in our game. In a perfect world, these backgrounds would be based on the MovingSprite class, but it turns out that the background designer has designed her classes differently. She has a set of classes that are arranged like you see in **Figure 15-3**.

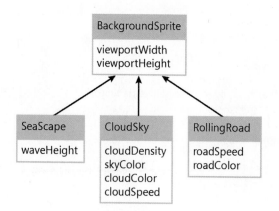

Figure 15-3 Background sprite designs

The problem we will have with these backgrounds is that the parent class is Back-groundSprite, so they are completely different classes from the ones in our game, which are based on the MovingSprite class. We can't easily add them to the list of sprites in our game because they won't fit with MovingSprite.

Adding abstraction

We have this problem because MovingSprite and BackgroundSprite are both sprites, but they are not in any way related. We could solve this problem by making a new parent class that both BackgroundSprite and MovingSprite extend. Our program can then manipulate game objects in terms of this type. In other words, everything in the game is a GameSprite, which can be either a MovingSprite or a BackgroundSprite. **Figure 15-4** shows how this would work.

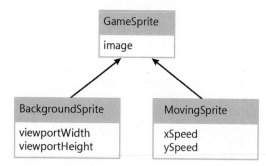

Figure 15-4 Combined class diagram.

The GameSprite class holds the image that is displayed, and the MovingSprite and BackgroundSprite classes are children of that class. Here is how the code would be written for the three classes.

```
class GameSprite                                    Parent class for all the sprites.
{
    ImageSprite image;
}

class BackgroundSprite : GameSprite                 Root of the BackgroundSprite hierarchy.
{

}

class MovingSprite : GameSprite                      Root of the MovingSprite hierarchy.
{
    double xSpeed;
    double ySpeed;
}
```

The GameSprite would hold the image (which every sprite needs), and the Moving-Sprite would hold the speed values and so on. The game would just contain a list of GameSprite objects:

```
List<GameSprite> sprites = new List<GameSprite>();
```

The problem with this approach is that it would be very time-consuming to implement if we already have existing classes. It is unlikely that the classes would have much in common. We need a way that we can use the abilities of these objects without our program caring about the particular kind of object that is being used. C# provides this in the form of the *interface*.

WHAT COULD GO WRONG

Make sure your most abstract class is abstract enough

Programmers use abstraction as a way of stepping back from a problem. For example, if I was creating an application to manage a clothes shop, I might talk to the shop manager about clothing rather than dresses, trousers, shirts, socks, and ties. Once I've discovered what the system needs to with the clothing items, I can then make child classes that are tailored (sorry) to the specific requirements of the different clothing types. For example, a dress would have a size value, whereas a pair of trousers would have a waist measurement and an inside leg measurement. However, when designing like this you need to make sure that your top-level class is abstract enough.

If the clothes shop sells handbags and purses (which it might do), these objects will not fit into my clothing class hierarchy at all. What I should have done is start with a more abstract class, perhaps called *Stock*, which holds all the information about an item in stock (for example, price, stock level, supplier), and then I can have child classes that describe different kinds of stock. This makes our application more "futureproof" because if the shop ever moves into something like jewelry, we can just add another child class.

Our design for the sprites reflects a lack of abstraction in that a game also needs to have sprites that don't move. We should really have made `GameSprite` the parent class of all the sprites from the very start. When you are picking the name and abilities of the top class in a hierarchy, you need to make sure that it is sufficiently abstract.

Interfaces

Interface is a confusing word. It instantly makes people think of desktop computers with mice, keyboards, and large flat-screen monitors. But in the case of a C# program, an interface is a set of things that a class can profess that it's able to do. When I think of interfaces, I think of the interface that defines the connection between a power socket and a plug. The interface defines the voltage that the socket will produce, the shape and size of the pins in the plug, and the purpose of each pin.

The interface specification does not say how the electricity in the socket is to be produced, and it doesn't say what the plug is to be connected to. A power socket can be driven by a nuclear power station or a battery-powered inverter, and the plug can be connected to a kettle or a flat-screen TV. Each side of the connection has a view of the other, which is entirely defined by the interface. They don't know or care what is actually producing the power or consuming it.

We want something similar for our software objects. We want a way that a single game can use sprite objects without caring exactly what type of objects they are. We can do this by identifying exactly what behaviors are required in a class and then expressing this in a C# interface. In the case of our game, we want the sprites in the game to be able to do two things: each sprite must be able to update itself (it must contain an `Update` method), and each sprite must be able to reset itself for a new game (it must contain a `Reset` method).

If an object can do those two things, we don't really care what it is: we can use it in our game. We can express these two abilities in the form of a C# interface:

```
interface IGameSprite
{
    void Reset();
    void Update();
}
```

Name of the interface.

Methods in the interface.

This code creates an interface named IGameSprite, which specifies the two methods that a class needs to provide to be a sprite in our game. Any class that contains Update and Reset methods can tell the compiler that it *implements* the interface by adding the interface name to the class name when it is declared:

```
abstract public class MovingSprite : IGameSprite
{
}
```

Objects based on this class will contain the methods in IGameSprite.

This tells the compiler that the MovingSprite class (and therefore any of its children) implements the IGameSprite interface. It is a way of saying that objects in the hierarchy *must* contain a Reset and an Update method or the program will not be able to make an instance of that class. Any class that wants to be treated like an IGameSprite can implement the interface. A program can also create references of type IGameSprite, and the references can refer to any class instance that implements the interface.

```
List<IGameSprite> sprites = new List<IGameSprite>();
```

My list of game objects is now a list of IGameSprite objects—that is, things that can update and reset. When the program runs, it performs these actions on the objects irrespective of what they are. All the background programmer needs to do is add a Reset and an Update method to her background drawing classes, tell the compiler that the classes implement the IGameSprite interface, and they can be used alongside the classes in our system. The interface has defined precise ways in which completely different objects can interact.

Interfaces allow you to regard objects in terms of what they can do, not what they are. They allow a lot more flexibility in program design. They allow you to specify how components can interact with each other and make it very easy for us to swap one component for another, without the system complaining.

Interfaces

Question: What do we mean by a list of interfaces?

Answer: The sprites list, which contains references to all the sprites in our program, is now a list of `IGameSprite` interfaces. This looks a bit confusing because an interface is not a "thing," it is just a collection of behaviors. However, this is exactly what we want. It is a bit like assembling a bunch of people who are all firefighters. We may have teachers, writers, artists, and beauticians turning up, but as long as they implement the "firefighter" interface (which is, basically, turn up, save people, and put out the fire) we don't care what they actually are. Remember, an interface provides a way of referring to an object based on what it can do, not what it actually is.

Question: What if we try to make an interface reference refer to an object that doesn't implement the interface?

Answer: To go back to the firefighter example, you are asking what would happen if we asked someone who isn't a firefighter to put out the fire. The answer is that the C# compiler keeps careful track of which classes implement which interfaces, and it checks to make sure that when you try to use an interface reference that the thing the reference refers to actually has the required behaviors.

Question: Can a class implement multiple interfaces?

Answer: Yes it can. Just like a beautician can be a firefighter and also a juggler. Each interface that an object implements provides a different "view" of that object.

Question: Why does the interface name begin with the letter *I*?

Answer: It is a convention in C# programs that the name of an interface always starts with *I*. This is so that a programmer can easily tell an interface from a class. An interface is quite different from a class. An interface doesn't actually tell the computer how to do something; instead, it gives a list of things that class must do.

PROGRAMMER'S POINT

Interfaces and abstract classes are deep stuff, but worth knowing about

Since you are just learning to program, you might find that abstract classes and interfaces are very hard to understand completely. We started off with programs that made simple decisions based on the contents of variables. Then we moved on to lumping data into objects so that we can manage related data more easily. Now we are moving on to making objects based on other objects (class hierarchies), template objects (abstract classes), and object-based components.

These are advanced programming and software design topics. You don't need to understand them completely right away. You can create awesome programs without using a class hierarchy. However, if are designing large and complex solutions made up of lots of different components, I'd strongly advise you to come back to the chapters in this part of the book and look at the ways that we fit together the elements in our game.

What you have learned

In this chapter we completed our exploration of the object-oriented features in C#, using the game Space Rockets in Space as the vehicle. You discovered how one object in a program can send a message to another and how complex programs can be made from a collection of cooperating objects. You have seen that a message is really just a method call with an agreed meaning and that an object can send messages in response to the ones that it receives. You have also investigated how objects can be given state, and that the state of an object sets the context in which incoming messages will be dealt with.

Sometimes, the design process will identify a need for objects to provide a certain set of behaviors in a manner appropriate to each specific object. You have seen how you can use C# abstract classes to create "templates" that specify an abstract requirement for a particular behavior without specifying exactly how the behavior should work in each child of the abstract class.

Interfaces take the idea of abstract classes even further. Abstract classes let us design templates that specify behaviors that all objects in a class hierarchy must implement. Interfaces, in contrast, specify a set of behaviors that any class can implement. Classes can implement the interface and then be managed in terms of this ability. Put simply, abstract classes let us manage objects in terms of what they are, whereas interfaces let us manage objects in terms of what they can do.

Programming is turning into an exercise in organization, and we can start to break down very complicated systems into a set of objects that each play a particular part in the implementation. It turns out that you can do a lot of your program design work by stepping back from the keyboard and drawing some diagrams that show what each element of the solution needs to do.

Here are some questions that you might want to ponder about software components.

What is the difference between an object and a component?

We started using objects as a way of gathering together data values to make them easier to manage. We created objects to represent musical notes in a tune, contacts in an address book, and similar things. You discovered that you can make objects more useful by giving them behaviors so that a musical note could play itself or a contact object could make sure that we never stored a contact with a missing name. You move into components when objects start to cooperate to make a system work. In our video game, the alien sprite sends a message to the rocket when it causes damage, and then the rocket sends a message to the game if this means that the rocket has been destroyed and the game has ended. As soon as you start to regard objects in terms of their abilities—rather than what they are—you are talking about software components.

Does using objects make my programs run more slowly?

Yes, but it doesn't matter. One of the fundamental principles of computing is that there are lots of ways to write a program. Every program that is constructed using objects could instead be written as one enormous method. It would be very hard to understand, and impossible to fix if it broke, but it would probably run slightly faster than an object-based solution. The benefits of an object-based solution are so great in terms of ease of construction, ability to test, and ease of modification that they are definitely the best way to write large programs.

Do I know all I need to know about objects?

I have been programming for a very long time. For the first part of my programming career I didn't use objects for the very simple reason that they hadn't been invented. However, I found that I tended to structure my programs in an "object-ish" way, using libraries of subroutines and data that I grouped together to make objects of my own. I've been using objects now for a long time, and I still don't consider my knowledge complete. One of the wonderful things about learning to program is that if you are programming you are always learning. The notes in this part of the text should give you plenty to think about when it comes to designing large systems, but you will only learn more if you write more code and make a habit of looking at code written by other people.

In Part 4, the final part of this book, you take your programming skills and learn how to use them to make fully fledged Universal Applications. You'll move from the Snaps framework to the world of user interface design, where you can create any kind of application you like. You'll also learn how modern applications are structured and even pick up some software engineering skills.

The ebook for Part 4 is included in the companion content you can download from *https://aka.ms/BeginCodeCSharp/downloads*.

Index

Symbols and numbers

/* and */ characters, 118
// characters, 117
& (ampersand), 114–115
&& (AND) logical operator, 114–115, 276
<> (angle brackets), 320
{} (curly brackets), 49, 58–59, 111, 215, 324
/ (division operator), 84–85
" " (double quotation marks), 48, 74, 324
= (equal), 73, 311–312
== (equal to), 107–108
\ (escape character), 228, 324
^ (exclusive OR) operator, 114
> (greater than operator), 104, 107
>= (greater than or equal to operator), 107
< (less than operator), 104, 106–107
<= (less than or equal to operator), 107
– (minus and unary minus sign), 84
* (multiplication operator), 84
! (not), 103–104, 131
!= (not equal to), 107–108
| (OR) operator, 114
() (parentheses), 48–49, 84, 98, 215
+ (plus sign), 77–78, 84, 88, 183
; (semicolon), 48
|| (short-circuit OR) operator, 114

A

abstraction, 460–462, 467–468
access to data, 346–351, 369
addition operator (+), 77–78, 84, 88, 183
AddLineToTextDisplay method, 139, 332
Alert method, 218–222
algorithms, 187
alphabetical sorting, 193–194
ampersand (&) logical operator, 114–115
AND (&&) logical operator, 276
angle brackets (<>), 320
animated behaviors in UI, 380, 414
announcer programs, 76–77, 79

applications (apps). *See also* programs
    building, 8
    continuously running, 10
    data-processing, 25
    game elements, 380, 414
    images, displaying, 358–359
    vs. programs, 15
    running, 7–10
    running again, 10
    starting, 7–8
    stopping, 10–11
    user-friendly, 355–356
arguments, 48–49, 86, 218, 221–222
    named, 96, 220–221
    number of, 64
    order of, 220
arrays, 176–179
    of class references, 317–318
    collections, storing, 294–296
    contents, displaying, 184–186
    elements, 177, 188–189, 294–295
    error detection, 209
    filling up, 295–296
    functionality, 208
    GetLength method, 204
    highest and lowest values, 194–196
    indexes, 177, 182–183, 200–201
    Length property, 180–181, 204, 322
    as lookup tables, 206–207
    multiple dimensions, 199–205
    multiple value types, 260–261
    preset, 262–263
    sizing, 319
    sorting, 187–194
    of structure values, 252–253
    three-dimensional, 205
    total value, 196–198
    two-dimensional, 200
    values, holding, 249
aspect ratio, 385
asset management, 127–132
assignment operator (=), 73, 311–312
assignment statements, 73–74, 158–159, 347
asterisk (*), 84, 118

B

backslash (/), 84–85, 117–118, 228
base classes, 424. *See also* inheritance
BeginToCodeWithCSharp folder, 5
BeginToCodeWithCSharp project, 7, 127
BeginToCodeWithCSharp solution, 11–15
behavior members of classes, 46–47. *See also* methods
bits and bit patterns, 36
black-box testing, 32–34
blocks of statements, 110–113
    copying, 138–139
    local variables, 111–113
    in loops, 143–144
    methods, 214. *See also* methods
    repeat conditions, 149–151
Boolean expressions, 103–104
Boolean (bool) type, 102–104
break statements, 163–168, 280
breakpoints, 151–155
bubble sorting, 187–194, 307
bugs, 138, 151–155
business rules, enforcing, 349–350

C

C# language
    case sensitivity, 59, 74
    clarity of, 12–13
    decision process, 102–104, 133
    keywords, 72. *See also* keywords
    program structure, 44–50
calculations, performing, 83–85
calling methods, 47, 49
camera, opening, 368
carriage return (\r) escape sequence, 228
case statements, 281
casting, 90, 92–94, 197–198
catch blocks, 353–354
catching exceptions, 353
central processing units (CPUs), 26
character codes, mapping to numeric values, 38
check codes, 370
child classes, 422–423. *See also* inheritance
    customizing, 426–427
    method overrides, 426–428
class definitions, 46
    object design, 310
    starting, 44–46
class diagrams, 441–442
class hierarchies, 429, 433–434. *See also* inheritance
    designing, 440–444

    width and depth, 444–445
class instances, 310. *See also* objects
class references as parameters, 318
class variables, managing by reference, 306
classes
    abstract, 462
    base, 424
    constructors, 316–317
    extending, 422. *See also* inheritance
    fully qualified names, 319
    helper, 319
    interfaces, implementing, 469–470
    methods, adding, 215–217
    methods, declaring, 47
    in namespaces, 320
    naming, 55–56
    partial, 411
    property behaviors, 382–384
    references, 311–318
    structures and, 306–318
ClearGraphics method, 276
ClearScreenTappedFlag method, 164
ClearTextDisplay method, 139
clock programs, 87–88, 360–361
cloud storage, 240
code. *See also* programs
    colored display, 14
    comments, 117–119, 125–126, 142, 241–243
    context, 341, 419
    debugging, 151–155
    indenting, 106
    inputs, 29–32
    low-level vs. higher-level instructions, 26–27
    machine, 26
    patterns, 78–79
    personalizing, 35
    pseudocode, 194
    reading, 39
    refactoring, 224, 244
    reusability, 147
code blocks, 110–113, 138–139, 143–144, 149–151. *See also* methods
code design, 463. *See also* design patterns
    class hierarchies, 440–444
    for debugging, 155
    lots of methods, 367
    object interaction, 448–456
    object-oriented design, 440
code development. *See* programming
code review, 34
coding. *See* programming
collections, 195, 323. *See also* arrays; lists
Collections namespace, 319–320

division operator (/), 84–85
documents, XML schema, 330
double quotation marks (" "), 48, 74, 324
double type, 82, 90–92, 98
DrawDot method, 269–270
DrawDotsUntilDrawInLeftCorner method, 366
DrawGamePage method, 378
drawing, 267–278
    clearing screen, 276
    in color, 274–276
    coordinates, 272–273
Drawing class, 362–363
drawing program, 267–278
drawings diary, 356–368
DrawLine method, 283–284

E

egg timer, 65
elements in arrays, 177
    null values, 294–295
    swapping, 188–189
else statements, 105–106, 114–115, 122
encryption, 369
enum keyword, 279
enumerated types, 278–282, 457–458
enumeration, 195
equal sign (=), 73, 107–108, 311–312
equal to operator (==), 107–108
equality operators, 107–108
error detection, 209
error reporting, 353
errors
    compilation, 58–60
    divide by zero, 85
    with loops, 171
    stack overflow, 217
    "unreachable code detected," 106
    "variable undefined," 309–310
escape character (\), 324
escape sequences, 228
exception handlers, 353–355
Exception type, 259–260
exceptions, 178–179
    catching, 353–354
    in constructors, 258–259
    error reporting, 353
    index out of range, 322
    invalid input, 258–259, 261–262, 349
    null references, 235–236
    prevention of execution, 349, 354
exclusive OR (^) operator, 114

execution, path of, 151–155
expressions
    evaluation, 84
    numeric, 83–85
    string, 77–78

F

fade-in behavior, 360–361
failure behaviors, 156
FallingSprite class, 422–427
false keyword, 103
faults, guarding against, 34
fetching data, 229–231, 235–236, 329–333, 357
FetchStringFromLocalStorage method, 229–231, 235–236
fields, structure, 250
file extensions, 54
file names, 56, 359, 361–362
finding data, 300–302
flags
    setting, checking, and clearing, 164, 192–193
    test, 203–204
float type, 82, 91–92, 94
floating-point values, 91, 197–198
FontFamily string, 403
FontSize value, 403
for loops, 160–163
    displaying array contents, 184–186
    for two-dimensional arrays, 201–203
foreach loops, 195–196, 262–263
fortune-teller program, 126
forward slash (/), 84–85, 117–118
fractional numbers, 80. *See also* real numbers
frames per second, 377, 381, 389, 404, 406, 421
fully qualified names, 319
functional design specification (FDS), 22
Funfair program, 119–126

G

game engines, 376–377
    hardware and, 393
    MonoGame, 393
    sprites, adding to, 381–382
games
    clamping values, 399–400
    creation, 414
    ending, 453–454
    frames per second, 377, 381, 389, 404, 406, 421
    game loop, 377–378, 389, 398

W

X

About the author

Rob Miles has spent more than 30 years teaching programming at the University of Hull in the United Kingdom. He's a Microsoft MVP, with a passion for programming, C#, and creating new things. If he had any spare time, he'd spend it writing even more code. He loves making programs and then running them to see what happens. He reckons that programming is the most creative thing you can learn how to do. He also reckons that in a battle between us and the Martians, we'd win, because we've got Visual Studio and they don't—and there isn't anything better in the universe for building software.

He claims to know a lot of really good jokes, but nobody has ever heard him tell one. If you want an insight into the Wacky World™ of Rob Miles, you can read his blog at *www.robmiles.com* and follow him on Twitter via @RobMiles.

rob@robmiles.com

Now that you've read the book...

Tell us what you think!

Was it useful?
Did it teach you what you wanted to learn?
Was there room for improvement?

Let us know at http://aka.ms/tellpress

Your feedback goes directly to the staff at Microsoft Press,
and we read every one of your responses. Thanks in advance!